GLAMORGAN CRICKETERS

GLAMORGAN CRICKETERS
1921–1948

Andrew Hignell

HALSGROVE

First published in Great Britain in 2020

Copyright © Andrew Hignell

All rights reserved. No part of this publication may be reproduced, stored in a retrieval system, or transmitted in any form or by any means without the prior permission of the copyright holder.

British Library Cataloguing-in-Publication Data
A CIP record for this title is available from the British Library

ISBN 978 0 85704 351 1

Halsgrove
Halsgrove House,
Ryelands Business Park,
Bagley Road, Wellington, Somerset TA21 9PZ
Tel: 01823 653777   Fax: 01823 216796
email: sales@halsgrove.com

Part of the Halsgrove group of companies
Information on all Halsgrove titles is available at: www.halsgrove.com

Printed and bound in India by Parksons Graphics Ltd

Contents

Acknowledgements

This book, once again, would not have been possible without the kind assistance of a number of people, cricket clubs and other organizations. In particular, the author would like to thank following for their assistance with research queries and/or photographs – Dr Dave Allan (Hampshire CCC), David Allen and colleagues at the Cardiff RFC Museum, Philip Bailey; Martyn Bevan; the late John Billot; Jeff Bird; Chris Brain; Judith Chandless; Jeff Childs; Guy Clarke; Kevin Clement; Katrina Coopey; Tony Davies; Bob Edwards; Susan Edwards; Jon Filby; Gerald Gabb; the late Bob Harragan; Stephen Hedges; Stephen Hill; the late David Herbert (senior); Lawrence Hourahane; the late David James; Jane James; David Jeater, John Jenkins; Bryn Jones; Mike and David Knight; Julian Lawton Smith; Brian Lile; Jon Lloyd; Tim Mathias; Bob Mole; Tony Percival; Tony Peters; Barry Phillips; Duncan Pierce; Gwyn Prescott; Edwina Smart; the late Hugh Thomas; Tony Webb; Prof. Gareth Williams; Sian Williams and Anthony Woolford, as well as the Archivists at Llandaff Cathedral School; Monmouth School; Christ College Brecon; Llandovery College; Exeter College, Oxford; Brasenose College, Oxford; Jesus College, Oxford; Glamorgan Archives, Dyfed Record Office; West Glamorgan Archives; The Cardiff Museum; The South Wales Miners Institute; Cardiff Local History Library and the National Library of Wales.

Main cover image – The Glamorgan side take to the field at Hove in 1939 for the Championship match against Sussex. (Photo Credit – Sussex CCC Museum.)

Top cover image – St Helen's, Swansea as seen for Glamorgan's match against the 1930 Australians.

Spine image – Wilf Wooller.

Back cover image – Maurice Turnbull.

Introduction

This is the second volume in a series of books containing biographies of all known Glamorgan cricketers. The first covered the period from 1889, when Glamorgan played their first inter-county fixture against Warwickshire at Cardiff Arms Park, until 1920 when the final batch of Minor County Championship matches took place. Through the efforts of 'Tal' Whittington (Volume 1, p199-201) sufficient home and away fixtures were secured for 1921 to allow the Welsh county to enter the County Championship.

There was great excitement on 18 May 1921 as Glamorgan played their inaugural first-class game at the Arms Park and, as Tal walked out with his opening partner at the start of the game there was a Celtic feeling to proceedings as the band of the Royal Welsh Fusiliers, who were gathered on the adjoining rugby field, played 'Men of Harlech.' Two days later there were further Cymric celebrations as Glamorgan defeated Sussex and, amidst the series of impromptu speeches given to the delirious crowd from the balcony of the pavilion, there was great anticipation that this 23-run win might mark the coming of age of cricket in Wales.

A view from the rugby field at the Arms Park of the pavilion and cricket ground alongside the River Taff where Glamorgan began life as a first-class county in 1921. (Photograph reproduced with the kind assistance and permission of the Cardiff RFC Museum.)

It sadly was not to be the case, as over the course of the next decade and beyond, Glamorgan CCC lurched from defeat to defeat like a drunk stumbling their way out of a bar, whilst visiting teams were so expecting to win that they did not book into their hotels for the full duration of the three-day matches. The series of heavy defeats affected gate receipts and the Club's flimsy finances proved to be a constant headache for their Treasurer and other officials, and their continued existence during the rest of the 1920s was only possible because of the generous nest egg of £1000 which Sir Sidney Byass had provided at the start of the decade in order to provide guarantees to English counties who were contemplating arranging fixtures with the Welsh outfit.

The spin-off from a playing point of view was that Glamorgan were rarely able to field a series of professionals and, as the following pages will outline, were heavily reliant of amateur talent. They could still call upon some of the stalwarts from the Minor County days, including Norman Riches (Volume 1, p.183-188) who agreed to lead Glamorgan during their inaugural summer of County Championship cricket as he took a sabbatical from his dental practice in Cardiff.

But the reliance on amateurs meant that the Glamorgan line-up was rarely the same from match to match – in fact, in 1921 there was a different line-up in each of the eighteen Championship fixtures, whilst some of the professionals who were hired were found to be badly wanting at first-class level. However, the perseverance of the Glamorgan officials paid off as they acquired some decent cast-offs from other counties, starting with Jack Mercer from Sussex and Frank Ryan from Hampshire, whilst Arnold Dyson and John Bell followed in the footsteps of Eddie Bates (Vol 1, p. 305-309) from Yorkshire to carve out a decent career as a professional with the Welsh county.

Eddie Bates, seen in 1924. The Yorkshireman was one of the stalwarts from the Minor County days who helped Glamorgan to eventually find their feet in first-class cricket.

Dai and Emrys Davies also emerged as homegrown professionals whilst Johnnie Clay and, later, Maurice Turnbull emerged as outstanding amateur talents with ball and bat respectively besides having spells as Glamorgan captain. Johnnie had begun life in 1921 as a tearaway fast bowler before switching to off-breaks, whilst Maurice had made his debut for the Welsh county in 1924 whilst still at boarding school in Somerset. The fresh-faced youngster duly played a match winning innings against Lancashire at Swansea and, with Cyril Walters from Neath Grammar School also impressing, there were hopes of greater success for the Welsh county during the 1930s.

Although Walters departed for Worcestershire, there were better days for Glamorgan during their second decade as a first-class county, but only after some dark times during the winter of 1932/33 when it seemed as if the Club would fold. It was only through the earnest efforts of Maurice and Johnnie, who by then were also the Club's Hon. Secretary and Hon. Treasurer respectively, that the financial crisis was averted. Each tapped into their wide range of contacts in the business and sporting worlds of South Wales to draw upon sufficient support to keep the Club afloat. The annual matches against the touring teams at Swansea also helped to swell the Club's coffers, with the St Helen's groundsman under strict instructions to create a decent wicket so that the match would certainly last all three days, whilst Maurice – with half an eye on empty spaces in the crowd – had to instruct his bowlers not to take wickets until every seat was filled!

The huge crowd at St Helen's for the visit of the 1930 Australians with some spilling over onto the rugby ground. In the background is the recently erected pavilion together with the balcony from which the great and good of Swansea cricket gazed down on proceedings.

Glamorgan also became more competitive during the 1930s as the young colts matured into high-quality county players, with Emrys forming a hugely productive opening partnership with Arnold, whilst Jack and Johnnie became two of the most successful bowlers on the county circuit. This decade also saw Glamorgan stage more games around South Wales. Having added games at Ynysyangharad Park in Pontypridd to their calendar during the late 1920s, it was largely through Johnnie's influence that the Welsh county briefly staged matches in the pleasant market town of Cowbridge in the Vale of Glamorgan. The wicket however at The Broadshoard left something to be desired and after some incident-packed matches, Cowbridge was deleted from the fixture liSt In its place were added The Gnoll in Neath and Stradey Park in Llanelli, with the latter

Stan Nicholls bowls to Dai Davies as Essex visit Cowbridge during August 1931 for their match against Glamorgan.

9

seeing Dai and Emrys play on their home soil in Carmarthenshire, whilst their presence in the Glamorgan line-up led to decent crowds at these western outposts of the county game.

1934 also saw Glamorgan merge with Monmouthshire whose finances as a Minor County had also been a source of worry. To some, it seemed strange that Glamorgan having just endured a torrid time with their finances should agree to join forces with another debt-ridden organization and agree to field a 2nd XI in the Minor County Championship. But as Maurice and Johnnie pointed out, you have to speculate in order to accumulate and the decision to merge with Monmouthshire proved to be a masterstroke. Not only did it mean that Rodney Parade, Newport and, later, The Welfare Ground in Ebbw Vale were added to Glamorgan's fixture list, but promising young Monmouthshire cricketers were now eligible to immediately appear in the Club's first-class fixtures.

The upshot was that the likes of Allan Watkins and Phil Clift, each from Usk, were able to play during the late 1930s in Championship cricket for Glamorgan having each honed their skills, alongside other emerging talent in the county's 2nd XI in Minor County games. No longer were they thrown in at the deep end as had happened to many of the young players during the 1920s whose story is told in the following pages. No surprise therefore that many of these promising young colts failed to make the grade, but with Glamorgan having also hired Bill Hitch, the ex-Surrey and England bowler to oversee the coaching and create a Colts team, the young cricketers of the late 1930s were in a far better position than their counterparts ten years or so before.

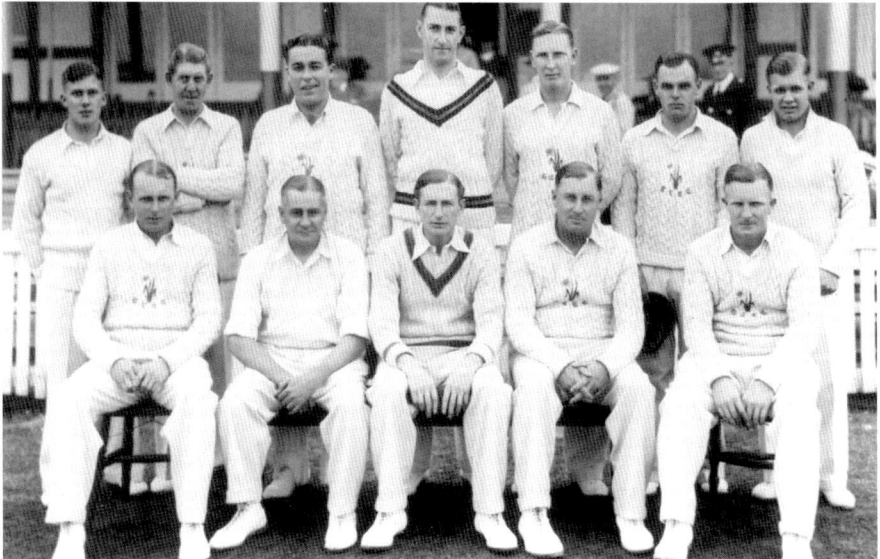

Phil Clift and Allan Watkins bookend the backrow in this Glamorgan team group from 1939. Proudly sitting in the middle of the front row is captain Maurice Turnbull in what tragically proved to be his final season of county cricket. Also in the photograph are, in the back row Cyril Smart, Haydn Davies, Peter Judge, Closs Jones and Tom Brierley, whilst sitting are Arnold Dyson, Dai Davies, Jack Mercer and Emrys Davies.

The proof of the pudding was the emergence of Allan Watkins as a leading all-rounder in county cricket after the Second World War and his selection for England in the Ashes series of 1948. However, by the time he rubbed shoulders with Don Bradman and his so-called Invincibles in their baggy green caps, there had been several changes in personal in Glamorgan's ranks. Tragically, Maurice had given his life to King and Country whilst serving with the Welsh Guards in Normandy having signed-off from Championship cricket in 1939 with a century against Leicestershire in what cruelly proved to be his final game for his beloved county.

The Club's leader in 1948 was another man who had endured a difficult War – Wilf Wooller, the former Welsh rugby international who had dabbled with county cricket in the late 1930s after leaving Cambridge University before being a Prisoner of War in the Far East and enduring life, and sadly death, in the dreadful camps such as Changi in Singapore.

Despite a significant loss of weight, the sporting all-rounder agreed to throw in his lot with the Welsh county and under the tutelage of Johnnie, as well as wicket-keeper Haydn Davies, Wilf became the dominant post-war personality in Glamorgan Cricket. To his delight and that of so many other passionate Welshmen and women, 'The Skipper' guided Glamorgan to their first-ever Championship title in 1948 and after the trials and tribulations of their first two decades as a first-class county, it was very fitting that Johnnie should take the final

Wilf Wooller (right) leads out the Glamorgan team, including veteran Johnnie Clay, into the field at Dean Park in Bournemouth in 1948 for the dramatic and historic conclusion of their match against Hampshire as the county title comes to Wales.

wicket in the game against Hampshire at Bournemouth as Glamorgan clinched the title.

For some of the pre-war veterans such as Emrys, they could scarcely believe what had happened at Dean Park and on the train journey back home to South Wales, he kept saying to his colleagues I will only believe it when I read it in the newspapers! By chance, Dai was also at the game, in his guise as a first-class umpire and he joined with his former colleagues as the celebrations went on, just like the name of famous Welsh folk song *Ar Hyd y Nos*, all through the night.

Emrys' own career also went on and on, with the yeoman all-rounder eventually calling it a day in 1954 shortly after celebrating his fiftieth birthday. By the time he hung up his bat, the Club's finances were in a far healthier state, whilst a series of ground improvements had also taken place. On the field, the next generation of homegrown Glamorgan cricketers had also come to the fore with the likes of Willie Jones from Carmarthen and Swansea's Gilbert Parkhouse occupying the engine-room of the batting. On the bowling front Len Muncer and Jim McConnon had each been recruited from outside Wales, but Don Shepherd from the Gower and Swansea's Jim Pressdee were making great forward strides as young cricketers.

By the end of the 1950s, Alan Jones from Velindre in the Swansea Valleys, Peter Walker, an all-rounder from a Welsh family who had been raised in South Africa and Tony Lewis, born in Swansea but educated at Neath Grammar School, were also making huge strides forward with each joining Don and others in writing the next chapter of success for Glamorgan during the 1960s, with the decade featuring consecutive victories over the Australian tourists and culminating in a second Championship title victory in 1969.

Johnnie Clay plus other players and Glamorgan staff excitedly look through the pile of telegrams and letters which flooded in to the Glamorgan office following their Championship success in 1948.

1921

The dream of first-class status had been finally achieved after several abortive attempts before the Great War, with the MCC rubber-stamping the application in February 1921. The post-War campaign had begun at the committee meeting held during the autumn of 1919 in Swansea in the offices of Club Treasurer Dyson Williams (Volume 1, p.193-196). As the Club regrouped and planned ahead following the end of the long and bloody warfare, the Club's officials discussed at length how to pursue the dream which had been there right at the outset of the Club's formation back in July 1888. Matters were left in the hands of Tal Whittington (Volume 1, p.198-201), the Neath-born solicitor, who had been at the forefront of the Club's affairs for many years.

It was fitting as well that he and Norman Riches (Volume 1, p183-188) should open the batting in the inaugural Championship match against Sussex at Cardiff Arms Park. After some spirited performances by the home side, including a stirring 96 from Jock Tait (Volume 1, p278-280), Riches left Sussex a target of 334 on the final afternoon. A fourth wicket stand of 166 in just ninety minutes between Ted Bowley and Don Jenner looked like laying the foundations of a Sussex victory, especially as there were several fumbles and dropped catches by the quite aged Glamorgan fielders. But Harry Symonds (Volume 1, p.247-248) took a fine catch on the boundary's edge as Jenner tried to dispatch a Glamorgan bowler in the direction of Cardiff Castle. It was then the turn of another Harry, Mr Creber – the veteran Swansea bowler (Volume 1, p.158-160) – to take centre-stage as he mopped up the tail and saw Glamorgan to a 23-run victory.

What followed on the Arms Park cricket field then resembled what had taken place so often on the adjoining rugby field after a Welsh rugby victory as the crowd, estimated

The ecstatic crowd surge onto the outfield at Cardiff Arms Park and gather in front of the pavilion after Glamorgan defeat Sussex by 23 runs, in May 1921.

at over five thousand swarmed onto the outfield and gathered in front of the pavilion to hear speeches from Norman, the victorious Glamorgan captain and his counterpart from Sussex.

Listening to these stirring words, and reading the celebratory words in the newspapers the following morning, it seemed as if it was the dawn of a brave new age in Welsh sport, fuelled by post-War euphoria and further growth in the local economy. But the dream soon turned into a nightmare as Glamorgan lost their next eight games in succession, including three by an innings, before defeating Worcestershire at Swansea in the last week of July. It proved to be their second and final victory of the summer and despite Norman ending up with 1080 runs to his name and Jack Nash (Volume 1, p.179-181) claiming 91 wickets, Glamorgan ended the summer in 17th and last place in the Championship table.

Despite gate receipts in excess of £700 at the Sussex match, the Club ended their first year of Championship cricket with a deficit of £447. Attempts to recruit and strengthen the playing resources were stymied by the lack of cash, and the Welsh county relied on a host of amateurs turning out and trying their best. Most had appeared in the Minor County matches in previous years, and were either past their best or not good enough for Championship cricket. Yet, there was still plenty of hope and optimism in these heady post-war years, and within the Glamorgan committee room, the Club's officials still believed that things would soon turn around. Surely things couldn't get any worse – unfortunately they did!

Glamorgan's team in their inaugural County Championship match, against Sussex at Cardiff in 1921. Back row standing – George Cording, Jack Nash, Eddie Bates, Edgar Cooper and Harry Symonds. Front row sitting - Arthur O'Bree, Tal Whittington, Norman Riches, Jock Tait and Percy Morris. Harry Creber is sat on the ground.

CLAY, John Charles ('Johnnie')

Born – Bonvilston, 18 March 1898
Died – St Hilary, 11 August 1973
Amateur
RHB, RM/OB
Ed – Winchester College
1st XI: 1921-1949
Cap: 1921
Captain: 1924-1927; 1929; 1946
England 1935 (1 cap); Monmouthshire 1919-1921
Clubs: Chepstow, Cowbridge, South Wales Hunts, Welsh Cygnets

Batting and Fielding Record:

	M	I	NO	RUNS	AV	100	50	CT	ST
F-c	358	536	88	6868	15.33	2	17	171	-
Wartime	17	14	6	158	26.33	-	1	4	-

Bowling Record:

	Balls	M	R	W	AV	5wI	10wM
F-c	59793	2335	25181	1292	19.49	105	28
Wartime	?	?	?	43	-	-	-

Career-bests:
First-class – 115* v New Zealanders at Cardiff Arms Park, 1927
9/54 v Northamptonshire at Llanelli, 1935

John Arlott summed up Johnnie Clay's natural ability as a bowler – "If you look at JC Clay, you will see that he looks like an off-break bowler. He is no hurler of thunderbolts,

Johnnie Clay.

no trafficker of that rather racy and rising delivery, or the leg-break with its even more raffish and deceitful by-product, the googly. The off-break is the classical and the traditional ball, and Johnnie was created to bowl it. The fast bowler and the leg-spinner were no more than phases designed to convince him of his natural bent."

In an illustrious career spanning almost three decades, Johnnie took 1,292 wickets for Glamorgan and with his clever off-spin, he teased and tricked several generations of county and Test batsmen. But had it not been for his efforts off the field with his great friend Maurice Turnbull, the Welsh county side might have folded because of financial difficulties in the early 1930s – a situation brought upon through poor results and a downturn in the economy.

Indeed, the position was so grim in the winter of 1932-33 for the county's Treasurer to resign and, as the club attempted to stay afloat by dispensing with the services of several professionals, a few cynics started to prepare Glamorgan's epitaph. But Johnnie, whose family had long been linked with sport in south-east Wales, was determined that the club should survive and, unlike the club's previous management, he opted for a proactive, as opposed to the reactive, approach towards fundraising and promoting the good name of Glamorgan Cricket.

For the next couple of years, Johnnie helped to mastermind the fund-raising scheme that eventually helped the club out of this pickle. Like his good friend Maurice, Johnnie's family owned a highly successful business in the bustling Docks at Cardiff and, with the dynamic and debonair personalities at the helm, a host of special events were staged across the region, with both men drawing on their vast range of contacts in the commercial and sporting community of Cardiff.

A measure of their success was that Glamorgan rose up to 7th place in the County Championship in 1937 with Johnnie enjoying an outstanding season, taking 176 wickets and establishing a club record which still stands today. He was widely regarded as amongst the country's leading spin bowlers, although his prowess with the ball had to be tempered at times with the financial needs of Glamorgan, especially when it came to a decent gate against the Australians in 1938. The first two days of the game were badly affected by the weather but the prospect of seeing the great Don Bradman bat at St Helen's had attracted a bumper crowd on the third morning, and during the afternoon, the crowd got their wish as out walked the great man in his baggy green cap. "Don't get Bradman out too quickly, as there are still a few places in the crowd" was the instruction from Maurice to Johnnie and the rest of the Glamorgan team.

Dutifully, Johnnie followed these instructions, as words spread like wildfire in Swansea that 'The Don' was at the crease. Scores of people headed for St Helen's – some no doubt with the flimsiest of excuses for leaving work, and many were rewarded with a glimpse of seeing 'The Don' play himself in as a record crowd now filled the historic ground. With a crowd over a dozen deep around the boundary edge, and the enclosures almost bursting, Maurice had a quick word with Johnnie and said that he could now try to get Bradman out.

It didn't take Johnnie very long either as Bradman – like so many other batsmen before and after – was lured down the track by Johnnie's subtle bowling and smartly stumped by wicket-keeper Haydn Davies. The Australian maestro departed somewhat crestfallen, but the crowd were happy as they had seen the great man bat, whilst the county's Treasurer was equally gleeful, counting the huge pile of coins in the pavilion!

Born in 1898, Johnnie was the eldest of four children born to Charles Leigh Clay, the owner of a coal exporting business at Cardiff Docks and a High Sheriff of Monmouthshire, whose home was at Wyndcliffe Court in Chepstow. The Clay's were enthusiastic sportsmen, with Johnnie's grandfather promoting cricket in the Chepstow area by arranging a three-day exhibition match in 1882 between a local XXII and the United Eleven of All-Eleven.

Charles Clay was also a useful cricketer with the Chepstow club, who on occasions fielded up to five members of the Clay family, and Johnnie therefore was introduced to the game at an early age. In 1911 Johnnie followed in his father's footsteps by attending Winchester, and four years later, he won a place in the school's 1st XI as a fast bowler. In 1916 – his final year at school – Johnnie was the school's leading wicket-taker, claiming 40 victims at just 10 runs apiece, including a haul of 8/86 against Eton.

After leaving Winchester, Johnnie spent the final years of the Great War serving in the Royal Fleet Auxiliary, before joining his father's business and supervising their business with clients in South America. During the summer, he continued to play cricket for Chepstow CC, whilst in the winter months he rode with the Glamorgan and Curre Hunts, in addition to riding in local point-to-points, and playing in goal for St Arvans AFC. Besides being a tearaway fast bowler, Johnnie developed his batting skills, and in 1919 he scored 150 against Cardiff Cliftonians.

In 1920 Johnnie impressed the Glamorgan officials when he played in two matches for Monmouthshire against the county who had secured first-class status for 1921, although the young all-rounder was not included in their inaugural Championship fixture at Cardiff. Instead, Johnnie went on the Glamorgan Nomads tour to South Devon where he scored a chanceless 144 against Torquay, and took 6/48 against Chudleigh, but he was duly included in Glamorgan's side for their match against

Johnnie Clay, seen standing second left with members of the Winchester XI of 1919.

Leicestershire at Swansea on 28 May, and although he failed to take a wicket in the match, it marked the start of his long, and loyal, association with Glamorgan Cricket.

In August 1921 Johnnie took his first five-wicket hauls, both on away grounds, with 5/37 against Derbyshire at Chesterfield, and then the following week 6/86 against Leicestershire at Aylestone Road. The latter game also saw Johnnie record his maiden first-class fifty as he flayed the Leicestershire attack for 71 before being stumped. He finished the summer with 41 victims – the third highest for the club, and one that could have been higher had the young pace bowler not been let down by some shoddy fielding and a string of dropped catches by the portly amateurs who stood in the slips. He also had to bowl some lengthy spells, simply because he was the youngest and fittest bowler in the Glamorgan side and, on occasions, he cut down on his pace after a lengthy spell and experimented with some leg-cutters and leg-spin.

Glamorgan got their value out of Johnnie again in 1922 as he claimed 83 wickets at just 22 runs apiece, and held together what was, at times, a piecemeal attack during another moderate season for the Welsh county. The highlight of the summer was a match analysis of 11/185 against Derbyshire at Swansea, and there were several occasions when Johnnie also cut back on his pace and bowled spin. A back strain severely affected him in

1923, and he could only bowl flat out for half a dozen overs, before switching to cutters.

A summer when he took just 45 victims may not at first glance appear to be a turning point in his career, but it was during 1923 that Johnnie began to bowl off-spin, largely as a result of some advice and coaching from Fred Bowley, the former Worcestershire cricketer who had been appointed as Glamorgan's coach. In mid-summer he bowled some lengthy spells of off-spin, including the game at Cheltenham College against Gloucestershire, for whom Alf Dipper struck 252*, and survived a chance early in his innings, when he played a ball from Johnnie which rolled back onto his stumps, but didn't dislodge a bail – a microcosm of the frustrations and disappointments which afflicted the jovial all-rounder early in his county career.

1923 was therefore a watershed year as it marked the dawn of a new and more successful phase as a specialist spin bowler, and there were stories that during the winter months Johnnie walked about Cardiff holding a small rubber ball and squeezing it tightly in his fingers in order to strengthen them for the new tasks which lay ahead. There was also another fresh challenge as he took over the captaincy for 1924, and proceeded to lead Glamorgan to five victories in their 24 Championship matches – their highest to date – and 13th place in the county table.

Johnnie Clay, the gentleman cricketer as seen in 1924 with his 'trademark' of a flower in the buttonhole of his cricket blazer.

Two years later, he had the delight of opening the morning paper in June after Glamorgan's victory over Derbyshire, and to see Glamorgan on top of the Championship table. It was not a fluke as a determined Glamorgan side, astutely led by Johnnie, remained in the top two until the end of July, with a group of promising young players, including Maurice as well as Cyril Walters, developing their skills and showing the benefit of Fred's wise words as coach, and the backing of Johnnie as the county's captain.

For several seasons, Johnnie had also been showing promise with the bat, and in 1926, he was left stranded on 84 in the match at Trent Bridge when the Nottinghamshire bowlers took the final wicket. However, he duly reached three figures the following July when batting at number five against New Zealand, he attacked the tourists bowling for two and a half hours in making an unbeaten 115.

There were other reasons for Johnnie to smile in 1927 as, during the course of the summer, he was promoted to a senior position within his father's business, and he announced his engagement to the daughter of Colonel Homfray of Penlline Castle. Given his new personal circumstances and increasing business commitments, he also stood down from the captaincy and handed over to Trevor Arnott.

Johnnie pledged to help out the county whenever he could but, having got married, and being involved in a growing number of business meeting, he was only able to play in nine games, all of them in Wales. It was a very disappointing summer for Glamorgan, as they won just a couple of games, and missed Johnnie's wise council. Trevor tried his best, but he did not enjoy the captaincy, so with Maurice – the other decent amateur – still in residence at Cambridge, and nobody else prepared to commit to a full summer of cricket, Johnnie agreed to share the captaincy with Norman Riches during 1929.

Fortunately, Johnnie was able to play in fourteen games, and during the course of 1929 he posted his maiden Championship century against Worcestershire at Swansea, and in the process shared in a remarkable ninth wicket stand of 203 with Joe Hills which still stands as a club record. The pair flayed the visiting bowling, with Johnnie dispatching several balls out of the St Helen's ground and into the goods yard of the Swansea Bay station which stood on the far side of Oystermouth Road.

During August, Johnnie handed over the reins to Maurice, and he was delighted when his young friend agreed to lead the side in 1930, when once again his business commitments restricted him to just nine games. Nevertheless, the summer of 1930 saw the pair forge a close partnership that was to successfully see Glamorgan through the Depression of the early 1930s. Indeed, Johnnie later said that he enjoyed playing with, and bowling under Maurice

A photo of Johnnie Clay's bowling action from 1948.

than any other captain, and the spinner proved this in 1930 with a fine seven-wicket haul from 53 overs of teasing off-breaks during the match with Somerset at Weston-super-Mare, followed in 1931 by another seven-wicket haul against Middlesex at Lord's.

But Johnnie aggravated his back during the match at Lord's and missed several matches before returning to the side in July, including the game with Northamptonshire at Cowbridge. The latter was a new venue for the Welsh club, just a couple of miles from Johnnie's home at St Hilary where he lived with his wife and young family. Johnnie was instrumental in organising the match on the ground where he regularly played club cricket, as the Welsh county sought to reduce their mounting debts by tapping into the support for cricket from fans in the Vale of Glamorgan.

But the club's finances failed to improve and, after the release of several professionals and the resignation of the county's Treasurer, Johnnie stepped into the latter's shoes and helped Maurice in a fund-raising campaign which preserved the club's status. As well as helping to raise some invaluable cash, Johnnie also agreed to turn out more regularly in the future, not least because Frank Ryan, the maverick left-arm spinner, had been released. Johnnie's reward were a series of highly productive seasons and a place in the England side.

He began the 1932 season with 11 wickets at Northampton, before recording a match haul of 9/47 on his home patch at Cowbridge as Somerset were dismissed for 88 and 40 on a crumbling wicket. He ended the summer with a career-best 82 victims, before adding a further 59 the following summer, during which he was hampered by a leg injury, and turned out on occasions when only semi-fit, bowling leg-breaks off one pace.

Thankfully, he was restored to full fitness in 1934, when he enjoyed a memorable season, finishing the summer with 103 wickets at just 17 runs apiece, and no less than thirteen five wicket hauls. He was also the leading amateur bowler in the country, and his success was marked by selection for the Gentlemen of England against the Australians at Lord's. During a fine season, he took 12/84 as Glamorgan defeated Surrey for the first-ever time at The Oval, as well as ten wicket hauls in consecutive Championship matches against Somerset at Swansea and Essex at Clacton. *Wisden's* correspondent was fulsome in his praise of the man widely regarded as the finest off-spinner in the country – "his flight and perfect length were the reasons for his success even more than ability to spin the ball and conceal the break. It has been frequently said that batsmen have often thought they were receiving a half-volley from Johnnie only to find to their surprise it was a perfect length ball."

He also had a hectic season off the field, as he played a leading role in the amalgamation of Glamorgan with Monmouthshire. His former county were now in dire financial straits, and unable to raise a team and honour fixtures, their officials approached Johnnie to see if Glamorgan were interested in an affiliation which would allow Glamorgan to field a 2nd XI in the Minor County Championship. Johnnie and Maurice agreed that it was an excellent offer, and on 4 July an agreement was brokered with Glamorgan replacing Monmouthshire in the Minor County competition the following year.

Not only was 1935 an important year for Glamorgan, with its 2nd XI acting as a nursery of promising talent, but it was an important year for Johnnie as well, as the off-spinner was called up into the England squad for the series with South Africa. He began the summer where he had left off in 1934 with a hatful of wickets, including 9/54 against Northamptonshire at Stradey Park, Llanelli; 8/46 against Leicestershire at Aylestone Road plus a match haul of 12/134 against Hampshire at Bournemouth.

JC Clay – the England and Glamorgan cricketer.

After such outstanding returns, the England selectors called up Johnnie for the Third and Fourth Tests of the series against the Springboks, but he was 12th man on each occasion. However, he was included in the squad for the Fifth and final Test at The Oval, and was duly included in the starting eleven. The game was staged on a placid surface – very different to the ones he often encountered on the county circuit – and the tourists had a more hard-nosed approach to batting than that adopted by some of the cavalier amateurs who Johnnie tricked and teased for Glamorgan. He duly delivered 32 accurate overs, without taking a wicket in what proved to be his only appearance at Test level.

He remained however in the selectors thoughts in 1936 when India were the summer visitors. Quiet words were made in his direction, but each approach was rebuffed with the answer "I'm too old, give someone younger a chance!" The reason for their interest were some further outstanding performances including 11 wickets in the match with Hampshire at Swansea, followed by 10/101 against Worcestershire at Neath, plus an astonishing return of 8/43 against the Indians at Swansea as Glamorgan defeated the tourists in a match that on the final morning seemed destined for a draw. But Johnnie took 8/14 in the space of eleven overs as the ball spun and lifted sharply to see his side to a remarkable victory.

His performance against the Indians was however merely the *hors d'oeuvres* before an astonishing summer in 1937 when he appeared in 26 out of the club's 30 fixtures and delivered 1103.3 overs of sheer artistry as he broke all of the county's bowling records with a haul of 176 wickets at 17 runs apiece. In his previous sixteen seasons with the county, he had recorded 54 five-wicket hauls, yet in 1937 he took five wickets in an innings on 20 occasions as Glamorgan ended the summer in 7th place in the table – their highest-ever position.

His finest hour in a season brimful of high-class performances came at Swansea against Worcestershire where he took a club record 17/212. In the visitor's first innings, Johnnie took 9/66, largely through intelligent variation of flight, rather than excessive spin, during a two and a half hour spell. Despite his exertions he had to bowl a further 34 overs when the visitors batted again as Closs Jones aggravated an injury which prevented him from bowling. Not surprisingly, he came in for a bit of punishment, but Johnnie had the last laugh as several visitors holed out on the boundary's edge. As Nomad wrote in the *Western Mail*, "Clay's performance was all the greater because he had no artificial aid and placed reliance on accurate length, combined with subtle variation of flight and pace. It was a triumph too for his temperament. If he was hit for a couple of boundaries, he walked to the wicket with that characteristic attitude of his – long arms hanging loosely and fingers twitching, and bowled the next ball as if nothing had happened."

With a thin and wiry frame, Johnnie retained his fitness by regularly riding with the Glamorgan Hunt during the winter months. In his youth he had ridden in local point-to-points, but by the 1930s, his involvement was reduced to just riding out whenever the Hunt met. His methods clearly worked as season after season, he was ready and raring to go, delivering long spells of testing off-spin. Johnnie therefore showed no ill effects after his exertions in 1937, and he began the following season with 9 wickets against Warwickshire followed by 12 against Hampshire.

With Johnnie in outstanding form, and Maurice now an England selector, it was no surprise that he received an invitation from chief selector Sir Pelham Warner to play in the First Test against the 1938 Australians at Trent Bridge. Maurice was optimistic that his pal would agree to play, but shortly before receiving the invite, Johnnie had injured his leg, ironically in the garden of his home on the outskirts of Cardiff, as he attempted to demonstrate to his children how Golden Miller had won the Cheltenham Gold Cup by leaping over a chair. But unlike the great racehorse, Johnnie came to grief and he duly had to withdraw from the squad as he feared his strained leg would not stand up to the rigours of a five-day Test.

This typified Clay's attitude in not wanting to let anyone down, least of all his great friend Maurice and, after several weeks of convalescence he was back in the Glamorgan side, ending with a haul of 94 wickets, including the prized scalp of Don Bradman in the match against the Australians at Swansea, at 17 runs apiece and the most-ever taken by an amateur for any county. As wicket-keeper Haydn Davies later recalled, "Johnnie valued the wicket of The Don more highly than any other he took for Glamorgan. Johnnie was all arms and legs and quite difficult to pick up unless you were used to him. This was a key factor in his dismissal as after beating Don through the air on several occasions, in sheer desperation, he went down the wicket, and was beaten by Johnnie's superb flight as I stumped him."

After his Herculean performances in 1938, a series of niggling injuries and business commitments meant that Johnnie only appeared in eight matches in 1939 – all of them in Wales. His final game of the summer – and tragically his last with Maurice – took place at Swansea against Leicestershire. Soon afterwards, he joined the Royal Artillery, serving initially as a Captain before rising to the rank of Major and being based in South Wales looking after the defense of several important settlements and ports.

Johnnie inspects the pitch for a county game at the Arms Park during 1954.

Based in South Wales, Johnnie was able to serve on the Emergency Committee which was created to oversee the running of the Glamorgan club during the War. He was also able to organise, and play in, a few fundraising matches in 1943 and 1944. Getting back into action after several blank years was a great delight, but in August 1944 Johnnie, like the rest of Glamorgan's supporters, were brought back down to Earth with the news that Maurice, now a Major in the Welsh Guards had been killed in action in Normandy.

Johnnie oversaw the arrangements for a Memorial Match the following year in memory of the great

Glamorgan captain and then, with the hostilities ceasing, he started organising the re-launch of county matches. The loss of Maurice had been a grievous blow to the club, but Johnnie was not going to give up, and out of a sense of duty to the club and his late friend, he agreed to taking over the captaincy as well as assembling a new squad of players, thereby ensuring that Maurice's efforts before the War would not be in vain.

Johnnie enlisted the help of Austin Matthews and Wilf Wooller as assistant secretaries, whilst his contacts in Cardiff Docks helped him persuade leading businessman Herbert Merrett to spearhead a fund-raising campaign to help restore the facilities at the club's various grounds. He also made contact with many of the amateurs and professionals who had appeared before the War, plus a couple of other rugby players and footballers who were decent cricketers.

Remarkably, Johnnie welded this motley assortment into one of the most successful sides in the club's history as in 1946 they won ten matches to finish in 6th place in the Championship table. His astute captaincy was the lynchpin in Glamorgan's success, to say nothing of his 130 wickets at 13 apiece, as the veteran rolled back the years to the pleasure of some decent crowds who flocked to see Glamorgan play, delighted that they were back in action after seven long years.

1946 was a turning point in the club's financial history as they ended the summer with their healthiest ever bank balance, besides having improved facilities and a pool of emerging talent. To further improve matters, Wilf had also accepted an offer to take over the captaincy and the following year, Johnnie was able to hand over the captaincy baton and move into semi-retirement.

Nevertheless, he still played in thirteen games, and continued to cause headaches for visiting batsmen with his subtle wiles. Hauls of 11/162 against the South Africans and a spell of 6/5 in 11 overs against Leicestershire at the Arms Park showed that he had not lost any of his skill. Many thought that when Johnnie agreed to serve as a Test Selector in 1947 his performance against the Springboks at Cardiff would be his last hurrah, but in 1948 Johnnie made a dramatic return as Glamorgan pressed for the county title. Wilf successfully persuaded the veteran spinner to return to the county side for the decisive match during August against Surrey at the Arms Park, with Johnnie responding to his recall in a magnificent way and claimed 10/65 as Glamorgan won by an innings and 24 runs.

The fifty-year-old remained in the side that travelled to Hampshire needing one more victory to clinch the title, and he proceeded to claim three cheap wickets as Hampshire were forced to follow-on. Wickets continued to tumble as the Glamorgan bowlers continued to work their way through the Hampshire batting and, after all that had happened during his illustrious career, it was most fitting that Johnnie should take the final wicket, trapping the last batsman leg before wicket, before returning to the pavilion, with tears of sheer joy running down his cheeks, to join in with the celebrations as Glamorgan became county cricket champions for the first time in their history.

This was the crowning achievement in a playing career that finally drew to a close the following year when, with Stan Trick unavailable and others injured, he played against Yorkshire at Newport, taking a wicket in each innings as the Tykes won by 278 runs. The curtain therefore came down on 29 August 1949 in a quiet and unspectacular way, back home on Monmouthshire soil where thirty years and countless overs earlier he had started his Minor County career. But Johnnie was never one for publicity, and he probably preferred playing his 358th and final game for Glamorgan without a huge fuss.

After retiring, Johnnie maintained his interest in cricket by serving on the committee as well as acting as one of the Club's Trustees and latterly their President. During the winter, he served as a secretary of the Glamorgan Hunt, besides acting as a Steward at Chepstow Racecourse and joining their Board of Directors. Johnnie also took great pleasure in owning, with his sons, a number of long-distance steeple-chasers who raced regularly at the Chepstow course. His business interests diversified as he joined the board of Wales Gas, in addition to being Chairman of the Board of the Park Hotel, as well as the High Street Arcade Company.

He still found time during the 1950s to turn out for the MCC, the South Wales Hunts, the Forty Club, Barry and Cowbridge, and fittingly he was present at Sophia Gardens in September 1969 when Glamorgan defeated Worcestershire to clinch the county title. For the second time in his life, his old eyes were full of tears of joy as Glamorgan, his team, celebrated their Championship success. He continued watching the side in the early 1970s despite failing health, and after a short illness he passed away peacefully at his home in St Hilary during August 1973. On his grave in the local church is a hand holding a cricket ball, as a lasting testament to one and all that John Charles Clay, of Glamorgan and England, was one of the finest cricketers and gentlemen the game of cricket has ever known.

243
JENKINS, Wyndham Leslie Trevor

Born – Newport, 26 August 1898
Died – Penarth, 14 June 1971
Amateur
RHB, WK
Ed – Bramshott School, Malvern College, plus Gonville and Caius College, Cambridge
1st XI: 1921
Club and Ground: 1922-1925
Cap: 1921
Clubs: Penarth, Cardiff

Batting and Fielding Record:

	M	I	NO	RUNS	AV	100	50	CT	ST
F-c	10	20	1	155	8.15	-	-	8	2

Career-best:
First-class –39 v Worcestershire at Kidderminster, 1921

A cigarette card of WLT Jenkins.

Leslie Jenkins made ten appearances for Glamorgan during their inaugural summer as a first-class county. He was the son of coal exporter Wyndham Trevor Jenkins, who had played for Monmouthshire from 1892 until 1899 and, after attending prep school in Hampshire, Leslie went to Malvern College where he won a place in their cricket XI during 1916. The College's magazine that July described him as "a very fair batsman, a good fielder and an efficient stumper."

On leaving school, Leslie joined the Royal Field Artillery, rising to the rank of Second Lieutenant by September 1917. His father's business had initially been based in Newport but, by the time he was in residence at Gonville and Caius, the Jenkins family were based in Penarth with Leslie showing promise as a top-order batsman and occasional wicket-keeper for the town's cricket club as well as for Cardiff CC.

In 1921 he was called into the Glamorgan side following an injury to Henry Symonds and made his first-class debut as a specialist batsman in the match against Gloucestershire at Swansea during the first week of June. Three weeks later, he also took over the gloves against Lancashire at the Arms Park before briefly returning to the role of specialist batsmen when school-master George Cording, one of his Cardiff team-mates became available at the end of term.

Leslie was back behind the stumps on Glamorgan's away matches in August against Sussex and Hampshire and, after a successful South Coast tour, he kept his place for the return match against Hampshire at the Arms Park. But the game ended in a two-day defeat for the Welsh county, who were led by Dyson Bransby Williams, the Swansea amateur, in his one and only appearance in Championship cricket. Glamorgan were dismissed before lunch on the opening day for 37 before the following day, their batsmen failed again as they went down to an innings defeat.

This game at Cardiff proved to be Leslie's final Championship appearance as the Welsh county, in a bid to bolster the batting and have a regular wicket-keeper, signed Hampshire's Jimmy Stone for 1922. Nevertheless, Leslie continued to turn out for the county's Club and Ground side, and was regarded as one of the best young amateurs behind the stumps in club cricket in South Wales.

Leslie duly succeeded his father in the family's coal exporting business in Penarth, and following his marriage to Joan Knight in May 1930, there were domestic as well as business commitments which left Leslie confined to largely playing club cricket at weekends. During the Second World War, Leslie served as a Special Constable, overseeing the protection of the town and docks which like nearby Cardiff, provided coal for the War Effort.

244
ARNOTT, Trevor

Born – Radyr, 16 February, 1902
Died – Ross-on-Wye, 2 February, 1975
RHB, RFM
Amateur
Ed – Monmouth School and Wycliffe College
1st XI: 1921-1930
Club and Ground: 1922-1929, 1935
Cap: 1922
Captain: 1928
Wales 1924-1930; MCC 1931-1934/35; Oxford and Cambridge Universities 1922;
South Wales 1922; LH Tennyson's XI 1926/27-1927/28; HDG Leveson Gower's XI
1927-1930; Gentlemen 1927-1928; South of England 1928; Sir J Cahn's XI 1929/30;
Monmouthshire 1931-1934
Clubs: Cardiff, Worthing, Incogniti, Welsh Cygnets
Rugby for Cardiff

Batting and Fielding Record:

	M	I	NO	RUNS	AV	100	50	CT	ST
F-c	188	321	25	4726	15.96	3	15	87	-

Bowling Record:

	Balls	M	R	W	AV	5wI	10wM
F-c	22123	646	11435	361	31.68	10	-

Career-bests:
First-class – 153 v Essex at St Helen's, Swansea, 1928
7/40 v West Indians at Cardiff Arms Park, 1923

In 1926 Trevor Arnott, a regular in the Welsh county's team during their first decade as a first-class county became the first Glamorgan cricketer to claim a hat-trick in the County Championship, achieving the feat against Somerset at the Arms Park. He also led the county during 1928 with what was described as debonair authority, but his leadership style was not to everyone's liking and, having falling out with several colleagues, notably Frank Ryan, the taciturn spinner, he was not re-appointed for 1929.

After a promising career as an all-rounder at public school, Trevor made his debut during Glamorgan's inaugural season of first-class cricket. Much was expected of the all-rounder who bowled at a lively medium pace and had earned a reputation as an aggressive strokemaker in club cricket. His maiden century eventually came during 1924 as he reached three figures century against Derbyshire at Swansea in 1924 in only 75 minutes, with Trevor reaching this personal landmark with a mighty six into the Mumbles Road.

His most successful summer with the ball had come the year before when Trevor claimed 64 victims. His hauls during 1923 included returns of 5/50 against Surrey, 6/98 in the match with Yorkshire plus a career-best 7/40 in the victory over the West Indians at the Arms Park as the Welsh county recorded their first-ever victory over an international team. However, the highlight of his career as a bowler in county cricket came in 1926 when he claimed the Club's first-ever Championship hat-trick during the match against Somerset at Cardiff Arms Park

In 1928 he accepted an offer to take over the Glamorgan captaincy from his good friend Johnnie Clay. His tenure began with a victory over Worcestershire at Cardiff but only one other success was recorded during a summer which saw the Welsh county remain in 15th place in the Championship table. More importantly, 1928 also saw some ill feeling emerge between Trevor and several of his colleagues, most notably Frank Ryan, the hot-tempered but talented left-arm spinner. After a series of arguments between the two, Frank was "rested" from the team and told that he might not get another contract with the Welsh county. However, his absence irked others in the team and, after some had discretely spoken to members of the Club's hierarchy, Frank was restored to the team, whilst Johnnie Clay and Norman Riches were appointed as joint-captains for the following season.

Trevor Arnott, as seen during 1925.

The summer of 1928 ended with a very bizarre game against Nottinghamshire at the Arms Park. As so often during 1928, the visitors were on top throughout and the final day began with Glamorgan's last pair, Emrys Davies and Frank at the wicket with sixteen runs still needed to avoid an innings defeat. So certain that the end would swiftly come that the other professionals in the Glamorgan side did not bother to change into their flannels and packed their coffins in readiness for their departure.

Trevor Arnott, Johnnie Clay and other amateurs head into a marquee for lunch with local dignitaries at a match during 1926.

But the two Glamorgan batsmen offered stout resistance and even managed to wipe out the deficit before, with a lead of one run, Emrys was caught and bowled by Bill Voce. It meant that Glamorgan would have to take the field again, and realising the chaos in the dressing room that might ensue, Trevor told his men not to unpack anything until he had spoken to Arthur Carr.

As the Nottinghamshire players came off the field, Trevor had a quiet word with Arthur who agreed to loan seven of his players as substitutes, as Trevor, Maurice, Emrys and Frank went out to field.

Arthur also agreed not to have the pitch rolled and, in turn, Trevor did not call for a new ball from the umpires, and tossed instead the old one to Maurice, as the Nottinghamshire openers took guard. There were plenty of chuckles from the rest of the Glamorgan players as Maurice marked out a small run-up, whilst Emrys took up position behind the stumps without any pads on. Maurice then sauntered up to the wicket, delivered a ball down the leg-side which was missed by both the batsman and wicket-keeper, with the two byes giving Nottinghamshire a ten-wicket victory. It was not though the last time Trevor captained the Welsh county as in 1929, with both Norman and Johnnie unavailable, he was the most experienced amateur in the ranks, and after his experiences the previous year, Trevor did his best to cajoul his colleagues.

During his career, Trevor played regularly for the MCC and also appeared for HM Martineau's XI against the 1928 West Indians. He also toured North America with Incogniti in 1924, Jamaica with Lionel Tennyson's XI in both 1926/27 and 1927/28 as well as South America with Sir Julian Cahn's XI in 1929/30. After retiring from county cricket with Glamorgan during 1930 at the premature age of 28, Trevor played Minor County cricket for Monmouthshire until 1934 when they wound up their activities and merged with Glamorgan.

He subsequently coached at Monmouth School and continued to be involved in sport by owning several useful greyhounds who regularly raced at the track which ran around the perimeter of the Arms Park rugby ground, besides becoming a low handicap golfer.

Trevor Arnott seen in 1939 when playing for Pat Brain's XI against a Glamorgan side at the Arms Park.

1922

Few would dispute that 1922 was Glamorgan's worst-ever season with the Welsh county losing a dozen matches in succession at the start of the season. The first four were by an innings and led several journalists to speculate whether Glamorgan were really a first-class side. The losing run eventually came to an end on 1 August as Harry Creber spun his team to victory over Somerset at Weston-super-Mare.

But it proved to be the sole victory of a truly dreadful summer which saw Glamorgan lose 18 of their 22 Championship matches. In all, 46 players appeared for the Welsh county in their first-class matches, and this total might have been even higher had doubts not existed over the eligibility of Dai Davies and other young players from Carmarthenshire to be chosen by Glamorgan. Amongst the myriad of amateurs who turned out was a fifteen year-old schoolboy called Royston Gabe-Jones who had impressed playing for the county's Colts and he won selection in the closing match of the summer at the Arms Park when several others declined approaches to turn out yet again for the struggling side and opted to play in club matches or go on end-of-season tours.

By September 1922 the Club's deficit had soared to a mammoth £2800 and to save on expenditure, the wives and girlfriends of the amateurs were asked to help out at the Arms Park and St Helen's by making sandwiches and cakes for their menfolk and the visiting team. Every penny was carefully counted by the Club's Treasurer, Ernest Tyler, the former schoolmaster and chemistry lecturer from Swansea University, with the twelfth man dispatched during the lunch and tea intervals to pay the money into the Club's bank account.

Glamorgan's three recruits for 1922 – Jack Mercer, Danny Sullivan and Frank Ryan, the irascible spin bowler who had hitch-hiked his way to Cardiff in search of a contract with the cash-strapped county.

Yet amongst the misery and gloom, there were some signs of hope, following the acquisition of Jack Mercer, Frank Ryan and Danny Sullivan All three spent the summer qualifying through residence, playing in club cricket and the friendly matches the Club had organized. Jack had opted the leave Sussex after hearing from colleagues about the game at the Arms Park the year before. With Maurice Tate blocking his way, Jack opted to head to South Wales. Danny was in a similar position at Surrey having served as Herbert Strudwick's understudy for many years and he was seeking further opportunities to display his talents behind the stumps.

The services of Jack and Danny had been secured through normal channels by the committee but as far as Frank was concerned, his arrival in South Wales was quite by chance. He had fallen out with his previous employers at Hampshire and duly hitch-hiked his way to see a friend in Bristol, before heading to South Wales in search of employment. It rather summed up the fortunes of Glamorgan that someone resembling a down-and-out and without two pennies to rub together should approach the Club. He duly secured a contract and, together with Danny, made his debut for his new employers in the friendly against an eleven, largely of Oxbridge cricketers, which HDG Leveson Gower had put together at the request of Tal Whittington who had taken over the captaincy from Norman Riches.

TRYING TO CATCH THE GREASY PIG.

DAME WALES: Cheer up, Glamorgan; you nearly had it that time.

A cartoon the Western Mail *newspaper which summed up Glamorgan's plight.*

EMERY, William ('Bill')

Born – Pentrebach, Merthyr, June 1897
Died – Gowerton, 13 December 1962
Professional
RHB, RM
1st XI: 1922
Colts: 1920
Clubs: Hill's Plymouth, Gowerton

Batting and Fielding Record:

	M	I	NO	RUNS	AV	100	50	CT	ST
F-c	2	4	0	5	1.25	-	-	-	-

Bowling Record:

	Overs	M	R	W	AV	5wI	10wM
F-c	34	6	111	2	55.50	-	-

Career-bests:

First-class –   5   v Nottinghamshire at Trent Bridge, 1922
          1/41 v Nottinghamshire at Trent Bridge, 1922

Bill Emery, who played twice for Glamorgan during 1922, was one of the leading professionals in South Wales during the 1920s and 1930s. The son of a colliery foreman in Merthyr, Bill had served with the Staffordshire Regiment during the Great War and, despite being wounded in the jaw and being gassed, he returned in one piece and resumed his fledgling cricketing career in Merthyr.

After demobilization, Bill secured a post as an apprentice blacksmith at the Hill's Plymouth works in his home town before accepting a position as Gowerton's professional for 1923. From then until 1940, Bill was Gowerton's leading bowler with one of his finest hours coming in 1928 when he took 9/22 against Swansea with seven of his victims being clean bowled. In subsequent summers, Bill continued to reserve some of his best performances for matches against Swansea, taking 7/5 as Swansea were bowled out for 21 in 1932 and four years later claiming 8/32 against the St Helen's club.

In 1924 Bill also took 7/3 against Brecon, and in 1937 claimed 8/4 against Clydach, yet despite this outstanding record in club cricket, he only played twice for Glamorgan during 1922 and claimed just a couple of wickets. His appearances also came during the Club's away matches against Lancashire at Old Trafford and Nottinghamshire at Trent Bridge so he never had a chance to play on home soil.

Bill Emery, seen in a team group from Gowerton CC during 1929.

Bill also played for Wales against the MCC at Lord's in 1925, leading some to speculate why the Glamorgan selectors had not made greater efforts to secure his services alongside the likes of Jack Mercer and Trevor Arnott. The Club's flimsy finances were the reason and had he played in a more prosperous period, there is no knowing what he had might have achieved, given his prowess with the new ball. During the 1930s he doubled up as groundsman and coach of Gowerton and, after retiring from playing in 1940, Bill worked as caretaker of the local Grammar School.

246
STONE, James

Born – Southampton, 29 November 1876
Died – Maidenhead, 15 November 1942
Professional
RHB, WK
1st XI: 1922-1923
Club and Ground: 1923
Other: 1923
Cap: 1923
Hampshire 1900-1914
Club: Briton Ferry Town

Batting and Fielding Record:

	M	I	NO	RUNS	AV	100	50	CT	ST
F-c	27	48	2	1047	22.76	1	5	26	12

Career-bests:
First-class –   108 v West Indians at Cardiff Arms Park, 1923

Jimmy Stone recorded Glamorgan's first-ever century against a touring team, with the wicket-keeper reaching this landmark against the 1923 West Indies at Cardiff Arms Park, and all at the ripe old age of 46! His innings came during a partnership of 136 in an hour and a half with Frank Pinch, and their stand laid the foundation for a 43-run victory for the Glamorgan side.

Jimmy had spent fifteen years on the Hampshire staff, during which time he passed a thousand runs on three occasions. He had also claimed over 300 dismissals in 274 first-class appearances for Hampshire between 1900 and 1914. After the Great War, Jimmy moved to South Wales and joined Briton Ferry Town, where he qualified by residence for Glamorgan.

The Welshmen had lacked the services of a regular wicket-keeper in their inaugural season, and had used a variety of amateurs and occasional keepers. They were very grateful to have the services of the Hampshire veteran, who became a

Jimmy Stone, seen at Worcester during 1923 – his final summer of county cricket.

regular in the Glamorgan side for the next two seasons after making his debut in 1922 against Northamptonshire at Swansea.

Jimmy retired from playing in 1924, but he remained in the county game by standing as an umpire in first-class cricket from 1925 until 1934.

247
GWYNNE, David Graham _Pugsley_

Born – Swansea, 8 December 1904

Died – Swansea, 11 December 1934

Amateur

RHB

Ed – Swansea Grammar School and Llandovery College

1st XI: 1922-1923

Colts: 1921

Club: Swansea

Batting and Fielding Record:

	M	I	NO	RUNS	AV	100	50	CT	ST
F-c	3	6	0	20	3.33	-	-	1	-

Career-bests:

First-class – 12 v Hampshire at Southampton, 1922

Pugsley Gwynne was a talented young sportsman in Swansea after the Great War, who played rugby to a decent club standard as well as appearing three times for Glamorgan during the early 1920s, albeit each time in a team that lost heavily, but whose life was cut tragically short just three days after his thirtieth birthday.

Born and raised in Swansea, Pugsley attended the local Grammar School before gaining a scholarship to Llandovery College. He showed great promise on both the cricket and rugby field whilst at Llandovery. The school's magazine was fulsome in its praise of his efforts in the summer of 1918 – "A beautiful batsman who shows remarkable promise. His off play is almost perfect, his strokes behind the wicket are very neat. A good field."

He met with less success with the bat for Llandovery in 1919 and developed a tendency to play too many square cuts rather than playing balls in more orthodox fashion with a straight bat. He bounced back to form during 1920, with the *Llandoverian* magazine commenting "so much better than last season. Excellent in the field." Pugsley had also shown much promise as a fly-half for the College and, on leaving Llandovery, he won a regular place at number ten in the Swansea Uplands XV.

His general athleticism as well as his prowess as a batsman saw Pugsley chosen to play for the Glamorgan Colts team against George Cording's XI at the Arms Park during May 1921 in the game the Welsh county's administrators used as a warm-up of the facilities ahead of the inaugural Championship fixture at Cardiff, besides using the contest to assess the emerging talent.

After yet another good summer at Llandovery, the schoolboy was chosen in the Glamorgan side during June 1922 for the away matches against Sussex at Hove and Hampshire at Southampton. Neither Pugsley or his team-mates covered themselves with glory on their Southern tour. He made 0 and 2 in the match at Hove which Glamorgan lost by 201 runs, before scoring 3 and 12 at Southampton as the Welsh county went down to a defeat by an innings and 106 runs.

A few critics argued that the teenager had only been chosen to make up for the inadequacies in the field of older and less mobile amateurs. Whatever the rights and wrongs of this standpoint was concerned, it was not until July 1923 that Pugsley appeared again at county level, following a series of decent innings for Swansea. But, once again, he could not transfer his good form from club cricket, but it was a mighty challenge in the first place against the powerful Lancashire side at the Arms Park. Pugsley made 2 and 1 as Glamorgan lost by an innings and 184 runs with the county's selectors subsequently opting to look elsewhere for fresh talent.

The son of William Gwynne, who owned a glass importers business in Swansea, Pugsley continued to play cricket for Swansea until 1931, besides acting as their captain between 1927 and 1929.

248
SPILLER, Cecil Willmington

Born – Roath, Cardiff, 19 August 1900
Died – Roath, Cardiff, 5 April 1974
Amateur
RHB, RM
1st XI: 1922
Club and Ground: 1920
Club: Cardiff

Batting and Fielding Record:

	M	I	NO	RUNS	AV	100	50	CT	ST
F-c	2	4	0	20	5.00	-	-	-	-

Bowling Record:

	Balls	M	R	W	AV	5wI	10wM
F-c	258	8	144	4	36.00	-	-

Career-bests:
First-class –   14 v Hampshire at Southampton, 1922
             3/50 v Sussex at Hove, 1922

Cecil Spiller was a useful all-rounder who played twice for Glamorgan during 1922 as the Welsh county's selectors desperately sought the winning formula in Championship cricket.

The son of William J Spiller, the Manager of the Spiller's Flour Mills in Cardiff Docks, and a leading Vice-President of Cardiff Athletic Club, Cecil showed promise with bat and ball whilst at school in the Welsh capital. After a brief spell with the Royal Flying Corps

from August 1918, he returned home to learn the milling trade and to play cricket for Cardiff.

With such an influential, and prosperous father, plus a noted cousin in Billy Spiller – the Club's first-ever Championship centurion (Vol 1, p.230-231) – it was no surprise that Cecil, as a talented amateur cricketer, played for the Welsh county's Club and Ground side during 1920, as well as for the Gentlemen of Glamorgan in their annual friendly against the Players.

During June 1922 Cecil was also given a chance to show his abilities during Glamorgan's South Coast tour. Although he claimed three wickets on debut with his brisk medium pace, he made 0 and 2 with the bat against Sussex at Hove followed by 4 and 14 against Hampshire at Southampton. Both games

Cecil Spiller.

ended in sizeable defeats and he was not called up again.

Later in the 1920s, Cecil spent some time in the Home Counties working for his father's business and appeared in AH Stockley's team which met the 1928 West Indies in a one-day game at New Malden. He made 9 and claimed a wicket in what proved to be his last major match. He continued to play in club cricket for Cardiff, but during the 1930s he suffered a depression of the skull during an accident at the mill and in the 1939 National Register was listed as "Incapacitated". He survived and lived until 1974 when he died during early April after a contracting bronchial pneumonia.

249
MADDEN-GASKELL, *John Charles Pengelly* MBE, OBE

Born – Llangibby, 1 March 1896
Died – Helston, Cornwall, 4 February 1975
Amateur
RHB
Ed – Haileybury School
1st XI: 1922
Somerset 1928-1930; Services XI 1944
Clubs: Penarth, Taunton, Somerset Stragglers

Batting and Fielding Record:

	M	I	NO	RUNS	AV	100	50	CT	ST
F-c	1	2	0	39	19.50	-	-	-	-

Career-bests:
First-class –   32 v Yorkshire at Headingley, 1922

John Charles Pengelly Madden-Gaskell, was a debonair batsman, born on St David's Day 1896 and educated at Haileybury who played once for Glamorgan during 1922 before – as an Army Major – being one of the key figures in the provision and dispatch of troops from ports across Southern England as part of Operation Overlord during June 1944.

The second son of Rev. Andrew Madden, John had overcome at the age of nine, the shock of finding out that his father, who was serving as a priest in Penarth, had eloped to Buenos Aires in Argentina with a twenty year-old girl called Maud Addams. He was duly raised in Newport by an aunt whose husband was a brewery manager with John changing his surname to Madden-Gaskell.

He also attended Haileybury School in Hertfordshire and won a place in the school's 1st XV between 1911 and 1913, as well as their cricket team in 1912 and 1913. After leaving Haileybury, John moved to live and work with his step-father, before joining the Second Battalion of the Welch Regiment as a Second Lieutenant in October 1914. The military records which have survived suggest that he never served on the Western Front and instead held a role in charge of training and logistics.

After being demobliised, the bespectacled amateur returned to Penarth and married Francis Lace, the daughter of the vicar of Exmouth and Budleigh Salterton. He also played cricket with credit for the Penarth club, besides earning a reputation as a cavalier batsman, who loved to attack either fast or slow bowling. His assertive approach to batting led to his selection for Glamorgan's away match against Yorkshire, in which he made 7 and 32, but it proved to be his only game for the Welsh county as the following year he moved to Somerset

JCP Madden-Gaskell.

to set-up a business in Taunton, selling fridges and radios, as well as hiring out public address systems for outdoor events.

John continued to play cricket and rugby for Taunton, and was chosen to play for Somerset on nine occasions between 1928 and 1930. The highlight of his county career came in his first season for the West Country side as he played a pair of accomplished innings against Nottinghamshire at Taunton, scoring 42 and 63 against an attack which boasted both Harold Larwood and Bill Voce, with the Welshman repeatedly driving the England fast bowlers on the up through mid-off and mid-on.

Business commitments prevented John from playing regularly in Championship cricket but he became a leading light with the Somerset Stragglers, and served as their secretary during the 1930s. John was attributed to breathing new life into the Stragglers, whilst his approach to batting won him many admirers – a journalist in a Taunton-based newspaper described him as "the gay cavalier of local cricket. To him, slow cricket was an abomination."

On the outbreak of the Second World War, John joined the Royal Artillery and his skills and acumen as an electrical engineer saw him promoted in 1942 to a position as Staff captain at the Artillery's headquarters in Hounslow. He subsequently became elevated to the rank of Major and Deputy Assistant Quartermaster General and, in this capacity in 1944 he was one of the military team who oversaw the provisioning of food and equipment for Operation Overlord. His efforts later saw him being awarded the MBE in the New Year Honours in 1947.

Despite his weighty duties for the military, he also found time to continue playing cricket and in 1943 appeared for Eastern Command against Northamptonshire at Wantage Road before in 1944 playing at Edgbaston for a Services XI against the Eastern Counties. John continued to serve with the Army until 1954 and shortly after his retirement he was awarded the OBE. His son, Robert John Seath, also played for Glamorgan Colts during 1939 before serving as an officer in the Indian Army during the Second World War.

250
MATHIAS, Frederick William, MC

Born – Abercynon, 7 August 1898
Died – Radyr, 19 April 1955
Amateur
RHB, OB
Ed- Cowbridge Grammar School; Clifton College, plus Gonville and Caius College, Cambridge
1st XI: 1922-1930
Club and Ground: 1923-1929
Cap: 1923
Clubs: Cardiff, Radyr, MCC
Rugby for Glamorgan Wanderers and Cardiff

Batting and Fielding Record:

	M	I	NO	RUNS	AV	100	50	CT	ST
F-c	28	46	5	457	11.14	-	1	7	-

Bowling Record:

	Balls	M	R	W	AV	5wI	10wM
F-c	96	0	84	1	84.00	-	-

Career-bests:
First-class – 58 v Lancashire at St Helen's, Swansea, 1929
1/16 v Oxford University at The Parks, Oxford, 1930

Freddie Mathias was a larger than life character who won the Military Cross at the age of twenty whilst serving with the Royal Flying Corps during the Great War. His wartime flying exploits and bravery also explain why the amateur, who played for Glamorgan during the 1920s and became a stock-broker in Cardiff, was known to one and all as 'Birdie'.

Born in Abercynon, Freddie was the grandson of William Henry Mathias, a railway entrepreneur and mining magnate who owned many collieries in the Rhondda Valley, and lived at Ty'n-y-Cymmer Hall in Porth. His father James managed this mining enterprise and in 1901 went into a partnership with George Insole, the Cardiff-based grandee whose sporting interests also included hunting and cricket, with George being a leading figure in the Fairwater club. James played cricket and rugby whilst at Christ College, Brecon

Freddie Mathias, whilst a pupil at Clifton College during 1916.

before living in Radyr, the popular suburb to the north-west of Cardiff where he made friends with former railway engineer Henry Oakden Fisher, who was also a kindly patron to the local cricket team as well as serving as a Vice-President of Glamorgan CCC. With such influential friends in the world of cricket, it must have delighted James to see Freddie take a keen interest in sport.

After boarding at Cowbridge Grammar School, Freddie attended Clifton College in Bristol and in 1915 and 1916, he won a place in the school's 1st XI as a spin bowler and batsmen. On leaving school he became one of many fresh-faced recruits in the Royal Flying Corps, having previously leant how to fly gliders at Filton Airfield whilst at Clifton. He swiftly passed his flying exams at the Beatty Flying School at Hendon during January 1917 with local legend having it that shortly after qualifying he crashed the last surviving training bi-plane, much to the glee of other trainees who had found it such a devil to fly!

He then joined Flight C of 34 Squadron, with his natural aptitude for flying the Sopwith Camels and Sopwith Pups seeing the eighteen-year-old swiftly rise to the rank of Temporary Captain. His elevation was also influenced by the loss of several colleagues over enemy lines, with Freddie also encountering a few hairy moments, including one mission during June 1917 over enemy lines when one of his plane's wheels was shot off in an attack with German forces. His skills in flying the two-seater Sopwith's saw Freddie and his navigator, another Welsh lad called Sylvester, safely land. Their only means of defense was a rostrum-mounted machine gun operated by the navigator who could not be too trigger-happy for fear of shooting off the tail.

Freddie was also involved with several skirmishes against the Imperial German Army Air Service, including Manfred von Richthofen, the notorious Red Baron who was a member of the deadly Jagdgeschwader 1. He also came face to face with one of the German pilots who was forced to make an emergency landing near the 34th Squadron's base and, subsequently disarmed him, but only after it transpired that the German was an old Cambridge pal of Freddie's commanding officer. The Luger pistol remained in Freddie's possession for many years, and fearing the leg-pulling which might follow, he was loathe to recount the precise events associated with his disarming of a German airman! Another incident saw Freddie being almost shot down by Italian forces as he was taking an RE 8 bi-plane down to Verona. After the spats with the Red Baron and his colleagues, Freddie was looking forward to some Italian hospitality but as he neared his destination the local gunners failed to recognize the unmarked plane as Freddie made a hastier than expected landing.

In September 1918, Freddie won the Military Cross for his gallantry in completing many hours of successful reconnaissance flights over the trenches in France and Belgium where he and Sylvester often had to fly without any air cover as the camera had replaced the machine gun in front of Sylvester. Whilst taking off and flying toward enemy lines, they had an armed escort, but when undertaking the reconnaissance over the combat zone the only protection the intrepid pair had was from a rifle which Sylvester had taken onboard.

The pair duly took a superb series of images allowing the Allied forces to know precisely where the weak links were in German lines and where dummy soldiers and decoy lines were situated. His citation duly paid tribute to his "conspicuous devotion to duty having carried out several successful shoots which did considerable damage to the enemy. He also successfully took a large number of photographs and obtained much valuable information."

At the end of the War, Freddie was offered a post helping to train pilots in India, but instead he went up to Cambridge University to read Geography at Gonville and Caius. Although he did well on the cricket fields for the College, he failed to make the Light Blues XI, but during the university vacations he met with further success playing for Cardiff as well as playing rugby for Glamorgan Wanderers. During one of these matches for the Wanderers against the Clifton Club, Freddie also won fame by travelling home to South Wales by train whilst sat on the roof of a carriage!

His feat – either daring or foolhardy depending on your outlook – was also sufficient for the youngster to gain entry to Cambridge's notorious Narkover Club and, after his wartime exploits, riding on the roof from Severn Tunnel Junction to Newport must have been a dream ride. However, by his own admission, his greatest moment whilst at Cambridge came during mid-November 1921 when together with fifty others from Gonville and Caius he took part in a daring raid which "obtained" the mounted gun from the Great War which had been placed in front of rivals Jesus College. Great planning and subterfuge took place with the gun carriage being towed by the students through the town at dead of night before being safely tethered at its new home.

Freddie, standing in front of the plane he flew at the Hendon Flying School.

It was during his days as an undergraduate that Freddie was first called into the Glamorgan team, for the match in July 1922 at the Arms Park against Nottinghamshire. Batting at number four, he made 9 and 0 as the visitors eased to an innings victory. He made further fairly nondescript appearances during what proved to be a troubled summer for the county club. It ended on a high though for Freddie as, during September, he joined Glamorgan colleagues Johnnie Clay and wicketkeeper Mervyn Hill on the MCC tour to Denmark, which comprised three matches in Copenhagen. Freddie thoroughly enjoyed the tour and during the second game, against a Combined Copenhagen XI he made 53 as the MCC secured an innings victory.

After coming down from Cambridge, Freddie became a stockbroker based in Westgate Street, a very convenient location given his sporting interests, and his close proximity to the Arms Park and willingness to turn out, almost at the

Freddie Mathias, as seen in a Glamorgan team photograph at Worcester in 1924.

drop of a hat, meant Glamorgan could easily call on his services if they found themselves short on the morning of a game. He continued to play for Glamorgan until 1929, and fully enjoyed life as an amateur on the county circuit, especially the after-play socialising with the opposition.

In the case of the rain-affected match with Lancashire at Cardiff during May 1927, this led to a spat with Ted McDonald, the Tasmanian fast bowler who was playing for the Red Rose county. Only a couple of overs in the Glamorgan first innings were possible on the opening day of the contest and, shortly after the umpires had called play off for the day, Freddie and Johnnie Clay took a group to Cowbridge where they had several drinks in the market town's pleasant hostelries. As the evening wore on, the conversation between Freddie and the fast bowler become less and less convivial, to the extent that after Freddie had told the Australian he wouldn't get him out the following day, the Lancastrian replied in no uncertain terms that he would knock his block off when play resumed.

When Freddie's turn came to bat the following afternoon, Ted was true to his word and unleashed a volley of bouncers against the Glamorgan man. But Freddie's response was to smile back and laugh in the Australian's direction. With steam almost coming out of his ears, Ted then unleashed another thunderbolt which Freddie hooked for four, with one local journalist writing that "he almost played the ball off his eyebrows." The Australian's verbal reply went unrecorded, but shortly afterwards, it started to rain again, washing out the rest of the day's play and, with rain still falling the following morning, the umpires abandoned the game. However, down in the amateur's changing room there was one member of the Glamorgan team who was eager to have another go at the Lancashire attack!

Another humorous incident came during the match against Hampshire at Southampton in 1923, when the opposition captain, The Hon. Lionel Tennyson, took exception to the grubby pads which Freddie wore as he made his way out to bat. The reason for their dirtiness was that Freddie had been in a purple patch of form in club cricket for Cardiff and, as quite a superstitious man, he didn't want to inadvertently do anything that might halt his good run. But the Hampshire skipper was so incensed by the state of Freddie's pads that he instructed his bowlers not to deliver another ball until the Glamorgan man had gone back to the pavilion to clean them.

With another devilish smirk on his face, Freddie duly walked back and found a large pot of white paint. With a great flourish on the pavilion steps, he theatrically daubed the offending marks before also whitening his boots and other bits of kit given to him by his grinning colleagues before resuming his place in the middle. One of those amused by Freddie's almost Oscar-winning performance was left-arm spinner Frank Ryan who had previously played for Hampshire and had fallen out with Tennyson. Frank had also been a pilot in the Royal Flying Corps and had traded gunfire with German pilots. Irked by Tennyson's petty attitude, the spinner shouted to Freddie " Doesn't he realise that there's more to life than worrying about a little bit of dirt?"

Freddie also played for Wales against Ireland at the Ormeau ground in Belfast during 1926, and posted a career-best 65 during a productive stand with his friend and Glamorgan colleague Norman Riches. The following September, Freddie also appeared for the Welsh Cygnets in a two-day game against the 1927 New Zealanders at Llandudno in a contest designed to take place in convivial surroundings in the North Walian resort and showcase the emerging talent in the Principality. However, the tourists adopted a more serious-minded approach with Freddie subjected to a torrent of caustic comments from Kiwi captain Tom Lowry. "This fellow can't bat" was the politest thing which Tom uttered as Freddie made an unbeaten 30 and ensured that after half-centuries from Norman Riches and Cyril Walters, the Welsh side were able to declare on 250-6. Freddie was also able to have the last laugh as Sam Jagger, the Denbighshire-born seam bowler took five wickets on the second day as the tourists were dismissed for 195.

July 1929 saw Freddie appear against Derbyshire at the Arms Park in what turned out to be his final Championship match for Glamorgan. It proved to be something of an inglorious finale as he was run out in each innings by Eddie Bates. In the first innings, he had made six when the grizzled Yorkshireman sent him back after Freddie had called for what appeared to be a straightforward single. Second time around, the pair were batting again with Freddie on 22 when Eddie called for an impossible single, leaving Freddie – who as the amateur was honour bound to respond to the professional's call – left hopelessly stranded for the second time in the game.

Freddie had continued to play at full-back for Glamorgan Wanderers, as well as briefly for Cardiff, largely because of a priceless ability to kick off both feet, allied to his speed and low centre of gravity. He was offered the captaincy of the 'Rags' – the Cardiff 2nd XV – but preferred to stay with the Wanderers. His final cricket match of note came in April 1936 when he played for Pat Brain's XI in their annual match against Glamorgan at the Arms Park as the county prepared for the forthcoming season. He claimed two wickets and made 16 before being bowled by his old friend Johnnie.

After the Second World War, and following an evening at the Ty Nant pub in Morganstown, Freddie agreed to turn out for Radyr the following day. He regretted his decision the following day, but his wife insisted that he kept his promise. A huge crowd though had gathered in the afternoon to watch the former county cricketer in action, but Freddie was clean bowled first ball!

He was also a well-known figure in social circles, hosting a number of parties at his home, initially at Ty Mawr in Marshfield and later at Brynteg in Radyr. Amongst those who attended with his sporting pals were members of the Tiller Girls review show plus a number of actors and actresses from Cardiff's theatres. Through his membership of Cardiff Aeroplane Club, he became a good friend of World War Two flying ace Guy Gibson who was wooing a girl from Penarth. The pair played golf several times together at the Glamorganshire Club, besides dining in the Cardiff and County Club with many of Freddie's pals, some of whom had marveled at his aerobatic skills when taking them for a spin in his Tiger Moth. On more than one occasion, Freddie had also flown to away matches in his bi-plane when called up by Glamorgan's selectors, and according to family legend, he also won the heart of Eileen Davies, later to be his wife, by flying over the valleys where her family owned several mines, as well as out over the Severn Estuary, although their first flight together had ended up with a forced landing owing to fog in the grounds of a country house.

When the Second World War broke out, Freddie was excited at the thought of going back into action against Germany and flying either Spitfires or Hurricanes with the Royal Air Force. He duly contacted the relevant personnel but, despite his distinguished record in the Great War, he was turned down. Undeterred, Freddie duly joined the Home Guard in Lisvane and took delight in manning the machine-gun positions and other gun

Freddie Mathias (left) and GV Wynne-Jones, the well-known BBC broadcaster and journalist, greet the mayor of Cardiff as he alights from a small aircraft during 1952.

batteries defending the port of Cardiff, besides regaling colleagues with tales of his time with the Royal Flying Corps.

Many tributes were duly paid to Freddie following his death in April 1955. In the words of one writer, "F was for Freddie as well as for Fun. He was endowed with whimsical humour, an impish nature and a loveable character." JBG Thomas, his good friend and sporting journalist, also commented how "his Peter Pan qualities have delighted so many who do not remember him on the field of play, and his courage and whimsy – even in his last illness – will never be forgotten." The Chairman of the Cardiff Stock Exchange also wrote "a friendly soul, generous to a degree, charitable in his judgements to everyone, never in my long association with Freddie did I hear him utter an unkind word of anyone. This world would be a happier place if we all possessed with the natural instincts of Freddie Mathias."

251
PEARSON, Dr Cecil Joseph Herbert

Born – Poplar, 22 January 1888
Died – Porthcawl, 14 September 1971
Amateur
RHB, OB
Ed – London University
1st XI: 1922
Clubs: Swansea, Porthcawl, Glamorgan Nomads

Batting and Fielding Record:

	M	I	NO	RUNS	AV	100	50	CT	ST
F-c	1	2	0	9	4.50	-	-	-	-

Bowling Record:

	Balls	M	R	W	AV	5wI	10wM
F-c	24	0	12	0	-	-	-

Career-best:
First-class – 9 v Nottinghamshire at Cardiff Arms Park, 1922

Dr Cecil Pearson, an expert in tropical medicine and later the Medical Director for Porthcawl, played once for Glamorgan during 1922. In contrast to his illustrious medical career, the bespectacled batsman and off-spin bowler enjoyed a modest first-class career, scoring 9 and 0 in his one and only Championship appearance and becoming one of eight victims in the county's second innings for Fred Barratt as the Welsh county capitulated to 47 all out and lost the match with Nottinghamshire by an innings and 125 runs.

Born on the Isle of Dogs during 1888, Cecil was the fourth son of Rev. John Pearson, the vicar of Bow, who had been brought up in Berbice in British Guyana before tending to the spiritual needs of the workers in the London Docklands.

Dr Cecil Pearson.

After leaving school, Cecil attended London University and trained as a doctor. Having graduated in 1911 with a specialism in tropical medicine, he worked initially in East Africa before joining the Nigerian Regiment in August 1914 on the outbreak of the Great War.

Dr Pearson also saw active service in the Cameroons before returning to the UK during July 1915. It was an important year for the young medic as in October, he married Anne David, the grand-daughter of William David, who had created the Pencoed Foundry and whose family were cousins of the David's of St Fagans whose number included Edmund David, Glamorgan's captain in their inaugural match in 1889 (Volume 1, p 21-23). Their wedding took place at St Stephen's, Spitalfields with Rev. Pearson proudly officiating.

Cecil spent a short period as Assistant House Surgeon at the Royal Devon and Exeter Hospital, before joining a practice in Pencoed, and subsequently in Porthcawl. He duly became a leading light in the resort town's cricket team and his performances for Porthcawl – as well as his family links with Edmund David – led to his selection in the Glamorgan side for the match with Nottinghamshire in 1922.

His home for many years was at Brynheulog in Victoria Avenue, Porthcawl and prior to serving as Medical Director for the town, he also served as Medical Officer for 'The Rest', the large seaside convalescence home in Rest Bay, on the western fringe of the town, which had been, created specifically during the 1860s by local philanthropists – and with the support of Florence Nightingale – for miners and others working in heavy industry. As one of the earliest examples of industrial welfare, the property has become a Grade Two Listed Building.

Dr Pearson served at 'The Rest' during the Second World War and also oversaw the addition of a wing at the care home for paraplegics. Sadly, Anne pre-deceased Cecil, passing away in 1938 at Porthcawl aged 53. They had one son, Arthur who later emigrated to New Zealand.

252
WORSLEY, Francis Frederick

Born – South Kensington, 2 June 1902
Died – Mile End, Stepney, 15 September 1949
Amateur
RHB, OB
Ed – Brighton College and Balliol College, Oxford
1st XI: 1922-1923
Club: Cardiff

Batting and Fielding Record:

	M	I	NO	RUNS	AV	100	50	CT	ST
F-c	2	3	0	34	11.33	-	-	1	-

Career-best:
First-class –   21 v Northamptonshire at Northampton, 1922

Francis Worsley, who played twice for Glamorgan – once in 1922 and again in 1923 – won great acclaim as the producer of the BBC radio programme ITMA (It's That Man Again) starring Tommy Handley, the well-known British comedian.

Francis was the son of cricket-loving Rev. Frederick Worsley, who played Minor County cricket for Cambridgeshire in 1912 and 1913 whilst acting as Vicar of Corringham. Born in Singapore in 1873, and educated at Cambridge University, Frederick had earlier served curacies in Barnes and South Kensington before taking a post at St Michael's Theological College in Llandaff. After the Great War, he also became a Canon at Llandaff Cathedral and his links with South Wales allowed Francis, through residence, to qualify to play for Glamorgan.

Born in the London area and raised in Cambridgeshire, Francis had attended Brighton College from January 1916 and subsequently played for their 2nd XI in 1917 and 1918, before representing the 1st XI in 1919 and 1920. In the former season, the College magazine noted how "his batting has shown great improvement, and he has learnt to play straighter and with more freedom. Is still too fond of trying to hook the good length ball, and has paid the penalty more than once. His fielding has always been good and keen." Francis also played for the College's Rugby XV in 1918/19 and 1919/20, besides representing the College at Fives, and captaining their VIII in 1920.

With such a sporting pedigree, he secured a place at Balliol College, but he failed to complete his first term and returned to Cardiff where he briefly worked as a motor tyre salesman. During August 1922 Francis made his first-class debut for Glamorgan, playing in the away match with Northamptonshire. His call-up followed some decent innings for Cardiff and in September 1923, Francis was called up for a second time for the match against Hampshire at the Arms Park after another decent summer in club cricket.

Francis had made a solid 21 on his county debut but did little of note against Hampshire and was called up again. This

Francis Worsley, seen in his days as a young cricketer.

was largely because his career had again changed course. At the time of his debut in 1922 Francis was teaching at Brightlands School in Newnham-on-Severn but early in 1924 he left academia and moved to Nigeria to work in the West African Colonial Service. He continued his rather nomadic and varied cricketing career by playing for the Gold Coast Europeans in 1926/27, before returning to Cardiff during 1927 and securing a post as a junior producer for BBC Wales

1924 had seen the formation of BBC Wales, and it was from a variety of makeshift studios in Park Place, Newport Road and other locations around Cardiff, that he cut his teeth in broadcasting, producing at first, public talks and religious services – no doubt using his father's contacts – besides acting as an Uncle on the Children's Hour programme and doing stints as an announcer.

In 1929 the BBC opened their South and West branch, and Francis was promoted to a new post in Bristol as a producer of drama programmes and theatre reviews. This saw him link up with productions taking place at the Bristol Old Vic and others theatres in the south-west. His close affinity with what was called the BBC Home Service saw him promoted yet again in 1938 to a post in London as a writer and producer of comedy programmes for network radio.

Francis Worsley, the producer of ITMA.

From his new home in Beaconsfield, the pipe-smoking Francis became the producer in 1939 of ITMA – a programme whose 300 episodes until 1948, broadcast from studios in Bristol and later Bangor in North Wales, have been credited for sustaining morale during the War Years. Francis is also credited for coining the acronym 'TTFN', short for "Ta Ta For Now" which was made famous by the show's Mrs Mopp, the Cockney charlady.

In 1949 Francis also was the author of the book *ITMA 1939-1948*, published by Vox Mundi of London, which was a history of the radio programme and a tribute to Tommy Handley who had died of a cerebral haemorrhage in January. Tragically, Francis also died later that year. His younger brother Cuthbert had also been a decent cricketer, and played for Glamorgan Colts besides keeping wicket for Cambridge University against Yorkshire at Fenner's in 1928.

253
MERCER, John ('Jack')

Born – Southwick, Sussex, 22 April 1893
Died – Westminster, 31 August 1987
Professional
RHB, RFM
Ed – Southwick Community School
1st XI: 1922-1945
Club and Ground: 1922-1939
Cap: 1923
Sussex 1919-1921; Players 1926-1934; MCC to India, Burma and Ceylon 1926/27; South of England 1928; Sir Julian Cahn's XI to Jamaica 1928/29; The Army 1942; British Empire XI 1943; Northamptonshire 1947
Clubs: Southwick, Barry, Cardiff

Batting and Fielding Record:

	M	I	NO	RUNS	AV	100	50	CT	ST
F-c	412	578	100	5730	11.98	-	10	124	-
Wartime	2	2	0	29	14.50	-	-	1	-

	Balls	M	R	W	AV	5wI	10wM
F-c	83773	3246	34058	1460	23.32	98	4
Wartime	?	?	?	2	-	-	-

Career-bests:

First-class –   72 v Surrey at The Oval, 1934

            10/51 v Worcestershire at Worcester, 1936

Jack Mercer was a colourful and larger than life character who enjoyed a long and distinguished career as a bowler for Glamorgan. In 1936 he became the first and so far only Glamorgan bowler to take all ten wickets in an innings in a first-class match besides being the first bowler in the Club's history to take over 1000 first-class wickets. But all of these fine achievements may never have happened had Lady Luck not been on his side during the Great War as he narrowly escaped death during the Battle of the Somme.

Born in Southwick, a thriving suburb to the west of Brighton, Jack was the second eldest of eight children, with his father Walt being a leading light with the local cricket club. Walt was still captain when Jack was old enough to play in senior games, and his success as a young seam bowler soon brought him to the attention of Sussex and he duly played for their Colts team, At that time, though, he had no ambitions of being a professional sportsman and, on leaving school at the age of fourteen, he became a postman. His father was a farrier and from a young age, Jack had been intrigued by the tales told by ostlers and stable lads when they brought their horses to his father's smithy. In particular, he became fascinated about Russia, the Cossacks and their magnificent steeds, so in 1913 he and a friend accepted an offer to become crew members of a sailing yacht heading to St Petersberg. It proved to be a highly enjoyable adventure with Jack meeting and falling in love with a ballerina. It meant, of course, that Jack had to teach himself Russian and, for a while, few of Jack's thoughts were about life back at home or playing cricket for Southwick. Everything changed however following the declaration of War during August 1914, and after receiving a letter from his parents, Jack and his pal returned home.

He duly joined the 12th Battalion (Second South Down) of the Royal Sussex Regiment and took part, like others in Lord Kitchener's newly-raised army, in an intensive course of military training at Witley Camp before in February 1916 travelling by train to Dover and onwards by boat to Calais. His Battalion then headed by train, lorry and on foot to Fleurbaix before taking part in the Battle of the Somme from late June onwards. Their role comprised a series of diversionary activities in the Richebourg and Ferme du Bois area, some twenty miles or so to the south of the main battlefield. But, after initial forays, it was clear the Regiment were facing superior German forces and as their supply of ammunition gave out, the 12th Battalion made a hasty retreat.

It was during this move back that Jack was wounded by an exploding shell, whose fragments struck him in the left arm, shoulder and chest, and whose defeaning noise caused him to lose hearing in his left ear. The soldier next to him was less fortunate as he was killed outright. Jack tumbled into the crater which the shell created, and was covered by the debris from the explosion. As well as being deafened, he was also disorientated and, at first, lay semi-conscious but increasingly aware that he had shrapnel in the upper part of his torso. He steadily regained consciousness, but lay prone for the next 48 hours, listening through his undamaged right ear to the cries of anguish from other injured troops as well as the harrowing groans of those who were dying from their wounds. It was a truly appalling time, and with the Germans poised to advance, Jack was fearful of what would happen if he was taken prisoner. In those dark hours, he would be forgiven for wanting to be put out of his misery as he saw through the flying dirt and clouds of smoke, the shells fly overhead.

After a day of constant shelling and gunfire, the German counter-attack ceased as their attention switched to the south and the main battle which had started in earnest. Jack was forever grateful for this lull in activities as, to his joy, a couple of troops – sent out to gather the bodies of the dead – found him in the crater. They dug him out and helped him limp back to where medical auxiliaries were based. Although being able to hobble around. Jack still had some nasty shrapnel wounds and, having inhaled various gases, the regimental doctor diagnosed Jack as having shell-shock and authorized his return to the UK.

Jack Mercer at Hove during 1921.

After returning by hospital train and ship, he began his recuperation at home in Shoreham. His physical wounds steadily healed but the mental scars remained, with Jack finding it difficult to sleep in his darkened bedroom as terrible flashbacks took place back to his time in the crater. Jack's recovery was not helped by news that Victor, his 20 year-old brother, had been killed during the bloody Battle of Cambrai. 1916 and 1917 were the darkest years of Jack's life and ones that, quite understandably, he wanted to swiftly forget. Indeed, it may have been no coincidence that Jack always gave his age as two years less than it was.

By the spring of 1918 Jack was in greater shape and, as life started to get back to normal, he secured a desk job in London with the Army, and was encouraged at weekends to further his rehabilitation by playing cricket. His success as a bowler with the Southwick club once again brought him to the attention of the Sussex coaching staff who offered Jack a place on the Sussex groundstaff in March 1919. At 25, he was the oldest of the new faces to be approached, but with nothing else on the horizon – and after the horrors of the War – Jack was only too delighted to get the chance of regularly playing cricket and to be paid for the privilege.

Under the direction of Head Coach Arthur Millward, Jack was able to hone his skills, besides bowling for hour after hour against the 1st XI squad. In early July 1919, he received a call to travel to Northampton when John Vincett was taken ill on the morning ahead of the Championship match at Wantage Road. It proved to be a low-key debut as well as being sole appearance of the summer but, at least, after the horrors on the Somme, Jack could now call himself a first-class cricketer.

He made sporadic appearances in the next couple of seasons including the game at Hove against Worcestershire during 1920 where he, and the other seamers, bowled under-arm lobs in the visitors' second innings. But with the emergence of Arthur Gilligan and subsequently Maurice Tate, it became clear to Jack that if he wanted to play regular county cricket, he would have to look elsewhere. He began talking with a couple of his fellow professionals who had been highly impressed by Glamorgan's victory over Sussex at the Arms Park in May 1921 and, aware that the Welsh county were on the lookout for fresh talent, he made contact with their officials and agreed terms.

For many years, Jack had been a gambler, with a love of horse racing nurtured by years of living in the lee of the South Downs, close to many fine training establishments. He knew several trainers and jockeys, and received during the course of his life many good tips, most of which failed to bring him the healthy financial rewards he craved. Joining Glamorgan in 1922 was the biggest gamble he ever took but it was comfortably the best, despite the fact they had enjoyed a torrid time in their first season in first-class cricket.

He initially played club cricket for Cardiff and Barry, as well as appearing in Glamorgan's non-county friendlies, plus Wales' first-class games, with the highlight being a return of 9/24 against Scotland at Perth in 1923 – a match which showcased both his bowling abilities and legendary stamina after a tiring all-day journey by train from Cardiff General. Soon after the game in Scotland, Jack completed his qualification period and duly became the Welsh county's opening bowler. In the words of RC Robertson-Glasgow, "for fifteen seasons, he opened, continued and closed the Glamorgan attack and welcomed with unfailing humour the reluctance of the batsmen to depart, the umpire to agree and the fieldsmen to bend. If there were a prize for continued excellence of skill and temper, surely Mercer would be on the shortest list of candidates. When hope was gone, he could still smile, when the seam was gone, he could still make the ball swerve."

Jack Mercer bowling in the nets.

After making his Championship debut against Leicestershire in August 1923, Jack was soon amongst the wickets, besides adding additional variations to his repertoire, realizing that he was going to be both the opening and stock bowler in Glamorgan's attack. After a series of chats over the winter months back home in Brighton with Maurice Tate, Jack worked assiduously on a leg cutter and other subtle variations. His hours of practice duly paid off, as in August 1925, Jack reached the seasonal milestone of 100 first-class wickets for the first time in his career during the match against Warwickshire at Swansea, with Johnnie Clay generously sending a couple of bottles of champagne into the professionals changing room so that Jack and his colleagues could celebrate his achievements. It was also a reward to Jack for pledging his loyalty to the Welsh county having turned down some lucrative offers to play in the Lancashire Leagues.

His tally of 105 wickets at just 20 runs apiece was very impressive, especially given the fact that in the previous six seasons his overall tally had been 92 wickets. Eager to stress that his achievements had not been a flash in the plan he told the Glamorgan captain "Don't worry Johnnie, I'll take 100 wickets for Glamorgan again next year!" These proved to be prophetic words as Jack proceeded to take 136 wickets and ended up second to the great Wilfred Rhodes in the national bowling averages.

1926 was certainly a coming of age for Jack as a bowler as he took five wickets in an innings on a dozen occasions and twice bagged a ten-wicket haul. He also appeared for the Players against the Gentlemen at the Scarborough Festival and was chosen as one of *Wisden's* Five Cricketers of the Year, before in the autumn being drafted into the MCC touring party who were visiting Ceylon, India and Burma, Not many cricketers can have heard of their selection for a MCC tour whilst at Longchamp Races, but that is exactly what happened to Jack whilst visiting the Parisian racecourse on a sojourn to France. He read about his call-

An extract from a brochure produced for the MCC tour of India in 1926/27.

up in the continental edition of *The Daily Mail* before heading back to his hotel to find that a telegram had arrived from Lord's. Injuries and fatigue had affected other players on the inaugural MCC tour to the subcontinent, led by Jack's former Sussex colleague Arthur Gilligan, and "Arthur and the boys need you" was the gist of the message which Jack received before hastily returning to England and heading off by boat and train to Bombay to join the tour party.

He enjoyed everything that the tour offered, both on and off the field. In one light-hearted contest he walked out to bat wearing a fez! He also toured Jamaica with Sir Julian Cahn's XI, but despite being chosen for these overseas tours and regularly appearing at the Scarborough Festival, Jack never got the opportunity to play in Test cricket.

Many believed his omission stemmed from an incident at the famous Festival when he inadvertently offended HDG Leveson Gower, a highly influential figure within MCC circles and a Test Selector. It came when Jack was fielding in a match for CI Thornton's XI, whilst Leveson Gower was perambulating with several high-ranking officials around the boundary. As Chairman of Selectors, Leveson Gower was keen to know which of the players in Thornton's team might be available as reserves for the MCC visit to South Africa. Jack was high in their thoughts so Leveson Gower tried to have a word with him at the end of an over when Jack was posted on the boundary's edge. In mid-conversation Jack realized that the next over was about to start so he said "Excuse me for a moment, but I must watch this delivery" and quickly turned around to walk in with the bowler. By the time, Jack resumed his post near the rope, Leveson Gower and his party had moved on. Later a colleague chided Jack for his actions saying "You were seen to turn your back on them in front of several thousand people. You'll never get picked now!"

From 1932 onwards, Jack served as senior professional with his sage advice about the strength and weaknesses of various batsmen greatly assisting Maurice Turnbull. He also helped to quell feelings of unrest in the professional's room when the Club's dire financial problems resulted in reduced salaries. Jack accepted the cuts and never queried the position and drawing on his wartime experiences told colleagues how fortunate they were to be outside playing cricket for a living. His reward for his devotion to the cause came at New Road during July 1936, and fittingly during his Benefit Year, as he took 10/51 against Worcestershire.

His record-breaking feat came during a two and three-quarter hour spell on the opening day of the contest and in quite humid conditions. With a decent-looking surface on which to bat, Bernard Quaife, the home captain, had earlier shown no hesitation in batting first, but his side were soon in trouble, collapsing to 59-6 before lunch with Jack delivering a superb spell of 13-7-7-5 as he gained lavish swing in the conditions. He was also ably assisted by some deft catching close to the wicket, with Cyril Smart holding a good catch in the slips, whilst Maurice held onto a sharp inside edge at short-leg.

The only batsmen to play with any certainty were Roger Human and Sandy Singleton, until the latter, after lunch, adopted more assertive tactics by trying to hit Jack off his length. The veteran was not cowed by these tactics and

Jack Mercer, as seen at the Arms Park during 1936.

51

simply asked wicket-keeper Tom Brierley to stand up, before having him stumped as he lost balance slashing wildly at a perfect away swinger. Jack swifty removed Dick Howarth and Reg Perks so with all nine wickets to his name, Emrys Davies – who had benefitted so much over the years from Jack's advice – deliberately sent his next few deliveries wide of the stumps in order that Jack would get a chance of claiming all ten.

The tension mounted and a couple of half chances were spilled in Jack's next couple of overs, before Peter Jackson skied a ball high into the outfield and George Lavis set off to get underneath it. Jack responded by standing at the end of his follow through with his hands raised up together, praying to the heavens. As the ball swirled around, Jack also turned to umpire Ernie Cooke and said "Its six bob to four that George will drop it." Ernie took the odds, but Jack was happy to settle his debts as George, after juggling with the ball for a few heart-stopping seconds, held onto it with an audible sigh of relief echoing all around the ground. As he was mobbed by his delighted colleagues, Jack nonchalantly shook the hands of the two batsmen and walked off with his sweater swung over his shoulder as if nothing out of the ordinary had happened.

Jack's success was based on several factors – firstly, the priceless ability to swing the ball either way and secondly, once the shine had disappeared, some clever cutters as he cut down on his pace. Evidence of how he became two bowlers in one came in 1929 during the match with the South Africans at Pontypridd. Jack initially took 4/26 during a seventeen-over spell with the new ball, before claiming four more as he switched to off-cutters, ending with a handsome return of 8/60 together with many plaudits from the Springboks.

In 1934 Jack also added a swiftly delivered leg-break to his armoury, so it was no surprise that on six occasions, his seasonal tally topped the hundred mark. Jack's career haul would have also topped 1500 wickets had there been assistance from more athletic and agile fielders. Many times, a greying and portly amateur would spill a catch close to the wicket, but unlike some modern bowlers Jack rarely lost his rag and went into histrionics if things didn't go his way. Instead he was a phlegmatic and jovial soul, saying "Bad luck and well stopped, Sir" to the red-faced fielder, before returning to his bowling mark.

A third factor was Jack's seemingly boundless stamina, with his leonine strength reputed to have been based on lengthy daily walks each winter along the sea front near his home in Seaford, during which he would also find time to throw pebbles into the sea in order to keep his right-arm strong. During July 1930 Jack bowled unchanged throughout the entire match against Worcestershire at the Arms Park, starting with 6/22 with his off-cutters in their first innings and operating with a ring of four close catchers on the leg-side. The following day, it was his swing bowling which hounded the Worcester batsmen as he took four of the first five wickets to fall as the visitor's collapsed yet again as his adopted county won by 215 runs.

Like other great bowlers, he also had a good memory and remembered the strengths and weaknesses of countless county batsmen. An example came in a match in the mid-1930s between Glamorgan and Yorkshire which was covered by BBC Radio. In the commentary team was Percy Fender and the former Surrey and England batsman was baffled at how Jack kept bowling out-swingers to Errol Holmes, and all whilst keeping a fielder positioned at deep square-leg. But no sooner had Percy shared his view with the listeners, than Errol miscued a pull against Jack and sent the ball lobbing a great arc straight into the hands of the man at deep square-leg. "I told you he was a cunning rascal," was Percy's on-air response.

Jack was also very superstitious and would frequently put a three-penny bit in his back pocket, believing that it brought him good luck. It led to a bit of leg-pulling, but on one occasion at Swansea, it seemed to do the trick. Jack had bowled without any luck before lunch against the Gloucestershire batsmen, so he decided to put his lucky charm in his pocket for the afternoon session. Remarkably, Jack proceeded to take seven wickets, and he duly kept the coin in his pocket for the next few matches. Despite his fine haul, Jack's colleagues continued to pull his leg about the coin's powers. "I'm out of luck myself" said Arnold Dyson, the opening batsman, "so let's see what good it does for me," putting the coin into his trouser pocket before going out to bat. To Arnold's delight, he posted his first half century for several weeks, and on returning to the dressing room he turned to the smiling Jack and said "Thanks – I now believe in fairies as well!"

Jack was also a capable tail-end batsman who, on several occasions, produced some brief, but ferocious spells of hitting. An example came in 1939, his final summer with Glamorgan, when he scored 31 off an over – which that summer spanned eight balls – delivered by Dick Howorth of Worcestershire. His lusty striking came in final half-hour of the match, which had seen Glamorgan's last pair come together with a lead of just ten. From Worcestershire's point of view, there was still enough time to claim the final wicket and then hit the winning runs, but Jack had other ideas as the last pair added 45 in the space of ten minutes. Jack struck the hapless Howarth for 6, 4, 2, 6, 6, 6 and 1 with each six coming from massive straight drives into the side of the North Stand, with each blow creating a loud clanging sound as it struck the metalwork of the enclosure.

Jack gave one chance early in his innings, and a somewhat straightforward one, as he drilled the ball straight to mid-off where the visiting captain Hon. Charles Lyttleton – later to be 10th Viscount Cobham – spilled the chance. The Worcestershire man was angry at his mistake and he continued to fume as Jack continued to unleash a volley of blows to take the game away from the visitor's. Shortly afterwards, Lyttleton called time before marching up to the stumps and vented his anger by hurling the stumps in the air and uttering a few choice phrases at which someone working a mile or so away at Cardiff Docks would have blushed.

Jack Mercer unwinds after a lengthy bowling stint against Somerset at Weston-super-Mare.

Cultured slogging was the description by one critic of Jack's batting style. A bit harsh maybe, but he stood quite firm-footed, with each mighty swish of the bat being accompanied with a jovial grin. Indeed, Jack had quite a whimsical attitude to his batting, joking that he only had two real shots. One a defensive shot he christened 'Cautious Caroline' which he usually played off the back foot into the offside, and the other called 'Saucy Sally' which was played off the front foot in an arc anywhere between mid-on and square-leg.

These were the times when Sunday was a rest day in between the first and second day's play of a Championship match, and there were many occasions after play on a Saturday night to socialize as Jack delighted guests with a series of humorous tales about life as a professional cricketer. As a member of the Magic Circle, there were times too when Jack could enthrall the guests, especially the ladies, with card tricks and other sleights of the hand which he had learnt as a young boy and had developed further on rainy days in dressing rooms all over England and Wales. In fact, Jack loved having an audience in front of him and, on numerous occasions in the pavilions or in the hotel bars, Jack would delight his younger colleagues by performing a magic trick, always with a whimsical glint in his eye, just as if he had baffled an opposing batsman or had struck another six high over long-on!

Unlike some of the other professionals, who spent every evening chasing any bit of skirt they could find, Jack was not a womanizer. He was instead a gentleman in the true sense of the word, always cutting a dapper appearance off the field with monogrammed silk shirts with French cuffs plus carefully tailored suits. He may have had the air of a wealthy charmer, but despite his refined accent, he was never that flush for cash, having gambled away much of the money made during his Benefit Year in 1936. His descendants still talk very fondly of the way "Uncle Jack seemed to forever be borrowing money from various friends and relatives." Despite being perennially short of money, Jack was still a kindly and generous soul, especially to his many nephews and nieces. Indeed, he always sent Melissa – his youngest niece – a pretty birthday card containing a ten shilling note and as befitted a young girl who kept ponies, a message saying "The money is for carrots for the 'orse!"

Each Christmas, he would dutifully return to his family's semi-detached home on the Shoreham seafront, and, on Christmas Day, he would always put on a magic show for all the young children, as well as the many adults, staying in the house. The only thing he couldn't magic up was money, and Jack was regularly hoping to improve his lot by having a flutter on the horses. He was also rather miffed about the very small amount of money he received from his Army pension. After receiving his campaign medals in the 1920s, Jack went before a War Office Pension Board to argue for an increase in the amount of money he received. After listening to Jack's reminiscences about events on the Somme and hearing of his circumstances, the Chairman of the Board replied that Jack couldn't be too badly off as at the time he was second in the national bowling averages. Jack immediately replied that without the injuries he would have been top of the bowling lists!

During the closing weeks of the 1939 season, Jack informed the Glamorgan committee that he would be seeking other opportunities for 1940, and expressed a desire to move into coaching. He had already been passing on plenty of advice to the young Glamorgan bowlers during the 1930s and spending time with the county's coach Bill Hitch, as they groomed the next generation of bowlers. He was also instrumental in recommending the bowling talents of Wilf Wooller to Maurice having watched the Welsh rugby international bowl in club cricket for St Fagans. But with Bill Hitch and Austin Matthews already lined up for coaching roles, the committee replied, much to Jack's pique that they might be not be able to offer him anything. To make matters worse, news of his departure was leaked to the Press, much to Maurice's anger.

It was not long though before there were other things on their mind as World War Two broke out. Jack served initially in the Intelligence Corps at Bletchley Park, assisting the hard-pressed staff as they translated, and sent, coded messages to colleagues in Eastern Europe, before his skills in speaking French and Russian saw him look after groups of POW's and other displaced nationals from Eastern Europe at an internment camp in Northern Ireland. He found time however to play in various fund-raising games, especially several with his former county colleagues in South Wales.

As life started to return to normal, Jack was offered some occasional coaching by both Glamorgan and Sussex, and once his duties at the internment camp in Ulster were over, he undertook some coaching in Cardiff and Hove. With no firm offers coming from either club, Jack successfully responding to a newspaper advert placed by Northamptonshire who were looking for a full-time coach, and someone who would help scout for new players. He duly joined the East Midlands side for 1947 and later than June made his 457th and final first-class appearance as he nobly stepped into the breach when his new employers found themselves at Southampton in the midst of an injury crisis.

A young Alf Valentine is coached by Jack Mercer in Jamaica during 1949/50.

During the winter months, he also coached in Australia and the West Indies. In particular, he spent several winters in Jamaica where he played a major part in the early career of one of the island's greatest cricketing sons, Alf Valentine, the left-arm spinner who became the first West Indian bowler to claim over a hundred Test wickets. Back in the winter of 1948/49, the tall, bespectacled youngster was a virtual unknown, living in a working-class suburb of Kingston. Jack was soon impressed by the amount of sharp spin Alf could impart from his long fingers. The pair duly spent many long hours in the nets, or on any patch of spare land in Kingston, with Jack helping the young spinner to perfect his skills and craft.

In 1963 Jack became Northamptonshire's 1st XI scorer – a position he filled until 1981 before spending a couple of seasons in a similar capacity with their 2nd XI. His new duties allowed him to retain close contact with cricketers young and old, as well as journalists with the scribes often frequenting the same area on the ground as the scorers. If bad weather was interfering with play, the Press Box would come alive with stories of yesteryear as Jack delighted the hacks with his tales. It also gave Jack a new and eager audience for his card tricks, with his scoring colleagues – sometimes frustrated by his loss of mathematical accuracy – now left wide-eyed in amazement by one of Jack's special tricks.

Indeed, he was one of the most popular scorers on the circuit with a cry of "everything's approximate" as he answered a Pressman's enquiry. Of course, these were of the days when scorers only used books and pencils and there were times after lunch, when Jack could doze off for a few overs – something that would be nigh impossible in this new digital era of computerized scoring. But Jack's colleagues the length and breadth of the country were more than happy for him to quietly copy up a few overs later having woken up from his nap. After all that Jack had done during his life, it was the least they could do!

Jack Mercer, seen with a friend at Scarborough, during his time as Northamptonshire's scorer.

RYAN, Francis Peter

Born – Tundla, India, 14 November 1888
Died – Highfields, Leicester, 5 January 1954
Professional
LHB, SLA
Ed – Bedford Grammar School
1st XI: 1922-1931
Club and Ground: 1922-1931
Cap: 1923
Hampshire 1919-1920; Wales 1923-1930; South 1925; HDG Leveson Gower's XI 1926
Clubs: Cardiff, Enfield, Barnsley

Batting and Fielding Record:

	M	I	NO	RUNS	AV	100	50	CT	ST
F-c	215	312	100	1699	8.01	-	-	78	-

Bowling Record:

	Balls	M	R	W	AV	5wI	10wM
F-c	39485	1323	19053	913	20.86	79	17

Career-bests:
First-class –   46 v Northamptonshire at Northampton, 1925
8/41 v Derbyshire at Cardiff Arms Park, 1925

Frank Ryan was one of the most colourful and charismatic characters ever to walk onto a cricket field. An extrovert with a larger than life personality, his exploits had they occurred in the modern era would have dominated social media and filled column after column in tabloid newspapers. Whilst some questioned Frank's tenacity when put under pressure, or when things were not going his way, few doubted his skills as a spinner and in 1927 his clever bowling, together with that of Jack Mercer, produced one of the greatest-ever upsets in county cricket as, in their end-of-season encounter at Swansea, bottom of the table Glamorgan unexpectedly trounced Nottinghamshire to prevent the East Midlands side from winning the County Championship.

The visitors had arrived at St Helen's with the county title virtually in their grasp and, with the East Midlands side only needing to draw with a team still seeking their first win of the summer, plans had already been set in motion for a civic reception in Nottingham to celebrate their title-winning season. But Glamorgan turned the formbook upside down and by mid-afternoon on

A photo of Frank Ryan taken during 1924.

the first day, Frank had claimed five wickets, as Nottinghamshire were dismissed for 233. Glamorgan's batsmen then garnered a lead of 142 runs leaving the visitors with the task of batting throughout the final day to secure the title.

But Jack claimed six wickets in their second innings, whilst at the other end, Frank tricked and teased the visiting batsmen with his subtle spin, as seemingly every false stroke brought a wicket. The net result was a steady procession of batsmen back to the Swansea pavilion, with each walking off in a state of disbelief, realising that their dream was turning into a nightmare. Indeed, there are tales that one of the Nottinghamshire tailenders sat on the pavilion balcony with tears flooding down his cheeks as his team-mates returned at regular intervals.

Frank was born in India where his Irish-born father, who worked as an engineer on the Indian railway, had been raised following the posting of Frank's paternal grandfather, who served in the Irish Army, to the sub-continent. His maternal grandfather, after whom Frank was named, was the son of the Chief of the Clan Macleod of Raasay, an island between the Scottish mainland and the Isle of Skye.

During the early 1900s Frank and his family returned to the UK to live in West Hampstead. Frank duly attended Bedford Grammar School where his love of cricket, based on his formative years in India, was soon to the fore. As a young boy he had reveled in bowling against whatever targets were available and, if no balls were present, he would pick up stones and bowl these instead. His accurate left-arm spin bowling duly won him a place in the School's 1st XI, as well as invites to the nets at Lord's and The Oval. Indeed, one year, he had the distinction of clean bowling CB Fry prior to the start of the Champion County match. In 1907 he also took 9/36 for the school against I Zingari and was approached by Gloucestershire.

Hampshire in 1920 with young Frank Ryan standing back right.

58

However, Frank turned his back on cricket and served an apprenticeship as an engineer in Glasgow before working on a steamship. According to his descendants, Frank got rather bored by life at sea and jumped ship in New York, where he subsequently lived with a German lady. Their relationship ended though in 1915 after Frank told her that he was going home to join up. Apparently, his partner said "But Frank you may be killed", to which he replied "But I have to do my bit for my country."

He initially enlisted with the Army in June 1915, but became a mechanic with the Royal Flying Corps during 1916, before becoming a spotter and taking part in a series of aerial battles with the German pilots. Whilst stationed at Aldershot, Frank was befriended by Kent's Colin Blythe who encouraged him to take up cricket. He won a place in the Aldershot Services team and in the match against The Guards Brigade, his potent spin bowling impressed the Hon. Lionel Tennyson, the Hampshire captain, who told Frank to contact him when the War was over. During 1919 Frank duly made contact with Tennyson and three days after being demobilized, he made his first-class debut for Hampshire against Sussex at Brighton.

It was quite a debut as Frank bowled Hampshire to victory during the final afternoon of the two-day match as he claimed five wickets in the closing twenty minutes as his new employers won with two minutes to spare. But his time with the South Coast club was not a happy one, with tales of a ready temper, a few excesses off the field, and several clashes with Lionel Tennyson. After one dispute in 1920, following a heavy night's drinking, Tennyson yet again questioned Frank about whether he was in a fit enough condition to play. Frank responded by literally walking out on the county club. After his binge the night before, he barely had two pennies to rub together, so Frank hitch-hiked his way to Bristol and approached his friend Charlie Tayler about the possibility of arranging an introduction to the Gloucestershire committee and a fresh start in the West Country.

After only a couple of years on the county circuit, Frank had already gained a reputation for heavy drinking and a tendency for flying off the handle if he did not get his way. Charlie therefore thought better of Frank's polite enquiry, and instead advised him to approach another old friend, Jack Nash, the groundsman-professional at Cardiff, knowing that the Welsh county were looking to bolster their attack. Frank duly headed on to Cardiff and, over the August Bank Holiday weekend, arrived at the Arms Park, where Nash and his son were marking out a pitch for Cardiff's afternoon fixture. By this time, Frank was in a quite disheveled state and, at first, Jack was unsure who the down and out actually was. After hearing his story about looking for employment, Jack took pity on his old friend, offered him a bath in the spacious Arms Park pavilion, provided him with a decent meal and even placed a few notes in his back pocket, before waiving Frank on his way to Swansea where Glamorgan were playing.

He continued his journey by foot and, on the Sunday, trudged through torrential rain, before arriving at the St Helen's ground, soaked through to the skin. Frank's efforts though were well worth it as, after a brief chat with the county's officials – who had been alerted by Nash that the taciturn spinner was on his way – an agreement was reached. Frank duly agreed terms with the Cardiff club before making his debut for Glamorgan in

1922 against a team raised by HDG Leveson Gower. Having completed his qualification period in 1923, he became a regular in Glamorgan's line-up. Frank soon proved to be a useful asset, especially as Jack Nash and Harry Creber had retired and he soon became Glamorgan's first choice spinner. After Johnnie Clay switched styles, the left-armer also formed a potent partnership with the off-spinner, and wary of not losing another county contract, he initially showed more self-discipline off the field.

Following his move to South Wales, Frank shared lodgings with three other professionals – Eddie Bates, Jimmy Stone and Dai Davies. Their house was close to the Riverside Conservative club, and the four thirsty cricketers enjoyed calling into the club, not through any political allegiance but because of the club's fine beer and excellent billiard table. It was here that Frank displayed another of his sporting skills, often winning handsome sums, or the promise of further drinks, as he displayed some amazing trick shots on the table.

On occasions, Frank and Eddie would also travel over by Campbell's Steamer from Pier Head for an evening's entertainment in Weston-super-Mare. The pair spent many happy evenings drinking and dancing in the Somerset resort, especially on a Saturday when they knew there was a day of rest ahead on the Sunday, but if their ventures came during the week, Eddie was quite prepared to act as something of a minder to Frank, ensuring that he was in one piece the next morning and could either practice hard in the nets or give his best out in the middle.

Frank Ryan, seen at Hove during Glamorgan's match against Sussex in 1925.

In all, Frank played in 215 matches for the Welsh county and claimed 913 wickets with his high flowing action. His best bowling figures of 8/41 came against Derbyshire at the Arms Park in 1925. This was his finest season as he claimed 133 victims, followed by 106 in 1926. One of Frank's first match-winning performances came at Swansea during 1924 as Lancashire chased a target of 146 on the final afternoon. Harry Makepeace and Ernest Tyldesley gave the Northern side a solid start and on 84-3 they appeared to have the measure of the bowling. But everything changed when Johnnie sauntered over to Frank, and told him that he would be coming on in, primarily in a bid to stem the flow of runs from the Lancashire bats. Frank had been very innocuous in his first spell, but Johnnie had great faith in the erratic and wayward genius. "Right, Frank", he said, "it's now or never," and much to Johnnie's delight, the left-armer responded with one of the finest ever spells of his career, taking 7/23 and proving to be virtually unplayable, as Lancashire fell 39 runs short of their target.

In the words of Jack Morgan, the correspondent of the *Western Mail*, "the Lancashire batsmen must have thought they were in the coils of a serpent. Bringing the ball down from his fine height, Frank spun it like a top on the dusty surface, and batsman after batsman groped and lunged in vain as the ball spun wickedly passed their bats." When the last wicket fell, Frank was carried shoulder high off the field by his fellow professionals, and much merry-making followed to celebrate the finest-ever Championship victory Glamorgan had recorded in their short history as a first-class county.

In 1926 Frank was the toast of his colleagues once again, albeit in rather unusual circumstances, after some fine early season bowling saw the Welsh county reach the heady heights at the top of the Championship after the spinner played a hand in an eight-wicket victory over Surrey at the Arms Park. There was little time for celebration after play as the Glamorgan squad had the prospect of a lengthy train journey to Yorkshire for their match the next day at Hull. In fact, it must have seemed like they were travelling to Hell as the Welsh cricketers had a nightmare journey with their train from Cardiff General being both late and overcrowded, as the national rail network still showed the side-effects from the General Strike.

The upshot was that the only room for the kit was in the guard's van, but Frank, Jack Mercer and the other professionals did not unduly mind the inconvenience as they stowed kit in between some milk churns, before turning other bags upside down to create a surface for a card school as they wiled away the hours heading north. Their train was then further delayed at Birmingham, and the knock-on effect was that they missed their connection at Derby. "Surely nothing else can go wrong boys," was Johnnie's message as the team waited in the darkness for the next service to the Yorkshire coast.

But things only got worse when the weary Welshmen eventually arrived at 2 a.m. at their hotel in Hull. To their horror, they discovered that the owner had let their rooms, believing that the cricketers were not coming after all, and with the Beverley race-meeting taking place, there were plenty of customers looking for a bed for the night. The news that the hotel was full was a bombshell to the tired players but, for the second time in the space of twelve hours, Frank was the saviour of the team. "Don't worry boys," said the spinner as Johnnie continued to remonstrate with the hotel owner, "I know a little place around the corner." He then disappeared for a few minutes to track down his friend's pub and, after waking up his pal, he successfully negotiated for everyone to sleep on the seats in the lounge.

After their long and frustrating journey, the team were only too happy to find somewhere to rest their weary heads for a few hours. "Good old Frank" was their toast the following morning as they heartily tucked into breakfast, but the rather spartan accommodation on board the train and later at the pub, plus his friend's late-night hospitality, meant that Frank woke up with a headache plus a rather stiff back. Johnnie regrettably had to leave the spinner out of the team when he tossed at the start of the match. The effect of the journey and the lack of a decent night's sleep also manifested itself in the Glamorgan batting, as the Welsh county were bustled out for 52 and 95 as Yorkshire recorded an innings victory to leapfrog Glamorgan and to the top of the county table.

This was only one instance when Frank's post-match socialising affected either his availability or his play the following day. On another away match, legend has it that Frank was found fast asleep under the covers having forgotten where the team were staying and decided to return to the ground where they were playing. Episodes such as these were quite frustrating for the Glamorgan hierarchy as, on his day, and given the right wicket, Frank would bowl any side out. But as Johnnie aptly put it, "there were times when he did not spin, nor did he toil, complaining of a sudden attack of lumbago if batsmen started to master him." But overall, Johnnie, and subsequently Maurice, appreciated Frank's maverick character as much as his bowling, and believed that more often than not he would try his best for Glamorgan.

However, fellow amateur Trevor Arnott found it harder to bond with Frank when he took over the captaincy in 1928 and by mid-season, the pair were at loggerheads. Frank's bowling form suffered and, as Glamorgan went from defeat to defeat, Trevor found it increasingly difficult to handle the short-tempered spinner. During mid-July, Frank was omitted from the side, with rumours circulating that a furious row had taken place between the two during which Trevor, who had the support of a faction on the committee who had been embarrassed by tales of the spinner's off-the-field excesses, had threatened Frank that he would recommend his release if he didn't curb his excesses.

Frank Ryan demonstrates his bowling action at Leicester.

The Club duly explained Frank's absence by announcing that he had been rested because of a loss of confidence, but eyebrows were raised as the out of favour spinner proceeded to take ten wickets in Wales' victory against the West Indians at Llandudno. In the tourist's first innings, he took 5/17 in 15.1 overs as he formed a potent, if potentially volatile, partnership with Sidney Barnes – the legendary former England bowler who was now running a hotel in Colwyn Bay – before claiming five scalps in their second innings as the West Indians were comprehensively defeated by eight wickets.

Wales' success was in stark contrast to the fortunes of the county club and, not surprisingly, there were stern calls for Frank to be immediately recalled to the side and to patch up his differences with Trevor and other officials. But Frank continued to be "rested" and in his absence, several of the professionals and amateurs alike spoke with trusted friends in the Club's hierarchy to express their dissatisfaction both at the spinner's absence and Trevor's style of captaincy. When the committee met during the autumn to review the situation, it was clear that a change of captain was needed.

Besides offering Frank new terms for 1929, they persuaded Norman Riches and Johnnie to share the duties in an attempt to lighten the mood in the camp. Each had the confidence and respect of the professionals, including Frank, but it was a far from ideal

situation, and on several occasions, neither Norman or Johnnie were available. The net result was that seven amateurs led the side during 1929 but, at least, Frank was able to return to the team and prove his worth to his doubters with a haul of 68 wickets.

Frank almost doubled this tally the following year as he enjoyed a renaissance under Maurice's leadership and his more gentle encouragement, although the Cambridge graduate had to use very subtle tactics to get the best out of the spinner. These were the days when Frank, like the other professionals, was paid a match fee at the end of each game. On the away trips, Frank would often have frittered away his fee, well before making the long journey home by train with his thirst quenched and a virtually empty wallet. If his wife was meeting him at Cardiff General Station, Frank would often sneak out of the back door of the station, and then find a friend who could lend him some cash, so that he could return home pretending that he still had his full fee.

Maurice was only too well aware of Frank's little peccadillo's and was more than happy to lend Frank a few pounds if he seemed down on his luck. He would even slip him a few fivers or tenners after a fine bowling performance, so it was no surprise that Frank enjoyed a wonderful return to form in 1930 with 127 wickets at 21 apiece.

1930 was also the summer when Frank claimed the wicket of Don Bradman when the Australians played at St Helen's. In later life, Frank admitted that it was the wicket he cherished most of all during his career as a professional and it came about in rather unusual circumstances after play had been delayed on the first day until 4.30 p.m. The great Australian arrived in the middle after an hour had elapsed with Dai Davies dismissing Bill Ponsford, but at the end of the over, Maurice called over Dai and Frank who was bowling at the other end, and said to the pair "Put your sweaters on boys, and have a breather." Frank was flabbergasted and replied "But skipper, let me have another go at him. I'll get him next over." Mindful of the huge cash cow which Bradman's presence at Swansea had created, Maurice duly retorted "But that's just what we don't want – can't you see that we've got to keep him in so that we have a good gate on Monday."

Bradman duly feasted against some gentle bowling for the rest of the evening and to the delight of Maurice and the Club's other officials, there were over 25,000 people shoehorned into St Helen's when play began on the Monday morning. As the Glamorgan team took their places on the field, Maurice threw the ball to the spinner, and said "OK, Frank, now you can have a go at him." "Don't worry, skipper," he replied, "I'll get him." True to his word, the left-armer breached the master batsman's defence and clean bowled him during his second over of the morning, before adding a further five wickets to earn a huge ovation from the enormous crowd as he led the Glamorgan team off the field. Frank's efforts with the ball also nearly set up a thrilling victory as the following day the Glamorgan batsmen put bat to ball in an effective way and, had it not been for some time-wasting tactics by the Australian captain, the Welsh county might have, in a very unexpected way, lowered the tourist's colours.

As far as Frank's batting was concerned, he could be something of an enigma. He would often execute some elegant and graceful strokes when standing in front of the mirror in the dressing room, but when out in the middle, he rarely played with any confidence or seriousness and never posted a Championship half-century.

One of Frank's most nonchalant and remarkable innings came at Trent Bridge when Harold Larwood was bowling at his fastest. The first two balls whizzed past the edge of Frank's bat, and also the stumps, as he attempted some airy and expansive drives. Then when Larwood delivered his third ball, Frank hit his own stumps with a resounding smack as he played a rather ungainly slog. The Nottinghamshire fielders could barely believe what they had seen and, as Frank returned to the pavilion, one of the member's shouted out "Bad luck, old boy" to which he retorted "Bad luck indeed – it was jolly good luck. Fancy standing up to Larwood for half an hour!"

After his fine summer during 1930, Frank suffered a loss of form in 1931 and frequently got rattled or lost his length when attacked by opposition batsmen. Despite some cajoling from Maurice, plus the odd fiver in his back pocket, there was a growing feeling that the 44 year-old was past his best. He had been less effective than before on the slow and sandy wickets at Swansea largely, in the view of some, because he did not travel home to his wife in Cardiff, preferring instead to stay down in Swansea at the Cricketer's Arms opposite the ground and drink away the night.

Having been one of his biggest allies, Maurice also became more than a bit embarrassed by Frank's off-the-field antics, especially his rather wanton way of socializing after play. In one match in 1931 when Glamorgan were playing in Lancashire, Frank had remained after play, drinking with friends and meeting up with old acquaintances. In the wee small hours of the morning, he remembered that the Welsh county were playing that day in Swansea, so he hired a taxi and told the startled driver to take him to South Wales.

Later that morning, there were a few raised eyebrows in the Glamorgan dressing room about his absence ahead of the game, but just as Secretary Arthur Gibson was preparing to ring his home in Cardiff to find out if he was ill, Frank's taxi arrived at the ground. The spinner told the driver to settle the bill with the rather red-faced official before strolling into the dressing room saying "Ryan never lets you down!"

Privately, Maurice was deeply upset at Frank's behaviour, believing that he had betrayed his kindness and tolerance of his occasional binges, and had now frittered away vital and much-needed cash. In public and the committee room, Maurice would not have a word said against Frank's bowling, and he had spoken up many times on Frank's behalf. But the dire financial situation during the winter of 1931/32 meant that the wage bill would have to be cut, and Frank was one of several professionals who were told they would not be offered a new contract. Hoping that the financial situation might improve, or that the Club would have a change of heart, Frank remained with his wife in their home in Cardiff until the spring of 1932, by which time it was clear there was no chance of a contract with the Welsh county and he agreed terms with Barnsley to play in the Yorkshire Leagues.

He continued to play in League cricket in Lancashire and Yorkshire for several summers, before moving to Blean in Kent where he worked as a Civil Service clerk in the RAC record office. During the Second World War he joined the Army once again and worked as a payroll clerk, besides moving to live in the East Midlands. Indeed, it was from his new home in Severn Street, Leicester that he wrote a letter in August 1944 in which he extolled, as follows, the virtues of Maurice Turnbull, following the Glamorgan captain's death in Normandy a couple of months after Operation Overlord:

"It had been an honour and a pleasure to me to have played under many grand captains, bit I unhesitatingly place Maurice Turnbull as not only the best under whom I have played but an outstanding captain in the history of the game. His tolerance and restraint under trying circumstances, his deep knowledge of the game, his intuition and far-sightedness remain indelibly imprinted in my memory."

Indeed, it was this more gentle and genial side of Frank's character that many outside the inner circle of Glamorgan players have forgotten, with many commentators at the time dwelling instead on his gregariousness and fondness for socialising. It would be wrong to consider him as a drunken oaf or alcoholic – more a charming and charismatic gentleman who enjoyed the company of others, and someone who got, often unwittingly, into a series of scrapes. Had it not been for these, his contemporaries believe that Frank would have won a Test cap or regularly gone on winter tours with the MCC.

255
ABEL, Thomas Ernest

Born – Kennington, London, 10 September 1890
Died – Lambeth, London, 23 January 1937
Professional
RHB, OB
1st XI: 1922-1925
Club and Ground: 1922-1925
Cap: 1924
Surrey 1919-1920; South Wales 1923
Clubs: Port Talbot, Maesteg Town

Batting and Fielding Record:

	M	I	NO	RUNS	AV	100	50	CT	ST
F-c	32	55	1	821	15.20	1	1	18	-

Bowling Record:

	Balls	M	R	W	AV	5wI	10wM
F-c	461	14	258	8	32.25	-	-

Career-bests:
First-class – 107 v Leicestershire at St Helen's, Swansea,1924
3/24 v Surrey at St Helen's, Swansea, 1924

Tom Abel was the son of Bobby Abel, the well-known Surrey and England cricketer, and the brother of Billy Abel who played for Surrey between 1909 and 1926. Tom had joined the Surrey groundstaff in 1913 and first appeared that year for Surrey 2nd XI in the Minor County Championship. The outbreak of the Great War halted his fledgling career as a professional cricketer as he joined the Royal West Surrey Regiment – in hindsight, his formative years as a young cricketer were lost to the War.

When county cricket resumed in 1919, Tom made his first-class debut against Somerset at The Oval – the first of eleven two-day games that summer in which the right-handed

Tom Abel.

batsman appeared, with Tom making one half-century. He re-appeared once for Surrey in 1920, against Warwickshire at Edgbaston, but with the renewal of his contract unlikely, he agreed terms with Glamorgan's officials to play in club cricket in South Wales during 1921 and to qualify by residence for the Welsh county.

In August 1922 Tom made his debut against the Combined Oxford and Cambridge XI at the Arms Park, before making his Championship debut in May 1924, ironically against his former employers at The Oval, opening the batting with Norman Riches. Tom ended the 1924 summer with an aggregate of 492 runs at an average of just 15. He only passed 50 once but on that occasion, Tom went on to post his maiden first-class century as he made 107 against Leicestershire at St Helen's in two hours and twenty minutes, with 16 fours. He retained his place as an opener in 1925 but only posted one fifty as he accrued 317 runs, once again, at an average of around 15 with his last appearance in county cricket coming at Bath during the final week of July against Somerset.

Tom was released by Glamorgan at the end of 1925 and returned to live in Clapham where he subsequently acted as a coach in local schools. He died in 1937 aged 46, with his body interred at Streatham Park Cemetery.

256
SULLIVAN, Dennis ('Dan')

Born – Mitcham, Surrey, 28 January 1883
Died – Harold Wood, Essex, 28 December 1968
Professional
RHB, WK
1st XI: 1922-1928
Club and Ground: 1922-1927
Cap: 1924
Surrey 1914-1921; South Wales 1922-1923; Wales 1922-1928; Tennyson's XI to Jamaica 1926/27 and 1927/28; Players 1928
Clubs: Mitcham, Briton Ferry Steel, Port Talbot

Batting and Fielding Record:

	M	I	NO	RUNS	AV	100	50	CT	ST
F-c	115	166	55	811	7.30	-	-	128	84

Career-bests:
First-class – 47* v Derbyshire at Queen's Park, Chesterfield, 1926

Dan Sullivan kept wicket for Glamorgan between 1922 and 1928, with his career tally of 84 stumpings bearing testament to his nimble abilities behind the stumps. He was regarded by contemporaries as one of the best glovemen in the country having spent time before, and after the Great War, on the Surrey staff.

His career as a professional cricketer stemmed from a friendship with Herbert Strudwick who lived two doors away from Dan's home in Mitcham. The Surrey and England wicket-keeper had seen the teenager (who was the youngest of seven children born to Irish-born James Sullivan who worked as a caretaker at a local school) throwing golf balls up against a garden wall and catching the returns. Impressed by his catching abilities, Herbert recommended that he joined the local cricket club. He subsequently kept an eye on Dan's development and in 1907 oversaw his selection for a Surrey Colts team.

An image of Danny Sullivan taken during 1927.

1907 proved to be an important year for Dan as during April he married his childhood sweetheart, Emily Mary Jane Hilliard, in Croydon shortly before joining Surrey's junior staff and acting as understudy to Fred Stedman, Surrey's reserve wicket-keeper. He also spent time watching the handling skills of Herbert, the Club's first choice keeper and the batting talents of Jack Hobbs, but one of his proudest memories of his cricketing education was playing in a match against WG Grace's London County at Crystal Palace. As he later recalled, "I squatted behind the great Doctor, who just gave me a friendly nod. Conversation between batsmen and wicket-keepers was practically unknown at the time, but after the match, he sought me out and told me to keep on with the good work."

During 1909 Fred Stedman moved to Ireland, with Dan making his debut for Surrey 2nd XI against Yorkshire 2nd XI at Horley. He duly became the regular wicket-keeper for Surrey's 2nd XI besides spending the winter months coaching and playing in South Africa. During the 1910/11 season, the young wicket-keeper also stood as an umpire in the Currie Cup match between Natal and Griqualand West at Durban when the gentleman originally appointed to stand in the contest was taken ill shortly before the game.

In mid-June 1914 Herbert was unable to play in Surrey's Championship match against Hampshire at The Oval, and Dan was called up to make his first-class debut. He duly claimed a notable first victim as he caught CB Fry off the bowling of Tom Bushby as the multi-talented sportsman, who played in 26 Tests for England, got a thick edge to a drive against the right-arm fast-medium bowler.

The outbreak of the Great War saw Dan initially join the Royal Irish Regiment before subsequently serving with the Royal Engineers on the Western Front. When cricket resumed in 1919, Dan made a further first-class appearance in Surrey's match against Cambridge University, besides standing as one of the umpires in the pair of one-day games which Surrey staged against the Australian Imperial Forces at The Oval.

1920 saw Dan being selected for Surrey's match against Oxford University, before appearing in a quartet of Championship matches during 1921 when Herbert was on

England duty, as well as Surrey's match against the Australians, but it was clear that despite some deft glovework he was still regarded as their second choice keeper. Surrey were keen for him to stay and offered a decent lump sum, but Dan was eager to achieve his long-held dream of playing regular Championship cricket so he opted for a change of scenery at the end of the 1921 season and agreed terms with Glamorgan.

Over the course of the next two years, Dan qualified through residence for the Welsh county by playing club cricket for Briton Ferry Steel and Port Talbot, besides making his Glamorgan debut in the match at the Arms Park in 1922 against a Combined Oxford and Cambridge XI. During August he also featured in the South Wales team which met North Wales, whilst the following year Dan also made his debut for Wales in their first-class match against Scotland at Perth.

1923 also saw him play for Glamorgan against the West Indians at the Arms Park, and featuring in the Club's first-ever victory against a touring team. His neat and tidy glovework was a breath of fresh air for Glamorgan's supporters who had seen a number of amateurs behind the stumps in previous years. What they lacked in ability, they more than made up for in enthusiasm, but with Jimmy Stone, the former Hampshire cricketer also on the staff, Glamorgan now possessed a pair of professional glovemen, and players who could make the most of standing up to the spin-heavy Glamorgan attack.

With Stone easing into retirement, Dan – at the age of 42 – became the Welsh county's first choice wicket-keeper in 1924 with his Championship debut for his new employers ironically coming on his old stamping ground as Glamorgan met Surrey at The Oval. The summer of 1924 saw Dan claim 36 victims, split equally between catches and stumpings, and his tally would have been much higher had Glamorgan not suffered a series of heavy defeats, and bowled only once in games. Nevertheless, Dan did not regret the move and as he later recalled "to play regularly at such grounds as Swansea and Cardiff was quite different from playing at The Oval. As first-choice, and without any competition, I was much more relaxed and assured about my cricket."

Danny Sullivan, as seen in 1924 wearing his wicket-keeper's kit.

A measure of his abilities can be gauged from the fact that 21 stumpings came Dan's way in 1925 as well as 26 the following year. But it wasn't just standing up where he excelled as during 1926 he also played a key role whilst standing back as Trevor Arnott claimed Glamorgan's first-ever hat-trick in Championship cricket. The seam bowler's feat came during the Welsh county's match against Somerset at the Arms Park and followed Dan taking a tumbling catch in front of the slip cordon as Guy Earle attempted an extravagant drive. Arnott followed this by clean bowling both George Hunt and Cuthbert

Godwin with the next two deliveries as Somerset subsided to 34–9, before some lusty blows by their last pair took the total to 59.

The catch to remove Earle was just one of many fine catches which Dan made during his four and a half years of regular Championship cricket with his adopted county. On many occasions, his efforts were even more praiseworthy considering the fact that he played with bruised and swollen hands. "Like many other 'keepers, I made use of raw meat to protect my hands," he later recalled. "A butcher would cut a few thin strips of steak and they would be kept in the pavilion in iced water until I needed them. Sometimes though my hands were so sore I could hardly hold my bat."

His efforts also won him selection in Lionel Tennyson's touring party to Jamaica in 1926/27. He thoroughly enjoyed himself on the tour, but was also involved in a car crash after the third match. As he recalled "Myself, Ernest Tyldesley and Jack O'Connor were taken for a motor ride to a place called Chinatown near Kingston. We were going to see the proprietress of a café who was reputed to be 127 years of age. She must have put over the evil eye as, on the way back, our car left the road and plunged into a banana plantation. Ernest Tyldesley dislocated a shoulder, O'Connor twisted his knee and I dislocated a thumb."

The accident ended Tyldesley's tour and saw him miss Lancashire's opening games in May, but Dan was only on the sidelines for a couple of matches as he rested his damaged digit. Despite also contracting sunstroke whilst bathing in the sea, the accident did not put Dan off from making further overseas visits and when Tennyson approached Dan later in the summer about making a return visit to Jamaica, he readily agreed.

Dan had celebrated his 45th birthday shortly before travelling with Tennyson's party on the SS *Changuinola*. Whilst at sea and chatting with his fellow professionals, Dan started to consider his career after county cricket. Ernest Tyldesley, the Lancashire batsman, had tipped him off the previous winter about a post that was shortly becoming available as coach and groundsman at Rossall School. After returning to the UK, Dan travelled to the Fylde Coast to discuss the post. The terms were favourable so Dan duly contacted the Glamorgan officials and told them that he intended to retire from playing and move to the Lancashire school.

Danny Sullivan on tour abroad with Hampshire's Phil Mead.

Fittingly, his final first-class game was the contest between Glamorgan and Surrey at the Arms Park which started on 11 August 1928.

His final summer of county cricket also saw him chosen for the Players against the Gentlemen in their annual encounter at The Oval in the first week of June. However, several counties were also involved in Championship matches so the teams were not fully representative of the amateur and professional talent. His call-up largely stemmed from the fact that Glamorgan were one of the counties not playing, but it was with immense pride that Dan walked out at the ground where he had learnt his trade. Dai Davies and Jack Mercer were also in the Players team and Dan was delighted to stump Alfred Jeacocke whilst standing up to Jack's cutters as his former Surrey colleague over-balanced and lost his footing trying to on-drive the wily Glamorgan bowler. Dan was looking forward to further opportunities in the Gentlemen's second innings, but the contest was badly affected by rain – with the last day being washed out without a ball being bowled.

'Mr Dan' was a popular figure whilst looking after the wickets at Rossall, coaching the young sportsmen and standing as an umpire in the school's games. Whilst based at Rossall, he also took great delight to see his son Leslie enjoy a decent career as a footballer. After playing as an amateur for Fleetwood and Blackburn Rovers, he turned professional and played as an outside-left for Lytham Town, Rochdale, Brentford, Bristol Rovers and Chesterfield. Dan remained at Rossall until the 1950s, before moving with his wife to Essex where he died in hospital in Harold Wood on 28 December 1968.

257
DAVIES, William Henry

Born – Briton Ferry, 7 August 1901
Died – Carmarthen, March 1973
Professional
RHB, RM
1st XI: 1922-1927
Other: 1923-1930
Clubs: Cardiff, Briton Ferry Steel

Batting and Fielding Record:

	M	I	NO	RUNS	AV	100	50	CT	ST
F-c	5	10	2	33	4.12	-	-	-	-

Bowling Record:

	Balls	M	R	W	AV	5wI	10wM
F-c	351	16	130	3	43.33	-	-

Career-bests:
First-class –   8* v Nottinghamshire at Trent Bridge, 1924
            2/35 v Leicestershire at Cardiff Arms Park, 1927

Bill Davies had a decent record as a professional in club cricket with Briton Ferry Steel and Cardiff during the 1920's, and appeared in five matches for Glamorgan – three at the Arms Park and two in away games at Trent Bridge.

He was highly regarded in club circles, especially as a lively seam bowler, and hard-hitting batsman. Had Glamorgan been able to have afforded to select more professionals, it is likely that Bill would have played on a more frequent basis in the County Championship.

His career had begun in the Neath area with his success for Briton Ferry Steel resulting in a lucrative contract with Cardiff in 1924. He enjoyed a fine summer with the city club in 1926 scoring 518 runs and taking 70 wickets – just four short of what, at the time, was the Club's record of 74 taken by Jack Nash in 1910. Whilst at the Arms Park, Bill also acted as assistant groundsman, working under Nash and Trevor Preece.

258
SHARPLES, James Everett

Born – Pendlebury, Lancashire, 26 December 1890
Died – Craven Arms, 23 August 1969
Amateur
RHB, OB
1st XI: 1922
Clubs: Bingley, Hythe, Briton Ferry Town, NOR Skewen, Craven Arms

Batting and Fielding Record:

	M	I	NO	RUNS	AV	100	50	CT	ST
F-c	1	1	0	0	-	-	-	-	-

Bowling Record:

	Balls	M	R	W	AV	5wI	10wM
F-c	6	0	1	0	-	-	-

Jimmy Sharples played once for Glamorgan during 1922 whilst working as an engineer at the National Oil Refinery in Skewen. He later worked in Turkey and Egypt before returning to England and spending the rest of his life in Shropshire.

The son of a Lancashire-born miner, Jimmy was brought up in the Bingley area of West Yorkshire where he showed great prowess at cricketer and football. Indeed, shortly before the Great War, Jimmy was a professional footballer with Leicester Fosse FC, before joining the 14th Cheshire Regiment and subsequently the 8th Border Regiment. After the War, Jimmy moved to work in Kent, where he played with success for the Hythe club, besides getting married in September 1919 to Mary Andrews.

During the early 1920s he moved to South Wales having secured a position at the National Oil Refinery in Skewen, and his run-scoring and off-spin bowling for the local team, as well as for Briton Ferry Town brought him to the attention of the Glamorgan selectors. With several regulars absent for the end of season encounter with Leicestershire at Cardiff Arms Park in 1922, Jimmy was drafted into the side. However, he was dismissed for a duck in what proved to be his only innings in first-class cricket.

Jimmy Sharples, seen when living in Shropshire.

Sadly, his marriage broke up, with Jimmy emigrating to work for several years in Turkey and the Middle East. During the 1930s he returned to the United Kingdom and settled in Shropshire, where he ran a tobacconists and newsagents in Craven Arms. Jimmy retained a keen interest in sport, playing cricket for the local club, in addition to owning several racehorses who ran in his colours under National Hunt rules. He also became involved in local politics and served as a councillor for Ludlow Rural District Council.

259
GABE-JONES, Arthur *Royston*

Born – Clydach Vale, 25 November, 1906
Died – Cardiff, 26 February, 1965
Amateur
RHB, RM
Ed – Blundell's School and Cambridge University
1st XI: 1922
Club and Ground: 1933-1935
Colts: 1922
Clubs: Clydach Vale, Cardiff, The Pterodactyls, Welsh Cygnets

Batting and Fielding Record:

	M	I	NO	RUNS	AV	100	50	CT	ST
F-c	1	1	1	6	-	-	-	-	-

Career-bests:
First-class 6* v Leicestershire at Cardiff Arms Park, 1922

In 1922 Roy Gabe-Jones became the youngest county cricketer during the twentieth century when he made his County Championship debut against Leicestershire at Cardiff Arms Park aged just 15 years and 9 months. Remarkably, it proved also to be his one and only appearance in first-class cricket.

Roy was the son of Rees Gabe-Jones, a prominent sportsman and doctor in the Rhondda Valley who played a handful of games for Glamorgan during the early 1890s (Vol.1 p.86-87). Educated at Blundell's School, he showed great promise as a young sportsman, playing rugby and cricket for the famous public school in Tiverton before returning each summer to play for Clydach Vale.

This was the case in 1922 with the teenager having few thoughts that he might ever play county cricket, never mind during that summer. But after a string of good scores, Roy was chosen to play initially for The Pterodactyls alongside other youngsters with South Walian links who were being privately educated as well as appearing in a Glamorgan Colts game during early August at the Arms

Royston Gabe-Jones, seen in his days at Blundell's School in Devon.

72

Park as the county's selectors, after a run of dreadful results by the 1st XI, desperately sought fresh, young talent.

His steady batting and outstanding fielding impressed the watching officials and when a number of amateurs opted out of the closing match of the season against Leicestershire, Roy was drafted into the side. He duly made a stubborn and unbeaten 6 against the vastly experienced Leicestershire bowlers and helped the depleted Glamorgan side to secure a draw. Roy's ground fielding also drew praise, yet he was never called up again to play in the 1st XI.

However, Roy did play for the Club and Ground side between 1933 and 1935, by which time he had completed his education at Cambridge University and had gone into business in Cardiff. A key factor behind his selection for the team was a good friendship with Club captain Maurice Turnbull with whom he played rugby for Cardiff.

Their friendship blossomed after time as a half-back paring in the Athletic XV during.1931/32. Roy was the good humoured captain of this team and following their success and good understanding they were chosen several times for the 1st XV during 1932/33. With Maurice's quick and steady passing, Roy became an astute and clever fly-half, who also proved to be an excellent foil for the strong running centres. By common consent, the Cardiff team possessed the best set of backs that season in Welsh rugby, and were even described by one writer as "the wonder team."

The Glamorgan side, as seen on the scorecard for the match against Leicestershire in 1922, including the 15 year-old Roy Gabe Jones.

1923

Just two Championship wins in 24 matches tells, yet again, another sorry story as Glamorgan languished in 16th place in the county table. Both of their victories during 1923 came at Swansea where Northamptonshire were defeated by four wickets and Gloucestershire were overwhelmingly beaten by 232 runs. But a third victory that summer reflected the mood of optimism which still existed within the Club's hierarchy and the belief that the good times were just around the corner.

The victory in question was the one by 43 runs over the touring West Indians in their match at the Arms Park over the August Bank Holiday and a match where the Welsh county's new recruits were to the fore. First, Jimmy Stone, the 46-year old former Hampshire wicket-keeper, wrote his name into the annals of his adopted county as he became the first Glamorgan player to score a hundred against an touring team. His efforts helped Tal Whittington set the visitors from the Caribbean a target of 239 and with George Challenor completing a fluent hundred, it looked like yet another defeat for the Welsh county.

But Frank Ryan and Jack Mercer then turned the contest on its head as the tourists lost their last six wickets for just 24 runs as Glamorgan completed their first victory over a touring team. The win crowned a fine summer for Frank who claimed 106 wickets for his new county and, much to his delight, reached the hundred-mark in the game against Hampshire, his former employers and with whose management he had clashed swords.

Cyril Walters, the product of Neath Grammar School, seen in his England blazer during 1934.

Eddie Bates also emulated Norman Riches' feats by amassing 1097 first-class runs and whilst the imports were earning their corn, there were encouraging signs shown by some of the new homegrown talent. Dai Davies had an eventful home debut at Swansea whilst Cyril Walters, the schoolboy from Neath, impressed many fine judges with his graceful batting.

Dai went on to become one of the stalwarts of Glamorgan, but Cyril – to the angst of many – switched to Worcestershire later in the 1920s before becoming in 1934 the first Welshman to lead England in Test cricket. How much better it might have been for the Welsh county in general that he was still allied to Glamorgan when he led out the England side for the opening Test of the Ashes series at Trent Bridge.

260
GEARY, Frederick William

Born – Hinckley, 9 December 1887
Died – Stoke Golding, 8 January 1980
Professional
1st XI: 1923
Clubs: Hinckley, Port Talbot

Batting and Fielding Record:

	M	I	NO	RUNS	AV	100	50	CT	ST
F-c	2	4	0	3	0.75	-	-	2	-

Bowling Record:

	Balls	M	R	W	AV	5wI	10wM
F-c	78	3	24	0	-	-	-

Career-best:
First-class –   2 v Surrey at Cardiff Arms Park, 1923

The son of a publican in the Hinckley area of Leicestershire, Fred Geary had a short spell on his native county's staff before playing in the Home Counties after the Great War. He then joined Glamorgan in 1923 and – funded by Club Chairman Sir Sidney Byass – Fred acted as the professional at Port Talbot besides looking after the wicket at the Margam Abbey ground.

During the first week of May 1923, Fred also played in a couple of Championship matches for Glamorgan at the Arms Park, despite having spent very little time in the region or being known to club captain Johnnie Clay. Indeed, Fred is believed to be the person referred to in the following exchange between Johnnie and a colleague. "One day this burly fellow, unknown to Johnnie or myself was chosen to play. Being a gentleman, Johnnie didn't like to ask him whether he was a batsman or a bowler. So Johnnie asked me and I didn't know either. 'Well,' said Johnnie, 'we'll put him in the slips. Even if he can't catch, he's a big chap – something might hit him!'"

Fred scored 2 and 0 on debut against Surrey, followed by 1 and 0 against Yorkshire. He did take a couple of catches, perhaps more by luck than judgement close to the wicket, but the all-rounder did not take a wicket in either game and returned to club cricket. During the 1930s he followed his father Kim into the licensed victualler's trade and became the publican of The George and Dragon in Stoke Golding.

DAVIES, David ('Dai')

Born – Llanelli, 26 August 1896
Died – Llanelli, 16 July 1976
Professional
RHB, RM
Ed – Pentip Church of England School, Sandy
1st XI: 1923-1944
2nd XI: 1935
Club and Ground: 1924-1948
Cap: 1923
Carmarthenshire 1920-1922; Players 1928; West of England 1944
Club: Llanelli

Batting and Fielding Record:

	M	I	NO	RUNS	AV	100	50	CT	ST
F-c	411	681	61	15008	24.20	16	71	193	-
Wartime	6	6	0	71	11.83	-	-	2	-

Bowling Record:

	Balls	M	R	W	AV	5wI	10wM
F-c	22011	774	9404	271	34.70	4	-
Wartime	?	?	?	1	-	-	-

Career-bests:
First-class –   216 v Somerset at Rodney Parade, Newport, 1939
6/50 v Essex at Westcliff, 1936

Dai Davies was Glamorgan's first home-bred professional to make an impact in Championship cricket. He was also the umpire in the Welsh county's title-winning game at Bournemouth in 1948 and uttered the immortal words "That's Out and we've won the Championship" when upholding an appeal for l.b.w. against Hampshire's last batsman.

Dai Davies from 1935.

During a first-class playing career from 1923 to 1939, the Llanelli-born all-rounder scored over 15,000 runs, and took 275 wickets. In addition, he held 195 catches and was described by Jack Hobbs as the finest cover point he ever saw. The youngest of eleven children, Dai's father was a staunch Calvinistic Methodist and three times each Sunday he and his family attended chapel. As Dai later observed with a wry smile on his face, "it meant I could only play cricket six days a week!"

The Davies family lived in Sandy Road and, with Stradey Park alongside, it was no surprise that Dai and his brothers were soon playing and watching rugby in the winter, followed by cricket in the summer. From the age of eight, Dai helped to put the tin plates on the scoreboard and reveled in his reward of a sandwich plus a bottle of lemonade. In 1910 he also stayed away from school for two days in order to operate the scoreboard at Stradey Park as the Gentlemen of Essex met the Gentlemen of Carmarthenshire. As he later recalled, "the lemonade and sandwiches kept coming thick and fast, and I was as happy as the larks singing high above. It was absolute heaven but hell lay just around the corner. When I returned to school, the Headmaster knew where I had been. I received four strokes of the cane, two on each hand, but I would have willingly taken forty more rather than miss that marvelous match."

His misdemeanors were soon forgotten as he was appointed captain of rugby and cricket, with his school winning the Llanelli Schools Challenge Cups in both 1909 and 1910. Against Old Road School, Dai took 7 wickets for 7 runs and after winning the trophies he was entertained to a lavish tea by the Headmaster, plus the vicar of Llanelli, Canon Watkin Morgan. Aged fourteen, Dai left school and became a pitman in the town's steelworks. During the summer, though, he did his best to ensure his work rota did not interrupt playing for Llanelli and completing his cricketing education under the tutelage of the Club's professionals, including ex-Hampshire spinner Ted Light and South African Bert Vogler.

He had first played for the Llaneli club in 1912 but it wasn't until 1919 that he became a regular in the 1st XI, largely because the cricket club did not play during the Great War with Dai, in a reserved occupation, spending many long hours at the steelworks, known locally as 'The Klondyke'. He swiftly made up for lost time and in his first appearance in 1919, against Briton Ferry Town, he took 6/44 with his brisk seamers. The next match, against Swansea, saw him claim 8/51, followed by 9/28 against Clydach.

Despite having secured a regular berth in the 1st XI, Dai still turned out on occasions for the 2nd XI, and against Parc Llewelyn in 1920 he made a whirlwind and unbeaten 183, striking 16 sixes and 17 fours. Later that summer, he also made his Minor County debut for Carmarthenshire and made a more composed half-century against Glamorgan at Stradey Park. In the return contest at Swansea, he claimed 9/82 with his name going into the notebooks of the county's selectors as someone to keep a close eye on.

Dai Davies demonstrates his pull stroke for a publicity photograph taken at the Arms Park.

The only fly in the ointment was that, as a resident of Carmarthenshire, Dai was ineligible under the residential regulations to play for Glamorgan in 1921 and it was two years later that his chance finally came to appear in Championship cricket. His debut in June 1923, against Northamptonshire at St Helen's, ironically came after Dai had completed a double shift. The previous night he had been ending his eight-hour shift in the hot and dusty environment of the local strip mill when he found out that his replacement had not turned up. Like the others, he had been paid a production bonus that afternoon, but had frittered much of it away in the White Horse Inn. The net result was that he was unfit to work, with Dai being persuaded to do the night shift as well.

He eventually arrived home at 6 a.m., and after breakfast went straight to bed. But Dai was woken by his mother shortly after eleven to say that a car was waiting outside to take him to St Helen's as Glamorgan were a player short after an injury in the warm-ups. In these days before mobile phones and text messaging, George Hay, the match secretary from Swansea, had telephoned Will Davies, the Borough Mayor of Llanelli in order to get a message and a vehicle as quickly as possible to Dai's home.

As Dai later recalled "I had never ever seen a Championship match and here I was playing in one. As I ran on, I looked at the scoreboard and saw that Northants were 57 for 0. At the end of the over, Mr Whittington tossed me the ball. 'You're bowling, Dai', he said and briefly discussed the field placing. With my fourth ball, I knocked the opener Bellamy's middle stump clean out of the ground. I'd been on the field five minutes and got my first wicket. I carried on bowling after lunch and got two more ......Glamorgan then had about an hour to bat after tea and I was beginning to feel very tired and I was more than thankful to sit on the dressing room bench. Just then Whittington said 'Get your pads on Dai, you're first wicket down!' I got my pads on and sat outside trying to summon up strength from somewhere. Thankfully, I wasn't needed because the openers held out until the close. I duly went home by train in the evening, very tired and very happy!"

As this story shows, Dai was never afraid of hard work, and over the next sixteen years he became one of the county's most consistent and reliable all-rounders, with a career best score of 216 against Somerset at Newport in 1939 during a match when Maurice Turnbull told his batsmen to occupy the crease for as long as possible after the visitors had, in his opinion, spurned the chance of setting up a game by batting for too long in their first innings.

Dai Davies relaxes at Weston-super-Mare.

His efforts also coincided with a miners strike at Bedwas Colliery and, as a staunch member of the Labour Party, Dai sympathized with their protests about working conditions and appropriate wage rates. Before the start of play, Dai purchased a copy of the *South Wales Argus* and carefully read about events at Bedwas under the heading "Welsh miners in stay-in strike." Dai duly cut it out and pinned it onto the door of the professionals' dressing-room. As he was doing so, Mr Dawson, a leading Cardiff shipowner, came up to him and said "£5 for a hundred today, Dai?" to which he replied "Thank you very much, Sir," before Dawson added "And it's £10 if you can make 200."

Unbeaten on 90, he duly went out and continued the rearguard action, telling Emrys

Davies to waive to him when there was news that the colliery strike was finally over. It was not until six o'clock that Emrys duly waived to Dai from the balcony – by this time, Dai had completed his double-century, and the signal from the dressing room prompted the end of his vigil too, as he advanced down the wicket to Arthur Wellard and was stumped for 216. Half an hour later Maurice brought an end to the innings, with their total on 547-7, and the weary Somerset fielders finally trudged off the field.

As it turned out, this was Dai's final major innings for the county, as he only passed 50 once more in the remaining seventeen games in 1939. In mid-July he was also left out of the team after he indicated to Maurice that he was contemplating his future and, on the boat journey home from Weston-super-Mare, he confirmed with Maurice that he had contacted the MCC to join the umpire's list for the following season.

However, Dai had to wait six years before becoming a first-class umpire, and during the War he spent time as cricket coach at Bromsgrove School, besides playing in some of Glamorgan's wartime friendlies which were arranged to raise funds for the War Effort, as well as for the West of England team. He duly officiated in 403 first-class matches from 1946 until 1961, with his career in a white coat starting with Worcestershire's game against the Indians at New Road. It was not though his first time umpiring as in 1927 he had stood in the match at Llandudno when the Welsh Cygnets played the New Zealanders.

Dai also stood in 23 Tests between 1947 and 1958, with his first international appointment coming at Lord's as England met South Africa. He also officiated in the Second, Third and Fifth Test of the 1948 Ashes series, standing at Lord's, Old Trafford and The Oval as Don Bradman and his Invincibles secured a famous series victory. Eighteen years before, Dai had been instrumental in taking Bradman and some of the 1930 Australians to the National Eisteddford, staged in People's Park in Llanelli, with Dai receiving a huge ovation as he went onto the stage with 'The Don'.

During the Fifth Test of the series with the 1951 South Africans, at The Oval, Dai also gave out Len Hutton for obstructing the field in a curious incident against Athol Rowan. As Dai stated in his memoirs, " He bowled a ball to Len Hutton which pitched on middle and leg. Hutton tried to sweep it, but the ball didn't connect properly. The ball ran off the top of his bat, on to his glove and went about six feet above him in the air. Russell Endean, the wicket-keeper was preparing to take the catch when Hutton took a second swipe at the ball and knocked it away from Endean's waiting gloves. There was a terrific appeal and I gave Hutton out… After the game, the match reporters came swarming into the umpires room. Sir Pelham Warner said it was unfortunate that a cricketer of Hutton's stature should be given out in such a manner. But laws are laws and he was out and that was all there was to it!"

Whether or not it was a coincidence, Dai only stood in one Test in 1952, but he was soon back in favour, standing in three Tests of the 1953 Ashes series, plus two of the 1956 series. During this period, Dai also accepted coaching appointments in South Africa and, in particular, spent time in Johannesburg, coaching schoolboys at Ellis Park. His rapid rise from Glamorgan batsman to Test umpire resulted from his excellent and firm decision-making – as shown by the incident with Hutton – as well as his affable manner, with the latter being important at a time when county captains marked umpires at the end of a game.

He was also renowned as an umpire who always took his time when making a decision. Not for him a trigger finger, but instead a slow death as he quietly weighed up all options. Beneath his white coat, Dai always wore his Glamorgan capped players sweater, plus a red tie bearing a Dragon motif leaving nobody in any doubt that he was a Welshman, and a very proud one at that! Indeed, at Bournemouth in 1948 after giving out Charlie Knott, Hampshire's last man, he quickly got changed into his civvies and then joined his former colleagues on the balcony of the Dean Park pavilion as Wilf Wooller and the Championship-winning team celebrated their success with the rendition of a series of Welsh songs!

The following week, Dai accepted an invitation from Wilf to join the squad on their end-of-season tour to Pembrokeshire where a series of friendlies took place at Narberth, Haverfordwest and Pembroke Dock. It was very much a social tour as each game was accompanied by a grand dinner and civic reception. Dai also stood as one of the umpires in the celebratory match at Swansea in mid-September at St Helen's as the great and the good of Welsh cricket joined Wilf and his – quite literally – merry team as they met a South of England XI at Swansea. The thought of his daily duties out in the middle – rather than the remains of a hangover from the jollities in West Wales – meant that Dai went a little bit more easy after play each evening when mixing with his former colleagues.

Dai was also known as the umpire who would turn away in between balls whilst standing at the bowler's end and break into song in an unique way to maintain his concentration. Indeed, Tony Lewis recalls a match against Kent late in Dai's career when he was facing the fast but erratic David Sayer. "All of my attention was based on trying to line up Sayer and having successfully seen off each delivery, I kept hearing a voice 'Singing high, high, high. Singing low, low, low' It took me about an hour to realise that it was Dai singing at the other end!"

In later life, Dai was badly affected by arthritis but he was able to collaborate with his son-in-law John Edwards in the production of his memoirs called *Dai Davies – not Out 78*, which were published in 1975. Indeed, Dai was a great raconteur, although he may have been prone to a little bit of embellishment, such as the tale of his club match against Swansea at Llanelli in 1922 which saw him claim six wickets as the visitors were dismissed for 48, with Dai's bowling also laying out three players in the dressing room – "Percy Morris played a rising ball onto his head and was caught by the wicket-keeper – caught out and knocked out. Willie Gemmill came in to bat without a box and I bowled him a ball which struck him in the target area – he retired very hurt. Then I bowled Jock Tait a yorker which pitched on his right foot – l.b.w., fractured bone and carried off."

Dai's recollection of his maiden Championship hundred, against Worcestershire at New Road also had plenty of colour. It came early on the third morning of a game when scores were level with Glamorgan's last pair at the wicket. Dai, unbeaten on 97 at the close the previous evening had been joined by Stan Hacker, the burly veteran whose county career had begun during the era of WG Grace. "I was facing the last ball of the opening over, and the thought crossed my mind of telling Stan to run a quick single. I looked at Stan and thought better of it. He was seventeen stone! As Fred Root walked back to his mark, the bells of Worcester Cathedral rang out to the tune of 'Abide with me. Fast falls the eventide.' I got the message. Root thundered towards me and bowled one down the line of middle stump. Left foot across, I clouted him through mid-wicket. Stan was bowled for a duck in the next over. I was 100 not out!"

This was the first of sixteen hundreds and during 1928 Dai made three successive centuries.

Dai Davies is the umpire as England's Jim Laker bowls to a New Zealand batsman in their Test Match at Lord's during 1958.

His sequence began with an unbeaten 126 against Sussex at Swansea, followed by 103 in the away match with Northamptonshire, before an unbeaten 165 in the game with Sussex at Eastbourne. As Dai recalled, "I now had visions of making six consecutive centuries to equal the record held by CB Fry, as we traveled from Eastbourne to Pontypridd to play Gloucestershire. Charlie Parker and Tom Goddard were two of the best spinners in the world on a wicket giving them any help and the Pontypridd strip soon crumbled. The first ball I received from Charlie Parker turned square and I gave Wally Hammond a thick edge in the slips and was out for a duck. In the second innings I was out in similar fashion and bagged a pair!"

His sequence of hundreds had begun at St Helen's in a match with gave Dai further material for an epic tale as the hard-hitting batsman, made one of the largest hits ever recorded in the Club's history. His feat came during a stand of 119 for the ninth wicket with Jack Mercer, with both batsmen taking great delight in putting the visiting bowling to the sword as the pair bravely counter-attacked after the loss of early wickets. Jack was also handicapped by a damaged calf muscle in his left leg, meaning that running quick singles was completely out of the question.

After seeing Dai secure a deserved century, Jack unleashed some furious blows as he looked to hit almost every ball he received for either four or six. But none were as massive as one blow unleashed by Dai against the bowling of James Langridge, which sent the ball sailing high over the rugby stand at the Mumbles Road End, and into a coal truck standing on the railway line At the time, nobody was quite sure where the ball had landed, and after a short delay, the game resumed with a replacement ball. But later that day it was discovered by a railwayman, albeit by the time the wagon was being unloaded at Craven Arms. The ball was duly returned to the Glamorgan officials and, for many years, Dai was able to dine out on the story of his feat of hitting a ball all the way from Swansea to Shropshire!

Another of Dai's hundreds came in the match with Nottinghamshire at the Arms Park in 1932 – the infamous game at Cardiff when Harold Larwood and Bill Voce, the visiting pair of England fast bowlers, announced prior to the game that they would be experimenting with fast leg-theory prior to touring Australia and hopefully quelling the prolific run scoring of Don Bradman. In front of a large crowd, Dai and Maurice enjoyed a double-century stand as they treated the Nottinghamshire bowling with utter contempt on a sluggish surface, as during three and a quarter hours' play, the pair added a record 220 for the third wicket, with Dai hooking and pulling a series of short balls to the boundary rope. Dai eventually departed for 106 but Maurice was unbeaten on 160 as his side ended a memorable day on 354-4.

In 1934 Dai only appeared in three Championship matches as during the away match with Kent during the second week of May, Dai suffered a severe haemorrhage from a stomach ulcer and was kept in hospital in Gravesend for three weeks. He returned to the side in 1935 and was awarded a Benefit Year. Dai nominated the game with Nottinghamshire at Swansea as his Benefit Match, but it rained for much of the three days. Dai incurred expenses of £586, and it could have been much higher had Swansea Corporation, who owned St Helen's, not agreed to charge Dai just one-sixth of the normal hiring rate. Fortunately, he had taken out an insurance premium against rain. From this he received £425, and together with collections at other home games, his end of year tally was £659. Many felt he deserved more, and a Glamorgan committee man offered to raise the question of another benefit for the popular Welshman. Dai though swiftly replied – "No thanks Sir, I can't afford it!"

262
ROGERS, Basil Leonard
Born – Bedford, 20 June 1896
Died – Claro, Ripon, 1 December 1975
Professional
RHB, RM
Ed – Bedford Modern School
1st XI: 1923
Club and Ground: 1922
Bedfordshire 1913-1924; Oxfordshire 1925-1935
Club: Swansea

Batting and Fielding Record:

	M	I	NO	RUNS	AV	100	50	CT	ST
F-c	2	4	1	46	15.33	-	-	-	-

Bowling Record:

	Balls	M	R	W	AV	5wI	10wM
F-c	60	0	33	1	33.00	-	-

Career-bests:

First-class –   16* v Northamptonshire at St Helen's, Swansea, 1923
              1/22 v Lancashire at Cardiff Arms Park, 1923

A member of a well-known family of cricketers in Oxfordshire, Basil Rogers played twice for Glamorgan during June 1922 whilst playing as a professional with the Swansea club. His contract however was not renewed at the end of the season and perhaps the all-rounder's greatest achievement whilst in South Wales was that he met Nellie Wilson, the step-daughter of a coal trader from Neath, with the pair getting married in Swansea during 1923.

Basil had become a cricket professional immediately after leaving Bedford Modern, whom he represented between 1911 and 1913. The latter year had also seen him make his Minor County debut for Bedfordshire in their away match with Norfolk at Lakenham, with the seventeen year-old batting at number eleven and opening the bowling with his medium-pace bowling.

In 1916 he and his brother enlisted with the Bedfordshire Regiment and served on the Western Front. He returned to the UK in 1919 and resumed his career in Minor County cricket with Bedfordshire. With Glamorgan having secured first-class status in 1921 he accepted an offer to play for the Swansea club and to qualify by residence for the Welsh county, living at Bryn Road, adjacent to the St Helen's ground.

He also represented South Wales in their friendly against North Wales at the Arms Park during August 1922, but he cut a rather anonymous role bowling four wicketless overs and not batting in the two-day game. Basil duly got an opportunity to play in Championship cricket on 1 June as he made his Glamorgan debut against Northamptonshire at St Helen's. It proved to be a rare victory for the Welsh county with the all-rounder being in the middle when the winning runs were struck, but the eleven-wicket haul of Frank Ryan contributed more to the Glamorgan victory than Basil's unbeaten 16.

He kept his place for the following match against Lancashire at the Arms Park and made 12 and 14 in a match where only two other batsmen – Jimmy Stone and Cyril Walters – got into double figures. Once again, his seam bowling had proved innocuous and whilst he had a respectable record as a professional with Swansea, few were surprised that he was not offered terms for 1924. Basil and his wife duly returned to Bedfordshire whom he represented again during 1924 before securing a post in Oxford and playing for the county until 1935. After retiring from playing he also acted as an umpire and stood in Minor County matches.

263
WALTERS, Cyril Frederick
Born – Bedlinog, 28 August 1905
Died – Neath, 23 December 1992
Amateur
RHB
Ed – Neath Grammar School
1st XI: 1923-1928
Club and Ground: 1923-1927
Cap: 1923
Worcestershire 1928-1935; England 1933-1934 (11 Tests); Tennyson's XI to Jamaica
1931/32; MCC to India and Ceylon 1933/34
Clubs: Neath, Welsh Cygnets

Batting and Fielding Record:

	M	I	NO	RUNS	AV	100	50	CT	ST
F-c	75	133	9	2146	17.31	2	5	23	-

Bowling Record:

	Balls	M	R	W	AV	5wI	10wM
F-c	32	0	37	0	-	-	-

Career-best:

First-class – 116 v Warwickshire at St Helen's, Swansea, 1926

Cyril Walters was one of the bright young hopes of Glamorgan cricket during the 1920s, and in 1934 he captained England against Australia at Trent Bridge. By this time however, Cyril was a Worcestershire player having joined the Midlands county in 1928 as their player-secretary. A batsman of elegance and charm, he was a renowned player of fast bowling and his career tally of 12,145 first-class runs would have been higher had his career not been prematurely ended by illness in 1935.

Educated at Neath Grammar School, Cyril had made his Glamorgan debut in 1923 as a 17 year-old against Lancashire, having a fine record in schoolboy cricket and having also impressed the Club's coaches when appearing for their Colts team. For a club who, in their early years of first-class cricket had relied so much on older players, the presence of a fresh-faced teenager in their ranks was a welcome addition.

It also took by surprise some of the over-zealous officials at away grounds, so much so that in the match at The Oval, the Surrey stewards could not quite believe that someone so young was actually playing, and they refused

Cyril Walters, as seen during 1929.

to allow Cyril into the pavilion. He politely pleaded with them that he was a member of the Glamorgan team, but was only let in after Johnnie Clay had been summoned downstairs from the dressing rooms above. "Yes, I know he's very young" Johnnie told the officious steward, "but he's in my team, and he's playing here today, so please let him in!"

Cyril appeared regularly for Glamorgan in 1924 and 1925, but only managed one half-century, against Worcestershire at New Road in 1924 and had a batting average hovering in the teens. However, there was no doubting his potential, nor his youthful flair in the field, which contrasted with the heavy girth and greying hair of several of his colleagues, so despite a lack of runs, his presence was greatly appreciated.

The elegant young batsman seemed to have turned the corner in 1926 as he struck a pair of centuries at Swansea, against Warwickshire and Leicestershire, besides recording assertive half-centuries against Somerset and Yorkshire, displaying a wide range of flowing stokes. Cyril had several business interests and in 1927 he only appeared in the opening six games, before making himself unavailable for the rest of the season as he concentrated on his career as an architect and surveyor.

Some within the Glamorgan hierarchy suggested that he turned professional, whilst others who were very mindful of the effect his departure might cause, were quite amenable to the youngster being offered a generous and long-term contract. But Cyril rejected these overtures and insisted he wanted to play as an amateur. He re-appeared briefly in 1928, before dropping the bombshell from a Glamorgan point of view that he – at the tender age of just 23 – had accepted terms with Worcestershire to act as their player-secretary.

He had to fulfil a two-year residential period and was therefore restricted to playing in non-Championship games. It was with some irony that on his debut in Worcestershire colours, the 1928 West Indians amassed 410-6 before the New Road batsmen replied with 439-2 with Cyril spending a long time in the pavilion waiting his turn to bat, but never getting a chance at the crease! He soon made up for lost time as in 1930 he scored over a thousand runs for his adopted county – a record he maintained throughout the rest of his time in the first-class game with a best of 2404 in all matches during 1933 and the following spring was chosen as one of *Wisden's* Five Cricketers of the Year. May 1930 had also seen Cyril captain Worcestershire against Glamorgan at New Road – the first time two Welshmen had been in charge of a County Championship match.

1931 also saw Cyril accepting the offer to lead the New Road side. It was also a season which saw him elevate himself to open the batting with 'Doc' Gibbons with the pair two years later sharing five century partnerships – a record for Worcestershire which went unchallenged until the advent of Glenn Turner in the 1970s and Graeme Hick during the 1980s. This was also the time when the loss of the gifted young amateur was most keenly felt by Glamorgan with Cyril making a career best score of 226 for Worcestershire against Kent at Gravesend during 1933, and in match when his side made 383 with 'Tich' Freeman claiming 8/110.

1933 was also the summer when Cyril played the first of his 11 Test caps, appearing in all three of the home Tests against the West Indies before touring India in 1933/34 with Douglas Jardine's England team and,

Cyril Walters opens the batting for England with Herbert Sutcliffe at Trent Bridge in the First Test of the 1934 Ashes series. Cyril was also the England captain for this match against Australia.

as an opening batsman, making his only hundred in Test cricket – and the first by a Welshman – with 102 at Madras and contributing much to an England victory. The

following summer, Cyril played in all five home Tests against Australia and became the first Welshman to lead England in a Test Match as he captained the side in the opening match of the Ashes series at Trent Bridge.

His elevation to the England captaincy, albeit for one game, came at a time when his former Glamorgan colleague Maurice Turnbull was also under consideration, having been invited to lead The Rest in the Test Trial at Lord's . Bob Wyatt was chosen to lead the England, whilst Percy Chapman who had taken the MCC party to the sub-continent over the winter was not selected in either side. On paper, it looked like a simple head-to-head between Bob and Maurice but, behind the scenes, the Test selectors had already taken a decision and, on the second morning of the Trial, Sir Stanley Jackson, the Chairman of the Selection Committee, told Bob he had been appointed to lead England in the First Test.

It was seen as something of a surprise decision as contemporary writers though were of the opinion that Bob was not a popular captain and was never at ease with authority. Whether or not this was the majority view, it proved to be a rather hasty decision as within half an hour of hearing of his elevation, Bob was back in the Lord's pavilion with a broken thumb, having been struck by Ken Farnes who extracted sharp lift from the damp wicket. In contrast, Maurice had a more productive Trial than Bob making an accomplished 46 in The Rest's first innings, and sharing a stand of 92 with Cyril.

For the Glamorgan supporters in the Lord's grandstand, it must have been a delight to see the two Welshmen in full flow in what was almost a throwback to the mid-1920s. The

Cyril Walters seen batting during 1931.

two gifted strokemakers took every opportunity to hit the ball, and keep the scoreboard ticking over with quick singles, with the talk in the Lord's Tavern being that a Welshman might be leading England the following week at Nottingham against Australia.

They were right, but it was Cyril who got the nod, and only after a prolonged saga over the fitness of Bob. Despite his cracked thumb, Bob was chosen to lead the side at Trent Bridge, with the Warwickshire man determined to play at all possible, realizing the enormity of the honour awaiting him and the prospect of securing the job for several matches. Medical opinion though was divided about his chances of playing, so Bob asked that a special aluminium shield be manufactured to protect his damaged digit. He also announced that as he was still experiencing pain, he would wait until the morning of the match before deciding whether or not he could play. It proved to be in vain as his injury forced him to withdraw and it was Cyril who went out to toss with Bill Woodfull, before leading out the rest of the England team.

Sadly, the following summer his career was ended – just as it had risen into the ascendancy – by ill health and domestic commitments as he was forced into retirement during 1935. He re-appeared in 1940 in Worcestershire's wartime friendly against Warwickshire but for the next half a century, he had only occasional contact with cricket as he focused on his family's business. As one observer wrote, "in what seemed a self-imposed exile, this private man with a puckish humour was lost almost permanently to cricket."

After his death in December 1992, a host of glowing tributes were paid to Cyril whose career in the county game was relatively short, spanning thirteen years, during two of which he played no Championship cricket. One of the most eloquent epitaphs came from the Rev. Mike Vockins, the former Secretary of Worcestershire who wrote "he was grace personified, elegant in appearance and manners, and in his cricket. With his handsome good looks, neatly groomed jet black hair (its change to grey in later life only added to his already distinguished appearance), allied to his attractive batting, Cyril was an outstanding amateur cricketer. He possessed that full, easy swing of the bat and immaculate timing which are the hallmarks of a class player."

Cyril Walters, seen during 1945.

With Glamorgan meeting the Australians at Neath in 1985, and again at 1989, Cyril was one of the guests of honour at the matches at The Gnoll, whilst in 1992 he was appointed as the inaugural President of the Worcestershire Old Players Association. As befitted his self-depracating wit, he accepted the position with genuine surprise and told his former players how he felt a mix of honour and amazement that anyone would remember him!

MOSS, Samuel Ernest

Born – Merthyr Tydfil, 25 November 1892
Died – Manchester, 1 December 1934
Professional
1st XI: 1923
Clubs: Birstall, Featherstone, Tong Park, Batley, Todmorden, Ramsbottom, Church
Son of Sam Moss

Batting and Fielding Record:

	M	I	NO	RUNS	AV	100	50	CT	ST
F-c	1	2	0	15	7.50	-	-	1	-

Bowling Record:

	Overs	M	R	W	AV	5wI	10wM
F-c	150	4	70	2	35.00	-	-

Career-bests:

First-class –   10 v Lancashire at Stanley Park, Blackpool, 1923
                   2/70 v Lancashire at Stanley Park, Blackpool, 1923

Ernie Moss was, like his father Sam, a journeyman professional in
Northern England and through his birthplace being in Merthyr Tydfil,
he was able to play at short notice for Glamorgan when they found
themselves a player short in 1923 for their match against Lancashire
at Blackpool. It proved to be his only first-class appearance but
the lively fast-medium bowler had an excellent record in both the
Yorkshire and Lancashire Leagues.

His first professional engagement had been in 1912 for
Birstall before joining Featherstone in 1913. After the Great
War was over, Ernie played for Tong Park and then Batley, and
it was whilst at the Yorkshire club in 1923 that he received the
message to help Glamorgan out at Blackpool. After Johnnie
Clay and Stan Hacker had opened the bowling, Ernie came on as

Ernie Moss.

second change and dismissed both openers. But the Red Rose batsmen went on to amass
441-8 before declaring and bowling Glamorgan out twice as they subsided to defeat
inside two days.

Had there been more money in the Club's coffers, Ernie might have played again, or
even moved to South Wales, but the lucrative offer of playing for Todmorden saw him
cross the Pennines for 1924, before moving to Ramsbottom in 1926 and then again to
Church for 1927. Whilst based in the Manchester suburbs he ran a cobblers shop but in
1934 he died of blood poisoning after badly cutting a finger at work.

His son Len was a noted footballer and played League matches for Burnley FC.

HILL, Mervyn Llewellyn

Born – Rookwood, Cardiff, 23 June 1902
Died – Westminster, 27 February 1948
Amateur
RHB, WK
Ed – Eton and Pembroke College, Cambridge
1st XI: 1923
Gentlemen of England 1920; Somerset 1921-1932; Cambridge University 1923-1924;
Devon 1935; APF Chapman's XI 1922; JH Doggart's XI 1922; WJV Tomlinson's XI
1923; GOB Allen's XI 1923; MCC to India, Burma and Sri Lanka, 1926/27
Clubs: Weston-super-Mare, Tiverton-Heathcote, Men O'Mendip, MCC and I Zingari

Batting and Fielding Record:

	M	I	NO	RUNS	AV	100	50	CT	ST
F-c	3	6	1	110	22.00	-	-	2	2

Career-bests:
First-class –   35 v Nottinghamshire at St Helen's, Swansea, 1923

Mervyn Hill was the eldest son of Vernon Hill and by keeping wicket for Somerset, Glamorgan and Cambridge University, he continued the good name of the family in cricketing circles. Mervyn also played a small but important part in cricket history when Surrey met Somerset at Taunton in 1926. With Surrey closing in on a ten-wicket victory and Jack Hobbs three short of his record-breaking century that would take him past WG Grace's record aggregate, Mervyn appeared to deliberately miss a stumping opportunity with Hobbs, having advanced down the wicket to a spinner, well out of his crease.

If this was indeed on purpose and not by accident, it was perfectly in keeping with Mervyn's jovial and good-natured personality, with the Old Etonian viewing cricket as a game to be enjoyed and played with a smile. Indeed, Mervyn was regarded as a "good tourist" visiting Denmark with the MCC in 1922, with the tour party also containing his father Vernon as well as two other Glamorgan players – Johnnie Clay and the fun-loving Freddie Mathias.

During the winter of 1926/27, Mervyn was also chosen by the MCC for their trail-blazing tour of India, Ceylon and Burma. Illness delayed his departure but he joined the party in mid-October for their third match, by which time they were in Karachi. So began the sequence of playing, junketing and travelling, all in searing heat, interspersed by the occasional day's shooting, fishing and sight-seeing until late February.

Mervyn Hill.

As with all MCC tours, there were plenty of humorous incidents as Arthur Gilligan and his intrepid party travelled, often by train for a day and through the night. Indeed, whilst they were making their way across the Sind Desert their express suddenly came to a halt. Lights went on and carriage windows were opened as the passengers looked out to see what had caused the sudden stop. It later transpired that George Brown in his attempts to clamber down from his bunk to answer a call of nature had clutched at whatever came to hand, only to lever himself down to the floor of his carriage by pulling on the communication cord, mistakenly thinking it was some kind of support!

Playing on matting wickets was also quite a novel and alien experience for Mervyn and others. As he wrote in a letter home "this was my first experience of matting and I shall never forget it. The ball never came quite at the height one was expecting it. It is true their (batting) style is not beautiful, for they have had no coaching and nearly all their runs were scored behind the wicket, just wide of second slip. They never looked like giving us a slip catch, as they would always cut the ball down."

Born in 1902 at his grandfather's home at Rookwood in Llandaff, Mervyn was educated at Eton where he won a place as wicket-keeper in the 1st XI in 1920 and 1921. In the former summer he made his first-class debut at Lord's by keeping wicket for the Gentlemen of England against the Combined Services. During 1921 he also

Mervyn Hill standing on the extreme right in a photograph which also includes his Glamorgan colleagues Johnnie Clay (standing second right) and Freddie Mathias (seated in the middle).

kept wicket for the Public Schools against The Army and made his Somerset debut against Sussex at Weston-super-Mare, with his father's cheery party being supplemented by other family members who had travelled from the Cardiff area across the Severn by Campbell's Steamer from Pier Head to support the nineteen year-old in his endeavors at the famous Festival and pretty tree-lined ground at Clarence Park.

June 1922 saw Mervyn play again for Somerset, this time amidst the bricks and mortar of the Aylestone Road ground in Leicester, before going up to Cambridge where he kept at Fenner's in the university's match with Lancashire. With Jimmy Stone recovering from injury and both Norman Riches and Tal Whittington in the veteran stage behind the stumps, the Glamorgan selectors called up the undergraduate for their matches against Gloucestershire at the Victoria Ground in Cheltenham, with Nottinghamshire at Swansea and, against Somerset at Taunton. Given his family's close connections with the West Country it was quite fitting that Mervyn's final appearance for the Welsh county should be at Taunton.

With more than a touch of irony, the wicket-keeper that day in early July for Somerset was none other than Jimmy Jones – a man who sounded in name more Welsh than his public school educated counterpart and a man who later switched to the Welsh county during the late 1920s. Mervyn regularly kept wicket for Somerset until 1926 before making a single appearance in 1927, and again in 1928, prior to bowing out of first-class cricket by playing during August 1932 against the Indians at Weston-super-Mare, and just a few miles away from his father's home and dairy farm at Woodspring Priory.

Besides the tale concerning Jack Hobbs and the merry-making on MCC tours, there are several other humorous stories relating to Mervyn's career. One relates to the time in 1925 in the match against Derbyshire when he hobbled out to the middle using his bat and a pair of walking sticks as aids after sustaining a leg injury. Another concerns the way Mervyn and his fellow amateurs would devour the racing newspapers before play, having been given tips by their sporting friends, with Vic Robson, the young son of spinner Ernie, often being sent on errands to the nearest bookmakers and, if Somerset were bowling, passing hand-written messages for the twelfth man to take onto the field so that Mervyn and his colleagues should know the outcome of their punts.

The most famous though relates to another game in 1925 at The Oval when Mervyn was chosen to appear for the Gentlemen against the Players. As someone who always stood up to the seam bowlers at Taunton and elsewhere, Gubby Allen was quite taken aback when Mervyn did the same against the Players with the England man believing that the Somerset keeper was taking the mickey about how fast he could bowl. Despite plenty of giggles and smirks on his colleagues faces, Mervyn unflinchingly stood up for the first couple of overs before a quiet word in his ear from captain Percy Fender saw him stand back. Any ill-feeling which may have existed between the pair soon dissipated as, coming in at number eleven, Mervyn stoutly held his end and allowed Gubby to record what was his maiden first-class hundred.

In 1933 Mervyn moved to Devon having secured a position as Land Agent for Sir John Heathcote-Amory who lived at Knightshayes Court in Tiverton. Sir John had become the Third Baronet on the death of his father in 1931, and the fellow Old Etonian was a keen cricketer himself having played for Oxford University and Devon, besides appearing for the West of England against the 1927 New Zealanders and for the Minor Counties against the 1928 Indians.

Mervyn succeeded Sir John as Devon captain in 1935 before marrying Patricia Barton, with whom he fathered three children. In 1945 the Hill's moved to live at Collipriest Farm to the south of Tiverton, with Mervyn also acting as Secretary of the Devon Landowners Association. However, during February 1948, Mervyn died unexpectantly whilst in a solicitor's office in Westminster. The cause of his sudden death at the age of 45 had been a congenital heart condition which he had endured since birth, but something that had not affected his sporting activities and gleefully enjoying all that life could offer.

266
WARNER, Claude Charles

Born – Cardiff, 31 March 1882
Died – Llanelli, 29 December 1965
RHB, OB
1st XI: 1923
Club: Llanelli

Batting and Fielding Record:

	M	I	NO	RUNS	AV	100	50	CT	ST
F-c	1	2	1	14	14.00	-	-	-	-

Bowling Record:

	Balls	M	R	W	AV	5wI	10wM
F-c	80	2	47	0	-	-	-

Career-bests:
First-class –   7* v Nottinghamshire at St Helen's, Swansea, 1923

Claude Warner was called up by Glamorgan for the visit to Swansea of Nottinghamshire during 1923 when other, more talented batsmen were unavailable.

Born in Cardiff and raised in Llanelli, he had first played for the cricket club based at Stradey Park during the early 1900s and, as an adult with long fingers, he developed a knack of bowling off-spin and leg-cutters without a noticeable change of grip. This ability, together with his decent record as a batsmen in club cricket for Llanelli, led to his selection for Carmarthenshire in 1920. In their match with Glamorgan at Stradey Park, Claude claimed 6/51 with his mix of off-breaks and cutters besides posting an accomplished 25 batting at number three for the West Walian side.

Claude Warner.

This impressive performance, plus a recommendation from Dai Davies, led to his call-up by Glamorgan in 1923 for the match at St Helen's against Nottinghamshire. He made 7 in each innings and failed to claim a wicket with his cutters in what proved to be his only opportunity at first-class level and a game which saw the hard-nosed professionals secure a comfortable victory over amateur enthusiasm.

Like many of his generation, Claude's best years as a cricketer were lost to the Great War with Claude serving with the Royal Flying Corps in the Middle East. He lived in Stradey Park Avenue, adjacent to the famous cricket and rugby ground, and ran a stockbroker's business with fellow Llanelli sportsman Percy Rees. He had started work when only fifteen and worked for 67 years in stocks and shares. He was also a devout member of the congregation at All Saint's Church where he sang in the choir for many years, besides being a leading member of Llanelli Operatic Society.

267
MEGGITT, Frank Claxton

Born – Barry, 17 February 1901
Died – Radyr, 9 October 1945
Amateur
RHB, RM
Ed – Mill Hill School and Emmanuel College, Cambridge
1st XI: 1923
Club: Barry

Batting and Fielding Record:

	M	I	NO	RUNS	AV	100	50	CT	ST
F-c	1	2	0	4	2.00	-	-	-	-

Career-best:
First-class –4 v Nottinghamshire at St Helen's, Swansea, 1923

Frank Meggitt, who played once for Glamorgan during 1923 in their match at Swansea against Nottinghamshire, was better known in sporting circles as a Welsh hockey international winning three caps during the mid-1920s.

He was the son of John Claxton Meggitt, a timber importer, Liberal councilor and former mayor of Barry who lived at Seacroft, a substantial property in Park Road. Frank was educated at Mill Hill and Emmanuel College, Cambridge where he also won a Hockey Blue in 1925. He had also been a very talented schoolboy cricketer, playing in the Mill Hill XI between 1917 and 1919, and this coupled with a decent record for Barry and in College cricket at Cambridge, led to his call-up for the Glamorgan side when they found themselves without Norman Riches and Tal Whittington for the visit of Nottinghamshire to Swansea in 1923. Frank made 0 and 4 as Nottinghamshire won by an innings and 108 runs, and was not called up again.

A photograph of Frank Meggitt taken during a club match at St Fagans CC.

In later life, Frank became a useful golfer, captaining the Radyr club, besides featuring in the Glamorgan Amateur Championships.

268
STEWART, Theophile Lecompte

Born – Brisbane, 9 May 1891
Died – Morriston, 14 December 1952
Amateur
RHB, OB
1st XI: 1923
Club: Llanelli

Batting and Fielding Record:

	M	I	NO	RUNS	AV	100	50	CT	ST
F-c	1	2	0	4	2.00	-	-	-	-

Career-best:
First-class –   4 v Derbyshire at Queen's Park, Chesterfield, 1923

Theo Stewart.

Theo Stewart can claim to have the most multinational background of any person to have played for the Welsh county, having been born in Queensland, Australia to an Irish-born civil engineer and his French wife.

His father, John Stewart and mother, Marie Francoise Lecompte, continued their travels during the late 1890s, spending time in India and also County Down in Northern Ireland, before settling in Llanelli around 1900. Theo showed promise as a schoolboy whilst at a local school and in the 1910s he made his debut for Llanelli 1st XI. 1914 also saw him play for the Gentlemen of Carmarthenshire against their counterparts from Glamorgan in a match in July at Stradey Park. Theo did not bat in either innings, with his off-spin yielding 39 runs in four expensive overs, but the Carmarthenshire amateurs won the game by five runs.

After the War, Theo became Llanelli's captain and Secretary and later the Treasurer as well. Theo had a reputation as a very precise and obdurate batsmen and this, rather than any prolific run of scores, led to his call-up for Glamorgan's match during 1923 against Derbyshire at Chesterfield. However, he made 4 and 0 and did not get a chance to display his talents as a spin bowler and purveyor of off-cutters.

Indeed, his abilities as a cricketer had been immortalised in the Llanelli area by a local bard who composed the following poem:

"TL Stewart – in short TL
Captains Llanelly very well
When Neath's All Blacks came down 'White'

He put them in a sorry plight.
They all went down for 30 – twice
TL's flights and his low cuts can tease mice."

An auctioneer by profession, Theo was married in 1917 and was an important figure behind the scenes during the 1930s when Glamorgan took County Championship cricket to Llanelli. He died in Morriston Hospital after a short illness in 1952 and was buried in Felinfoel.

269
SPENCER, Helm

Born – Padiham, 31 November 1891
Died – Lane Head, Burnley, 7 December 1974
Professional
RHB, RFM
1st XI: 1923-1925
Club and Ground: 1924-1925
Other: 1923-1924
Cap: 1924
Lancashire 1914
Clubs: Padiham, Lowerhouse, Saltaire, Eccleshill, Llanelli, Bacup, Colne, Belvedere

Batting and Fielding Record:

	M	I	NO	RUNS	AV	100	50	CT	ST
F-c	39	68	2	743	11.25	-	1	29	-

Bowling Record:

	Balls	M	R	W	AV	5wI	10wM
F-c	5067	170	2270	101	22.47	4	-

Career-bests:
First-class –   56 v Nottinghamshire at Cardiff Arms Park, 1924
                7/33 v Northamptonshire at St Helen's, Swansea, 1925

Helm Spencer enjoyed a profitable time in League cricket in Lancashire either side of a short county career with Glamorgan during the 1920s. Had the Welsh county possessed deeper financial reserves, Helm might have remained longer in South Wales.

The son of a cotton weaver, Helm impressed with bat and ball for Padiham and Lowerhouse in the Lancashire Leagues, and played twice, primarily as a fast bowler for his native Lancashire during 1914. He appeared against Gloucestershire at Old Trafford and Kent at Canterbury, but despite many warm recommendations when county cricket resumed in 1919, the ambitious professional failed to agree terms with the Red Rose county and played instead with Saltaire in the Bradford League. His wicket-taking prowess duly alerted a number of scouts with the officials of Llanelli winning his signature, at a handsome fee for 1921.

Glamorgan's administrators were pleased to see his acquisition by the Stradey Park officials for 1922 with one report outlining how "in the bowling attack, his lightening deliveries played havoc and the stumps were lifted right out of the ground. He is the best all-round professional that has served the club for many years. Let us hope that his smile, which never fades, has brought the Club a change of luck."

But there was a stumbling block towards his availability for Glamorgan as he lived five miles inside the Carmarthenshire border. He duly moved east to Lougher and duly set his sights on a new career with Glamorgan. In the meantime, he played for Wales against Scotland at Perth in 1923, scoring 33 and taking a trio of wickets, before in September making his Championship debut for his adopted county against Hampshire at the Arms Park.

A photograph of Helm Spencer dated 1925.

Helm duly enjoyed a decent first summer in Glamorgan's ranks, claiming 64 wickets at 18 runs apiece with his finest hour coming against his native county at Swansea, and a match where a Lancashire victory, seemed a formality. After Glamorgan were dismissed for 153, Helm claimed 6/44 in 21 hostile overs. with Frank Ryan keeping things tight at the other end. Lancashire were left with a seemingly straightforward target of 146 and began well, reaching 84-3 before Frank Ryan entered the attack. He responded with one of the finest ever spells of his career, taking 7/23 and proved to be virtually unplayable, as Lancashire fell 39 runs short of their target, with Helm helping to carry Frank shoulder-high off the field to the delight of the Swansea crowd.

1925 saw the tall bowler claim just 37 wickets at 29 runs apiece for Glamorgan and, with Jack Mercer having secured a regular first team berth, Helm opted to accept an offer from Colne to return to the Lancashire Leagues. He remained up north for the rest of his career playing as a professional until 1930 for Colne, and then as an amateur from 1931 for Lowerhouse.

In 1937 he was involved in a series of incidents in Lowerhouse's match with Burnley Initially, he walked away from the stumps as the bowler released the ball, asking for the sight-screens to be moved. Despite the stumps having been hit he was recalled after a discussion with the Burnley captain only for a few overs later another heated argument to ensue as the crowd, upset by his earlier actions, booed and barracked the former Glamorgan professional.

Irritated by the noise, Helm pulled away again as Manny Martindale was in his delivery stride. The ball cannoned into the stumps, but Helm's response was to sit down on the ground for over ten minutes as he had a protracted exchange of views with the fielding captain and others about what he perceived to be unsporting behavior from the Burnley contingent. Eventually, he got up and walked off believing that he had made his point, but he was subsequently reprimanded by the club and League officials, and left to join the Belvedere club for the following season.

Helm returned to the Lowerhouse club during the 1960s and acted as their Treasurer, besides serving on their committee. He also undertook a spell of coaching and advised Roy Marshall when the West Indian was a young League professional.

1924

Some of the optimism from the committee room had clearly rubbed off on Glamorgan's players during 1924 as they fared a little bit better, winning five of their 22 Championship matches. They also rose up to 13th place after Johnnie Clay had succeeded Tal Whittington as the county's captain.

The omens though did not look great as the summer of 1924 began with innings defeats against Surrey and Yorkshire before a week or so later another reversal, this time by 128 runs during an extraordinary match with Lancashire at Liverpool. The game had started very well for Glamorgan as they dismissed the Red Rose county before lunch for just 49. Helm Spencer caused the havoc in the home team's ranks with the bespectacled seamer claiming 5/9 against his former employers. But just as the congratulatory telegrams started to arrive at the Aigburth ground, Helm and his colleagues were going out to field for a second time after Lancashire's bowlers took just 15.3 overs to bowl out Glamorgan for 22 – a total which is still their lowest-ever in first-class cricket.

The following match at Derby saw an end to the losing sequence as Glamorgan completed a seven-wicket victory. This was followed by an innings win over Leicestershire at Swansea, before Johnnie Clay's team beat Somerset at Taunton prior to doing the double over the Peakites by defeating Derbyshire at Swansea. The fifth win of the summer and easily the most dramatic in Glamorgan's short history of Championship cricket then followed as a full-strength Lancashire side travelled to St Helen's. With several regulars out of form, the selectors gave youth its head as Maurice Turnbull, the seventeen year-old batsman from Downside School, made his county debut. The fresh-faced teenager, from a well-known ship-owning family in Cardiff, duly played his part in a handsome victory over one of the strongest teams in the Championship, with the teenager's steady and nerveless batting in both innings belying his inexperience at first-class level.

Maurice Turnbull, who made a dramatic Glamorgan debut during 1924, seen wearing his Downside cap.

DAVIES, David _Emrys_

Born – Sandy, Carmarthenshire, 27 June, 1904
Died – Llanelli, 10 November, 1975
Professional
1st XI: 1924-1954
2nd XI: 1935
Colts: 1923
Club and Ground: 1923-1954
Cap: 1925
Benefit 1938; Testimonial 1947
Wales 1926-1929; British Empire XI v Combined Universities 1944; Northern
Command 1944; Northamptonshire 1944; Leicestershire 1944-1945; Combined
Services 1946; The Rest 1949;
South of England 1949-1950
Club: Llanelli

Batting and Fielding Record:

	M	I	NO	RUNS	AV	100	50	CT	ST
F-c	612	1016	79	26102	27.85	31	148	211	-
Wartime	1	2	0	47	23.50	-	-	-	-

Bowling Record:

	Balls	M	R	W	AV	5wI	10wM
F-c	62621	2484	26030	885	29.41	32	2
Wartime	?	?	?	2	-	-	-

Career-bests:
First-class – 287* v Gloucestershire at Rodney Parade, Newport, 1939
6/24 v Leicestershire at Rodney Parade, Newport, 1935

Some nicknames are mischievous or based on leg-pulling, but for Emrys Davies, a man with 26,102 runs and 885 wickets to his name during his first-class career with Glamorgan, the

"The Rock" – Emrys Davies.

sobriquet of 'The Rock' could not be more fitting. Indeed, for three decades, the doughty left-hander opened the batting for the Welsh county against the finest new ball bowlers in England and, together with Arnold Dyson between 1932 and 1948, formed one of the most prolific opening partnerships in the Club's entire history.

In 1935 Emrys became the Club's first-ever player to perform the Double of a thousand runs and a hundred wickets during a first-class season, besides scoring a hundred and taking a hat-trick in the game against Leicestershire in 1937. However, out of all of his record-breaking feats, Emrys' finest achievement was scoring an unbeaten 287 against Gloucestershire at Newport in

1939 – the highest-ever score in the Club's history and a record which stood for 61 years.

But such a glittering array of achievements seemed unlikely at first as he clung on to a place on the professional staff, more through potential rather than performance. He made his Championship debut in a rain-ravaged contest in June 1924 against Gloucestershire at the Arms Park. Batting at number ten Emrys made 5 and later took a solitary wicket with his left-arm spin as play eventually got underway on the final day.

It was not until eight years later that he made the first of his 31 centuries, whilst his inaugural ten-wicket haul did not come until 1936. Emrys' early years with Glamorgan were quite modest ones, with Frank Ryan acting as the front-line left-arm spinner whilst the former steel-worker from Llanelli occupied a berth in the lower middle-order with his bowling role being to deliver chinamen, from over the wicket and to a full length with a predominantly legside field.

By the start of the 1929 season, Emrys had made 71 first-class appearances, but only had two fifties to his name and no five-wicket hauls. Not surprisingly, there were calls for his contract to be terminated, but both Johnnie Clay and Maurice Turnbull believed that Emrys' batting technique was sound enough to make the grade. He also imparted plenty of spin on the ball and had developed his skills under the wing of Frank.

The consensus was all that was needed was greater experience and confidence and Emrys duly got more opportunities in the early 1930s following the release of both Frank and veteran batsman Eddie Bates, chiefly on cost-saving grounds. But the departure of the two former English professionals was also part of a scheme devised by Maurice and Johnnie to promote the Welsh identity of the Club. Emrys was one of several homegrown players to be given greater opportunities, with the left-hander moving up the order to open the batting with Arnold Dyson.

As Maurice himself later wrote "I can think of few committees who would have persevered with Emrys for eight years as ours did, and Emrys, realizing this fact, has repaid his debt by exemplary service at all times. Refusing to run before he could walk, he has learnt the art of batsmanship

Emrys Davies batting in the Arms Park nets during 1924.

bit by bit. His style may not be orthodox in every respect, but he is quick on his feet and watches the ball as closely as the great ones. Indeed, he rivals the very best on difficult wickets."

1932 proved to be the turning point in his career, with Emrys scoring what contemporaries regarded as a "brilliant knock" of 175 in the fourth innings of the game against Essex at the Arms Park, eight years to the day, and on the same ground, as his first appearance for the Daffodil county. Even his most ardent supporters in the Glamorgan hierarchy could not have forecast the dramatic headway the all-rounder made in subsequent years. The advice imparted by Arnold boosted Emrys' confidence, whilst the release of Frank meant he was now Johnnie's spin partner on turning wickets, and could bowl in a much more classical style than before.

Knowing that Maurice also had a great belief in him, was another important factor, allowing Emrys not to unduly fret or worry if things went wrong. This anxiety had affected some of his play in earlier years but, with greater self-belief, most things went right rather than wrong for the Carmarthenshire-born professional. He added further shots to his repertoire, especially the late cut to third man, whilst extended spells as a left-arm spinner helped Emrys to add flight, dip and plenty of cunning to his bowling. 1932 was the last season when Emrys failed to claim a five-wicket haul, and he ended the summer with a tally of 70 wickets.

A second hundred followed in 1932 against Leicestershire on a capricious wicket at Cowbridge, followed by 100* against Middlesex at the Arms Park in 1934 and three more in 1935 – against Gloucestershire, Warwickshire and Somerset. Indeed, 1935

Emrys Davies and Arnold Dyson, Glamorgan's formidable opening pair, seen at Swansea in 1937.

was a landmark summer for Emrys as he completed the Double of 1000 runs and 100 wickets – the first Glamorgan player to achieve this feat. Emrys reached the landmark at Worcester on the final afternoon of the season, albeit in rather contrived circumstances. Rain had fallen overnight, and with Emrys on 99 wickets, he was champing at the bit to get into action. Worcestershire's Frank Warne also needed 42 runs to reach a thousand for the first time in his career so after lunch Maurice and Bernard Quaife, the Worcestershire captain, told the umpires that they wanted to stay at the ground rather than head home, even though there was no chance of a positive outcome in the contest.

The umpires duly waited on during the afternoon, and eventually made a start at 5.20 pm, with the two captains doing what they could to see the two players to their landmarks. Glamorgan declared their second innings at 4-2, leaving Worcestershire with around half an hour or so to bat. Warne was promoted up the order from his usual berth at number seven, and with some generous bowling and sympathetic fielding, he duly reached his personal landmark. A couple of balls later, it was Glamorgan's turn to celebrate as Emrys bowled Peter Jackson, who attempted a rather ungainly slog. The umpires then called time and everyone trooped off knowing that the two players had reached their milestones.

Four more centuries followed for Emrys in 1936, before three more in 1937 plus a record stand of 237 with Arnold against Leicestershire during which the left-hander making 139 at Aylestone Road, followed by a hat-trick in the home team's second innings as they subsided to an innings defeat. Emrys removed George Geary thanks to a smart catch by Cyril Smart before next ball Herrick Bowley spooned a ball to Dai Davies. A subtle change of pace of flight saw Haydon Smith depart l.b.w. as Emrys completed his hat-trick and a return of 3/31 from 22 miserly overs. When questioned by journalists after completing this relatively unusual feat of a century and a hat-trick in a match, Emrys was typically modest and self-effacing – "I had a bit of luck with bat and ball, and today I'm glad that my colleagues took some good catches. The most important thing though was that Glamorgan won the game."

In all, Emrys amassed 1765 runs during 1937, and in his own modest way, he was quite pleased by his efforts. By his own admission, he took more delight by events of 1939 – another vintage summer for the Glamorgan opener who made 100 against Lancashire at Old Trafford, 134 in the game with Nottinghamshire at Swansea, and 102 on another damp surface at Pontypridd against Sussex. However, the summer also saw his record-breaking 287 against Gloucestershire at Rodney Parade as he occupied the crease for seven and a half hours and in the closing overs went past the Club's previous best of 280, made by Dick Duckfield against Surrey at The Oval in 1933.

Had the attitude of Gloucestershire captain Wally Hammond been less churlish, Emrys might have recorded a triple hundred. Wally had already completed an unbeaten 302 in Gloucestershire's first innings and, with a sizeable cash prize for the batsman who made the highest score of the summer, it was not just the home supporters and the Glamorgan team, who were keeping a close eye on the Rodney Parade scoreboard during the closing minutes.

But to the disgust of the home side, Wally deliberately slowed down proceedings and posted a series of fielders near the boundary ropes as the weary Welshman tried in vain to strike some boundaries. At the time, Wally was the England captain, whilst Maurice had become a Test Selector, and there were many that late afternoon at Rodney Parade who felt that the actions of the Gloucestershire man were unbecoming of someone in such an elevated position in English cricket.

Whilst there was plenty of back-slapping for Emrys from his colleagues and the home supporters at the end of the game, only the briefest of handshakes took place between the two teams. There was also a rather frosty and brief exchange of words between England captain and Test Selector with their terse conversation not being lost on the Media, several of whom passed comment on it in their match reports.

These events, in the closing overs at Newport, duly became the talk of the county circuit for several days. A number of the Gloucestershire side had also been embarrassed by their captain's time-wasting antics and deliberately negative field-placings to deprive Emrys of reaching 300. Wally Hammond was certainly not a universally popular figure and when Sir Pelham Warner asked one of his Gloucestershire colleagues his thoughts about his captain , Basil Allen replied "If you want my honest opinion, Plum, I think he's an absolute shit." After what happened at Rodney Parade, all of the Glamorgan side and the majority of the spectators would have wholeheartedly agreed.

But Emrys' efforts with bat and ball were not lost on the MCC selectors who, during 1939, sounded him out about his availability for the winter tour to India. But almost as soon as Emrys had started to think about the prospect of playing for England, War was declared and the tour was cancelled. At the end of the summer he joined the Army and was attached to the Northern Command Battalion. Emrys subsequently appeared for the British Empire XI against the Combined Universities in 1944, as well as guesting for a Northamptonshire XI and scoring 101 besides taking 3/14 against his old adversaries from Leicestershire, for whom he also appeared during 1944 and 1945 whilst based in the East Midlands.

During the spring of 1946, Emrys was still in the East Midlands, but thanks to the persuasive efforts of Johnnie Clay, who served as a Colonel in the Territorial Army, Private Davies was transfered to Cardiff Barracks and, despite not being demobilised until late July, he managed to play in all of Glamorgan's Championship matches that summer by doing guard duty all night, thereby allowing him to play during the day in the home fixtures besides 'obtaining' privilege leave which conveniently coincided with the away games!

Emrys responded with hundreds against Hampshire at Swansea, as well as against Warwickshire at Edgbaston, before the so-called 'Peter Pan' of county cricket made

An image of Emrys Davies batting in a County Championship match during 1954.

five centuries during 1947, with three figure scores against Essex at the Arms Park, Sussex at Hove, Hampshire at Southampton, Worcestershire at New Road, and Nottinghamshire at Trent Bridge, with his partner Arnold Dyson reveling in a renaissance-like summer as the pair took their tally of opening stands to the thirty-mark – an unprecedented level not only for Glamorgan Cricket but the wider county game as well.

The Championship-winning summer of 1948 proved to be a joyous one for Emrys as the fruits of his hard labour during the difficult years of the 1920s bore fruit. His consistency of run-scoring that summer as Glamorgan's senior professional saw him amass 1,708 with 105 against Lancashire at Old Trafford, plus 215 in the match with Essex at Brentwood as he and fellow-Welsh-speaker Willie Jones added a record 313 for the third with the pair confounding the fielders by their conversation in their native tongue.

Out of all of Emrys' achievements, he later admitted that this stand during the Championship winning summer with his good friend Willie Jones was amongst his greatest days as a player. As he later reflected, "the crowd at Brentwood that day grew silent as Willie and I added more and more runs. The cheers from our balcony, as well as from a few loyal Glamorgan supporters, gave us great support, and by the time I had reached 200 I wondered quite how far I could go! Dai Davies was also one of the umpires that day, and I can remember him saying to me in Welsh, keep going, keep going, as Willie kept finding the boundary. The message from Wilf was to bat out the day, but after five hours at the crease I was caught by Ken Preston off the spin of Bill Dines for 215 and I returned, quite weary, to the changing rooms at Brentwood, knowing that I had done my bit to lay the foundation of what proved to be a match winning total."

Although no other centuries followed during 1948, Emrys' consistency at the top of the order remained an important weapon in Wilf Wooller's armoury, with Emrys being the Club's leading run-scorer that daffodil golden summer with 1636 runs to his name in Championship cricket. An injury to the fingers on his left hand meant that Emrys did not take any wickets that summer and barely bowled at all, but with Stan Trick, Johnnie Clay, Willie Jones and Len Muncer all in good form, the loss of Emrys' spin was not a major handicap. He was able instead to focus on his batting and still prolific partnership with Arnold, as the experienced duo watchfully blunted the new ball attack of several opposing sides who having viewed the grey hairs in Glamorgan's top-order, believed they could easily make early inroads. How wrong they were, as Emrys lived up to his monicker of 'The Rock' and thwarted their spritely but largely ineffective efforts.

His innings at Bournemouth in 1948, during Glamorgan's decisive Championship match against Hampshire, may not have seen Emrys convert a half-century into yet another hundred, but his 74 in even time, after rain interference on the opening day, helped to kick-start the Glamorgan innings on the second day as the Welsh county gained the upper hand and allowed others including Willie and later Len to play with freedom as Wilf's team reached what proved to be both a match-winning and Championship-winning total.

There were tears in Emrys' eyes, as well as in his good friend and namesake Dai's who was umpiring the game at Bournemouth, as together with the rest of Wilf's side, they assembled on the balcony of the Dean Park pavilion to toast one of the greatest-ever days in the Club's history and the first-ever Championship title coming to Wales. "Am I dreaming?" he said to colleagues as they toasted their success with champagne, before adding. "I won't believe this is really happening until I read it in the newspapers back home!"

Emrys Davies, at mid-off valiantly stops a ball driven to him by Bob Herman during Glamorgan's decisive Championship match at Bournemouth in 1948.

He whimsically repeated this phrase several times as the happy Glamorgan party made their way by train from Bournemouth back to Cardiff General and as a result, when their express arrived at Newport, George Lavis and Jim Pleass saw a group of well-wishers who were standing on the platform with a couple of crates of beer for the team to enjoy on the final leg of their epic journey, plus copies of the last edition of the local newspaper which was carrying banner headlines about the Welsh county's success. George and Jim duly brought the crates and papers onto the train, so it was with a bottle of beer in one hand and the final edition of the *South Wales Argus* in the other, that Emrys – with tears running down his cheeks once again – finally believed that Glamorgan were the County Champions of 1948.

A round of parties and special functions then followed, plus a series of interviews with a host of journalists, many of whom from Fleet Street had doubted the Welsh county's resolve during the second half of the season, believing that their bubble would burst before the closing weeks and allowing, in their eyes, the more established counties to hold sway. But Emrys gave no hint of ill-feeling towards these writers for what they had put into print when he spoke to them. Instead, like the other stalwarts in the squad, Emrys was at pains to give credit to Maurice for what he had done collectively as well as individually for Emrys. With due deference to the distinctions between amateurs and professionals, Emrys said to one reporter "Mr Wooller has been our outstanding leader during 1948 but, for many of us in the team, we also owe a massive debt of gratitude to Mr Turnbull for what he did during the 1930s. I only wish he had been there at Bournemouth when we lifted the title."

The match against Hampshire was the penultimate time that Emrys opened the batting with Arnold, with the pair coming within five runs of their 33rd opening stand of a hundred or more in Championship cricket. Hampshire had been the opposition when the pair posted their last three-figure stand for the first wicket as they added 201 at the Northlands Road ground in Southampton during the last week of July 1947 and laid the platform for a comprehensive ten-wicket victory, with Emrys making 119 and Arnold 96.

After Arnold's retirement at the end of 1948, Phil Clift became Emrys' regular opening partner. The pair had opened for the first half of the 1948 and when Hampshire visited the Arms Park for the opening Championship match of 1949, it proved to be a case of business as usual as the pair added 113 for the first wicket. Emrys went on to add further centuries against Warwickshire at Swansea and Nottinghamshire at Trent Bridge.

With illness preventing Phil Clift from playing in 1950, Emrys had a series of new opening partners, starting with Stan Montgomery, and then Wilf himself, with the pair adding 116 for the first wicket against Kent at Gillingham as the Welsh county won by six wickets. An injury to 'The Skipper' at the start of June saw Gilbert Parkhouse move up from the number three berth to join Emrys, who also led Glamorgan in a series of games during mid-summer. The return to health and fitness of Clift the following summer saw a resumption of the Davies-Clift pairing at the top of the Glamorgan order and the Usk-born batsman was Emrys' partner as he scored his final hundreds in Championship cricket during 1951 against Derbyshire at the Arms Park, as well as Nottinghamshire at Trent Bridge.

Fred Trueman bowls for England in a Test Match watched by umpire Emrys Davies.

Phil remained Emrys's opening partner until August 1952 – a summer when the 48 year-old opener was one of the most consistent batsman in county cricket, scoring 13 half-centuries and amassing 1678 runs without a hundred (a record aggregate for a Glamorgan batsman not reaching three figures). Gilbert then moved up from the number three slot to become Emrys's regular partner for the rest of his career, with Emrys having another decent summer in 1953 with 1174 runs, eleven half-centuries and a top-score of 77.

1954 however proved to be a less productive summer for Emrys and a week or so after celebrating his 50th birthday he travelled to Peterborough with the Glamorgan squad for what proved to be his final-ever innings. At the time he had just 180 runs to his name in eight matches, and a top score of just 27. With the Glamorgan spinners having enjoyed a purple patch of form during the previous month, it came as no surprise that the surface for the away match with Northamptonshire had a green hue. The home side also boasted Frank Tyson who was swiftly building up a reputation as one of the most hostile bowlers on the county circuit. He duly lived up to his nickname of 'The Typhoon' by bowling Emrys with a scorching delivery which beat the veteran for sheer pace and venom.

The veteran duly made his way back to the pavilion without having made a run and sat down amidst stony silence in the professionals changing room. With his colleagues looking on, Emrys took off his gloves and cap, unbuckled his pads and then with tears welling up in his eyes, turned to Wilf – who had popped in from the amateurs room to speak to the batsman about his dismissal – and said the fateful words "Skipper, I think I'm finished, I didn't even see that ball!" He never batted again in first-class cricket for Glamorgan with Wilf opening the batting in his place in the second innings.

Later that summer, Emrys applied to the MCC to join the first-class umpires list and in early May 1955 he stood in his first game as Warwickshire met Somerset at Edgbaston. He soon made a favourable impression and in June 1956 he stood in the Second Test of the Ashes series at Lord's. Earlier in the summer, he had stood with Dai Davies for the first ever time, as the Australians opened their tour at Worcester.

In July 1956 he officiated in the Fourth Test of the Ashes series – the famous match at Old Trafford when Jim Laker took 19 Australian wickets as England won by an innings to retain the historic urn. The Surrey off-spinner followed a first innings return of 9/37 with 10/53 in the second, but Emrys was standing at the other end where in his opinion Tony Lock was bowling equally as well, claiming one wicket in the first innings and then in the second innings returning figures of 55-30-69-0.

During 1957 Emrys stood in three of the matches in England's series with the West Indies, followed by two more Tests against the 1958 New Zealanders, and then in 1959 two games in the rubber with India. None were as dramatic as the Old Trafford Test in 1956, but they all carried their due amount of pressure and tension – all of which started to weigh heavily on Emrys' mind. He was a very gentle and conscientious soul and, as more and more of the Tests came under the microscope of the Press, he started to suffer from bouts of ill health and at the end of the 1960 season he stood down from the umpires list.

As Dai Davies later reflected, "the electric atmosphere of a Test Match is a pretty good breeding ground for ulcers and the turnover in international umpires is quite considerable. Emrys, who was a far more sensitive soul than I ever was, resigned on account of ill health, and I am convinced that Test umpiring contributed in no small measure to his illness. Umpiring and refereeing are thankless tasks – if you make mistakes you come in for a lot of stick: if you do well no-one says a word."

Having umpired in 148 first-class matches, Emrys left the county circuit and acted as a cricket coach at Llandovery College. For many years since the Second World War, he had spent the winter coaching in South Africa, especially at Kimberley Boys High School.

Emrys' younger brother Gwynfor, also played for Glamorgan during 1932, whilst his son Peter won a rugby Blue at Cambridge University, besides playing for Glamorgan 2nd XI between 1948 and 1958, in addition to captaining Llanelli during 1956.

Emrys Davies meets HM The Queen whilst standing as an umpire in a Test Match at Lord's.

271
HARRISON, George Benjamin

Born – Dalton, Cumbria, 14 September 1895
Died – Manchester, March 1945
Professional
LHB
1st XI: 1924-1925
Club and Ground: 1923-1925
Cap: 1925
South Wales 1923
Clubs: Ulverston, Barrow-in-Furness, Cardiff

Batting and Fielding Record:

	M	I	NO	RUNS	AV	100	50	CT	ST
F-c	9	17	0	109	6.41	-	-	2	-

Bowling Record:

	Balls	M	R	W	AV	5wI	10wM
F-c	15	0	10	0	-	-	-

Career-best:
First-class – 34 v Surrey at The Oval, 1925

George Harrison had a brief career as a batsman with Glamorgan during the mid 1920s. Despite a career average of just 6.41, he won his county cap having appeared in nine games as the sole criterion at the time was a minimum of six appearances.

Born in the hamlet of Dalton, near Kendal in Cumbria, George played his early cricket for Ulverston and Barrow-in-Furness, besides working as an apprentice shuttle-maker at a local mill. During the Great War, he served with the King's Lancashire Regiment before returning to the UK and becoming a professional cricketer. His success as a batsman in the Lancashire Leagues saw him recommended to Glamorgan in 1921 and he duly qualified by residence by playing for Cardiff.

During this period, George played in Club and Ground matches, besides appearing for South Wales in 1923 against North Wales at the Arms Park. He duly made his first-class debut in 1924 as he opened the batting with Norman Riches against Gloucestershire at the Victoria ground in Cheltenham. Despite making 8 and 4, George kept his place for the visit to Bradford Park Avenue where he opened with Tom Abel against Yorkshire. However, he bagged a pair and dropped down to number three for the next match, against Leicestershire at Aylestone Road. The weather though prevented any play on the first two days, and when his turn came to bat on the final afternoon, he made a far from convincing 9 and was dropped from the side.

George Harrison.

With Glamorgan's officials in quite advanced discussions with other English professionals, the committee informed George towards the end of the summer that it was unlikely he would be offered terms for 1925. However, he had already agreed terms with Cardiff for 1925 and decided to stay in South Wales in the hope that something might turn up. Discussions with Norman Kilner had already fallen through and when discussions were terminated with another batsman, Glamorgan gave George a second chance as they offered him a two-month trial during May and June.

Club coach, Fred Bowley had supported this offer as George had always impressed him in the nets at the Arms Park and had played some decent innings for Cardiff in club cricket. George duly appeared in a further six matches for Glamorgan, but he struggled yet again making 88 runs in a dozen innings. Perhaps nerves got the better of him, or the pressure of knowing he had to impress in order to secure a long-term contract became too great. For whatever reason, he failed to cut as fine an impression in the nets when out in the middle against fellow professionals, and his final county appearance came in the away match with Northamptonshire, where batting at number three, he made 6 and 2. After completing his appointment with Cardiff, George subsequently returned north where he played in the Durham League.

272
BELL, John Thomson
Born – Batley, 16 June 1895
Died – Guiseley, 14 August 1974
Professional
RHB, OB
1st XI: 1924-1931
Cap: 1926
Yorkshire 1921-1923; Wales 1924-1930; HDG Leveson Gower's XI 1926
Clubs: Yeadon, Farsley, Cardiff

Batting and Fielding Record:

	M	I	NO	RUNS	AV	100	50	CT	ST
F-c	166	281	18	7324	27.84	10	34	61	-

Bowling Record:

	Balls	M	R	W	AV	5wI	10wM
F-c	245	3	205	2	102.50	-	-

Career-bests:
First-class – 225 v Worcestershire at Dudley, 1926
         1/2 v Sussex at Hove, 1930

John Bell followed the example of fellow Tyke Eddie Bates by moving from Yorkshire to South Wales during the 1920s and qualifying for Glamorgan after also failing to secure a place in his native county's side. Like Bates, he flourished in his new home and came of age as a batsman during his mid-thirties, besides carving a niche in the Welsh county's record books by becoming their first-ever double-centurion in County Championship cricket as he made 225 against Worcestershire at Dudley.

Born in Batley during June 1895, John grew up in the Yeadon area and shortly before the outbreak of the Great War he showed much promise as a batsman in the Airedale and Wharfdale League. In November 1915 the 20 year-old enlisted at Ripon with the Royal Artillery and, after training at Catterick Camp, he went in May 1916 to the Western Front. However in August 1917 he contracted trench fever and returned to British soil as he was treated at South Camp in Ripon.

John had recovered sufficiently by July 1918 to return to active service and he was amongst a battalion of Artillerymen to assist the Italian forces in their assault on Vittorio Veneto. It was during these actions that John was mentioned in dispatches, with his commanding officer noting how "during a

John Bell, as seen during 1927.

four-hour bombardment, he continually visited each gun-pit, and supervised the fitting of new springs under heavy fire. It was largely through his untiring efforts that the guns of this battery were all kept in action. Later in the day, when ammunition was running short, he took charge of a party and carried ammunition for two hours along a heavily shelled track."

BATES AND BELL OPEN GLAMORGAN INNINGS.
The two Yorkshiremen, opening the batting for Glamorgan against Lancashire during 1926.

After being demobilised, he returned to the UK and resumed his cricket-playing career. His rich promise as a batsman led to him joining the Yorkshire groundstaff in 1920 and playing for their 2nd XI. The following summer John made his first-class debut, playing initially against Hampshire and later Leicestershire. He re-appeared in five matches during the middle of the 1923 season, but despite some steady performances, his limitations in the field were exposed, and at the end of the season, the 28 year-old was released from the Yorkshire staff.

Aware of Eddie Bates' success in South Wales, John accepted an offer to play as a professional with Cardiff in 1924 and to start a qualification period with Glamorgan. Despite being unable to play in Championship matches, and playing mainly in club matches, he showed great promise on his debut for the Welsh county against the 1924 South Africans, as well as in matches for Wales. Having complied with the MCC regulations, he duly became Eddie's regular opening partner in 1926 and responded to his new role by recording centuries against Warwickshire, Northamptonshire and Somerset.

In addition, John became the first Glamorgan batsman to score a double-hundred for Glamorgan as he posted 225 against Warwickshire at Dudley. At the start of his record-breaking innings, John initially adopted a watchful approach, but the longer he remained in the middle, the more expansive his strokeplay became and he played with great freedom and panache as he shared a rapid partnership of 177 in just 70 minutes with Trevor Arnott.

John Bell, the umpire.

He confirmed his ability to compile long and steady innings as he scored another double-hundred in 1927, this time 209 for Wales against the MCC, before notching up a pair of Championship hundreds in 1928 during Glamorgan's games with Leicestershire and Nottinghamshire. 1929 saw John add two more – against Lancashire and Derbyshire – besides making a majestic 157 for Wales in their first-class friendly against Sussex.

1930 was a quiet year for John, with a solitary Championship hundred against Warwickshire at St Helen's. With only one more hundred coming his way during 1931, the Glamorgan committee decided to release both John and his long-standing opening partner from their playing staff at the end of the summer. It was a difficult decision for Maurice Turnbull and the Glamorgan hierarchy to make as the 36 year-old had enjoyed some productive times, but it was felt that his best years were now behind him and, with wafer-thin financial reserves, contracts were offered instead to younger players.

John duly returned to Northern England and re-joined Yeadon. In 1948 John returned to county cricket, standing as an umpire before retiring in 1951 and becoming a male nurse at Menston Hospital in Yorkshire.

273
TURNBULL, Maurice Joseph Lawson

Born – Cardiff, 16 March 1906
Died – Montchamp, France, 5 August 1944
Amateur
RHB, OB
Ed – Heathfield House, Cardiff; Downside School and Trinity College, Cambridge
1st XI: 1924-1939
Club and Ground: 1925-1939
Cap: 1925
Captain: 1929-1939
Cambridge University 1926-1929 (Blue 1926, 1928, 1929); England 1929/30-1936
(9 Tests); MCC; Gentlemen; The Rest; Army
Clubs: Cardiff, St Fagans, The Pterodactyls
Rugby for Cambridge University, Cardiff and Wales (2 caps); Hockey for Cardiff and
Wales (3 caps); Squash for Wales; Wisden's Five Cricketers of the Year for 1931

Batting and Fielding Record:

	M	I	NO	RUNS	AV	100	50	CT	ST
F-c	314	504	25	14431	30.12	22	74	253	-

Bowling Record:

	Balls	M	R	W	AV	5wI	10wM
F-c	262	2	266	2	133.00	-	-

Career-bests:
First-class –   233 v Worcestershire at St Helen's, Swansea, 1937
        1/4 v Somerset at Bath, 1931

Maurice Turnbull was one of Wales' finest all-round sportsmen. His sporting deeds could have come straight from the pages of a *Boys Own* magazine. Maurice's sporting CV was indeed a most impressive one – county cricket for Glamorgan, captain of Cambridge University and Glamorgan, 9 Test caps for England and a Test selector, rugby for Cardiff, London Welsh, and twice for Wales, hockey for Cardiff, Cambridge University and Wales, founder member of Cardiff Squash Club and squash champion of Wales. In the view of many, he remains the most complete all-round sportsman Wales has ever produced and one can only wonder at what else he might have achieved had he not given his life to King and Country as he was shot through the head whilst serving with the Welsh Guards in Normandy during 1944 and leading a small detachment of troops in trying to halt a column of Panzer tanks as they launched a counter-offensive on the town of Montchamp.

Today, such a diverse and Corinthian sporting career would simply not be possible, with the modern demands of professional sport limiting Maurice to one – cricket, the game which meant most to him and his Yorkshire-born father who was a leading ship-owner at Cardiff Docks, as well as for the Club he helped to save from extinction. Without his dynamic presence, the Club would not have survived a period of extreme financial hardship during the 1930s with Maurice masterminding a series of fund-raising functions across the length and breadth of South Wales.

Together with Johnnie Clay his great pal and another member of the shipping elite in Cardiff Docks, he helped to convert Glamorgan's finances from a parlous state of near bankruptcy into one with a healthy balance in excess of a thousand pounds. Maurice put his heart and soul into the affairs of the county club, so much so that he refused an invitation in 1933 to tour India with the MCC and forego chances of winning further Test caps. It was also claimed that during that winter, he danced more miles than he had scored runs the previous summer – an impressive feat considering that he had passed the 1300 run mark.

If his efforts off the field were vast, then his presence as a top-class batsman and wise captain were even greater. He inherited a Glamorgan side in 1930 which had rarely tasted back-to-back victories in Championship matches and could boast a highest position of just eighth, This was all to change with Maurice at the helm on a regular basis from 1930. The previous summer he had had a short trial as captain with some of the Glamorgan hierarchy wondering if Maurice, despite his excellent record as a leader at Downside and Cambridge, would cut the mustard when dealing with hard-nosed professionals rather than students. They need not have worries as right from the outset, he skillfully got the best out of the motley assortment of journeymen professionals and cavalier amateurs at his disposal. As RC Robertson-Glasgow later wrote, "he wrenched stability from chaos, gave them runs and leadership, and re-kindled interest that lay feebly smouldering under a mound of defeats and deficits."

Maurice Turnbull.

His outlook was always positive, quietly chivvying his bowlers, no matter what the scoreboard read, and always telling them that a wicket was just around the corner. When batting, his rallying cry was "let's get on with it, we must try and win, even if we lose." As typified a man of great energy, he worked and played hard, but always ensured that everything was done in the right spirit. An example came against Kent at Tonbridge in 1937, when newcomer, Phil Clift, was given a gentle ball from Frank Woolley, as he tried to help the youngster get off the mark. Unaware of this gentlemanly agreement, Phil duly smashed the ball for four, much to the amazement of the Kent side. Maurice was the non-striker, and was also annoyed at Phil's apparent disrespect. He duly marched down the wicket and issued a stern rebuke to the young batsman.

Even in his civilian dress – pin-striped suit and brown felt hat – he gave the impression of neatness, correctness and everything in order. His cheerful outlook became infectious, with others playing with smiles on their faces, Woe betide any opponent who played in a negative way, as Maurice was quite prepared to shame them for their boorish methods by encouraging someone to bowl slow, underarm lobs. Many jolly japes also took place, with the skipper reveling in the jollity, such as the time against Somerset at Weston-super-Mare when at Maurice's behest Johnnie bowled a bouncy rubber ball to their good friend 'Box' Case.

His inspirational leadership came at a time when sharp social divisions still existed between the amateurs and professionals with each using separate dressing rooms and entrances onto the pitch. But Maurice went out of his way to mix with the professionals off the field, and often entertained the entire team at his own expense on away trips, especially if they had done well and ensured that they thoroughly enjoyed themselves. Once at Clacton, he accepted an invitation for the side to appear on stage and, despite a long day's play, his colleagues did Maurice proud by singing their hearts out in the seaside review.

This paternalistic attitude was also evident during the early 1930s, when he went out of his way to ensure that his players were never out of pocket when attending fund-raising functions. An example involved Dai and Emrys Davies who travelled from

Maurice Turnbull seen with Patsy Hendren of Middlesex and England during a match at the Scarborough Festival.

their homes in Llanelli to a dance in the Patti Pavilion in Swansea. As the function ended, Maurice went up to them and asked "How are you getting home boys?" to which Dai replied "There is a mail train at four a.m. – we'll catch that." "Rubbish," said the skipper, "come on, I'll drive you both home," and he duly drove both back to Llanelli, before turning his car around and driving home to Cardiff.

Like all good leaders, he knew when to stand back and distance himself, especially if things threatened to get out of hand, or when a joke had gone far enough, and was going to result in embarrassment. This was the case with what had started as a harmless prank when Jack Mercer had spotted an item in a shop in Bristol which resembled an MCC tie. Jack then dared JH Morgan, the *Western Mail's* journalist, to wear it at Hull when Glamorgan were playing Yorkshire. Morgan bore more than a passing resemblance to Lord Lionel Tennyson, the former Hampshire captain, who at the time, was a columnist for a Sunday newspaper. Morgan duly accepted the wager, and strutted like a peacock

around the ground, fooling the crowd and journalists alike. But Maurice did not like the prank, and at the close of play told Morgan in no uncertain terms that he was upset.

Later in the 1930s, Maurice became more distant and aloof, preferring on occasions to drive on his own to away games whilst the rest travelled by train. "Snotty nosed bastard!" some professionals would mutter as Maurice arrived at grounds in his open-top sports car, This mix of envy and jealousy arose again in the late summer of 1944 when news of Maurice's tragic death reached South Wales, with some of his county colleagues erroneously claiming that he had been shot through the head by a sniper whilst gallivanting around in a staff officer's jeep.

However, the majority of Glamorgan's professionals thought the world of him, and even agreed to endure a salary cut when he instigated a series of cash-saving measures. For Frank Ryan, the mercurial spinner, Maurice was always there to support him with a quiet word of advice or even a few pound notes to get the heavy drinking bowler out of a scrape. Frank hit on hard times both on and off the field, yet despite a few contretemps over his drinking habits, Maurice always spoke up in support of him, and it deeply upset the skipper that the financial circumstances eventually forced the club to dispense with Frank's services.

Under his tenure, Glamorgan also acquired a stronger Welsh identity in the belief that this was the key to boosting gate receipts besides not wasting money on old, has-beens from English counties. He also ensured that the club were more clearly representing Wales by playing Championship fixtures at a variety of out-grounds, not just at Cardiff or Swansea, Through his encouragement, Glamorgan amalgamated with Monmouthshire in 1934,

Maurice Turnbull seen batting for England against India at Lord's during 1933.

thereby broadening the club's catchment area from which players and financial support could be garnered The merger also allowed Glamorgan to enter a 2nd XI in the Minor County Championship, where the youngsters could quietly learn their trade.

From an individual point of view, Maurice was a gifted and stylish stroke-maker, who hated to be dominated or contained by any bowler. He believed that attack was the best form of defense and was often at his best when others failed, or when quick runs were needed, mixing textbook strokes and the unorthodox in an effort to dishearten the bowlers. It had been clear for many years that Maurice was destined for higher honours, and during 1929 he was approached by the MCC selectors about his availability for the winter tour to Australia and New Zealand. He had enjoyed an *annus mirabili* for

Cambridge University, amassing over a thousand runs for the University and ending his final term with an average in excess of 50. He also made an unbeaten 167 for Cambridge against a powerful Yorkshire attack during what *Wisden's* correspondent described as "a brilliant display of hitting", reeling off some elegant drives, and by scoring at a run a minute, he showed that he was not in the slightest bit cowed by the wily professionals.

He was delighted to receive the MCC invitation, especially as he had not made any definite plans over the winter months. There were offers of work in the City of London, but the prospect of a winter tour and maybe even a Test cap, was very tempting so he accepted their invitation and waited for final confirmation. It duly came during late August, by which time Maurice had rejoined his Glamorgan colleagues and, for the second consecutive summer, did not taste success in any Championship matches. He was delighted when his old Cambridge pal Maurice Allom was also chosen and the pair departed with the rest of the party on the SS *Orford* having the previous night attended a special dinner in St Pancras attended by various dignitaries, MCC officials and the New Zealand High Commissioner. A very jolly evening was had by one and all, so after the dinner was over, the two Maurice's, plus several other members of the tour party, went into Regent's Park in the early hours of the morning for a patriotic sing-song.

This helped to set the tone for the *apres cricket* on the tour, which Maurice took part in aplenty on the Australian leg. When the party reached New Zealand in early January, Maurice was drafted into the England side for the First Test at Christchurch, thereby becoming the first Glamorgan player to win an England Test cap. To his delight, Maurice

The Cambridge University team of 1929 captained by Maurice Turnbull (seated centre). Trevil Morgan is sat to Maurice's right.

Allom took four wickets in five balls, including a hat-trick on the opening day. After rain interruptions, his turn came to bat on the third day and, with instructions to go for quick runs, he duly followed the orders and hit a quick seven before holing out at extra cover. He didn't get another chance to bat as England went on to win by eight wickets – in fact, he didn't get another chance to play in the further Tests as other batsmen were chosen in his place.

Having been disappointed at not getting another chance, he returned to the UK in April and focused his efforts on a first full season in charge of the Glamorgan team. It proved to be a fine summer for both the team and their captain as they rose up from the bottom of the table to finish in 11th place whilst Maurice amassed 1665 runs and was nominated as one of *Wisden's* Five Cricketers of the Year. During June he was sounded out by the MCC regarding his availability for the winter tour to South Africa. Once again, he answered in the affirmative and once again he spent the winter in the company of Maurice Allom having departed Southampton in late September on board the *Edinburgh Castle*. But shortly after the Union Castle liner had completed a brief stopover in Madeira, Maurice received the totally unexpected news that his father had collapsed and died in Cardiff.

He sat quietly in his cabin, consoled by Maurice Allom, fellow Catholic Patsy Hendren and one of the priests onboard the liner. With his world having crashed down around him, he talked about heading back home, but his friends persuaded him that there was really nothing that he could do, as the funeral would have been over by the time he got back to Cardiff. They also told him that his father would have wanted, above all else, for him to carry on and enjoy a successful tour in South Africa. After quiet contemplation, Maurice realised they were right, and remained on board. His father would have been proud, as Maurice ended up playing in all five Tests and made a handsome 61 in the second innings of the opening Test at Johannesburg as England chased a target of 240 to win.

There was however a certain amount of controversy over his dismissal, especially as Maurice had enjoyed a promising partnership with Wally Hammond that had rescued England from the parlous state of 30-3, and looked like turning the game around in the tourists favour. But after adding 101 in under an hour and a half with Wally, he was "bowled" by Buster Nupen as, in the words of watching journalists, "the wicket-keeper's hands, the ball and the leg stump all became jumbled up together". There were initially cries of 'well bowled' so Maurice, as the perfect gentleman, started to walk off towards the pavilion, but the umpire at the bowler's end shouted to him to return as he was not quite sure what had happened.

After consulting with his colleague at square-leg, the umpire gave Maurice out, much to the displeasure of his colleagues in the Pavilion. Allom later wrote "all that it is certain is that both bails fell forward and the ball finished in the middle of the pitch. Now it is a physical impossibility for that to happen unless the stumps are hit right at the bottom, but it was agreed on all sides that the ball had passed the batsman on the leg side and either hit, or missed, the leg stump high up." Maurice retained his place in the remaining

Tests but didn't post another half-century as South Africa won a series dogged by bad weather and questionable umpiring.

Maurice turned down other tours, largely because of the gravity of Glamorgan's financial worries, but in 1933 he was recalled to the England side for the Tests against the West Indies at Lord's and The Oval, largely as a result of a purple patch of form during which he made an unbeaten 200 against Northamptonshire at Swansea. Unable to ignore Maurice's sheer weight of runs, he was included in the team for the opening match of the series against the West Indies. Batting at number six, he shared in a breezy partnership with Douglas Jardine, before he attacked once too often against Ellis Achong and was caught

Maurice (at the rear) seen speaking to business contacts in the Cardiff and County Club during a fund-raising event on behalf of Glamorgan CCC in 1939. BHS Davis is on the right of this image.

for 28. Once again, he didn't bat again in the game as the bowling of Walter Robins, George Macauley and Hedley Verity saw England to a comfortable innings victory.

A nasty bout of lumbago forced Maurice to withdraw from the side for the Second Test at Old Trafford, but his replacement James Langridge had an inauspicious debut, and Maurice was restored for the Third and final Test of the series at The Oval. By this time though he was in a more barren patch at county level, and facing Manny Martindale during a spell of leg theory, he made just four before losing his off stump. 'Father' Marriott, the Kent leg-spinner then took eleven wickets on his Test debut as the West Indians followed on, before England wrapped up the series with another comfortable innings win.

Some thought he might have led England in the series against the 1934 Australians, but it was not until 1936 that Maurice played his ninth and final Test Match, against the Indians at Lord's. His selection followed cultured hundreds against Kent at the Arms Park and Yorkshire at Swansea, plus an elegant century in the rain-affected Test Trial at Lord's. His reward was a slot at number three in the opening Test but he was comprehensively bowled for nought by Amar Singh as India secured a 13-run lead on first innings, Gubby Allen and Hedley Verity then produced a match-winning spell, sharing nine wickets between them to leave England with a victory target of 106. After the loss of Arthur Mitchell without a run on the board, Maurice calmly played himself in, and played second fiddle to Harold Gimblett as their century stand saw England to a comfortable victory by nine wickets. Nevertheless, the selectors made wholesale changes to the batting for the second Test, where the new line-up amassed 571-8 with Wally Hammond making 167. With Maurice's form having completely fallen away, he was not called up again.

He bounced back to form the following year with a career-best 233* against Worcestershire at Swansea but, by now, his time had gone to stake a claim for a regular berth in the England team. With a career tally of over 18,000 runs to his name, plus 29 centuries, contemporaries believed his defence was not quite tight enough to allow him such profligacy at Test level, especially against spin bowlers, where Maurice was sometimes too impetuous for his own good. Even so, his contemporaries regarded him as the best captain of his generation never to lead England in Test cricket. He led the Rest in the 1934 Test Trial and, with good luck, might even have led the side for at least one Test in the Ashes series. Had he shown more selfishness in his approach to batting, and put himself first, he might have led out an England side in a Test.

But for Maurice, it was the team that counted, rather than the individual, and the needs of the team always came first. He was also quite prepared to risk censure by the authorities if it meant that Glamorgan had a chance of winning and the crowd got value for their attendance money. An example came in 1931 when he had an unfortunate spat with the MCC authorities over what they deemed to have been an illegal declaration in a rain-affected Championship match at Cowbridge. Maurice's honest alibi was that he was trying to stage some entertaining cricket to please the crowd, rather than play out a boring draw, besides trying to force a victory. Other spats followed as he did the same in other games, but by the late 1930s, these brushes with the authorities had been long forgotten. In 1938 he was appointed a Test selector, before in 1940 being appointed onto the MCC Select Committee which was reviewing the future of the county game. In the minds of some, Maurice was being groomed as a future Secretary of the MCC, or even Chairman of the Test selectors. Tragically, events on the outskirts of a pretty French town meant that neither took place.

Out of the 504 innings he played for Glamorgan, his finest innings came against Nottinghamshire at the Arms Park in 1932, and during a game when Harold Larwood and Bill Voce, the England fast bowlers who were experimenting with fast leg-theory which they hoped to employ on the winter tour to Australia and quell the run-scoring of Don Bradman. As an experiment, it was a spectacular failure as Maurice thrashed the bowling for an imperious 205, and during his five hour innings, single-handedly mastered the bowlers who over the winter months created such a controversy with 'Bodyline' bowling.

Sitting in the crowd at the Arms Park was a young man called John Arlott, who had travelled by train and bicycle with a friend from London to watch the fiery Nottinghamshire bowlers. Arlott subsequently became the doyen of English cricket writers, and wrote in his memoirs how Maurice "was wonderful to watch that day. As the ball rose along the line of his body, he hooked it so fiercely that it went with a single, fierce, skiding bounce for four to the square-leg or long-leg boundary. He scored a quite brilliant double century and punished those two England bowlers as I believe no other batsman ever did."

Arlott had travelled to South Wales to watch this match because Maurice had been his childhood hero and had revelled in the schoolboy's achievements, both at Downside School, the Roman Catholic boys boarding school to the south of Bath and on his quite remarkable county debut in August 1924 after he was chosen in the side to play the mighty Lancashire at Swansea. To the delight of the Glamorgan committee, Maurice made the highest individual score of the match – a composed and confident 40 – and together with typically razor-sharp fielding, he helped to set up a 38-run victory, described by *Wisden* as "the biggest thing done for the county since their admission to the Championship," with Maurice gleefully joining in with the celebrations in the Swansea pavilion that went on long into the night.

Sitting in the crowd was his proud father and, like a true Yorkshireman, he was delighted to see the Red Rose county subside to defeat. After setting up a thriving shipping business in Whitby, Mr Turnbull senior had moved to Cardiff. He also continued to closely follow the fortunes of the White Rose county and regale his offspring with tales of the great Yorkshire players. Around their home in Penylan in Cardiff, were coloured and sepia prints of some of the great names of Yorkshire cricket, but for Maurice, it was a Surrey batsman who left perhaps the most lasting impression on the teenager, as he marveled at the experience of having watched Jack Hobbs score a century at Bath on a school outing to the Recreation Ground.

Maurice, like so many other siblings, was greatly influenced by his elder brother Lou who also won rugby Blues at Cambridge as well as six Welsh caps, before leading the Cardiff 1st XV, Indeed, it was Lou who Maurice turned to when things were not quite going to plan, with Lou always being there to lend a helping hand or pass on a word of advice. Maurice followed Lou into the Cardiff team in 1928/29, and developed into a brave scrum-half. In his first two years up at Cambridge, the History undergraduate was the reserve scrum-half in the Varsity XV, and would have won a rugby Blue in 1928 had he not damaged the cartilage in his right knee. This injury also affected his hockey career at Cambridge, and had he remained fully fit, he would have also won a hockey Blue as well. '

The highlight of his career with the oval-ball was being a member of the Welsh side in 1932/33 that recorded Wales' first-ever victory at Twickenham. One of the reasons for his inclusion in the side was his steady and consistent passing of the ball from the base of the scrum or line out. He formed a fine partnership for Cardiff with fly-half Harry

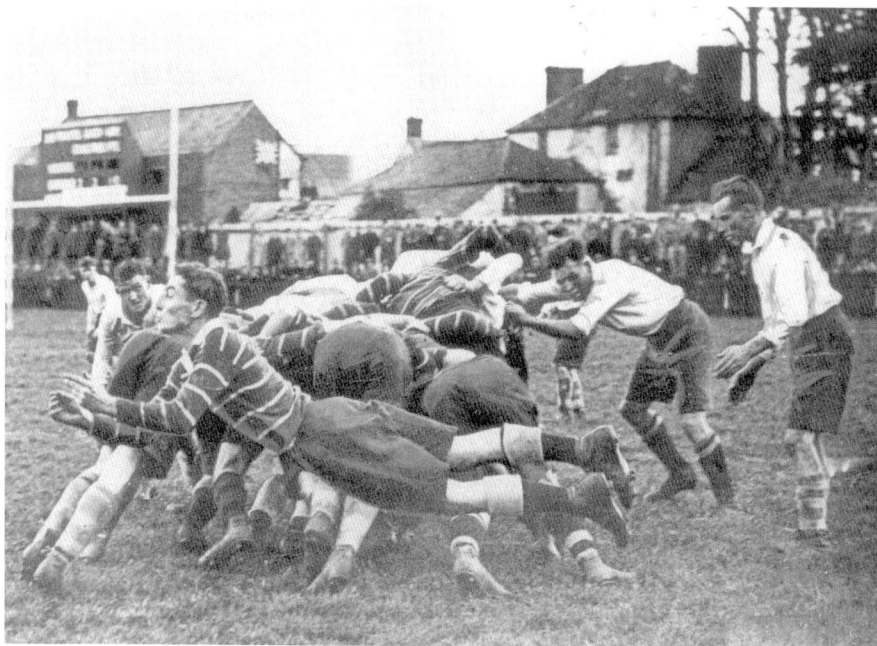

A dive-pass by Maurice Turnbull playing at scrum half for Glamorgan during the early 1930s.

Bowcott, with Maurice's fast and consistent service always giving Harry plenty of time to decide whether to kick or run. After being chosen in the Possibles XV in the Final Trial, their side defeated the Probables with one journalist writing how "Turnbull's service was perfect, and Bowcott's was the most skilled and versatile of all the attackers."

The star of the show though was Wilf Wooller and the North Walian schoolboy, plus the Cardiff half-backs were chosen in their side at Twickenham, as the selectors pinned their hopes on Maurice unlocking the immense potential of a swift back line which was untried at international level. It was asking a lot in front of a likely crowd of 60,000, and on a ground where a Welsh side had never won. But the Twickenham hoodoo was dispelled by a side containing seven new caps and, in contrast to modern intensive training, had a solitary run-out the afternoon before the game at their base in Richmond.

After both teams had been presented to HRH The Prince of Wales, the English applied plenty of early pressure on their opponents. As Maurice later wrote, "when play started, everything seemed utterly unreal. I've never known tackling so hard and swift. I took one bang on my shoulder which slowed my pass up and really hurt." It came as no surprise when England scored an early try but Watcyn Thomas, the Welsh captain, gathered his team together under the posts, told them to relax and simply play their natural game. Wales had spent the first half playing into the wind, but with no further breaches of their defense, it dawned on the Welsh tyro's that England had squandered their chances. At half-time, Watcyn spoke to his men again and praised Maurice for his swift service, even under intense pressure, which had allowed Harry to kick faultlessly off his left foot. The captain asked for more of the same in the second half and, with barely a minute having elapsed, the Welsh made a strong attack into English territory which resulted in winger Ronnie Boon, who had also played cricket for Glamorgan, calmly drop kicking a goal.

The men in red maintained their attack with Maurice twice tackled inches short of the try-line as he made some sniping bursts at the base of the rucks and mauls. The burly Welsh pack also won more and more possession, allowing Maurice to quickly feed Harry, who cleverly alternated between unleashing a series of ranging kicks, or slipping the ball to Claude Davey or young Wilf to run at their opposite numbers. From one of their attacks, the ball quickly reached Ronnie and the Welsh amateur sprint champion ran behind the posts to score a fine try. There were loud cheers from the Welsh contingent as the Twickenham scoreboard changed to 7-3, and after spirited defence, they swarmed onto the field when the referee blew his whistle to end the game. A long evening of hearty celebrations then followed for the players and their supporters as they literally attempted to paint the town red!

Maurice and his colleagues were retained *en bloc* for the match against Scotland at Swansea, but Maurice's badly bruised shoulder was now restricting his arm movements and, unable to swing his arms or pass the ball, Maurice had no option but to withdraw from the side.

Happily, Maurice was soon restored to full fitness and returned to the Welsh side for the journey to Ireland to play at Ravenhill, Belfast. The home pack and a swirling wind however made it a much more difficult game for Maurice and his colleagues. Late in the game, Maurice fired out a quick pass to Harry and the fly-half scythed his way through flat Irish defense and over the line for a good try. But his effort came too late as the Irish ran out the victors 10-5 and shortly after the game Watcyn Thomas, who had argued with the selectors over playing people out of position, was stripped of the captaincy. With the Press being critical of the Welsh backs being unable to string together any attacking moves, it also proved to be Maurice's final appearance in a red jersey.

Maurice and Elizabeth Turnbull on their wedding day.

Two seasons later a broken wrist forced Maurice to retire from rugby, ironically just as he was enjoying a fine run of form and squash became his main winter recreation. He had enjoyed the racquet sport as a means of staying fit whilst up at Cambridge or abroad on an MCC tour, but there was a paucity of decent courts in Cardiff. He typically rectified matters during 1935/36 by financing the creation of Cardiff Squash Club, and it was at the new courts in Ryder Street where he duly played against, and socialized with, his many acquaintances from the world of cricket, rugby, as well as other sports.

Like Johnnie, he was a close follower of National Hunt racing and, whilst a student at Cambridge, became friends with Jack Jarvis, the Newmarket trainer. He was also a good friend of champion boxer Jack Petersen, and attended many of his title bouts, besides using his illustrious contacts when raising cash for Glamorgan and even covered the travel costs incurred by Petersen to be guest of honour at a fund-raising rugby match at Blaenavon.

Away from sport, Maurice was a charming and debonair man, with business interests in both the insurance world and journalism. He had enough acumen and drive to have carved out a brilliant business career had he not devoted so much of his time to Glamorgan CCC. He was also something of a gourmet and wine buff, and even as a student, had a great fondness for good claret. Indeed, Viv Jenkins, recalled the time at a top hotel in London when "Maurice, after several sips from his glass, sent for the wine waiter and gave him a fierce rebuke on what he felt was a rather poor bottle!" He also held interests in poetry and literature, and had extended his studies at Cambridge to complete an extra year studying the English novel.

During the 1930s, he contributed a regular editorial for the Welsh-based *Catholic Times*, and wrote on rugby for the *Sunday Telegraph*. In addition, he oversaw the creation of the Glamorgan Yearbook and, in his role as editor, contributed many features, besides writing a pair of books with Maurice Allom during their tour with the MCC to Australia and New Zealand during 1929/30, and to South Africa the following winter. Indeed, it was whilst writing these charming volumes that the Glamorgan captain acquired the nickname "Little Maurice", and the finished works with Big Maurice contain wry and subtle comments about life on tour during the inter-war period.

Through their shared experiences and writing, Maurice was best man when his pal got married in April 1934. Allom remembers how "Maurice was a great and intelligent companion, and there was never a dull moment with him. He was quietly mirthful, reveling in the absurdities of life. He enjoyed a sense of the ridiculous which I think is the truest form of humour." However, Maurice could also be prickly at times and he did not enjoy criticism, especially when playing rugby. One week, he devoted several paragraphs in his weekly column in the *Catholic Times* to voice his displeasure at the jibes he had received the previous weekend when playing for Cardiff against Swansea. "I was booed as hard probably as a man can be. It makes me sick. All because when I put the ball into the scrum, Cardiff usually heeled it!"

Behind this public persona lay a man with a firm Catholic belief, and an indication of his faith came on the 1929/30 MCC tour, when Maurice was deeply aggrieved when missing Mass on a Sunday for the first ever time. Another measure of his devout faith came later in life, when he refused to take Communion when he thought his wife was using contraception. Maurice would also put his faith before his sport, and during one rugby season, Maurice took a week's holiday from playing for Cardiff to spend seven blissful days in Rome. Each day, he dutifully visited St Peter's Basilica, and queued up for hours, just to have a brief moment with the Pope. He also led a group of Catholics from South Wales to a Papal mass and congregation in Dublin, and all whilst being in the middle of a Championship match at Cardiff, traveling over by ferry to Ireland after the close of play on Saturday, and returning overnight on Sunday to be back on the field on Monday morning.

The Turnbulls were amongst the most prominent Catholic families in South Wales, and fervent supporters of all the good things that St Peter's RC Church attempted to do. Together with his brothers and father, he regularly returned to Downside to take part in the Easter Retreat, and in his own words "to spend Holy Week at Downside is always a source of grace and inspiration. I only wish everyone could be as fortunate as I am." Maurice was very grateful for the support of this strong family unit, and in his diary on the 1929/30 MCC tour, he wrote the following dedication – "To my mother and father who with what great sacrifices of self, equipped me and sent me out, rich upon the voyage of life."

This voyage indeed proved to be a rich and highly successful one, but it ended most abruptly in Northern France during August 1944 where, as always, Major Turnbull led from the front. Having arrived on the Continent a fortnight after D-Day, he led a number of successful raids on Nazi troops as the Allied Forces moved forward through Normandy. However, on the outskirts of Montchamp, he paid the highest price for his bravery, as he was shot and killed instantly by gunfire from an advancing German tank as he and his colleagues fearlessly crawled alongside a line of hedges overlooking the sunken road along which the Panzers were advancing.

Even in these final, grim hours, Maurice's faith and his belief in the family remained foremost in his mind. The final entry in his diary dutifully records taking Mass and Holy Communion on the morning of his abrupt death and, prior to leading the fateful raid on the German tanks, Maurice took

A wartime image of Maurice Turnbull.

MAJOR M. J. TURNBULL

Maurice Turnbull Killed In Action

out his wallet from his pocket, and looked at the photograph of Elizabeth, his wife and Simon, Sara and Georgina, their three small children.

News of his death reached South Wales over the next few days, and during the rest of August, many glowing tributes were paid to Maurice. Amongst the touching tributes to Maurice was written by Maurice Allom in *The Times*. It summed up the feeling of his many friends and others who he had been involved with during his diverse, varied and tragically short life: "The thought of war was to Maurice distasteful; nevertheless, his sense of duty was such that when the need was there, his self-appointed place was in one of our finest regiments. We shall miss Little Maurice sadly, but he has left an indelible mark in our hearts which will serve to keep the memory of him green."

The Western Mail *carries the awful news of Maurice's death in Normandy.*

124

1925

After the euphoria of their thrilling victory in 1924 over Lancashire at Swansea, it was back to earth with something of a bump for Glamorgan during 1925. The Welsh county slipped back to the basement of the Championship table and secured just one victory during a long and tiring summer when – not for the first time, or the last – the Club's wafer-thin finances were at the forefront of everyone's mind.

Their sole victory came at the Arms Park over Derbyshire but only after an embarrassing sequence of thirteen consecutive defeats between 9 May and 14 July, during which the time the old chestnut of whether or not Glamorgan were a first-class county was frequently aired within the pages of the local newspapers.

The losing sequence ended as Glamorgan inflicted their third victory in a row over the Peakites with their handsome victory by 200 runs following an outstanding spell of bowling by Frank Ryan who returned figures of 5/19 and 8/41. The spinner enjoyed a stellar season during 1925, claiming in all 133 wickets but for the second season in a row his batting colleagues were not in their best form and, once again, no batsman topped the 1,000-run mark.

By mid-season, the Club's deficit had already topped the £2000 mark and, in the absence of a lucrative tourist fixture during 1925, a series of austerity measures were introduced in order to keep the Club afloat. These cost-saving measures saw reduced terms being offered to the professionals with Eddie Bates, Emrys Davies and Helm Spencer all rejecting at first what they saw as inadequate terms. Eddie and Emrys subsequently had a change of heart, but Helm failed to reached an agreement for 1926 and left the Club.

An aerial view of Cardiff Arms Park dating from the mid 1920s showing the adjoining rugby ground and properties in Westgate Street.

MORGAN, William <u>Guy</u> (later STEWART-MORGAN)

Born – Garnant, 26 December, 1907
Died – Carmarthen 29 July 1973
Amateur
RHB, RM
Ed – Christ College, Brecon; St Catharine's, Cambridge and Guy's Hospital, London
1st XI: 1925-1938
2nd XI: 1935-1937
Club and Ground: 1933-1937
Cap: 1927
Cambridge University 1927-1929; Perambulators 1929; Wales 1929
Rugby for Cardiff, Swansea, London Welsh, the Barbarians, Cambridge University,
Guy's Hospital and Wales

Batting and Fielding Record:

	M	I	NO	RUNS	AV	100	50	CT	ST
F-c	45	66	11	976	17.75	-	7	6	-

Bowling Record:

	Balls	M	R	W	AV	5wI	10wM
F-c	357	4	257	3	85.67	-	-

Career-bests:
First-class – 91* v Sussex at Horsham, 1929
1/15 v Essex at St Helen's, Swansea, 1928

Guy Morgan, at 21 years and 185 days, holds the record of being Glamorgan's youngest-ever captain in Championship cricket as he led the Welsh county against Warwickshire at Edgbaston in 1929. At the time, it was the established practice for an amateur to lead the county side, yet despite being the youngest in the team, and with both Johnnie Clay and Norman Riches unavailable for selection because of business commitments, it was Guy who led out the Welsh county.

It proved to be an inauspicious debut for the Cambridge graduate as, after losing the toss, he then saw Warwickshire's batsmen rattle up 536 with Bob Wyatt posting 150. To make matters worse Dai Davies was injured whilst fielding and was unable to bat when Glamorgan took to the crease on the second day. They were soon in trouble and were bowled out for 166 before being invited to follow-

Guy Morgan.

on. Wickets continued to tumble but, thanks to some lusty blows from Jack Mercer, Glamorgan were 110-8 when stumps were finally drawn on the second evening. Frank Ryan and Wilf Jones added a further 13 runs the next morning before Wilf was bowled, and with Dai still *hors de combat*, Warwickshire were able to celebrate victory by an innings and 247 runs.

Born in Garnant in Carmarthenshire on Boxing Day 1907, Guy was the nephew of Teddy Morgan (Vol 1, p.217-218). He made his Glamorgan debut whilst still at school at Christ College, Brecon with the right-handed batsman and seam bowler playing against Somerset at Cardiff Arms Park on 3 June, 1925. At 17 years and 186 days old, he became the second youngest player to appear for the Welsh county, though probably he was the youngest ever on ability and performance as the previous youngest, Roy Gabe-Jones, had only been called up for the end-of-season encounter when a host of other players were either injured or unavailable.

In contrast, Guy had produced a string of excellent performances for the Brecon school, both on the cricket field and in their rugby team. In all, he scored over 2,000 runs and took in excess of 150 wickets whilst a pupil at Christ College besides making the first-ever double hundred at the school's ground. Contemporaries remember how Guy was quick on his feet whilst batting and in the field. He excelled at cover point and, with bat in hand, had a particular relish for the pull and cut. With the county selectors looking to blood fresh talent, the prodigiously talented young sportsman got the nod.

Guy subsequently went up to Cambridge University and made his debut for the Light Blues against The Army at Fenner's in May 1927. It proved to be his only appearance as a Freshman, and, once term was over, he was a regular face in the Glamorgan side, where his nimble and athletic fielding again caught the eye. A similar pattern occurred in 1928 with Guy playing once for Cambridge, against the West Indians at Fenner's, before appearing for Glamorgan during August.

By this time, Guy had also won honours on the rugby field for Wales. After a fine season as a Freshman in the Cambridge XV, he made his debut in a red jersey against France at Swansea on 26 February, 1927, with the young centre enjoying a fantastic debut, scoring a try himself and being prominent in the creation of four others as the visitors were routed – all to the delight of a delirious crowd of 25,000. In all, Guy won eight Welsh caps and during 1929 also led the side duly becoming the only man to have ever led both Wales at rugby and Glamorgan at cricket during the same calendar year.

Indeed, 1929 was quite a red letter year for Guy the cricketer as at Horsham in June, he made his highest first-class score and played a leading role in a historic victory by the Welsh county who defeated Sussex after having been invited to follow-on. Such an outcome had seemed unlikely at the close of the first day when the visitors were languishing on 57-5 after the home side had posted 306, and when Glamorgan followed-on shortly before lunch, it looked like another heavy defeat was looming.

Second time around, Glamorgan offered much more in the way of resistance, with John Bell making a stubborn half-century before Guy arrived in the middle and proceeded to play the innings of his life, counter-attacking the tiring bowlers with glee. He shared useful stands with both Trevor Arnott and Frank Ryan, with the latter helping Guy to add 85 for the final wicket as Glamorgan amassed a 203-run lead. Guy remained unbeaten on 91 with his spirited efforts galvanizing the Glamorgan attack. Sussex duly wilted against some fine bowling by Jack Mercer and Emrys Davies who each proved almost unplayable on a wicket which a couple of hours earlier when Guy was at the crease had seemed a featherbed. The Sussex tailenders offered brief resistance, but when Walter Cornford was dismissed by the spin of Eddie Bates, Glamorgan had won by 56 runs, and it was fitting that Guy was invited to lead the victorious side off the field.

His medical studies meant that Guy did not appear again for Glamorgan until August 1933 when the West Indians visited Swansea. Despite not having played first-class cricket for four years, Guy top-scored in the first innings with a spritely 69 before being run out. His efforts could not prevent Glamorgan from losing by ten wickets, but it led to a further five Championship appearances that month, with the highlight being an unbeaten 79 against Sussex at Hove.

August 1934 saw Guy appear in a couple of Championship matches, including the rain-affected match at Bristol where Gloucestershire's Wally Hammond made an unbeaten 302. The following year, he played in a further four games and made a doughty 56 against Nottinghamshire at Trent Bridge before being felled by Bill Voce and dismissed 'hit wicket'.

In 1936 Guy was chosen for the match against the Indians at St Helen's, as well as in two Championship matches, plus a series of matches for the 2nd XI in the Minor County Championship and for the county's Club and Ground side. 1937 saw him play again for the 2nd XI and during the season he scored his only century for the Welsh county, scoring 110 with sixteen fours and a six in the game against Berkshire at Reading. Guy was chosen again for the 1st XI in May 1938 for the friendly at The Parks against Oxford University, as well as the match

A cigarette card of Guy Morgan, the Welsh rugby international and Glamorgan cricketer.

during August against Gloucestershire at Bristol. However, he was injured during the latter and was unable to bat in either innings of what proved to be his final first-class appearance.

Guy had also played rugby with distinction for Guy's Hospital, Swansea, London Welsh and the Barbarians. In his youth, Guy had also been a decent golfer besides representing St Catharine's College in a variety of athletic pursuits whilst in residence at Cambridge. His elder brother Noel also played for Glamorgan during 1934. In addition, Guy changed his surname to Stewart-Morgan by deed poll on 21 May, 1941.

Sadly, he was crippled with rheumatoid arthritis from his late thirties, but he taught with great fortitude at Radley for 32 years, despite being confined to a wheelchair in his later years. On retiring from Radley, Sir George Mallaby, the chairman of the College's board, paid him the following tribute – "the school had never seen [some]one who understood the real value of games and the right attitude which should be adopted towards them…. This sinewy, tenacious little man had gifts of character quite out of the ordinary. He was shrewd, he was fearless, he was never deceived by vanity or pretences; he was of all men, the best debunker ever."

275
JONES, Thomas <u>Charles</u>

Born – Llandovery, 1 April 1901
Died – Westminster, 19 July 1935
Amateur
RHB
Ed – Llanyre Hall, Llandrindod Wells; Llandovery College and Shrewsbury School
1st XI: 1925-1928
Colts: 1922
Carmarthenshire 1919-1920; RMA Woolwich 1920; RMC Sandhurst 1921
Club: Llandovery

Batting and Fielding Record:

	M	I	NO	RUNS	AV	100	50	CT	ST
F-c	3	6	0	36	6.00	-	-	-	-

Career-best:
First-class – 21 v Warwickshire at Edgbaston, 1928

Charles Jones, an Army officer, played twice for Glamorgan during 1925 and once more in 1928. Had he not had military duties, the former pupil of Llandovery College and Shrewsbury School might have secured a regular place in the Glamorgan middle-order.

Cricket was in the blood of Charles Jones with his father, Douglas Thomas Mayberry Jones being a leading figure in the closing years of the South Wales CC during the late nineteenth-century. Educated at Cheltenham College, Douglas had played for the South Wales team between 1883 and 1885, besides playing for Radnorshire and later Carmarthenshire in 1908 and 1909 when the West Wales side had a brief, and largely unsuccessful, foray in the Minor County Championship.

By this time, Douglas was a leading solicitor in Llandovery, with Charles being educated initially at Rev.

Charles Jones.

Potts preparatory school at Llanyre Hall in Llandrindod Wells, before gaining a place at Llandovery College. Charles showed promise on both the rugby and cricket field, before gaining a scholarship to Shrewsbury School where he won a place in their 1st Xi in 1918 and 1919.

After leaving school, Charles attended the Royal Military Academy in Woolwich in 1920, followed by a couple of years at the Royal Military College at Sandhurst. He represented both seats of learning in their cricket XI as well as playing for Carmarthenshire in 1919 and 1920 where he played some assertive innings.

He subsequently became a Second Lieutenant in the South Wales Borderers, but despite his military duties, he played for the Glamorgan Colts in 1922 before making his Championship debut in June 1925 during the Club's match against Somerset at the Arms

Park. During the second week of July, he appeared again in Glamorgan's away match at the Fry's ground in Bristol against Gloucestershire, but it was not until almost three years later that he played again, appearing against Warwickshire at Edgbaston.

It proved to be another heavy defeat for Glamorgan, losing to the West Midlands side by ten wickets, with his two appearance in 1926 ending up in a 230-run victory for Somerset and a loss by 296 runs to Gloucestershire. Charles made an assertive 21 against Warwickshire in what proved to be his final appearance for the Welsh county. A bachelor, he lived with his parents at Nantyrhagfaen, near Llandovery, but died prematurely in Belgrave Square, London at the age of 34.

276
THOMAS, Arthur Emlyn

Born – Neath 1901
Died – Neath, June 1956
RHB, RM
1st XI: 1925
Colts: 1922
Clubs: Briton Ferry Town

Batting and Fielding Record:

	M	I	NO	RUNS	AV	100	50	CT	ST
F-c	1	2	0	15	7.50	-	-	-	-

Career-best:
First-class – 11 v Northamptonshire at St Helen's, Swansea, 1925

The all-rounder from Briton Ferry Town made one appearance for Glamorgan in Championship cricket, appearing against Northamptonshire at Swansea during 1925.

Arthur had an outstanding career in club cricket, and his work commitments, rather than any questions about his cricketing abilities, resulted in the match against Northamptonshire being his sole appearance at first-class level.

An image of Arthur Thomas.

DAVID, Rodney Felix Armine

Born – Llandaff, Cardiff, 19 June 1907
Died – Hellingly, Hailsham, 2 July 1969
Amateur
RHB
Ed – Limpsfield School, Wellington College and RMA Sandhurst.
1st XI: 1925-1929
Colts: 1925
Club and Ground: 1928-1933
Clubs: Margam, Cowbridge, Free Foresters, South Wales Hunts, Royal Welch Fusiliers

Batting and Fielding Record:

	M	I	NO	RUNS	AV	100	50	CT	ST
F-c	3	5	0	20	4.00	-	-	-	-

Career-best:
First-class –   17 v HDG Leveson Gower's XI at St Helen's, Swansea, 1925

Rodney David was the second son of Edmund Usher David (Vol. 1, p.21-23), the man who led Glamorgan in their inaugural fixture in 1889 against Warwickshire at the Arms Park. He had been a fine schoolboy batsman whilst at Wellington College, and during 1925 Rodney led the XI and topped the school's averages. Later that summer he also made his first-class debut, playing against HDG Leveson Gower's XI at Swansea. Batting at number four, he made 17 in what proved to be his sole innings on Welsh soil.

Rodney pursued a career in the Royal Welch Fusiliers after leaving Wellington, but during May 1929 he appeared twice for the Welsh county, firstly in the away match with Cambridge University followed by the Championship match starting immediately afterwards at Northampton. Later that year, Rodney also toured India with the Free Foresters.

He subsequently rose to the rank of Major before living in Surrey, and during July 1940 marrying Lois Keitha Ritchie whose family hailed from Tasmania. They had two daughters – Susan and Angela – and lived in Kensington and Chelsea before moving to Sussex, where Rodney died in hospital during the summer of 1969.

Rodney David, sitting front left, with his brothers.

MORGAN, William Percival ('Percy')

Born – Abercrave, 1 January 1905
Died – Neath, 3 March 1983
Amateur
RHB, RM
Ed – Christ College, Brecon
1st XI: 1925
Colts: 1923
Club and Ground:1924
Clubs: Neath, Swansea
Rugby for Neath

Batting and Fielding Record:

	M	I	NO	RUNS	AV	100	50	CT	ST
F-c	1	2	0	4	2.00	-	-	-	-

Bowling Record:

	Balls	M	R	W	AV	5wI	10wM
F-c	6	1	0	0	-	-	-

Career-best:
First-class – 4 v Nottinghamshire at St Helen's, Swansea, 1925

Percy Morgan was an outstanding schoolboy sportsman at Christ College, Brecon during the 1920s. He led the cricket XI during 1923 and was described in the College magazine as "one of the best cricketers ever turned out at Christ College. We fully expect to hear of his representing Glamorgan before very long."

Percy Morgan, seen aged fourteen when playing in the Christ College 1st XI of 1919.

Indeed, after becoming the first Breconian to score a hundred in the annual match with Llandovery College, Percy was chosen to appear for the Glamorgan Colts in 1923. Appearances for the Club and Ground side followed in 1924 before some impressive innings by the trainee accountant for Neath led to his selection in the Glamorgan side for the closing Championship match of 1925, against Nottinghamshire at Swansea.

It proved to a chastening experience as, batting at number 7, he faced the raw pace of Harold Larwood and the clever off-spin of Sam Staples. Indeed, the latter dismissed him for a duck in his maiden innings, with Percy making 4 second time around. He also bowled a maiden over with the visiting batsmen closely watching the short and wiry seamer with a corkscrew run-up.

Despite his outstanding record at Christ College, this proved to be his sole appearance at first-class level. He subsequently played for the Club and Ground side, as well as for the

2nd XI in the Minor County Championship, against Oxfordshire and Dorset in August 1935. By this time, Percy had switched allegiances to Swansea, whom he had captained during 1933. By his own admission, he enjoyed playing in these lesser games, and told friends in later life "I did play once for Glamorgan but in the 2nd XI it was more fun."

Percy was the son of Edwin Morgan, a colliery owner in Ystradgynlais. He also played rugby for Neath, whilst his younger brother John Wynston Powell, also played for the Glamorgan Colts team during 1925.

279
PERKINS, Arthur _Lionel_ Bertie, OBE

Born – Swansea, 19 October 1905
Died – Umlanga, Natal, South Africa, 6 May 1992
Amateur
RHB
Ed – Bromsgrove School
1st XI: 1925-1933
Colts: 1923
Club and Ground: 1924-1925
Cap: 1933
Club: Swansea

Batting and Fielding Record:

	M	I	NO	RUNS	AV	100	50	CT	ST
F-c	6	10	3	102	14.57	-	-	4	-

Career-best:
First-class – 26* v HDG Leveson Gower's XI at St Helen's, Swansea, 1925

Lionel Perkins was a talented young sportsman from Swansea, playing cricket and rugby for the town side. The Swansea-born batsmen however spent many years working as an engineer in the Colonial Service in South-East Asia and East Africa, so his appearances for Glamorgan were restricted to two during 1925, and four further games in 1933 when on holiday back in South Wales.

He was the son of Bertie Perkins, a captain and secretary of Swansea Cricket and Football Club, besides being a committee member of Glamorgan CCC, who was a merchant at Swansea Docks specializing in the importation of iron ore, silver, gold, lead and copper. Lionel's uncle Frank was also a colliery agent at the Docks, besides being a leading member of the South Wales CC. With the playing of sport in his genes, Lionel shone as a young sportsman captaining Bromsgrove School on 1923 besides playing at scrum-half for Swansea RFC.

Some decent innings for Swansea saw Lionel win selection for Glamorgan's Colts side in 1923, followed by their Club and Ground side in 1924, and again in 1925 when he posted a stylish half-century against Llandovery College. The latter saw him being chosen in the county's side for the three-day friendly against HDG Leveson Gower's XI over the August Bank Holiday at St Helen's. At the end of the month, Lionel also made his

Championship debut against Warwickshire, again on his home patch, but the match was affected by rain and he only made a single in his solitary innings.

For several years this looked like being his sole taste of county cricket as after qualifying as an engineer, Lionel emigrated to work in Singapore and Malaysia. However, he continued his cricket career whilst in South-East Asia, and played some forthright innings as an opening batsman for both Singapore and Penang. During May and June 1933, he spent time on holiday with his father and family in Swansea. News of his brief return reached the ears of Maurice Turnbull, the Glamorgan captain who had seen at first hand Lionel's prowess whilst playing for the Colts. A measure of the impact that Lionel had made was that he was chosen to bat at number three for the visit to Northampton, but he only made 4 and 3, dismissed each time by Austin Matthews, another friend from their time in the Colts set-up.

Few eyebrows were raised as Lionel dropped down the order for the match the following week against Essex at Swansea. He made a fluent 14 and kept his place for the visit of Gloucestershire to Pontypridd. Again, Lionel impressed with an unbeaten 25 before playing in the next match against Lancashire as Glamorgan made the Red Rose county follow-on before Ernest Tyldesley and Jack Iddon saved the game for the visitors. Maurice had hopes that Lionel might stay on for a few more weeks, but he had to return to South-East Asia and his innings of 9 against Lancashire was his final one in first-class cricket.

After the Second World War, Lionel moved to work in East Africa and subsequently was based in Nairobi as Assistant Secretary of the Roads Division of the Kenyan Ministry of Works. He was awarded the OBE in the Queens New Year Honours in January 1963.

280
SPENCER, Charles Richard

Born – Llandough, 21 June 1903
Died – South Havant, 29 September 1941
Amateur
RHB, WK
Ed – Clifton College and Magdalene College, Oxford
1st XI: 1925
Club and Ground: 1924
Oxford University 1923-1924
Clubs: Cardiff, Penarth

Batting and Fielding Record:

	M	I	NO	RUNS	AV	100	50	CT	ST
F-c	1	1	0	0	-	-	-	-	1

Charles Spencer was the son of a well-known Cardiff solicitor and, as a wicket-keeper, he played one match for Glamorgan against HDG Leveson Gower's XI in 1925 as the county's selectors gave opportunities to local talent. However, he failed to score on what proved to be his sole appearance for the Welsh county.

At the time of his selection for Glamorgan, Charles was a student at Magdalene College, Oxford having previously impressed in the Clifton College XI and playing for the Glamorgan Club and Ground side. The previous two seasons had also seen Charles play for Oxford University against the West Indian tourists as well as against Leveson Gower's XI at Eastbourne.

During May 1924 he was also chosen by the Dark Blues for their match at The Parks against Middlesex, but George Abell got the nod by the Oxford selectors as wicket-keeper for the Varsity Match. Charles returned to South Wales without a Blue but his neat wicket-keeping for Penarth resulted in his selection for the county side in their friendly against Leveson-Gower's side at the Arms Park.

After graduating from Oxford, he taught at Stowe School, before accepting a post during the late 1930s at a school in Eastbourne. The outbreak of War saw Charles become a captain in the Royal Marines, but he tragically took his

Charles Spencer.

life in South Havant during September 1941. According to the *Portsmouth Evening News,* "Captain Charles Spencer, Royal Marines, who was found shot on the footpath in Park Road South about daybreak yesterday, was 38 and unmarried. On Sunday night he had supper at a local hotel and chatted with one of his fellow officers. He left the hotel about nine o'clock to catch a bus, which would have taken him to his destination within half an hour. His body was still warm when found. A service revolver was close by."

Military records noted that Charles committed "suicide by revolver (wound to head) whilst his mind was unbalanced." His grandfather Richard had been a leading member of the South Wales CC during the late nineteenth century.

281
MORGAN, John _Trevil,_ MBE
Born – Cyncoed, Cardiff, 7 May 1907
Died – Leigh Woods, Clifton, 18 December 1976
Amateur
LHB, RM, occ WK
Ed – Llandaff Cathedral School; Mr Robathan's Prep School, Newnham-on-Severn;
Christ College, Brecon; Charterhouse School and Jesus College, Cambridge
1st XI: 1925-1945
2nd XI: 1935-1951
Club and Ground: 1926-1936
Cap: 1925
Cambridge University 1927-1930 (Blues 1928-1930); Wales 1928; Western Command
1942; Lord's XI v West of England 1944
Clubs: Cardiff, South Wales Hunts, Free Foresters, Pterodactyls

Batting and Fielding Record:

	M	I	NO	RUNS	AV	100	50	CT	ST
F-c	39	52	3	792	16.16	1	2	9	2
Wartime	1	2	0	33	16.50	-	-	1	-

Bowling Record:

	Balls	M	R	W	AV	5wI	10wM
F-c	1013	32	535	11	48.63	-	-

Career-bests:

First-class – 103* v South Africans at St Helen's, Swansea, 1929
3/16 v Warwickshire at Edgbaston, 1933

Trevil Morgan was the first Welshman to score a hundred in the Varsity Match at Lord's, besides being the first homegrown Glamorgan batsman to score a hundred against a Test-playing side. A member of the famous family who owned the well-known department store in Cardiff, his business commitments prevented him from playing regularly for the Welsh county, but he became a highly successful captain of the Glamorgan 2nd XI, and under his astute leadership, many young players flourished before going on to even better things in the County Championship.

JT Morgan, seen taking guard in the nets at Fenner's whilst an undergraduate at Cambridge.

The third son of J Llewellyn Morgan, the Managing Director of the department store in The Hayes, his second Christian name came from the Trevil Mountain on the border between Breconshire and Monmouthshire from where his father hailed. However, he never liked the name and was universally known as 'JT'. He began his schooling at Llandaff Cathedral School, before joining Lionel Robathan's prep school in Newnham when the former Head of the Llandaff school decamped to Gloucestershire (Volume 1, p.269). He also had a brief spell at Christ College, Brecon before joining Charterhouse where he soon impressed as a left-handed batsman and right-arm medium pace bowler, besides being an adept and agile wicket-keeper. Indeed, as a fifteen-year-old he made an unbeaten 148 against a strong Harrow XI.

He made his Glamorgan debut during August 1925 whilst still a pupil at Charterhouse and appeared in six Championship matches starting with the visit to Leyton to meet Essex. Like his good friend Maurice Turnbull, JT had been identified by Johnnie Clay as a potential Glamorgan cricketer, and had played for The Pterodactyls – the team comprising public schoolboys which had been formed to showcase the emerging talent. JT also shared two of Maurice's interests – history and horse-racing. Their friendship blossomed in the unlikely surroundings of a first-class carriage on the journey from Leyton to Chesterfield, as the two young sportsmen discussed the form of the day's racing, before talking about the merits of various Cambridge colleges to which JT was planning to apply. The pair remained close friends, with JT acting as a wise advisor to the Glamorgan captain during the 1930s.

He led Charterhouse during 1926 before going up to Jesus College, Cambridge where he won Blues in 1928, 1929 and 1930. As a Freshman, he made an impressive 60 against a full strength Yorkshire attack and was unlucky not to win a Blue. He made amends during 1928 and also capably kept wicket both for the Light Blues, as well as in a couple of Championship matches for Glamorgan.

His finest summer as an undergraduate came in 1929 as JT acted as Secretary of the University team, with his good friend Maurice as captain of the Cambridge side. Once again he had an extended run as their wicket-keeper, including the match against HDG Leveson Gower's XI at Eastbourne. There was something of a festival air to this contest as the students gained valuable practise in readiness for the Varsity Match, and it was in these light-hearted conditions that Maurice dismissed Miles Howell for six with the deft assistance of JT, who removed the bails as the England amateur football international essayed an abortive slog. The dismissal also led to whoops of delight from Maurice and JT, as they had placed wagers with their colleagues that Maurice would get a wicket with his gentle leg-breaks.

Despite the fun and frivolity, there were more pressing matters on Maurice's mind as the Varsity Match approached, especially the question of who should keep wicket. JT had capably kept wicket but was in poor form with the bat, and there were claims for the inclusion of other 'keepers as the Varsity Match approached. Maurice received over 100 letters in the run-up to the match advocating other keepers, but he stuck to his guns and selected JT. His friend repaid Maurice's loyalty with an innings of 149, described by *The Cricketer* magazine "as one of the finest ever seen in the Varsity match." He had come in with the Lord's scoreboard on 137-5, before counter-attacking the Dark

A sumptuous drive by JT Morgan whilst practising at Cambridge.

137

Blues bowling with a series of powerful drives that forced CK Hill-Wood, their fast left-arm bowler, to have a mid-off and mid-on on the boundary's edge. Even with another man at deep mid-off, and an orthodox mid-on, Hill-Wood could not stem the flow of runs from the Welshman.

Wisden's correspondent was also fulsome in his praise of Morgan's innings, writing how "he drove hard, cut brilliantly and used leg strokes with such an effect that he scored 41 in an hour before tea, and then with Harbinson a steady partner, he completed his 50 in 75 minutes. Morgan went on hitting all round the wicket so freely that he reached his century in two hours and ten minutes, and completely turned around the game." In all, JT batted for three and a half hours as he became the first Welshman and the first wicket-keeper to score a century in the Varsity match. Even more remarkably, it was made with a bat borrowed from Maurice. Over dinner the night before the match, JT had told his friend that he was thinking of changing his bat in a last ditch bid to bring about a change of luck. "Have one of mine", Maurice jovially told his friend, little knowing what his generosity would produce!

Later that summer JT also hit an impressive century for Glamorgan against the 1929 South Africans, again with Maurice's bat in a three-hour innings striking two 6's and eleven 4's.

In 1930 Morgan led the Cambridge side to a wholly unexpected victory over Oxford before returning to South Wales and joining the family business. This limited his opportunities to play for Glamorgan, and judging by his form for Cambridge, JT would have become a highly successful county batsman had he been able to find enough time to play Championship cricket on a regular basis. Contemporaries remember JT as "a left-handed bat with a sound defense. He played well off his legs and was a tremendous driver and cutter of the ball. He bowled medium-pace off-cutters and, as a wicket-keeper, never regarded himself as more than a useful stop-gap. He also had the advantage of being ambidextrous and some of the Yorkshire professionals, seeing him bowling left-arm slows in a net, advised him to cultivate that and abandon his right-arm bowling."

He also played a key role in the creation of a Glamorgan 2nd XI in the Minor County Championship following the merger with Monmouthshire during 1934, and the subsequent development of homegrown talent. JT had sizeable business commitments, but realised the importance of a 2nd XI to the future of the Glamorgan club. With Maurice having proposed the scheme, JT also did not want to let his good friend down so during the following spring a host of young players turned up at the Arms Park, and to be vetted by club coach Bill Hitch, JT and other senior Glamorgan players. Their actions were successful and on 5 June 1935 Glamorgan 2nd XI played their first match in the Minor County Championship under JT's leadership against their counterparts from Middlesex at Ynysangharad Park in Pontypridd.

There was a significant cost though for Glamorgan to bear and the following year, with gate receipts at 1st XI level falling by £3000, Edgar Arnott, who shared the Treasurers duties with Johnnie Clay, announced "until revenue starts to come in again with membership subscriptions for the new season, assuming that is, that the club should continue, I regret to say that I am of the opinion that perhaps it is the time for the club to gracefully wind up as a first-class county and return to the Minor County ranks." Maurice and Johnnie were aghast to hear this, especially after all of their hard work both on and off the field, and having dragged the club through one financial crisis already and argued against this. "But our costs are so high at the moment", replied Arnott. "We need to seriously reduce these costs, and in my opinion, if we are to continue in the County Championship, we should scrap the 2nd XI and release Mr Hitch as the club's coach."

Maurice was adamant that the 2nd XI fulfilled an important role, and duly read out a report from JT pointing out that it would always be expensive to run the Minor County side, but that it ultimately allowed the club to unearth new talent, which would save the club money in the long run by not hiring talent from other counties. His view held sway but after further financial concerns, they withdrew the 2nd XI at the end of 1937. It was a difficult decision for the Glamorgan hierarchy to make, especially as JT was quick to point out, youngsters such as Haydn Davies and Closs Jones had each found the 2nd XI to be an excellent training ground, and had easily adapted to life in the County Championship.

JT duly suggested a clever solution – hiring out the young professionals to the top cricket clubs and the first division sides in the South Wales Cricket Association. His shrewd business brain was to the fore as he pointed out that such a course of action would help to defer the costs of running a nursery and, with the young professionals still being

JT Morgan is the wicket-keeper in this image of a match at Lord's during 1929.

free during the week, they could continue to have specialist coaching by Hitch, and play in occasional friendlies with neighbouring counties. This is what unfolded in 1938 and again in 1939, whilst in the post-war era, the attachment of Glamorgan's professionals to League teams continued with much success.

JT served as a Major in Royal Artillery during World War Two and oversaw anti-aircraft duties in South Wales, especially the defense of the vital ports along the coastal strip. His sterling efforts were also recognized by the award of the MBE in April 1945. Ten years later, JT took over as Chairman of David Morgan's, besides serving as a Governor of Christ College and a Director of the Welsh National Opera.

JT's father, Llewellyn, had been a member of the South Wales CC, besides playing for Cardiff during the 1880s and 1890s, whilst his elder brother Aubrey played for Glamorgan in 1928 and 1929. His younger brother Gerald also appeared for the Colts between 1935 and 1937.

In 1945 JT also turned out in some of Glamorgan's wartime friendlies before captaining the Welsh county's 2nd XI when it was resurrected in 1946. His final match for them came during June 1951 against Worcestershire 2nd XI at the Arms Park. Despite having stopped playing at a county level, JT still turned out for the South Wales Hunts during the 1950s. He was also a talented golfer and acted as President of the Royal Porthcawl Golf Club from 1968 until his sudden death in December 1976 at the age of 68. His obituary in *Charterhouse* magazine noted how JT had "always taken life as it came. Never unduly elated by success or depressed when things were going badly, he was an extraordinary reassuring person: one always felt that his judgement was extremely sound and that he was the least likely person to do anything silly."

The Glamorgan players practice on the outfield at the Arms Park during 1925. The fielders include Johnnie Clay (left), Norman Riches (third left), Trevor Arnott (fourth left) and Emrys Davies (right).

1926

1926 was a seminal summer in the history of Glamorgan CCC as for the first time in the Club's history they staged major fixtures away from their traditional bases at the Arms Park and St Helen's. The winter months had seen the Club's officials grapple with ever-rising debts and a series of discussions took place over how to further reduce expenditure. One way was to broker a lower rent for the use of the grounds at Cardiff and Swansea, but there was a lobby on the committee who believed that the Club should look further afield to stage games.

Encouraging noises duly came from Pontypridd who offered Glamorgan the use of Ynysangharad Park, the valley town's purpose-built recreational complex which had been laid out on the flood plain of the River Taff as a tribute to the young men of the area who had lost their lives during the Great War. With Pontypridd only wanting 10% of gate receipts, Johnnie Clay led a delegation to inspect their facilities. There were further smiles when the Glamorgan captain heard about the promises of support from businesses in the Taff and Rhondda Valleys. It seemed too good an offer to refuse so the committee allocated the fixture with Derbyshire in 1926 to Pontypridd.

The game ended in a draw and ended the winning sequence against Derbyshire which earlier in the summer had seen an eight-wicket victory for Johnnie's men at Chesterfield. This was one of nine victories in the 24 Championship fixtures as Glamorgan enjoyed a joyous summer and allowed all concerned to think about something else apart from the finances. They ended the summer in eighth spot in the table and, for a short while after their win at Chesterfield, Glamorgan were on top of the Championship table.

1926 proved to be a memorable summer for the emerging young amateurs as both Cyril Walters and Maurice Turnbull registered their maiden Championship hundreds. Several of the professionals also enjoyed a fine year, not least John Bell whose aggregate of 1547 runs included Glamorgan's first-ever double-hundred as he posted 225 against Worcestershire at Dudley. This game also saw Jack Mercer claim 13/98 to steer the Welsh county to an innings victory. The lion-hearted seam and swing bowler also claimed a ten-wicket match haul against Somerset at the Arms Park in a game made notable by the fact that Trevor Arnott became the first Glamorgan cricket to claim a hat-trick in first-class cricket.

A cartoon of Trevor Arnott who, during the game in 1926 against Somerset at Cardiff, became the first Glamorgan bowler to claim a Championship hat-trick.

282
HILLS, Joseph John.

Born – Plumstead, Kent, 14 October 1897
Died – Westbourne, Hampshire, 21 September 1969
Professional
RHB, WK
1st XI: 1926-1931
Club and Ground: 1924-1930
Cap: 1926
Club: Barry
Football for Cardiff City, Swansea Town and Fulham
Umpire in first-class cricket 1939-1956

Batting and Fielding Record:

	M	I	NO	RUNS	AV	100	50	CT	ST
F-c	104	165	7	3252	20.58	6	11	92	3

Career-best:
First-class – 166 v Hampshire at Southampton, 1929

Born in Plumstead in Kent, Joe Hills showed great promise as a schoolboy sportsman but on leaving school in 1915 he initially trained to be an electrician before enlisting with the Royal Engineers during mid-May 1916. The eighteen year-old then spent time at Hitchin Signals Depot before going to France in January, 1917 with the BT Cable Section. He soon

saw active service on the Western Front, ensuring that cabling and other wiring from Brigade HQ reached the forward positions.

During the summer of 1918 Joe was involved in manoeuvres associated with the Hundred Days Offensive and on 27 August, 1918, during heavy shelling and gunfire during the Battle of Amiens, he showed great bravery in ensuring that the communication links were maintained between Brigade HQ and the forward lines in what proved to be a decisive passage of warfare. His efforts did not go unnoticed and he duly received the Military Medal for his brave deeds on 11 December, 1918.

Joe subsequently returned to civilian life in Kent and continued to show rich promise in both football and cricket, before securing a place on the Kent groundstaff as well as having trials as a goalkeeper with various Football League clubs. In the mid-1920s, Joe secured a professional contract with Cardiff City, and on New Year's Day 1925 he made his debut for the Bluebirds against Sunderland.

Joe Hills demonstrates his batting stance.

Following his move to South Wales, he also secured a professional post with Barry, and his fluent strokeplay, classical cover driving and neat wicket-keeping attracted the attention of Glamorgan's officials who were looking for a young and agile person behind the stumps. Terms were agreed for the 1926 season, and Joe soon proved to be a useful acquisition for Glamorgan, recording his maiden hundred against Nottinghamshire on a quite lively Trent Bridge wicket.

As befitted someone who had been decorated for gallantry, this was one of many brave and gutsy innings that Joe played, and he took part in several stubborn lower order partnerships, adding 202 for the eighth wicket with Dai Davies against Sussex at Eastbourne in 1928, as well as an unbroken 203 with Johnnie Clay for the ninth wicket against Worcestershire at Swansea in 1929 – a partnership which still remains as the Club's best for that wicket in first-class cricket. Both men scored feisty hundreds, as they added 150 in just 65 minutes with each striking the ball with gay abandon all around the wicket.

One of Clay's massive sixes rivalled those struck by recognised batsmen, as the spinner lofted a ball from Fred Root high over the rugby grandstand, before landing in the goods yard of the Swansea Bay station opposite the ground, and then bouncing up through a glass window of a nearby office, startling the clerk who was sat nearby. Their efforts saw Glamorgan to 506-8, before Trevor Arnott produced a five-wicket haul to dismiss the weary Worcestershire side for 240 and allowing Johnnie to gleefully enforce the follow-on. But then it was the turn of Worcestershire's batsmen to mount a rearguard action on the final day as a defiant century from Leslie Wright helped to see his side to the safety of a draw.

In 1926/27 Joe had a spell as goalkeeper with Swansea Town, before joining Fulham as their reserve goalkeeper, but in September, he broke his forearm and ruptured elbow ligaments in a reserve team game. Although he was able to return to action later in the season, he was increasingly handicapped by the injury, so he retired from football, and concentrated on cricket. The injury also meant that he had to give up keeping wicket, and he played as a specialist batsman for the next few seasons. Giving these ailments, his innings at Swansea in 1929 with Johnnie becomes even more impressive

By the early 1930s, Glamorgan's finances were in a sorry state, and with ever increasing costs, the Club regrettably released Joe and other professionals as an economy measure. Joe duly returned to club cricket, but he missed the *bonhomie* of the county circuit. During the mid 1930s he started umpiring, standing in Minor County games in 1936, before being promoted to the first-class list the following summer. The highlight of

Joe Hills, seen during his days as a first-class umpire.

his new career came in 1947 when Joe stood in the Fourth Test of England's series against South Africa.

Joe remained on the umpire's list until 1956, during which time he earned a reputation as a cheerful and popular official and, perhaps drawing on his grim experiences in the trenches, he was always ready to pass on a word of encouragement to a young player who was down on his luck. He retired from umpiring in 1956 after standing in 273 first-class matches, and subsequently died in Bournemouth during September 1969, just a few weeks after gleefully celebrating his former county winning the Championship title for the second time in their history.

283
JONES, Edward _Cyril_

Born – Cardiff, 11 March 1896
Died – Cardiff, 23 December 1978
Amateur
RHB
1st XI: 1926
Club and Ground: 1922-1926
Clubs: Cardiff, Barry, JHP Brain's XI, Welsh Cygnets

Batting and Fielding Record:

	M	I	NO	RUNS	AV	100	50	CT	ST
F-c	1	-	-	-	-	-	-	1	-

There is an apocryphal story that the Glamorgan team were once travelling by coach to an away match with only ten fit men. According to the tale, they stopped off near a valley pub and duly made enquiries about whether anyone fancied playing for them – the volunteer duly travelled with them, but did not bat or bowl, before being dropped off on the return journey and never being seen again!

Nothing of the sort actually happened, but during 1926 Cyril Jones, a policeman from Cardiff, did make a solitary appearance for the Welsh county without batting or bowling during their away match with Leicestershire. Owing to the General Strike, the Glamorgan travelled to the East Midlands in an open-topped charabanc, rather than by train, with Cyril, being a late call-up, owing to an injury to another amateur. Indeed, the seeds for the mischievous story above may have been sown whilst the team were travelling to this rain-affected game, with the participants conveniently forgetting that Cyril did get his name into the scorebook by catching George Geary off the bowling of Frank Ryan.

Cyril Jones.

Cyril had a decent record in club cricket for Cardiff and Barry besides having played for Glamorgan's Club and Ground side in 1922. He also appeared between 1927 and 1936 in Pat Brain's XI when the county undertook their pre-season practice games against the scratch side, formed of club cricketers, at the Arms Park.

284
TYSON, Cecil Thomas

Born – Brompton, Yorkshire, 24 January 1889
Died – Leeds, 3 April 1940
Professional
LHB, LM
1st XI: 1926
Yorkshire 1921
Clubs: Bridlington, Castleford, Whitwood, Gowerton, Scarborough, Bankfoot,
Tong Park

Batting and Fielding Record:

	M	I	NO	RUNS	AV	100	50	CT	ST
F-c	2	4	0	88	22.00	-	1	-	-

Bowling Record:

	Balls	M	R	W	AV	5wI	10wM
F-c	80	1	32	0	-	-	-

Career-best:
First-class –   79 v HDG Leveson Gower's XI at Cardiff Arms Park, 1926

Cec Tyson hit the headlines in 1921 as he became the first-ever batsman in Yorkshire's history to score a century on his first-class debut. His feat came against Hampshire at Southampton in 1921, but disagreements over financial terms and his lucrative commitments in the Yorkshire Leagues meant he only played for the White Rose county on two further occasions.

His outstanding batting record in the Bradford League – where he became, at the time, one of only two men to pass the thousand runs mark in a season – came to the attention of Gowerton, and with the club poised to participate in the newly-instigated South Wales and Monmouthshire League, officials from Gowerton made contact with him about joining them for 1926, and like Eddie Bates and John Bell before him, qualify for Glamorgan.

It was a very generous offer, but Cec was something of a tactiturn character and had not informed the Whitwoood club about the discussions, so there was plenty of surprise in local circles as Cec, shortly after impressing for a Pontefract and District side against the full Yorkshire team, upped sticks and moved with his wife Florrie, and their two young children, Reggie and Florence, to Gowerton.

The left-hander continued his prolific run-scoring with Gowerton and was duly chosen for Glamorgan in their match against the Australians at Swansea. The contest drew a crowd of 25,000 but Cec, batting at number three, had few opportunities to show his abilities against the quicker bowlers and was dismissed for 8 and 0 by the spinners Arthur Mailey and Clarrie Grimmett. However, he fared much better three weeks later in the friendly at the Arms Park against HDG Leveson Gower's XI making an elegant 79 and sharing a partnership of 119 for the third wicket with Maurice Turnbull.

But just when it seemed that Glamorgan had unearthed another batting gem, Cec announced at the end of the season that he was returning North. Various reasons were cited, including being disappointed by the modest sum of money which Gowerton were offering for 1927, whilst in another newspaper he claimed that his wife Florrie had suffered from phases of bad health whilst in Gowerton and had not settled.

This was not the first time there was an element of smoke and mirrors over Cec's disappearance from the county scene. After falling out with Yorkshire in 1921 he had

Cec Tyson.

claimed that, as a miner, he could earn more money working down the pit, plus a weekend engagement with a club, than playing county cricket. On another occasion, he had told a journalist that he "preferred club cricket as it is not, physically speaking, so strenuous as the county game." And all from a man who during the match between Yorkshire and the 1921 Australians at Bradford Park Avenue caused something of a stir in front of the pavilion by refusing to let his four-year old son Reggie drink ginger-beer straight from the bottle, insisting instead that he used a glass, much to the youngster's vocal disapproval as he smashed the glass on the terraces.

The son of Richard Tyson, a stonemason, Cec had grown up in the Scarborough area and had first made a name for himself before the Great War when playing for Bridlington. Cec made his debut for Yorkshire 2nd XI during 1911 and continued to play for the White Rose's second string until the outbreak of War. As he held a reserved occupation, he continued his work as a miner besides playing for the Bradford League XI between 1917 and 1919, as well as the Yorkshire Cricket Council against Yorkshire 2nd XI in 1920 at Castleford.

During November 1915 he had married Florence Fox at St John the Evangelist Church in Baildon, a suburb of Bradford. His brother Reginald, was also a useful cricketer in Northumberland and appeared for the county's 2nd XI during the 1920s. Cec remained in the Whitwood area of Castleford, and started coaching duties with the local club during the late 1930s. However, he was taken ill in the spring of 1940 and died aged 51 in Leeds General Infirmary during the first week of April.

285
DYSON, Arnold Herbert

Born – Halifax, 10 July 1905
Died – Goldsborough, 7 June 1978
Professional
RHB, RM, occ WK
1st XI: 1926-1949
2nd XI: 1935
Club and Ground:1925-1947
Cap: 1929
Sir Julian Cahn's XI 1938/39; Appleyard's XI 1941
Clubs: Kingcross, Lidget Green, Neath

Batting and Fielding Record:

	M	I	NO	RUNS	AV	100	50	CT	ST
F-c	412	696	37	17920	27.19	24	92	243	1
Wartime	1	2	0	83	41.50	-	1	-	-

Bowling Record:

	Overs	M	R	W	AV	5wI	10wM
F-c	195	2	160	1	160.00	-	-

Career-bests:

First-class –   208 v Surrey at The Oval, 1932
1/9 v Lancashire at Old Trafford, 1938

Arnold Dyson holds the record for 305 consecutive appearances in Championship cricket between 1930 and 1947. During this period, the steady right-handed opening batsman formed productive partnerships initially with Eddie Bates, and subsequently Emrys Davies. Indeed, the Dyson-Davies combination is still amongst the most successful opening pairing in the club's history with the pair sharing 32 century partnerships

The son of Joseph Henry Fox Dyson (an engineer who later became a publican!), Arnold grew up in the Halifax area where he soon shone at cricket. His neat and stylish batting were the results of coaching from George Hirst and he impressed many good judges. But Yorkshire's officials believed that he might be a bit too flamboyant for the county game, and with questions over the tightness of his defensive play in Championship cricket, others wondered if his modest and slightly reticent character would hold him back in the cut and thrust of professional sport. During his early years on the Glamorgan staff, it looked as if these observations had been correct.

An image of Arnold Dyson on his Glamorgan debut during 1926.

147

Arnold had moved to join Neath in 1925, and for the next couple of years appeared in Club and Ground games, besides making his first-class debut in the three-day friendly in August 1926 against HDG Leveson Gower's XI at the Arms Park. The following summer he made his Championship debut but he failed to set the world on fire, amassing 179 runs in his 20 innings. He fared better with 618 runs in 34 innings in 1928, with a few wags suggesting that his swift and agile fielding rather than his batting was keeping him in the team. But all the time his confidence was growing, whilst he had significantly tightened up on his technique.

These tangible signs of improvement saw Arnold move up the order and in 1929, whilst at number three between fellow Tykes, Eddie Bates and John Bell, Arnold made his maiden century with 106 against Gloucestershire at Swansea during the last week of June. A fortnight later, he moved up to open with Eddie and seemed poised to register his second Championship hundred in the match with Worcestershire, also at St Helen's, only to be dismissed by Humphrey Gilbert for 98.

He continued his development during the next couple of seasons, amassing 935 runs during 1930, followed by 1126 in 1931, before being paired at the top of the order with Emrys Davies, another man whose early years had been lean. The pair blossomed in 1932 with Arnold scoring 100 against the Indians at the Arms Park, followed by a superb and career-best 208 against Surrey at The Oval and single-handedly dominated a high-class attack, with Viv Jenkins being the only other Glamorgan batsman to get past fifty.

Just for good measure, Arnold also made centuries in 1932 against Worcestershire at Stourbridge, plus Middlesex at the Arms Park, whilst in the match with Northamptonshire at Swansea he shared an opening stand of 131 with Emrys – the first of 32 three-figure partnerships the doughty pair shared during their career as they skillfully blunted the new ball efforts of the likes of Bill Voce, Harold Larwood, Maurice Tate, Fred Root, Ken Farnes, Hopper Read, Alf Gover, Alec Bedser and a host of Test bowlers in touring teams from overseas.

When asked by a journalist to nominate his finest innings, he was quick to nominate his career-best double-hundred at The Oval in 1932, but added that a similarly dominant innings against Lancashire at the Arms Park in 1934 had given him much pleasure, making an unbeaten 191 with the next highest score being Maurice Turnbull's 44. He had also greatly enjoyed his 147 against the 1933 West Indians at the Arms Park, but he felt that his other great knock in Glamorgan's ranks was his century before lunch against Kent at Swansea in 1937 when he shed his obdurate and poker-face image to merrily play a sparkling cameo, full of graceful and well-placed strokes.

Another highlight in 1937 was an opening stand of 274 with Emrys against Leicestershire at Aylestone Road. Both men made hundreds with Arnold amassing 126 before adding another hundred to his tally against Worcestershire at Stourbridge. The highlight of the 1938 season for Arnold was a career-best tally of 1884 runs during a summer which also saw him score four centuries, the best of which was an unbeaten 170 against Sussex at Eastbourne. He took a well-earned Benefit in 1939 and during the

One of Glamorgan's most prolific opening batsmen, seen walking out to bat at Bournemouth in 1948 in the historic victory over Hampshire.

course of another run-laden season he also shared an opening stand of 255 with Emrys against Gloucestershire.

Besides being a fine opening batsman, Arnold was an agile fielder, especially close to the wicket. As Johnnie Clay later recalled, "he had few superiors in the game. Slip or short-leg, the 'suicide squad' – as he affectionately termed it, to our guileful off-spinners, he missed little. He was indeed a snapper-up of unconsidered trifles to the irritation of defaulting batsmen."

Between the August Bank Holiday match of 1933 and the middle of 1947, Arnold was an ever-present in the Welsh county's side – a testament to his fitness, durability and consistency as a batsman. Once again, Johnnie was fulsome in his praise of the Halifax-born cricketer – "never has any county been served by a cricketer who was so conscientious in all of his duties. Seldom has a captain had such a fund of experience and quietly thought out knowledge on which to draw at will. Here is a player who has studied the game from all its interesting angles and who can devise a plan to remove the most obstinate batsman."

Always immaculately turned out and meticulous in his preparations, Arnold also toured New Zealand with Sir Julian Cahn's XI during 1938/39. During the Second World War, he and his wife Sarah, who he had married on St David's Day 1933, moved back to Yorkshire with Arnold playing for Lidget Green in the Bradford League in 1940 and 1941, before joining the RAF and playing for their representative side against the Army and a Sussex XI.

Some thought his run-scoring days might be over when cricket resumed in 1946, but Arnold yet again proved his doubters wrong as he amassed 1371 runs in 1946 and 1607 the following year. It proved to be a daffodil-golden swansong for the stalwart opener as he shared double-century stands with Emrys against Sussex at Hove and Hampshire at Southampton, besides posting hundreds against Kent at Newport, Warwickshire at Swansea, as well as Sussex in the games at Hove and Cardiff.

A gleeful Arnold Dyson, as seen in 1948.

At the end of the season, he informed the Glamorgan selectors that he had a coaching post lined up at Oundle and that 1948 would be his final summer of county cricket. He duly bowed out on a high as, under Wilf Wooller, the Welsh county lifted the county title at Bournemouth with the opening making 51 in the match with Hampshire and sharing a stand of 95 with Emrys which set his side on their way towards an historic victory.

1927

From the euphoria of 1926 and a finishing position in the top half of the Championship table to the despair of 1927 as Glamorgan sank back to 15th place and recorded just a solitary victory in their first-class matches. It duly came in their 26th and final Championship match against Nottinghamshire at St Helen's as, against expectations, they turned the tables on the East Midlands side with Jack Mercer and Frank Ryan each producing stellar bowling performances.

Jack Mercer bowls Sylvester Kirk as another Nottinghamshire wicket falls in their dramatic end-of-season match at Swansea.

In their defence, Glamorgan lost a fair amount of playing time during 1927 with August being an especially damp month. Two games – against Northamptonshire at Pontypridd and Lancashire at Blackpool – were washed out completely without a single ball being bowled. The loss of the game at Ynysangharad Park was very frustrating for all concerned with the Pontypridd club, especially as the good attendances at previous games had seen the Glamorgan officials decide to award a second game to them that summer.

After the to-ing and fro-ing in previous summers, there was greater stability for Glamorgan during 1927 with just one Championship debutant in Cyril Smart, the former Warwickshire cricketer, whilst John Chandless (Volume 1, p.277-278) of Cardiff

A cigarette card of Glamorgan's new colours and logo introduced during 1927.

re-appeared for the county in their match with Somerset at the Arms Park having made his most recent appearance back in 1920 during their days as a Minor County.

1927 also saw the death of JTD Llewelyn, the grand old man of Glamorgan Cricket, and the person who had convened the meeting during 1888 at the Angel Hotel in Cardiff when the Club was formed. With a tragic sense of coincidence, JTD died at his home at Penllergaer on the 39th anniversary of the meeting. The 91 year-old had proudly watched his sons Willie (Volume 1, p.30-31) and Charlie (Volume 1, p.80-81) play for the Welsh county, whilst in 1921 he had been overjoyed at Glamorgan gaining elevation into the County Championship. Glamorgan were playing in Yorkshire at the time of JTD's death but the following week they were back in South Wales, meeting Warwickshire at Swansea – the town which he had served as a Conservative MP – and the ground at St Helen's whose creation he had helped to finance over fifty years before.

SMART, Cyril Cecil

Born – Lacock, Wiltshire, 23 July 1898
Died – Abertillery, 21 May 1975
Professional
RHB, LBG
Ed – Westbury Church of England School
1st XI: 1927-1946
Club and Ground: 1924, 1934-1935
Cap: 1928
Warwickshire 1920-1922
Clubs: Trowbridge, Porthcawl, Briton Ferry Town

Batting and Fielding Record:

	M	I	NO	RUNS	AV	100	50	CT	ST
F-c	190	301	35	8069	30.34	9	46	123	-
Wartime	23	25	2	566	24.61	1	2	5	-

Bowling Record:

	Balls	M	R	W	AV	5wI	10wM
F-c	13070	302	6943	169	41.08	1	-
Wartime	?	?	?	2	-	-	-

Career-bests:
First-class – 151* v Sussex at Hastings, 1935
5/39 v Somerset at Weston-super-Mare, 1939

Cyril Smart, one of the most explosive hitters in county cricket during the 1930s, was the first Glamorgan batsman to create a world-record. He was also the first, and so far the only, cricketer from the Welsh county to be immortalized in a major piece of poetry.

Cyril's world record came after tea on the opening day of Glamorgan's match with Hampshire at the Arms Park in July 1935. It was a match in which the hard-hitting batsman made his third first-class hundred and during the final hour's play he struck Hampshire's Gerry Hill for 32 in an over. The earlier proceedings had been quite drab but the run rate picked up in the final session with Dick Duckfield and Cyril each putting bat to ball with great purpose, adding 130 in the final hour.

As Hill later recalled, "Smart was going along like a normal batsman, when he suddenly let loose on me. His six-scoring strokes were from straight to deep square-leg; they were all clean hits and he wasn't dropped once". His scoring sequence was 6, 6, 4, 6, 6 and 4, with the latter blow just inches short of crossing the boundary for a fifth six.

Earlier in the season, Cyril had also made an unbeaten 114 against the touring South Africans over the Whitsun Bank Holiday, with another display of carefree hitting as he shared a partnership of 131 in an hour and a half with debutant Wilf Hughes. Their efforts not only created a club record for the tenth wicket, but also helped to save Glamorgan from defeat. At first, Hughes had been the dominant partner, but as the bowlers became demoralised, Smart started to join in with the big-hitting and struck some massive sixes, one of which sailed out of the ground and straight through the plate glass window of the foyer of the Angel Hotel in the adjoining Westgate Street.

Sitting enraptured in the crowd during Cyril's innings against the tourists was an eleven year-old schoolboy called Dannie Abse. He later trained as a medic and won fame as a poet, with one of his works, entitled *Cricket Ball* commemorating the feats of the Glamorgan batsman:

Cyril Smart.

> 1935, I watched Glamorgan play
> especially, Slogger Smart, free
> from the disgrace of fame, unrenowned,
> but the biggest hit with me.
> A three-spring flash of willow
> and suddenly, the sound of summer
> as the thumped ball, alive, would leave
> the applauding ground.
> Once, hell for leather, it curled
> over the workman's crane
> in Westgate Street
> to crash, they said, through a discreet
> Angel Hotel windowpane.
> But I, a pre-war boy,
> (or someone with my name)
> wanted it, that Eden day,
> to scoot around the turning world,
> to mock physics and gravity,
> to rainbow-arch the posh hotel
> higher, deranged, on and on, allegro,
> (the Taff a gleam of mercury below)
> going, going, gone
> towards the Caerphilly mountain range.
> Vanishings! The years, too, gone like change.
> But the travelling Taff seems the same.
> It's late, I peer at the failing sky
> over Westgate Street
> and wait. I smell cut grass.
> I shine an apple on my thigh.

Cyril's first hundred for Glamorgan had also come at the Arms Park, against Worcestershire the previous year, at the ripe old age of 37. In his early years on the Glamorgan staff, he had fretted about not making a century and had a reputation for unleashing one of his big hits too soon in his innings. His leg-breaks had become his weaker suit and, with a solitary five-wicket haul to his name and no hundreds, some questioned whether he should be retained. His 128 against Worcestershire in 1934 was therefore a monkey off his back and he followed up his big-hitting efforts against Hampshire and the South Africans with an unbeaten 151 against Sussex at Hastings, besides earning the epithet "an autumn crocus" from Johnnie Clay in his review of a season which saw the Wiltshire-born batsman set a new Club record with an aggregate of 30 sixes.

His six-hitting feats at the Arms Park had won him many admirers and he did not let his fan club down in 1936 by making 123 against Northamptonshire and 121 in the match with Lancashire. On both occasions, to a great roar, he sent balls clanging into the metalwork of the recently-erected North Stand. But as Clay pointed out "he is not by any means a hitter, pure and simple. His defensive play is correctness itself and that bat, straight as a plumb line, is a model for all young batsmen." Indeed, the more reserved and cautious side of Cyril's batting was to the fore at The Oval in 1936 when he added another century to his tally, but there were some lusty blows again at Rodney Parade in 1939 when Cyril completed what proved to be his penultimate hundred for his adopted county with 141 against Somerset.

During the Second World War, he was one of the regulars in the Glamorgan side which played matches during 1943, 1944 and 1945. Again the words of Clay in the 1946 Yearbook pay tribute to his efforts in helping the Club to raise funds for the War Effort – "he could always be relied upon, played in all the matches, often at very great inconvenience to himself and invariably made runs." In many ways it was for this, just as much as his big-hitting

Cyril Smart demonstrates his forward defensive stroke.

for Glamorgan before the War, that the county awarded him a Benefit Year in 1946. He duly played in nine matches that summer, taking his bow from the county game after the away match with Northamptonshire at Rushden.

His grandfather had been the groundsman at Trowbridge, whilst his father Thomas had also been a professional cricketer, keeping wicket for Wiltshire between 1895 and 1912, besides acting as the professional at Marlborough College. His elder brother Jack had also appeared for the minor county before joining Warwickshire in 1919, with Cyril following him to Edgbaston, where he impressed as leg-spinner in a trial game during August. He duly spent three years on the Warwickshire staff, with the Smart brothers making their Championship debuts together in the game against Surrey at The Oval in May 1920.

Whereas Jack played in over 200 further games for Warwickshire, Cyril played in a further 44, making two fifties but only claimed nine wickets and was released from the staff at the end of 1923. Aware of his bowling abilities, rather than with the bat, officials from Briton Ferry Town offered him professional terms for 1924, Together with his wife Victoria Julia Fanny Pomphrey, who he had married in Nuneaton in 1919, he moved to South Wales hoping to resurrect his career. His batting flourished in League cricket and he was duly offered terms for 1927 after completing his residential qualification.

During the Great War, Cyril had served with the Machine Gun Corps. After retiring from cricket, he became a publican in Neath.

1928

With Johnnie Clay's business commitments preventing him from committing to playing regularly for Glamorgan, Trevor Arnott took over as Glamorgan captain for 1928. It did not see an upswing in the Club's fortunes as the Welsh county won just two of their 26 Championship matches.

On the batting front, several of the Glamorgan players enjoyed a good summer, with John Bell ending the season with a decent tally of 1551 runs. Eddie Bates and Dai Davies also topped the thousand mark with the latter also hitting three consecutive Championship hundreds, including an unbeaten 165 against Sussex at Eastbourne.

During the summer, discussions also took place with officials from Monmouthshire who, owing to their precarious finances, were likely to drop out of the Minor County Championship in 1929. Following discussions involving Johnnie, a plan was put forward for Glamorgan to amalgamate with their neighbours and run a 2nd XI in the competition allowing the young cricketers to gain valuable experience.

But Glamorgan themselves had their financial worries and were finding it expensive to run just one side, never mind two. Whilst agreeing with the principle of Johnnie's suggestion, the Club's committee decided that the practicalities and increase in expenditure made it a non-starter.

A cartoon from a local newspaper for the Welsh county's match with Derbyshire at the Arms Park rather sums up Glamorgan's hapless summer.

LAVIS, George

Born – Sebastopol, Monmouthshire, 17 August 1908
Died – Pontypool, 29 July 1956
Professional
RHB, RM
1st XI: 1928-1949
2nd XI: 1935-1954
Club and Ground: 1926-1953
Cap: 1928
Coach: 1946-1956
Forfarshire 1938-1939
Clubs: Panteg, Barry Athletic, Broughty Ferry

Batting and Fielding Record:

	M	I	NO	RUNS	AV	100	50	CT	ST
F-c	206	312	43	4957	18.42	3	23	71	-
Wartime	1	1	1	116	-	1	-	-	-

Bowling Record:

	Balls	M	R	W	AV	5wI	10wM
F-c	16452	517	7768	156	49.79	-	-
Wartime	?	?	?	2	-	-	-

Career-bests:
First-class – 154 v Worcestershire at Cardiff Arms Park, 1934
4/55 v Sussex at Cardiff Arms Park, 1933

George Lavis was the first in a long line of highly respected Glamorgan coaches who, after the Second World War groomed a steady stream of homegrown talent. From 1946 until his sudden death in 1956 George acted as Glamorgan's Head Coach, and a host of young cricketers owe their later success in the Club's 1st XI as well as for England, to his wise words and enthusiastic advice in the winter nets.

After some promising performances as a teenager with Panteg, George made his first-class debut in 1928 as a right-handed batsman and seam bowler. It was not though until the early 1930s that the young all-rounder secured a regular place in the Glamorgan middle order. After some fluent fifties, George struck his maiden century against Worcestershire at Stradey Park in 1933 before the following year completing a career-best 154 during the match with Worcestershire at the Arms Park.

1934 also saw George share in what at the time was a record tenth wicket stand with Jack Mercer in what proved to be a quite remarkable contest against Surrey at The Oval. The pair joined forces after tea on the first day following an afternoon collapse which had seen Glamorgan slump to 232-9. George had been the only batsman to hitherto offer any resistance, but everything changed during an hour's play as the pair added 120. Jack set the tone by unleashing a series of mighty blows including a massive straight six against Percy Fender which sent the ball into the pavilion enclosures, before George played some more orthodox and expansive drives. In a bid to end their merry spree Errol Holmes, the Surrey captain, recalled England seamer Alf Gover, but Jack greeted his return by driving and pulling the first four deliveries for four, before swatting the fifth to mid-wicket for three. George then played a silky cover drive against the last delivery, with his textbook efforts sending the ball, accompanied by loud cheers from Glamorgan's contingent of supporters to the boundary for another four as the over yielded 23 runs.

Soon afterwards, there was more hearty applause as another cultured off-drive by George brought up the 300. The runs kept flowing as it seemed none of the Surrey attack could contain the pair, but when Eddie Watts, returned in place of a disconsolate Gover, the seamer bowled Jack for 72 as the Glamorgan batsman attempted another massive blow in the direction of the pavilion. The pair left to a standing ovation and much applause as well from the Surrey players, who no doubt were quite glad to head back to the pavilion after the torrent of runs.

Their efforts saw Glamorgan to their first-ever victory at the London ground as a weekend deluge completely changed the complexion of the pitch. As a result, Surrey's batsmen found it well-nigh impossible batting against Johnnie Clay on what had become a damp and spiteful surface with the off-spinner returning match figures of 12/84 as the Welsh county won by an innings inside two days.

George Lavis.

Later that evening, there was plenty of rejoicing at the team's hotel and, not for the first or last time, George led the singing. He had a fine baritone voice and on several occasions was in demand when the jolly band of Glamorgan cricketers were invited to appear after play on stage at various shows and reviews. "George could be the life and soul of the party," recalled Viv Jenkins," and whilst some of our chaps seemed more eager to chase after the dancing girls, George was quite content to keep rolling out the Welsh melodies."

In 1935 George struck another hundred at Llanelli, as he made 101 against Northamptonshire and, with a 2nd XI taking part in the Minor County competition, George readily helped Bill Hitch with some of the coaching duties, especially with some of the young lads he knew who had been recommended to the county from clubs based in Monmouthshire.

All seemed well in his world, but the arrival of Austin Matthews during 1937 changed things. Austin had a fine track record as a coach at Cambridge University and Stowe School, and the former Northamptonshire bowler started to undertake more and more coaching with Bill. With Jack Mercer nearing the end of his illustrious career, and Wilf Hughes still opting to mix teaching with cricket, the lion-hearted Matthews became

George Lavis seen batting against Surrey at The Oval during 1936.

the flavour of the month, resulting in George getting fewer and fewer opportunities to augment his batting talents with his medium-paced bowling.

To make matters worse, the pair had crossed swords on a few occasions, whilst George's winter wages were cut during 1936/37 whilst there was also a reduction in his summer salary. Realizing that his face no longer fitted in the coaching set-up, George sought opportunities elsewhere and opted to take up an appointment with Broughty Ferry in Dundee and also help coach Forfarshire.

His move to play in Scotland had been with a heavy heart as George had many good friends in South Wales and he was overjoyed during the spring of 1946 to be contacted by Johnnie Clay about the possibility of returning to the Glamorgan set-up and to assist with the coaching and overseeing the creation of a 2nd XI as the Club regrouped after the War. By this time, several of his young friends from Monmouthshire, including Phil Clift and Allan Watkins had secured a regular place in the 1st XI, whilst Austin Matthews was deployed more as an Assistant Secretary than a coach. It was an offer he could not refuse, and with Johnnie adding that George might also get another chance to play for Glamorgan again if they found themselves short, it didn't take him long to accept the offer.

As it turned out George re-appeared on a further 37 occasions, besides playing in the Championship-winning season of 1948 and, as twelfth man, being on the field at Dean Park when Glamorgan clinched the title. Having readily patched up his differences with Austin, and secured his much sought after niche in the Glamorgan set-up, George thoroughly enjoyed the revelry which accompanied the success of Wilf Wooller's team during 1948, with his singing once again being the highlight of the post-match celebrations as well as the special functions across South Wales which went on long into the autumn months.

His final first-class appearance came in 1949, with Glamorgan recognizing his efforts on their behalf by awarding him a well-earned Testimonial in 1950. It saw many warm tributes to George with John Arlott writing how "George was one of the Clay-Turnbull disciples. He played strokes and hit the ball hard, bowled his medium pace stuff, a little short of a length, as long and as often as was asked and fielded hard all day – and in those days, it often *was* all day!"

After hanging up his whites, George concentrated on his duties as Glamorgan's coach and chief talent scout. Bernard Hedges had been amongst the many schoolboys on whom George devoted so much of his time in the late 1940s. As captain of the Pontypridd Boys Grammar School, Bernard had proudly been presented at the end of a successful and run-laden summer in 1946 with a cricket bat by George. The coach duly kept a close eye on the talented schoolboy, often visiting his home to hear about his progress and it was on George's advice that Glamorgan offered Bernard terms

George Lavis, in his post-War guise as Club coach, passes on a few tips to another George, young spinner GB Shaw.

of £6.10.0 a week for 22 weeks during 1950.

Given the kindness George had shown, Bernard readily accepted the offer and the pair remained friends, with George – later that summer – also sending the young batsman a congratulatory telegram when he posted his maiden Championship hundred against Sussex at Chichester.

During the early 1950s George's good friend Phil Clift started to lend a hand as an Indoor School was opened in Ebbw Vale to augment the facilities at the Arms Park. The pair worked many long hours together, happy in the knowledge that they were grooming the next generation of county players but in July 1956 George died after a short illness.

288
JONES, James

Born – Blackwell, Derbyshire, 15 February 1895
Died – Bristol, 19 December 1953
Professional
LHB, WK
1st XI: 1928-1929
Cap: 1928
Somerset 1922-1923
Clubs: Manton Colliery, Chard, Briton Ferry Town, Neath, Gowerton

Batting and Fielding Record:

	M	I	NO	RUNS	AV	100	50	CT	ST
F-c	8	13	1	326	27.16	-	4	12	8

Career-best:
First-class –   75 v Essex at Leyton, 1928

Jimmy Jones, a wicket-keeper born in Derbyshire, played for Glamorgan during 1928 and 1929 after a short spell six years before with Somerset. Despite a long-standing injury to his right arm, he proved to be adept behind the stumps and would have enjoyed a longer career with the Welsh county had it not been for the emergence of the outstanding Trevor Every from Llanelli.

The son of a miner, who was a decent club cricketer, Jimmy sustained a nasty injury at the age of fourteen as his right arm was crushed in a mining accident at Blackwell Colliery. He returned to work after several months in hospital but remained above ground as an engine driver, at Manton Colliery near Worksop besides playing with credit as a forceful left-handed batsman for the works team.

Despite still having restricted movement in his right arm, Jim's feisty batting and tidy glovework drew the attention of several talent scouts, including those from Chard and in 1920 he was offered professional terms with the Somerset club. Some forthright innings in the West Country caught the eye of the Somerset selectors and during August 1922 he made his first-class debut against Warwickshire at Taunton. Whilst in Somerset, he also met his future wife Madge, with the pair having two children.

Jimmy started the 1923 season as first-choice gloveman, playing in a further sixteen games and

Jimmy Jones seen in his Somerset blazer.

proving himself to be a very tidy keeper. However, 1924 saw Dar Lyon and New Zealander Tom Lowry share the wicket-keeping duties as Jimmy, following a winter coaching in Bermuda, joined Gowerton for whom he played until 1927 before joining Neath.

Whilst attached to the Neath club for two seasons, Jimmy played in eight matches for Glamorgan as well as in a couple of games for Wales, against Sussex and the 1929 South Africans as he acted as understudy for Danny Sullivan, the veteran gloveman, who had kept for Surrey before moving to South Wales.

By the end of 1929, with Danny Sullivan having taken a coaching appointment in Lancashire, Trevor Every became Glamorgan's first choice as the Welsh county looked to promote their homegrown talent. Jimmy duly joined Briton Ferry Town for the next two summers. As a contemporary at Briton Ferry remembered, "he was the total professional. Honest in the complete fulfilment of his contract, and dedicated to the correct upbringing of his young charges. He hated gamesmanship and many a bowler was made to look foolish when seeking to upset a young batsman by delaying delivery and shifting fielders around. Jimmy – as the non-striker – would loudly tell the offending bowler that as soon as he was ready, his colleague wouldn't be and would prefer to pat the pitch or consult the seagulls! He was a splendid wicket-keeper, unfussy, sure and magical on the legside – an artist who could convey and teach all his skills to the wicket-keepers that were destined to follow him."

In 1932 Jimmy accepted a coaching appointment at Denstone College. His duties at the Staffordshire school also saw him prepare the pitches and as the College's magazine records Jimmy was " a class left-hand bat and wicket-keeper, who had the gift of imparting his knowledge and instilling confidence in the boys, whilst the match wickets he prepared were really good – too good in the opinion of some who saw the heavy roller used so constantly and pitches shaved almost completely devoid of grass."

Jimmy Jones seen with his son Arwyn at Gowerton during 1929.

Jimmy left Denstone at the end of the 1934 season having secured a similar post in Hammersmith. In 1944 Jimmy became the licensee of The Old Duke in King Street, Bristol where he mixed with many of the actors appearing on stage at the nearby Bristol Old Vic Theatre. His brother Harry was a decent footballer and played professionally for Notts Forest and Sutton Town as a left-back. He also won a solitary England cap against France in Paris in 1923. Jimmy died of heart failure during December 1953 whilst working at the public house in Bristol.

289
MORGAN, Aubrey Niel

Born – Llandaff, 30 January 1904
Died – Ridgfield, Washington, 14 December 1985
Amateur
RHB, RM
Ed – Charterhouse School and Jesus College, Cambridge
1st XI: 1928-1929
Colts: 1924
Club and Ground: 1928
Wales 1929
Clubs: Cardiff, JHP Brain's XI, Welsh Cygnets

Batting and Fielding Record:

	M	I	NO	RUNS	AV	100	50	CT	ST
F-c	5	9	0	83	9.22	-	-	1	-

Bowling Record:

	Balls	M	R	W	AV	5wI	10wM
F-c	384	8	263	3	87.67	-	-

Career-bests:
First-class –   35 v Oxford University at The Parks, Oxford, 1928
              2/93 v Yorkshire at Hull, 1929

Aubrey Morgan was the elder brother of 'JT' Morgan and a member of the Cardiff-based family who owned the famous department store in Cardiff. Educated at Charterhouse and Jesus College, Cambridge, he showed fine promise as an all-rounder and was regarded by some as a future captain of Glamorgan. He duly had an eventful foray into the world of county cricket during 1929 before emigrating to the United States and became a Diplomat based in New York.

During July 1929, when captaining Cardiff, he answered an SOS from Glamorgan to lead the county in their away match against Nottinghamshire. It came about because neither Johnnie Clay, Norman Riches or Trevor Arnott were available for the visit to Trent Bridge. To some, it seemed a strange decision, especially as the all-rounder had only played for the Welsh county twice before, and both times against student opposition – Oxford University in 1928 and against Cambridge University at the start of the 1929 season. But Aubrey was well-regarded as a captain in club circles and with doubts over who was going to lead Glamorgan on a regular basis in 1930, the county's hierarchy considered him as one of the contenders.

Despite having never played before in a Championship match, he duly went out to toss at Trent Bridge on the morning of 3 July, and after losing the toss, Aubrey partnered Jack Mercer with the new ball. However, Aubrey's debut in the county competition only lasted thirty minutes as, after bowling half a dozen overs, he strained a hamstring and limped off the field, leaving Eddie Bates in charge with

Jack as his deputy. His departure also meant that Glamorgan were down to just one seamer, and a host of spin bowlers. No surprise that Nottinghamshire made 512-6 before Harold Larwood scythed through the Glamorgan batting, claiming 11/73 as the visitors were dismissed for 107 and 78 to give Nottinghamshire victory by an innings and 327 runs.

Aubrey Morgan.

Aubrey remained with the Glamorgan party for the next match, against Leicestershire at Loughborough, but played solely as a batsman. The return of Trevor Arnott as captain however made very little difference to the fortunes of the Welsh county as they subsided to another innings defeat inside two days, with Aubrey, batting at number ten in the order and despite limited footwork, hitting a lusty 20 in Glamorgan's first innings.

A fortnight later, and now restored to full fitness, he was chosen again for Glamorgan's match with Yorkshire at Hull as well as Wales' match against the MCC at Lord's. Norman Riches was captain for both games and during the game in Yorkshire, Aubrey opened the bowling with Trevor and lost little in comparison with his new ball partner as he claimed the wickets of Arthur Mitchell and Wilf Barber, but once again, Glamorgan went down to another innings defeat. A month later at Lord's, Aubrey featured in a Welsh side that boasted the veteran SF Barnes and, as a result, operated as first-change in the attack. He duly claimed three wickets and helped his colleagues draw the match.

By this time, Maurice Turnbull, his friend from their Cambridge days, had commenced what proved to be a successful trial as Glamorgan captain, so Aubrey returned to club cricket and was not called up again by the Welsh county's selectors. He briefly worked in his family's department store in Cardiff before emigrating to the United States to act as an assistant to the British Ambassador in Washington.He soon became an acquaintance of Dwight Whitney Morrow, a senior partner in the JP Morgan investment bank and later a Republican politician and US ambassador to Mexico.

In December 1932 Aubrey married Dwight's daughter Elisabeth, but sadly she died two years later of an incurable heart disease in Pasadena, California. During June 1937, Aubrey married Dwight's youngest daughter Constance and with Dwight's other daughter Anne being the wife of Charles Lindbergh, Aubrey had become brother-in-law of the US aviator.

In the summer of 1939, Sir Robert Vansittart, the British government's chief diplomatic adviser, privately recruited Aubrey as well as John Wheeler-Bennett, the historian and future biographer of King George VI, to revitalise the moribund British Library of Information in New York, so that the British voice might be effectively heard in the United States in the event of war.

Aubrey and Con, together with a few friends, had virtually at their own expense established a daily survey of the American media for the use of the Foreign Office and the Ministry of Information. In an office in Rockefeller Center, the British Press Service, nicknamed "the Clip Club", comprised a team of writers under Con who collated the material from various British consulates in the United States. It was a valuable source both for British officials in London and for Isaiah Berlin, then working at the British Embassy in Washington, for his weekly report on trends in America, which Winston Churchill always read with great interest.

The activities of the British Library of Information and the British Press Service were eventually transformed into the British Information Services with Aubrey acting as its Controller. By this time, his brother-in-law Charles Lindbergh was head of America First, the leading isolationist pressure group. Herman Goering had convinced Lindbergh shortly before the war that Britain could not withstand the might of the Luftwaffe, and his wife Anne shared her husband's views. The Morrow family therefore were deeply divided at this time but it did not deflect Aubrey from his work.

Around this time, he and Con also purchased a large property at Ridgefield in the south-west of Washington State, and quietly drew up plans for the farm, which they renamed Plas Newydd (or new place) as a possible retreat for Welsh relatives, including JT, should Britain be invaded by the Nazi's.

After the hostilities were over, Aubrey and Con took up residence at Plas Newydd where they raised a large herd of dairy cattle and marketed timber from huge Douglas firs. But in 1947 John Wheeler-Bennett contacted Aubrey and persuaded him to fly to the UK on what he described as "a matter of national interest". It was to urge Aubrey to become the personal advisor and counsellor on Anglo-American relations to Sir Oliver (later Lord) Franks, the new British Ambassador to the United States.

The Welshman was, at first unsure, believing that he had done his stint as a government servant and was now enjoying a quieter life in farming. But Sir Oliver's charm and his remarkably lucid mind won Aubrey over. He and Con duly moved back to Washington and remained there until finally retiring from the diplomatic service in 1953. It had proved to be a fine appointment and it was largely for this work, as well as his stance on Germany against his brother-in-law, that Aubrey was subsequently awarded the CMG.

As a youngster at Charterhouse and Cambridge, he was – like his brother Trevil – known by his middle name of Niel which was a shortened version of his grandfather's name Nathaniel. But perhaps because of Con's influence, he was known as Aubrey for the rest of his time in the United States. He died at Plas Newydd in September 1985 after a varied but very happy life.

WILLIAMS, Lewis Erskine Wyndham ('Tip')

Born – Bonvilston, 28 November 1900
Died – St Hilary, 24 April, 1974
Amateur
RHB
Ed – St Anthony's Prep School, Eastbourne; Oratory School and
University College, Oxford
1st XI: 1928-1930
Club and Ground: 1929
Clubs: Cowbridge, South Wales Hunts CC, Welsh Cygnets, JHP Brain's XI

Batting and Fielding Record:

	M	I	NO	RUNS	AV	100	50	CT	ST
F-c	4	8	2	145	24.16	-	1	1	-

Bowling Record:

	Balls	M	R	W	AV	5wI	10wM
F-c	42	1	42	0	-	-	-

Career-best:
First-class – 53* v Oxford University at The Parks, Oxford, 1928

'Tip' Williams, who played four times for Glamorgan, was a well-known figure in the sporting and legal world of South Wales. His grandfather Richard Wyndham Williams had been a leading solicitor in Cardiff in the mid nineteenth century, besides being the founding President of the Cardiff and County Club, as well as being related to the Homfray family.

A young 'Tip' Williams.

His father, Lawrence Gardner Williams also worked as a solicitor in the Welsh capital and, whilst living in Bonvilston, enjoyed hunting with the Glamorganshire Hunt, serving as its secretary from 1898 until 1934. Indeed, it was the love of the equine world and a close interest in steeple-chasing that led to Lewis being known to everyone as 'Tip'. A great character, he was also a close friend of Johnnie Clay and his brother Peter, with whom he founded the South Wales Hunts in 1926.

Tip had first played for Cowbridge whilst an undergraduate at Oxford, and subsequently reveled in the more social form of the game, playing alongside other young gentlemen from the Vale of Glamorgan and talented amateur sportsmen. He was a decent batsman in his own right and after some good innings for Cowbridge, the forceful right-hander was chosen in the Glamorgan side in May 1928 for the three-day friendly against Oxford University at The Parks. His good friends Pat Brain and Aubrey Morgan were also in the eleven, with Tip scoring an unbeaten 53 in the second innings after the Dark Blues had enforced the follow-on. With the Welsh county handicapped by the absence of the injured Norman Riches, Oxford won the game by eight weeks.

In May 1929 Tip was chosen again in the Glamorgan side, this time for the friendly with Cambridge University at Fenner's. His good friends Maurice Turnbull and Trevil Morgan were captain and secretary of the Light Blues at the time, so there was plenty of jolly banter amongst the young Welshmen in the drawn game with Tip unbeaten on 31 when time was called. In mid-May 1929 Tip made his Championship debut against Somerset at the Arms Park having answered a late call from Johnnie Clay when the county found themselves short of a batsman for the game. Despite these pre-match alarms, Glamorgan won the contest by 128 runs, but Tip's contribution was a modest one, making 0 and 13.

He would have loved to have played more Championship cricket alongside his sporting friends, but his training and subsequent duties as a solicitor prevailed. He did though make one further appearance, this time under Maurice's leadership, against Oxford University over the Whitsun Bank Holiday in 1930. But like his previous visit to The Parks, he featured in a scratch side which were beaten by the students.

Given his friendship with the Clays and his close links with the Cowbridge club, he helped to set-up and organize Glamorgan's matches at The Broadshoard. He also continued to play until 1939 for Pat Brain's XI in their annual pre-season game at the Arms Park against the county side and after the Second World War, he still turned out for the South Wales Hunts, besides being a familiar face at local point-to-points and the meetings at Chepstow Racecourse, often in the company of the Clay family.

In June 1933 Tip married Mary Eleanor Knight of Tythegston Court, who was the daughter of Robert Lougher Knight, the

A jovial Tip Williams, seen during 1937.

Clifton-educated barrister who had played for Oxford University, the MCC and the South Wales CC between 1880 and 1886. Prior to the Second World War, Tip and his wife lived at Verlands, Cowbridge whilst they later lived at The Manor House, St Hilary.

BOWEN, Elfyn

Born – Llannon, Llanelly, 10 July 1907
Died – Brynlliw Colliery, Gorseinon, 24 August 1965
Professional
LHB, SLA
1st XI: 1928-1933
Club: Gowerton
Rugby for Swansea

Batting and Fielding Record:

	M	I	NO	RUNS	AV	100	50	CT	ST
F-c	3	5	1	40	10.00	-	-	-	-

Bowling Record:

	Balls	M	R	W	AV	5wI	10wM
F-c	30	2	14	0	-	-	-

Career-best:
First-class –   22 v Lancashire at St Helen's, Swansea, 1928

Elfyn Bowen was a talented left-handed batsman and spinner who played twice for Glamorgan during 1928, before re-appearing five years later in a match at Swansea. His fine record in club cricket with Gowerton and the search for homegrown talent initially led to Elfyn joining the county's staff in 1928 as an understudy to Frank Ryan, the maverick spinner.

Elfyn Bowen.

Elfyn duly appeared in the pre-season friendly for Pat Brain's XI against his county colleagues at the Arms Park in April, before making his first-class debut during June against Lancashire at Swansea, scoring 22 and bowling five overs.

With Frank very much the number one left-arm spinner, and Johnnie Clay as his off-spin partner, Elfyn's opportunities were restricted to just one further appearance, six weeks later when Glamorgan visited Leyton to play Essex. He scored just 2 and 5 and didn't bowl as the game ended in a draw. The following summer, Elfyn suffered problems with his action and, with a loss of confidence, he was released from the county's staff.

He returned to club cricket with Gowerton, and regained his confidence both with the bat and ball in the South Wales and Monmouthshire Leagues, so much so that in June 1933 Elfyn re-appeared for Glamorgan in the match against Northamptonshire at Swansea. However, he only scored 7 and once again didn't bowl in what proved to be his final county appearance. Elfyn was also a talented rugby player playing in the centre and at fly-half for Swansea RFC, for whom he was a regular in the 1928/29 season.

292
SHEA, Alfred James

Born – Briton Ferry, 7 November 1898
Died – Neath, 21 May 1969
Professional
RHB, RM
1st XI: 1928
Club: Briton Ferry Town

Batting and Fielding Record:

	M	I	NO	RUNS	AV	100	50	CT	ST
F-c	2	3	0	22	7.33	-	-	-	-

Bowling Record:

	Balls	M	R	W	AV	5wI	10wM
F-c	246	7	171	1	171.00	-	-

Career-bests:
First-class – 10 v Nottinghamshire at Trent Bridge, 1928
1/130 v Gloucestershire at Bristol, 1928

Alf Shea was a stalwart with Briton Ferry Town with the all-rounder having a fine record for the club during the inter-war period, besides playing twice for Glamorgan in 1928.

A slight figure, Alf was tough as teak and extolled supreme self-confidence in his abilities either with bat or ball in hand. A classic example of his never-say-die attitude came during his Championship debut against Gloucestershire at the Greenbank ground in Bristol during the last week of June. Glamorgan did not have their first-choice attack on show that day, no doubt because both Alf Dipper and Wally Hammond were in decent form. The former duly scored 188 and the latter an unbeaten 218 against an attack which featured Alf and the gentle seam of George Lavis with the new ball, followed by Cyril Smart's leg-breaks, Emrys Davies' chinamen and Dai Davies' medium-pace.

Alf Shea.

Without Johnnie Clay or Frank Ryan, there was no devil in the visiting attack as Gloucestershire reached 300 for the loss of just three wickets. But Alf typically felt he could still make an impression and walked up to captain Norman Riches saying "We are not doing so well, Skipper," "No Alf" said the Cardiff amateur, to which Alf replied "Do you want to change all that?" Norman replied in the affirmative to which Alf said "Then give me the bloody ball!"

Norman duly re-introduced the Briton Ferry man who for the next three-quarters of an hour, bowled his heart out in tandem with Emrys Davies, before being rewarded with the wicket of Billy Neale who was trapped l.b.w. by a ball which fizzed through from Alf's high and text book action. Gloucestershire batted on well into the second day, before

167

declaring on 653-6 and hoping to cheaply dismiss Glamorgan. Perhaps Alf's tenacious attitude rubbed off on his new colleagues as John Bell, together with Norman, stoutly defended and saw the Welsh county to the safety of a draw.

He retained his place for the visit later in the week to Trent Bridge, where Harold Larwood and Fred Barratt exploited a wicket with pace and bounce. Batting at number ten, Alf made a spirited 10 with his reminiscences of facing Larwood, told many times after play at the Briton Ferry ground, having gone down into the Club's annals. "I thought I had gone blind. But I realized that I couldn't be. I could see everything, except the ball! I didn't see the second one either so I made a plan. When he was five yards from the wicket, I counted one – two – three and then let fly with an uppish late cut. Some watching thought differently and said the ball instead had cannoned into the shoulder of the bat. Anyway, it almost carried for six into the stand, and I believed I had his measure!"

It was not to be as the English bowler removed him shortly afterwards as Alf was caught flaying at a delivering from Larwood. Later that day, Alf's seven overs of seam were then treated with disdain by Dodger Whysall who struck him for 41 *en route* to a century, before on the final day, Alf was dismissed hit wicket as he played a typically unorthodox swipe at the leg-spin of Len Richmond. It proved to be his final action for Glamorgan having tasted the other side of life in county cricket as Nottinghamshire completed an innings victory.

Alf met with more success as a batsman in club cricket and in 1928 scored a century against Swansea in the space of just 45 minutes, hitting 8 massive sixes and 13 fours. After retiring from playing, Alf coached at the Briton Ferry club and gleefully passed on tips to the next generation including his nephew Dennis who played for Glamorgan after the Second World War.

His father, Henry Alfred, had been born O'Shea but in adulthood opted just for Shea. Henry worked as a moulder at the local ironworks – a trade into which Alf also followed until retiring during the late 1950s. He had married Elsie Ridd in 1923, but sadly she predeceased him during 1942.

293
HOWARD, Alan Raymond

Born – Clarendon Park, Leicester, 11 December 1909
Died – Hounslow, March 1993
Professional
LHB, RM
1st XI: 1928-1933
2nd XI: 1936-1938
Club and Ground: 1927-1933
Cap: 1929
Clubs: Hill's Plymouth, St Fagans

Batting and Fielding Record:

	M	I	NO	RUNS	AV	100	50	CT	ST
F-c	59	97	2	1153	12.13	-	3	35	-

Bowling Record:

	Balls	M	R	W	AV	5wI	10wM
F-c	108	2	70	0	-	-	-

Career-best:

First-class – 63 v Derbyshire at St Helen's, Swansea, 1930

Alan Howard was a member of a well-known cricketing family in Leicester with his father Arthur playing for the East Midlands county during 1921 and his younger brother Jack also appearing for Leicestershire between 1946 and 1948.

Alan had impressed as a schoolboy batsman in local cricket in his native Leicestershire during the mid-1920s and had joined the Glamorgan staff in 1928 with the county's officials hoping that the forceful and attractive left-handed batsman could fill the void left by the departure of Cyril Walters.

His county career began promisingly with a fluent 21 batting at number eight against Worcestershire at New Road in August 1928, whilst the following May at Pontypridd, he top-scored with 33 in the first innings against the South Africans. His technically correct style led to his elevation to opening batsman in 1930, and during the match against Derbyshire at Swansea, Alan made his maiden half-century, scoring 63 in the first innings and 37 in the second. But this proved to be the pinnacle of his county career, as he struggled in other games and ended the summer with a modest average of 15.

His experiment at the top of the order ended in 1931 as Alan dropped back into the middle order. He remained an agile fielder and held many brave catches standing at short-leg, but he only scored two further fifties and failed to establish a regular place in the side. After six appearances at the start of the 1933 season, he was released from the county's staff as the Club looked to reduced their costs.

Alan remained in South Wales, and continued to be a heavy scorer in club cricket for St Fagans and the Hill's Plymouth club in Merthyr. Some wondered whether his greater maturity and experience would see Alan get a second chance on the county's staff later in the 1930s but with homegrown batsmen such as Willie Jones, Allan Watkins and Phil Clift all emerging, nothing came Alan's way. Nevertheless, he did play for Glamorgan 2nd XI in their Minor County match against Berkshire at Reading in 1936 as well as in their friendly against the Phoenix Club of Ireland at Barry Island during August 1938.

Alan Howard.

1929

Three wins from 28 Championship matches was an increase of one from the previous summer but even so, the Welsh county sank back to the bottom of the championship table during a summer when the lack of regular captain proved to be a major handicap for Glamorgan at the end of their first decade as a first-class county.

Whilst Norman Riches and Johnnie Clay were the nominated captains for 1929, each were unable to play on several occasions with the upshot that Trevor Arnott, Guy Morgan and Aubrey Morgan also led the team at various times during the first three months of the summer. Finding a regular captain for 1930 was therefore at the top of the committee's agenda and, with Maurice Turnbull having graduated from Cambridge and capably led the university side, he was given a short trial as the Club's during August. He passed with flying colours and was appointed for the following year, by which time he had become the first Glamorgan player to appear in Test cricket .

Earlier in the year, the Glamorgan committee had also decided to allocate the match over the Whitsun Holiday against the South Africans to Pontypridd instead of the Arms Park. Their decision upset several senior figures in the Cardiff club, but the sizeable charges they levied in renting their facilities at the Arms Park to the county organization had been a source of frustration for the Glamorgan Treasurer for several years. With the eager officials at Pontypridd saying they would do all they could to promote the game, and charge Glamorgan very little for the use of Ynysangharad Park, the experiment got the green light.

Seating for 12,000 was duly installed with posters placed around Pontypridd and district promoting the match. However, only 4500 were present on the opening day with the entrance fee of two shillings – twice the normal admission – deterring many, who opted instead to find other vantage points around the Park from which to watch the action. There were also issues over the pitch preparations with seventeen

wickets tumbling on the first day for 272 runs after heavy rain had fallen the day before when the groundsman was putting the finishing touches to the surface.

Fortunately, the game went into a third day, but saw the Springboks record a facile victory. But the arguments over the admission charges and the lack of a regular captain, led to questions being asked about the way the Club was being run.

The Two Maurices – Messrs Allom (left) and Turnbull.

294
JONES, Wilfred Edward

Born – Pontardawe, 2 February 1912
Died – Ogwr, October 1992
Professional
LHB, SLA
1st XI: 1929-1933
Colts: 1928-1930
Club and Ground: 1928-1933
Cap: 1929
Clubs: Pontardawe, Neath

Batting and Fielding Record:

	M	I	NO	RUNS	AV	100	50	CT	ST
F-c	50	73	30	300	6.97	-	-	21	-

Bowling Record:

	Balls	M	R	W	AV	5wI	10wM
F-c	6122	202	2754	77	35.76	3	-

Career-bests:

First-class –   27 v Sussex at Cardiff Arms Park, 1931
        6/93 v New Zealanders at Cardiff Arms Park, 1931

Wilf Jones was a talented left-arm spin bowler who was on Glamorgan's staff between 1929 and 1933. He had first impressed as a spinner during the early years of the South Wales and Monmouthshire League, and duly appeared for Glamorgan's Colts side in 1928, as well as their Club and Ground side. Wilf made his debut against the 1929 Springboks at Pontypridd, and was initially Frank Ryan's understudy.

During 1931 Jones took a career-best 6/93 against the New Zealanders at the Arms Park, and subsequently got an extended run in the Glamorgan side after Frank had been released. However, Wilf subsequently lost form and confidence taking only 29 wickets, and no more five-fors during 1932.

A photograph of Wilf Jones taken during 1933.

He re-appeared in seven further matches during 1933 but Wilf continued to struggle, claiming only six wickets as preference was increasingly given to Emrys Davies' left-arm bowling. At the time, Glamorgan were also facing severe financial hardship and the county committee realized that they could not afford to have both Wilf and Emrys on their professional staff. With Emrys having cemented a place at the top of the order, and Wilf having modest abilities as a batsman, it was the latter who parted company Glamorgan.

He subsequently enjoyed a decent career as a professional with Pontardawe and Neath.

171

295
EVERY, Trevor

Born – Llanelli, 19 December 1909
Died – Newport, 20 January 1990
Professional
RHB, WK
Ed – Llanelli Boy's School
1st XI: 1929-1934
Colts: 1929
Club and Ground: 1929-1934
Cap: 1929
Clubs: Gowerton, Maesteg Town, Llanelli

Batting and Fielding Record:

	M	I	NO	RUNS	AV	100	50	CT	ST
F-c	128	198	44	25188	18.35	1	8	108	70

Bowling Record:

	Balls	M	R	W	AV	5wI	10wM
F-c	48	0	49	0	-	-	-

Career-best:
First-class – 116 v Worcestershire at Stourbridge, 1932

Trevor Every.

Had he not lost his sight and been forced into sudden and premature retirement, Trevor Every might have been one of the finest batsmen/wicket-keepers in the Club's history. During his short, six-year career in county cricket, Trevor claimed 108 catches, and 70 stumpings, with his record behind the stumps showing that he had an almost innate understanding with spinners Johnnie Clay and Frank Ryan.

On leaving school, Trevor had worked in the tinplate works at Llanelli, and had few thoughts of ever becoming a professional cricketer. The youngster had satisfied himself by keeping wicket cricket for Llanelli's second string in the South Wales and Monmouthshire League, but everything changed early in 1929 when Trevor got the chance to guest for Gowerton when they arrived at Stradey Park to play Llanelli without their regular keeper. He duly took two fine catches and made three smart stumpings, and, mindful that Joe Hills, Glamorgan's first-choice keeper had suffered an arm injury, some of Gowerton's professionals wrote to the county officials, suggesting that they have a look at the young wicket-keeper.

A few weeks later, a trial was arranged at the Arms Park, along with other young colts, in front of county coach Fred Bowley and several committeemen. Trevor was understandably quite nervous, but he had nothing to worry about as, at the end of the session, Fred walked up to him and said "Where have you been hiding?" The upshot was a two-year contract, and Trevor duly made his first-class debut later in the season, against Yorkshire at the Arms Park and displayed great skill and dexterity standing up to the wily spinners, nonchalantly taking each ball with the minimum of fuss. as Frank and Johnnie went through their repertoire of deliveries.

With Hills unable to continue behind the stumps, Trevor played in all of Glamorgan's Championship matches during 1930 and within a couple of years had over a hundred dismissals to his name. The fact that he had almost as many

Trevor Every seen in his full wicket-keeping kit.

stumpings as catches to his name bore testament to his dexterity and nimbleness behind the stumps, as it did to the canny skills of the county's spinners.

During 1932 another hundred came Trevor's way as he displayed his batting prowess by posting a match-saving century against Worcestershire at Stourbridge. Such a scenario had seemed highly unlikely as, at the start of the final day's play, Glamorgan were 188-6 and with Trevor at the crease alongside Arnold Dyson, they were staring defeat in the face. As he padded up on the pavilion balcony on the final morning Arnold turned to Trevor and said "Stay with me till I get a hundred and I'll give you ten bob." Several other members of the Glamorgan side overheard this, including Maurice Turnbull, so the skipper added "Score fifty Trevor, and I'll give you a decent bottle of champagne", whilst Jack Mercer chipped in "Do that and I'll give you fifty fags!"

Buoyed up by this friendly banter, Trevor duly helped Arnold to his century, before launching a counter-attack himself, unfurling some beautifully-timed cover drives, as well as a series of delicate cuts and glances off his legs. After nearly two and a half hours at the wicket, the dapper little wicket-keeper reached his maiden Championship century, much to the delight of his team-mates who were only too pleased to honour the wagers they had struck before play. Trevor was eventually dismissed for 116, and on returning to the dressing room, he found alongside his bags a pile of cigarettes from Jack, plus a case of champagne from Maurice. As Trevor unbuckled his pads, the Glamorgan captain walked over and said, "You've really earned this Trevor, and thank you very much."

By the end of 1933, Trevor's name had entered the notebooks of journalists and MCC selectors alike as he established himself as one of the best young keepers on the county circuit. Many good judges were forecasting a bright future for him, but during the pre-season nets in 1934, Trevor started to experience a few difficulties seeing the ball in flight. He initially put this down to a lack of concentration and being disturbed by the noise of traffic in the adjoining Westgate Street. But in the opening match of the season against Kent at the Arms Park, Trevor missed several balls whilst standing up to the stumps besides made several uncharacteristic fumbles as the ball came in from the fielders.

After play Jack spoke with Trevor about his poor day behind the stumps. "I think it's simply because I wasn't concentrating properly," said Trevor. But after being bowled for a duck the next morning, Jack spoke to him again at lunchtime and said "Trevor, I think you've got a problem – go and speak with the captain." Jack had already alerted Maurice about the situation and his concerns about Trevor's vision, so at the close of play the wicket-keeper went to see an eye specialist at Cardiff Infirmary. The doctor duly undertook several tests and then told the 24 year-old the awful news that his optic nerve was deteriorating, and that there was nothing that could be done for him.

Trevor remained in the infirmary overnight as further tests were undertaken. With the plucky keeper absent from the ground the following morning, Maurice gathered his team together in the Arms Park pavilion and quietly told them about the wicket-keeper's condition. "Let's raise some money to help our pal" was Jack's heartfelt response as the entire team agreed to immediately set up a fund to raise some cash for the popular wicket-keeper. He never set foot on the ground again as a player as Tom Brierley took over behind the stumps. The scorebook for the 2nd innings of the match with Kent simply records Trevor as being 'absent ill'.

Within a few weeks of the diagnosis, Trevor had completely lost his sight, but through the kindness of his colleagues, he was able to train as a stenographer with the RNIB in Cardiff and adjust to life as a blind person.

296
CREBER, Arthur Brynley

Born – Sketty, 11 October 1909
Died – Colwyn Bay, 10 August 1966
Professional
RHB, RM
1st XI: 1929
Scotland 1937
Clubs: Swansea, Llandudno, Longsight, Ferguslie, Heriot's FP

Batting and Fielding Record:

	M	I	NO	RUNS	AV	100	50	CT	ST
F-c	1	2	0	7	3.50	-	-	-	-

Career-best:
First-class –   4 v Leicestershire at Loughborough, 1929

Arthur Creber, was the son of Harry Creber, the long-serving Glamorgan professional and groundsman at St Helen's. Whereas his father was a left-arm spinner, Arthur was a right-arm seam bowler and a hard-hitting batsman. He made one appearance for Glamorgan, against Leicestershire at Loughborough in 1929 whilst attached to Llandudno, but his bowling skills were not called upon as Glamorgan subsided to an innings defeat with spinners Frank Ryan and Cyril Smart sharing eight wickets between them. Batting at number seven, Arthur made 4 and 3 as George Geary claimed ten wickets to hurry the Leicestershire side to victory inside two days.

Arthur subsequently left South Wales to play as a professional with the Longsight club in Manchester before joining Ferguslie in 1935. In August 1937 he re-appeared in first-class cricket, opening the bowling for the Scottish side against Yorkshire at Harrogate, and claiming the wicket of Arthur Mitchell. He also appeared in both of the Scots games that summer against Sir Julian Cahn's XI at Stanford Hall and West Bridgford, claiming three wickets and a pair of catches in the latter contest.

He joined the Anti-Aircraft Command in World War Two and featured in their cricket teams during 1943, playing against Northern Command at Sheffield and Blackpool, besides travelling to South Wales to feature in the match against a Glamorgan XI

Arthur Creber.

at Barry Island. The following year he played for an Anglo-Scottish XI against the British Empire XI at Kilmarnock whilst his last match of note came in 1945 as he featured in the Scottish Services side which met the Royal Australian Air Force at Selkirk.

Arthur and his wife Grace – whom he had married during 1935, plus their son Harry Valentine – remained north of the border after the War as he secured a post as groundsman and professional at George Heriot's School in Edinburgh. During the 1950s, he returned to North Wales having secured a similar post at Rydal School in Colwyn Bay.

RHYS, Hubert Ralph John ('Jack')

Born – Aberdare, 31 August 1897
Died – Llandaff, 18 March 1970
Amateur
RHB
Ed – Shrewsbury School
1st XI: 1929-1930
Cap: 1930
Free Foresters 1929
Clubs: Cardiff, St Fagans, MCC, Welsh Cygnets

Batting and Fielding Record:

	M	I	NO	RUNS	AV	100	50	CT	ST
F-c	7	13	1	147	12.25	-	-	5	-

Career-best:
First-class –   35 v Surrey at St Helen's, Swansea, 1930

Jack Rhys was a stockbroker from the City of London who played twice for Glamorgan in 1929, and five times during 1930 after impressing Maurice Turnbull by making a superb 149 for the Free Foresters against Cambridge University in June 1929.

His father, Watkin Llewellyn Rhys, was a GP in Aberdare with young Jack being sent to school at Shrewsbury. His free-flowing batting saw him win a place in the cricket XI during 1913 whilst he captained the side in 1915. He also captained the football and fives teams, besides being a gifted athlete, excelling in the half-mile as well as the sprints. On leaving Shrewsbury, Jack initially joined the Royal Horse Artillery before joining the Royal Garrison where he rose to the rank of Lieutenant.

When hostilities were over he moved to work in Cardiff, besides resuming his cricketing career with both Cardiff and St Fagans. In April 1920 he also married Ethel Violet, the daughter of Sidney Sweet-Escott, the Chairman elect of Brain's Brewery, who had played regularly for Glamorgan during the 1890s (Volume 1, p65-66).

Opportunities duly came Jack's way to work in the City of London so he and Ethel moved to south-east England, and for many years lived with their four children at Eltham in the Royal Borough of Greenwich. Whilst based in the Home Counties, Jack played for a number of cricket clubs, and wandering elevens, as well as for the MCC for whom he appeared against Ireland at Lord's during 1929.

That same year, he was chosen to bat at number four for the Free Foresters in their annual encounter with Cambridge University at Fenner's. With Maurice leading the Light Blues, the Welshman could not have picked a finer moment, or person, in front of whom to display his talents as a batsman, hitting a sublime 149 as he put to the sword a decent Cambridge attack. After play, Maurice sounded out the stockbroker about his availability to play for Glamorgan, with Jack agreeing to turn out during his holidays in August. Maurice duly passed out these messages to Johnnie Clay, who was sharing the captaincy duties that year with Norman Riches, and the upshot was that Jack made his Championship debut against Leicestershire at Pontypridd, batting at number seven, followed by playing in the match with Surrey at the Arms Park and appearing in the same slot.

With Glamorgan eager to promote home-grown talent, and save on their expenditure on professionals, Jack was duly sounded out over his availability in 1930 and, to the delight of Maurice, the stockbroker made himself available for selection during May, and June. During this short sabbatical from his work in the City, Jack made a fluent 35 in the match against Surrey at St Helen's, besides making 73 once again for the Free Foresters in their match against Cambridge University.

Jack also played for Wales against the MCC at Lord's in 1930, and batting at number three, he made 7 and 0 in what proved to be his final first-class match. He also turned out for Monmouthshire in 1934 in their Minor County Championship match with Berkshire at Rodney Parade but did not get a chance to bat as rain played havoc with the two-day contest.

During the Second World War, Jack served with the Royal Regiment of Artillery, before moving back to live in South Wales. His son Bill – who also attended Shrewsbury School – played with much success for St Fagans as well as for Glamorgan 2nd XI during 1948 and 1949, before working for Brain's Brewery and becoming the company Chairman from 1971 until 1989.

The Ynysangaharad Park cricket ground, where Jack Rhys made his Championship debut, as seen in 1925.

1930

1930 saw Glamorgan rise back up the table to 11th place after a couple of years in the doldrums. Five of their 28 Championship matches ended in victory, with a further fourteen games ending in a draw. There were just nine defeats during Maurice Turnbull's first summer in charge as the renaissance in Glamorgan's fortunes began under the Cardiff-born captain.

Although the first Championship win did not come until the first week of June, it was apparent to all that there was now a firm hand on the tiller. Right from the outset there was a buoyant and optimistic mood in the Glamorgan camp, as shown by the way Eddie Bates and Joe Hills posted forthright centuries against Surrey as the Welsh county posted 474 and all despite having only had one practice match before the start of the season and limited outdoor nets at the Arms Park.

The collective spirit was also evident at Worcester where Dai Davies, Trevor Every and Jack Mercer all defended stubbornly during the final day to help save a game where previous Glamorgan team's would have meekly folded. No longer was it a case of the Glamorgan side being a collection of individuals bereft of the essential team spirit. Instead, Maurice cultivated a sense of togetherness with his cheerful manner allowing less confident and more complex personalities, such as Frank Ryan, to return to decent form. Indeed, the spinner made a wonderful return to form in 1930 with 127 wickets at just 21 runs apiece, having claimed only 68 victims during 1929.

1930 therefore saw the start of the Welsh county's second decade in the world of first-class cricket and with Maurice at the helm, further progress was expected both in terms of results on the field and the Club's finances. Both duly came but only after many long hours of application on behalf of Glamorgan CCC.

A view of the St Helen's ground in Swansea during the 1930s.

BRAIN, Michael Benjamin

Born – Cyntwell, Cardiff, 13 April 1910
Died – Trelech, Monmouth, 24 August 1971
Amateur
RHB, WK
Ed – Repton School and Trinity College, Cambridge
1st XI: 1930
2nd XI: 1935-1947
Colts: 1925
Clubs: Cardiff, South Wales Hunts, Repton Pilgrims, Welsh Cygnets

Batting and Fielding Record:

	M	I	NO	RUNS	AV	100	50	CT	ST
F-c	1	2	0	9	4.50	-	-	-	-

Career-best:
First-class –   9 v Oxford University at The Parks, 1930

Michael Brain was the youngest son of Sam Brain, the outstanding Glamorgan wicket-keeper (Vol. 1, p.84-85) from their days as a Minor County and the younger brother of Pat Brain (Vol. 1, p.351-352). To their father's delight both maintained the family tradition by keeping wicket for the Welsh county, with Michael's sole appearance being in Glamorgan's contest in 1930 against Oxford University at The Parks

His selection for Glamorgan came whilst Michael was an undergraduate at Cambridge, having capably kept for Repton in 1928 and 1929. After coming down from Cambridge, he married Daphne Blanche Hoghton, the daughter of a London stockbroker, during the summer of 1935 before working for a while in the Home Counties. A career with the family business soon beckoned, with Michael serving as Chairman of Brain's Brewery from 1955 until his death during 1971.

Despite his business commitments, Michael took every opportunity to play cricket, turning out for Cardiff, the South Wales Hunts and the Repton Pilgrims, besides playing for Glamorgan 2nd XI in the Minor County Championship in 1935 and again in 1947, with the match against the counterparts from Worcestershire in the latter season at the Arms Park being his last match of note.

His son Chris followed in his father and grandfather's footsteps by keeping wicket for Cheltenham College and St Fagans, besides serving as Chairman of Brain's Brewery between 1989 and 2009, during which time he oversaw the move of the Brewery in 1999 from its traditional site in Cardiff off St Mary Street to the southern side of the Cardiff Central railway station on the site of the former Hancock's brewery, thereby allowing the redevelopment of The Old Brewery into the hugely popular Brewery Quarter, full of restaurants and bars, in the heart of the Welsh capital.

Michael Brain.

DUCKFIELD, Richard George ('Dick')

Born – Maesteg, 2 July 1907
Died – Bridgend, 30 December 1959
Professional
RHB, RM
1st XI: 1930-1945
2nd XI: 1926-1938
Cap: 1931
Players 1934
Clubs: Maesteg Town, NOR Llandarcy
Rugby for Maesteg

Batting and Fielding Record:

	M	I	NO	RUNS	AV	100	50	CT	ST
F-c	191	301	39	6894	26.31	9	37	26	-
Wartime	4	3	0	1	0.33	-	-	-	-

Bowling Record:

	Balls	M	R	W	AV	5wI	10wM
F-c	318	1	255	0	-	-	-

Career-best:
First-class – 280 v Surrey at The Oval, 1936

Dick Duckfield still holds the record for the most number of runs in a first-class match for Glamorgan having made 280* and 50* against Surrey at The Oval in 1936. At the time, his double-century was the highest individual innings in the club's history, and a very bright future was being predicted for the Maesteg-born batsman. Yet within two years, Dick had retired from the county game after a complete loss of confidence.

Dick had also been the first homegrown batsman to successfully emerge from the South Wales and Monmouthshire League, inaugurated in 1926. One of the aims of the new competition was to improve the standard of play, besides helping the Glamorgan selectors to identify new talent. As an eighteen year-old he had already played for Maesteg Town against the county's Club and Ground side in June 1925 and two years later, after some promising innings in the new League, he played against Glamorgan in a combined Maesteg Town and Celtic XI.

Various approaches were made to the young batsman over the course of the next few years to join the County's professional staff. At first, the terms were too modest for Dick to throw his lot in with Glamorgan, but an agreement

Dick Duckfield.

was duly reached for 1930 and later that August he made his debut, batting at number three, as the Welsh county visited Bramall Lane to play Yorkshire followed by the visit to Derby.

With Eddie Bates and John Bell being released, Dick got further opportunities in the next couple of years and, by 1932, the right-handed batsman had secured a regular place in the county's middle order. The following year he continued his development by scoring a thousand runs for the first time in his career, besides recording his maiden first-class hundred with 121 against Middlesex at Lord's.

His efforts also helped Glamorgan to save the game after following-on, with Dick sharing a stubborn fourth-wicket partnership of 146 with Dai Davies.

Two further hundreds followed in 1933 with Dick making 128* against Gloucestershire at the Wagonworks Ground as well as 100 against Leicestershire at the Arms Park. He consolidated on this headway in 1934 with a century against Cambridge University at Fenner's as well as an unbeaten 155 against Kent at Gravesend. Glamorgan lost the latter game but Dick's classical strokeplay and well-placed boundaries had impressed many influential people and journalists.

Given his good form, it came as no surprise when in mid-July Dick was chosen to represent the Players in their annual match against the Gentlemen at The Oval. He duly celebrated his selection by scoring an impressive 106 as the Players amassed 651-7 before twice dismissing the Gents and wrapping up an innings victory. With his name being mentioned in high circles, his form dipped in 1935 and despite further hundreds against Cambridge University and Hampshire – each at the Arms Park – he ended the season with a tally of just 895 runs.

He returned to form early in 1936 with half-centuries against Northamptonshire and Sir Julian Cahn's XI before making his record-breaking 280* against Surrey at The Oval. In all, he occupied the crease for five and a half hours and helped Glamorgan to their best ever total of 550-6. It looked as if the 28 year old

An image of Dick Duckfield taken at the Arms Park during 1935.

181

from Maesteg had turned the corner, and was poised for further success. But once again, he lost form and, in the course of his next 28 innings, only passed fifty on three occasions. Maurice Turnbull tried to help by steadfastly continuing to select Dick in the belief that he would come out of his slough of form, and that dropping him would only do more harm than good. But none of this worked and, after eight single figure scores in August, Maurice reluctantly dropped the despondent batsman who like his angry captain, had been upset by taunts of "Here comes Dick Duck" from opposing players when the out-of-form batsman made his way to the middle.

He worked steadfastly in the nets at the Arms Park over the winter months and his efforts appeared to have paid off as, in the fourth game of the summer, he made 101 against the 1937 New Zealanders at the Arms Park and helped the Welsh county to a six-wicket victory. By the end of the season, he passed a thousand runs again and had added nine half-centuries to his tally, but a new problem started to emerge as he made a series of fielding blunders and dropped a couple of catches.

Things had got worse by 1938 as Dick completely lost confidence in the field, and developed a psychological inability to catch a ball. His blunders in the field during the previous summer had weighed on his mind over the winter months, and by early 1938 they were affecting his batting as well as he lost form again and only passed fifty on two occasions. It did not help that his contract was up for review at the end of the summer, and things reached a head when Dick approached Maurice, asking not to field in any position where his problems might be exposed. Maurice responded with some honest and frank advice, in an attempt to boost his colleague's confidence, and arranged for him to have extra catching practice with Bill Hitch on day's off behind closed doors at the Arms Park. After these sessions with the Club's coach, Maurice chose Dick for the closing games of the summer against Sussex at Eastbourne and Essex at Clacton-on-Sea, hoping that the less-pressured atmosphere at these Festival grounds, plus the seaside air, would provide the tonic which Dick needed.

Despite Maurice's encouragement, Dick completely went to pieces again in the field, and was a shadow of his former self with bat in hand. He ended the season with just 462 runs in his 16 appearances and, after the Glamorgan captain had taken medical advice, it was with a heavy heart that he told Dick that he would not be offered terms for 1939.

He returned to club cricket and also featured during 1944 in a number of Glamorgan's wartime friendlies, playing against the British Empire XI at the Arms Park, the West of England at Clifton College, Western Command at Pontypridd and Sir Learie Constantine's West Indian XI at Barry Island. After the war he also ran a sports shop in Maesteg. In his youth, he had played rugby as a strong-running centre three-quarter for Maesteg Harlequins and Maesteg RFC.

1931

The summer of 1931 began with Glamorgan recording a stirring 161-run victory over Warwickshire at Edgbaston, but only three of the remaining 27 Championship encounters ended in victory for Maurice Turnbull and his team. His side had to wait until 21 July for their next victory as Worcestershire were defeated at Pontypridd by seven wickets. Another victory soon followed at Cowbridge as the inaugural game at the ground in the Vale of Glamorgan resulted in a controversial five-wicket win for the Welsh county.

The following week, Surrey were also beaten in a rain-affected match at the Arms Park with Viv Jenkins, the Welsh rugby international playing a match-winning role with the bat as the South London outfit were defeated by three wickets. As far as the team based to the north of the River Thames was concerned, 1931 was an important year as Middlesex had eventually agreed to fixtures with the Welsh county after refusing previous requests during the 1920s. The inaugural match at Lord's however saw Middlesex win by 135 runs but the return encounter at Swansea ended in a draw.

1931 was a landmark season as well for the Welsh county in that the match against Northamptonshire at Kettering during June saw Glamorgan field an all-professional eleven for the first time in their history, with Eddie Bates in charge as neither Maurice Turnbull or Johnnie Clay were unavailable.

The two amateurs though had plenty on their minds at

Their innings were over – Frank Ryan (left) walks off with John Bell at the Arms Park during 1926. Both were released as cost-saving measures by the Club at the end of 1931.

the end of the summer, not least the Club's rising deficit which now stood at £4,271 and, with falling gate receipts, yet another cost-saving exercise was undertaken with professionals Eddie Bates, Frank Ryan, John Bell and Joe Hills all being told they would not be re-engaged for the following summer.

300
JENKINS, Vivian Gordon James

Born – Port Talbot, 2 November 1911
Died – Harpenden, 5 January 2004
Amateur
RHB, RM, occ WK
Ed – Llandovery College and Jesus College, Oxford
1st XI: 1931-1937
Colts: 1925-1930
Club and Ground: 1930-1934
Cap: 1931
Oxford University 1933 (Blue)
Clubs: Cardiff, Bridgend, Optimists, Stanmore
Rugby for Wales (14 caps), Cardiff, Bridgend, London Welsh, Dover, Kent
and the Barbarians

Batting and Fielding Record:

	M	I	NO	RUNS	AV	100	50	CT	ST
F-c	44	69	9	1072	17.87	-	3	10	7

Bowling Record:

	Balls	M	R	W	AV	5wI	10wM
F-c	61	0	54	2	27.00	-	-

Career-bests:
First-class –   65 v Surrey at The Oval, 1932
                1/13 v Surrey at The Oval, 1932

Viv Jenkins was one of the true all-round sporting
gentlemen of the 1930s. Besides batting, bowling and
keeping wicket for Glamorgan, Viv won a Double Blue at
Oxford, played club rugby for Cardiff, Bridgend, London
Welsh, Dover, Kent and the Barbarians, won 14 Welsh
rugby caps as full back between 1932 and 1938, and toured
South Africa as the vice-captain of the British Lions party
in 1938.

His father Thomas Gordon Jenkins was an elementary
school teacher, initially in Port Talbot before securing a
headship in Neath. He grew up near the Aberavon RFC
ground and, as a young boy, Viv used to crawl through
the club's perimeter fence to catch a glimpse of the town's
rugby side. His life-long love-affair with sport was further
fuelled at Llandovery College where he played with great
success for the College's 1st rugby XV and 1st cricket XI
between 1925 and 1929.

*Viv Jenkins, seen whilst coaching
at Dover College.*

The College magazine in 1926 described the youngsters cricketing talents as follows – that summer he played "an excellent bat with every stroke. Always consistent. Should became very dangerous in a couple of years." No surprise that by the time he went up to read Classics at Jesus College, Oxford, Viv had already impressed whilst playing for the Glamorgan Colts. In 1931 when Trevor Every was injured, Viv was called up to make his Championship debut against Middlesex at Swansea. In his second appearance for Glamorgan, against Worcestershire at Pontypridd, the Oxford undergraduate pulled off three sharp stumpings as the visiting batsmen struggled against the clever spin of Johnnie Clay and Frank Ryan.

Viv also batted with confidence making an unbeaten 27 on his Championship debut and retained his place in the side when Trevor regained fitness. Later that summer he played a match-winning innings in the rain-affected match with Surrey at Cardiff as Glamorgan chased 215 runs to win in 165 minutes. With the Arms Park scoreboard on 146-6, a Surrey victory looked a formality, but Viv – showing no sign of nerves against his far more experienced opponents – played a series of forcing strokes, with his unbeaten 40 seeing Glamorgan home by three wickets with just minutes to spare.

It was a measure of the strength of university cricket at the time that Viv did not make the Oxford XI again in 1932 but he played in thirteen further games for Glamorgan and in the match at The Oval treated the Surrey bowlers with disdain once again as he made his Championship best score of 65 and shared in a fifth wicket stand of 172 with opening batsman Arnold Dyson. Just for good measure, he also claimed the wicket of Percy Fender in the closing over of what had become, largely through their doughty stand, a drawn game.

Viv did make the Oxford XI in 1933 having been called up at the eleventh hour to keep wicket in the Varsity Match. His defensive batting on the final day of a rain-affected match earned Oxford a draw besides allowing Viv to add a cricket Blue to the ones he had won at rugby. He also left Oxford having never been on a losing XV in the Varsity Match.

After coming down, he became a Classics and Games teacher at Dover College in Kent, and only played for Glamorgan during his school holidays in 1934. Two further appearances took place during 1936 with his final appearance for the Welsh county coming in the match against Surrey at Neath in 1937. Given his previous form against the South London club, his father gleefully attended the game at The

A photograph of Viv Jenkins, seen in his cricket whites in 1933.

Gnoll, just a short distance away from where he was now a Headmaster, hoping to see his talented son put the Englishmen to the sword. But there was only play on one day as the game became a rather soggy end to Viv's career as a county cricketer.

Fortunately, Viv's father had plenty to smile about when watching his gifted son play rugby having won fourteen caps for Wales, all at full-back. He featured, alongside Maurice

Turnbull, Wilf Wooller and Ronnie Boon in Wales's first-ever victory over England at Twickenham in 1933, and was also in the Welsh XV which secured the famous triumph over the All Blacks in 1935 at Cardiff. His two conversions and a heroic try-saving race against Kiwi winger George Hart helped Wales to a 13-12 victory against New Zealand, and "by that lovely point," Arthur Rees, the Welsh pack-leader and his lifelong friend since schooldays, used to say. Viv always maintained that it was the most nerve-wracking sporting contest in which he had ever taken part.

Viv went on to become the leading full-back of the day, noted not just for his kicking and defensive qualities but also for his flair for attack, the legacy of his days at Llandovery College as a centre. Indeed, in 1934 Viv became the first-ever Welsh full-back to score a try in an international, achieving the feat against Ireland at St Helen's, and just a few yards away from where he had made his Glamorgan debut.

In 1938 he won selection as vice-captain of the British Lions tour to South Africa. Unfortunately, he was hampered by hamstring trouble whilst in the Cape, but in his only Test, at Ellis Park, Johannesburg, he kicked a prodigious penalty goal from eight yards inside his own half of the field. For many years the eight-panelled leather ball from that match had pride of place among the hats and brollies in the porch of his Hertfordshire home – a talking point for new visitors or old playing colleagues.

His last Welsh cap came against England at Twickenham in 1939, with Viv retiring after the game, aged just 27, and eager to carve out a new career. He briefly worked in the City with the Land Law Company before joining the Territorial Army and serving in the anti-aircraft command. He still found time though to feature in a number of rugby and cricket matches, including the match in February 1940 when he kicked six conversions as the British Army beat France 36-3 at Parc des Princes. As far as cricket was concerned he played for The Army against Oxford University in 1942 as well as the Metropolitan Police the following year.

When hostilities were over, Viv became a sports journalist with *The News of the World*. In later years Viv, who was a great raconteur, would regale his colleagues in the Press Room with tales of his early adventures as a journalist, including his journey to cover Wally Hammond's England tour of Australia in 1946/47. While the tour party and officials travelled by steamship, Viv went out by flying boat, dressing for dinner each night and going ashore at exotic venues such as Rome, Cairo and Singapore. His trip was also enlivened by a group of female dancers and mannequins who were making their way to Sydney – even fifty years after his escapades, the memories of this visit still brought an impish glint to Viv's eyes.

During the early 1950s, Viv joined the *Sunday Times* as its chief rugby writer; and remained in this position until retiring in 1976, having been on every Lions and Welsh overseas tour. By his own admission, he must have set the world record for attending rugby dinners and parties – the only one he reckoned he missed was the traditional Twickenham post-match banquet after his first cap in 1933, when he had to retire to his bed with a 100-plus temperature and was in hospital for the next five days. As his good friend JBG Thomas recalled, "He partied hard. His stamina was legendary. On tour, he was the last to his bed and the first to rise. You could judge how boisterous the evening had been by the size of the flowers he dispatched the following morning. He always apologized in style."

Viv also edited *Rothmans Rugby Annual* and did a stint as chairman of the Rugby Union Writers' Club. At the time of his death, he served as President of Glamorgan's Former Players' Association. His wife, Sue, the niece of the former Richmond and England forward George Fraser, died in 1984 and

Viv Jenkins (right), with cravat, reminiscences on the victory by the Welsh rugby team over New Zealand in 1935 with Wilf Wooller (left) and former All Black Jack Manchester.

thereafter he divided his time between the two Hemispheres having become the companion at her Queenstown home of Elinor Stewart, the widow of former All Black Ron Stewart who had toured Britain and South Africa with the New Zealand teams of the 1920s.

301
BOON, Ronald Winston

Born – Barry, 11 June 1909
Died – Waipukurau, Hawke's Bay, New Zealand, 4 August 1998
Amateur
RHB, RM
Ed – Barry Grammar School ; Trinity College, Carmarthen and Dunfermline College of Physical Education
1st XI: 1931-1932
Colts: 1929
Cap: 1932
Clubs: Barry, Cardiff, XL Club
Rugby for Wales (12 caps), Cardiff, London Welsh, Ayr, Dunfermline, New Brighton and the Barbarians

Batting and Fielding Record:

	M	I	NO	RUNS	AV	100	50	CT	ST
F-c	11	19	2	229	13.47	-	-	4	-

Bowling Record:

	Balls	M	R	W	AV	5wI	10wM
F-c	60	0	40	0	-	-	-

Career-best:
First-class – 33 v Surrey at The Oval, 1932

Ronnie Boon was another sportsman for all seasons, excelling in team games as well as individual events in both summer and winter. During his illustrious career, he was a Welsh champion sprinter, a county cricketer with Glamorgan, and a Welsh rugby international. Indeed, it was in the red rugby jersey that Ronnie's finest sporting moment came as, during January 1933, the winger helped to lay to rest the Twickenham 'bogey', by scoring all of Wales' points – with a try and a drop-goal – in their first ever victory in a rugby international at England's headquarters.

The dapper Boon had a fine record for Cardiff RFC, scoring seventy-six tries in ninety-eight games, playing mainly on the wing, but he had such outstanding ball-handling abilities and running skills that he could play anywhere in the three-quarter line, or even at stand-off, as he did in the late 1930s for New Brighton.

His sporting prowess was evident from an early age, as he represented Welsh Secondary Schools at both rugby and cricket, besides winning junior honours in athletics before winning, at the age of twenty the 220 yards in the Welsh Amateur Athletic Association's championships. He subsequently played cricket for both Barry and Cardiff, besides winning selection for the county's Colts side in 1929. His lightning-fast speed over the ground, and swift throwing, as much as his capabilities as a batsman, were responsible

Ronnie Boon, seen during 1931.

for his selection by Glamorgan in 1931 – a time when the county fielded several plump amateurs who, whilst worth their place as strong-armed batsmen, were something of a liability in the field.

The fleet-of-foot youngster made his Glamorgan debut against Gloucestershire at the Arms Park, and compiled an assured 23 before making 24 and 22* against Nottinghamshire. Soon after, Ronnie completed his training as a games teacher and moved to Scotland, but Maurice Turnbull remained in touch with the gifted athlete, and persuaded him to play for Glamorgan during his school holidays during July and August 1932. Ronnie played in a further nine matches, including the contest with Surrey at The Oval where, batting at number nine, he made a sparkling 33 and revealed some deft footwork as he advanced down the wicket to the leg-spin of Percy Fender.

The rugby selectors from Cardiff and Wales also persuaded Ronnie to travel south from his base in Dunfermline to turn out for club and country and, after events at Twickenham, and Wales' inaugural win, in January 1933, Welsh rugby fans were eternally grateful for his willingness to regularly return home.

Ronnie continued to teach in Scotland until 1938, before moving to work in London, Cornwall and Denbighshire. He also participated in fund-raising cricket matches during the Second World War, appearing for Denis Compton's XI in 1943, besides playing for Sussex in friendlies in 1944 and 1945. He subsequently became an Inspector of Schools, and also secretary of London Welsh RFC. between 1961 and 1969, before returning to his native south Wales, where he was Chairman of the South Glamorgan Education Committee. He emigrated to New Zealand with his daughter during 1995 but three years later Ronnie died at his new home near Hawkes Bay.

302
WILLIAMS, Ieuan

Born – Brynamman, 17 March 1909
Died – Eastbourne, 3 March 1964
Amateur
Ed – Liverpool University
RHB, occ WK
1st XI: 1931
Club: Glanamman

Batting and Fielding Record:

	M	I	NO	RUNS	AV	100	50	CT	ST
F-c	2	4	0	10	2.50	-	-	-	-

Career-best:
First-class –   7 v Gloucestershire at Cheltenham College, 1931

Ieuan Williams was a 22 year-old dental student at Liverpool University who played twice for the cash-strapped Glamorgan during 1931 as the Welsh county's selectors blooded a number of young and homegrown amateurs rather than spending what little cash they had on aged and over the hill professionals from England.

The student had impressed in club cricket in his native Carmarthenshire as well as at Liverpool University, and after further impressing Maurice Turnbull during a Colts Trial, Ieuan was called up to make his first-class debut against Gloucestershire. Batting at number five, he made 1 and 7 and kept his place for the friendly against Nottinghamshire at Swansea where he met with less success, scoring a single in each innings.

Ieuan was also a capable wicket-keeper and, with the Club looking for an understudy to Trevor Every, this was another reason behind his sudden elevation into the world of professional cricket. However, the acquisition of Tom Brierley, plus the emergence of fellow West Walian Haydn Davies meant that Ieuan was not called up again. After qualifying as a dentist in 1935, Ieuan worked in practices in his native Glanamman, as well as in Bridgend, Chester, London and Poole.

During the Second World War, Ieuan worked as an Army Dentist besides playing in some of the fund-raising games involving service teams. In 1943 he kept wicket for The Army which played a Glamorgan XI at the Arms Park, before appearing the following year for the United Services against the West of England at Clifton College.

303
BRIERLEY, Thomas Leslie

Born – Southampton, 15 June 1910
Died – Victoria, British Columbia, 7 January 1989
Professional
RHB, WK
Ed – Manchester Grammar School
1st XI: 1931-1939
Colts: 1931-193
Club and Ground: 1932-1933
Cap: 1933
Lancashire 1942-1948, British Empire XI 1942; North 1942-1944; South 1942;
Combined Counties 1942-1943; Cheshire 1942; The Rest 1943; England XI 1943;
Hampshire XI 1945; British Columbia 1949-1952; Canada 1951-1954
Clubs: Cheadle, Urmston, Barry, Manchester, Vancouver, Cowichan

Batting and Fielding Record:

	M	I	NO	RUNS	AV	100	50	CT	ST
F-c	181	292	25	4760	17.82	3	20	153	72

Bowling Record:

	Overs	M	R	W	AV	5wI	10wM
F-c	38	0	33	0	-	-	-

Career-best:
First-class –   116 v Lancashire at Old Trafford, 1938

Tom Brierley was Glamorgan's first-ever player to appear in Championship cricket as well as the Olympic Games. He was also one of the few players from the inter-war era to secure a contract with another English county as, after playing for the Welsh county from 1931 until 1939, he joined Lancashire after the Second World War.

Tom Brierley.

Tom joined the Glamorgan staff in 1931 as a specialist batsman after success as a young cricketer growing up in the Whalley Range area of Manchester. His father had been a naval officer based in Romsey so having been born in Hampshire, Tom had to spend two years qualifying for the Welsh county. Even so, he was still able to play in their non-Championship friendly against Nottinghamshire in August 1931, and kept wicket because Trevor Every was indisposed with a minor ailment. He also played in 1932 against the Indians.

During 1932 Tom was also given three weeks of leave in order to appear for Canada in the Olympic

Games in Los Angeles where lacrosse was one of the demonstration sports. He had spent the past few years playing and coaching cricket in Canada, besides learning the rudiments of lacrosse. Although cricket was his number one sport, the chance to appear in the 1932 Olympics was a once in a lifetime opportunity for the Southampton-born cricketer, and he was very grateful that Maurice Turnbull and the Glamorgan management agreed to his request. Playing in front of 75,000 people at the Los Angeles Memorial Coliseum proved to be a very different experience for Tom than appearing in front of a few thousand supporters at the Arms Park, or barely a hundred at a club ground in South Wales.

In May 1933 Tom made his Championship debut against Essex, and later in the summer he also recorded his maiden half-century against Worcestershire. In 1934 Brierley got a chance to secure a regular place in the Welsh county's line-up but only after Trevor Every, the county's brilliant young wicket-keeper, tragically lost his sight. Having experience behind the stumps in the Lancashire Leagues, Tom duly took over behind the stumps, and it was a measure of his abilities that he retained the position for the next four years, until handing over the gloves to Haydn Davies during 1938. With a century to his name the year before against Sussex at Hastings, Tom duly retained is place in the Glamorgan line-up as a specialist batsman.

In 1938 he made a career-best 116 against Lancashire at Old Trafford, before adding a third century to his tally the following year with 113 against Nottinghamshire at Swansea. During the Second World War, he played for a number of Service teams and other scratch elevens.

In 1946 Tom decided to join Lancashire, largely as a result of the possibility of a coaching position at Old Trafford. He made his first appearance for the Red Rose county during 1945 in their friendly against the Royal Australian Air Force. A further 45 appearances followed over the course of the next three years, with Tom making an unbeaten 116 for his new county, ironically against Glamorgan at Liverpool in 1947, giving him another unique distinction of having posted his career-best scores both for, and against, Glamorgan.

At the end of the 1948 season, Tom decided to emigrate to Canada to become coach to the British Columbia Mainland Cricket League, which was based in Vancouver. In addition, he served as a parks supervisor with a focus on developing cricket grounds.

An image of Tom Brierley taken during 1939.

He subsequently played for British Columbia besides, in 1951, making his debut for Canada against the MCC and the following year, appearing in their annual encounter against the United States. In 1954, the 44 year-old was a member of the Canadian side that toured the UK, with Tom appearing in their side that played against the Pakistani's. His final first-class appearance came at Lord's during September 1954 as he played for Canada against Middlesex.

At the end of the tour, he remained in the UK after securing a post in Birmingham as a cricket coach and groundsman, before returning to Canada in 1959 to take up a post as cricket coach and economics teacher at Shawnigan Lake School on Vancouver Island. He subsequently

Tom Brierley enjoys a rest after play against Somerset at Weston-super-Mare.

played club cricket for Cowichan CC in the Victoria and District League until 1970 before acting as their umpire and overseeing the creation of a new ground. During the 1960s he also organised summer cricket schools for youngsters in British Columbia and Alberta, and was regarded as one of the leading coaches in Canada.

A cigarette card from 1932 showing Tom's colleagues in the Glamorgan squad.

1932

Another difficult summer, both on and off the field, for the Welsh county who continued to languish in the lower echelons of the Championship table, securing just three wins from their 28 games in the three-day competition. Two of these victories came in low-scoring games at Cowbridge, with the first in early June against Leicestershire with the visitor's losing by an innings as Jack Mercer and Johnnie Clay fully exploited a worn surface.

The second came against Somerset during July after torrential rain on the Sunday and first thing on Monday morning, made batting a lottery with the West Country side dismissed for 88 and 40. But the mopping up operations by the enthusiastic locals and Glamorgan groundstaff had damaged the surface of the pitch. Not surprisingly, the umpires were pretty damming in their post-match report and later in the season the MCC informed Maurice Turnbull, the Glamorgan secretary that they did not believe that Cowbridge should be allocated further matches.

Earlier in the year, Maurice had received far happier news from the corridors of power at Lord's as the 1932 Test Trial was allocated to the Arms Park. The influential Glamorgan leader had reasoned that the presence of the country's top names would lead to a bumper crowd and a healthy profit. But the weather gods were not shining on the daffodil county as play was restricted by rain to just three hours on the opening day, and nothing else on days two and three. The game therefore did not help to reduce the Club's deficit.

The autographs of the Glamorgan players who played Kent at Canterbury during 1932.

304
DAVIES, Gwynfor

Born – Sandy, Carmarthenshire, 12 August 1908
Died – Llanelli, 10 March 1972
Professional
RHB, RM
Ed – Pentip Church of England School
1st XI – 1932
2nd XI – 1936-1937
Club and Ground: 1930-1934
Cap: 1932
Club: Llanelli

Batting and Fielding Record:

	M	I	NO	RUNS	AV	100	50	CT	ST
F-c	7	9	1	77	9.62	-	-	2	-

Bowling Record:

	Balls	M	R	W	AV	5wI	10wM
F-c	312	15	134	3	44.67	-	-

Career-bests:
First-class –   44 v Surrey at St Helen's, Swansea, 1932
2/18 v Surrey at St Helen's, Swansea, 1932

Gwyn was the younger brother of Emrys Davies and a decent all-rounder in his own right who spent a year on the Glamorgan staff in 1932 during which time he played in seven matches during May and June.

Gwyn had followed his elder brother into the Llanelli side during the mid-1920s and after some decent performances with bat and ball, he played against Gowerton for the Glamorgan Club and Ground side in June 1930. He got further opportunities the following year, and in May 1931 against Hill's Plymouth he claimed three wickets with his off-cutters with one of the Merthyr batsmen being caught by Emrys.

He agreed terms as a junior professional for 1932 and in May he made his first-class debut against Lancashire at Blackburn. The match was decimated by the weather with Gwyn not having a chance to bat or bowl. The rains seemed to be following him around as his next appearance ten days later against Warwickshire at Pontypridd saw the young all-rounder participate in another watery draw, but at least he got a chance to bat, at number eleven, and was unbeaten on one.

He met with better luck the following week at Swansea when Surrey were the visitors. He began by claiming a couple of wickets, before featuring in a spirited last wicket stand of 99 with Dick Duckfield after Glamorgan had nosedived to 57-9. His partner made an unbeaten 62 whilst he scored a career-best 44, containing some flowing drives and fierce cuts against the more experienced attack. Gwyn then returned figures of 7-4-5-1 in Surrey's second innings and kept his place in the side for the next month.

Gwyn's doughty efforts with the bat at Swansea also saw him undertake the role of night-watchman in both innings against Essex at the Arms Park, as well as the match with Leicestershire at Aylestone Road. The latter though proved to be his final first-class appearance. With Glamorgan lacking pace and penetration in their bowling options, the Club's selectors gave Ted Glover and subsequently Harold Dickinson extended opportunities.

Gwyn left the Glamorgan staff at the end of the season and trained as an electrical linesman. In September 1933 he also married Jean Gay. Gwyn continued to play with good effect for Llanelli besides appearing for Glamorgan 2nd XI in their Minor County Championship fixtures during 1936 against Middlesex at Finchley and Cheshire at Neston, as well as the visit to Finchley once again the following year.

Gwyn Davies seen with his wife Jean.

305
GLOVER, Edward Robert Kenneth ('Ted')

Born – Worcester, 19 July 1911
Died – Cardiff, 23 March 1967
Amateur
RHB, RFM
Ed – Sherborne School
1st XI: 1932-1938
Club and Ground: 1930-1937, 1947
Cap: 1933
Clubs: Cardiff, Welsh Cygnets
Rugby for Glamorgan Wanderers

Batting and Fielding Record:

	M	I	NO	RUNS	AV	100	50	CT	ST
F-c	47	73	23	406	8.12	-	1	18	-

Bowling Record:

	Overs	M	R	W	AV	5wI	10wM
F-c	7247	175	4284	118	36.30	3	-

Career-bests:

First-class –   62 v Somerset at Downside School, 1934
                 5/79 v Northamptonshire at Kettering, 1935

Ted Glover was a popular all-round sportsman during the 1930s, playing cricket for Glamorgan CCC and rugby for Glamorgan Wanderers RFC. In later years, he became an influential sports journalist and, after retiring from county cricket, he helped to promote the game in the post-war era by editing *The South Wales Cricketers' Magazine.*

Educated at Sherborne School, Ted had shown rich promise as a schoolboy cricketer and in 1929 he was chosen to play for the Lord's Schools against The Rest. With Glamorgan searching for new home-grown talent, it was no surprise that shortly after leaving school in 1930 Ted was invited to play for the county's Club and Ground XI. Some useful spells of fast-medium bowling for Cardiff, allied to some bold innings, full of assertive strokeplay saw Ted make his first-class debut for Glamorgan in 1932 against the Indians at Cardiff Arms Park.

Ted Glover seen on his Glamorgan debut during 1932.

He played more frequently during 1933 and took part in some moments of light relief with his rugby-playing friend Viv Jenkins, most notably with a sign saying 'Wanted – a Respectable Girl'. They had first spied the sign in the window of a newspaper shop in Hinckley when popping in for newspapers and cigarettes before play. On leaving the small shop, Glover discretely filched the sign, which he duly gave a border of sticking tape.

The fun with the sign then started as the pair of amateurs placed it gently on the back of Harry Ditton, the cricket correspondent of the *Western Mail*. Harry spent the day with the card on his back, and several times walked around the ground, blissfully unaware of what was causing the crowd to smile and laugh. At the close of play, Ted and Viv recovered the notice from Harry's jacket, with the cricket writer thankfully seeing the funny side of the prank.

The sign was subsequently place in the windows of railway carriages and dining saloons as the happy band of Glamorgan cricketers made their way to Clacton for the game against Essex. It came during the festival week at the seaside ground, and when many of the celebrities and entertainers from the theatres took the opportunity of dropping in to watch some cricket during the afternoon sessions. One of the star attractions at the resort was Billy Merson and his troupe of dancing girls, so after a visit on the Saturday afternoon by one of Merson's colleagues, the Glamorgan team were given free tickets to the evening performance, plus a special invitation to an after-show party.

But before all of this, the pair, plus their good friend Maurice Turnbull had a dinner engagement with the Essex captain and various dignitaries from the Clacton club. The three Glamorgan amateurs duly socialised with these officials before heading off, admittedly quite well-oiled to meet up with the rest of the team at the theatre where Merson and the troupe were appearing. They arrived with their naughty notice just in time before the dancers made their appearance on stage, with Ted making a most dramatic entrance. He ran down the central aisle and, as he placed the sign on the apron of the stage, a loud cheer rang out from the Glamorgan contingent, gleefully sitting and also well lubricated in their free seats. Various stagehands, thinking that Ted was going to accost the dancing girls, swiftly ushered him back to his seat, and the performance went on, much to the pleasure of all the Glamorgan side.

The highlight though was meeting the troupe and the other performers in the backstage party with the singing and revelry going on long into the night. Despite all of the merriment, Ted remembered to recover his sign from the stage before they left the theatre it duly appeared again in railway carriages as the team headed north for their next match against Yorkshire at Scarborough. However, Maurice had to step in to end the jokes as things went a little bit too far after Ted and Viv attached the sign to the back of umpire John King as the elderly official was walking out from the pavilion. John was one of the oldest umpires on the circuit, and there were many smiles on the faces of the players and the crowd as he spent the entire session with the sign on his back.

But Maurice felt that things had gone too far by making one of the senior umpires should have been made a laughing stock and, after the various episodes

Ted Glover seen at Cardiff Arms Park during 1936.

following the so-called "illegal" declarations at Cowbridge in 1931 and 1932, he did not want to get into more hot water with the MCC authorities. He duly spoke to Ted and Viv after play and said "A joke's a joke boys but I think that this one has gone far enough." The pair agreed and duly disposed of the sign.

The incident was never raised again at a cricket ground, but Maurice did – in most jocular terms and with a little bit of elaboration – recall these events a couple of years later when speaking at the marriage of Ted to his sister Ever. "He's most definitely found a respectable girl," said the Glamorgan captain before toasting the newlyweds with a glass of his favourite champagne. Ted and Maurice remained close friends throughout the 1930s and shared an insurance brokerage at Cardiff Docks, with their office based at the Coal Exchange in Mount Stuart Square. He also deputised on two occasions for his brother-in-law as Glamorgan's captain – against Sussex at Hove in 1936 and Cambridge University at Swansea during 1938.

When War was declared Ted joined the RAF and was posted to the South coast. This explains his appearance for Billy Griffiths' XI against Kent in 1941 as well as for the Anti-Aircraft Command during various fund-raising matches two years later. After the War and the tragic death of his good friend, Ted became a journalist, writing on rugby and cricket for both the *South Wales Echo* and the *Western Mail*.

Bowled! Ted Glover loses his middle stump whilst batting in a County Championship match for Glamorgan.

With the encouragement of Wilf Wooller, another of his rugby-playing friends, Ted also did his bit to help promote club cricket in South Wales and to continue the good work of his late brother-in-law by helping to edit *The South Wales Cricketers' Magazine*, besides writing a series of articles giving coaching advice to young cricketers.

306
HARRIS, George Joseph

Born – Underwood, Notts, 22 January 1904
Died – Swansea, 28 December 1998
Professional
RHB, RM
1st XI: 1932
Club and Ground: 1945
Clubs: Swansea, Briton Ferry Town

Batting and Fielding Record:

	M	I	NO	RUNS	AV	100	50	CT	ST
F-c	1	1	0	0	-	-	-	1	-

George Harris was the younger brother of Charlie Harris, the famous Nottinghamshire batsman, with George making a solitary appearance for Glamorgan during 1932. It was an inauspicious debut as he was bowled by Freddie Brown for nought in what proved to be his only appearance at first-class level.

He had spent time during the mid-1920s on the Trent Bridge groundstaff, during which time George mixed cricket for Nottinghamshire 2nd XI with playing football as a goal-keeper, initially for Netherfield Rovers before joining Mansfield Town, for whom he made five League appearances during the 1925/1926 season when the team finished second in the Midland Counties League.

George's sporting career then saw him spend time in Northern Ireland playing for various football teams as well as cricket for North Down. During the early 1930's George joined Swansea Town as their reserve goalkeeper, with his move to South Wales resulting in him playing cricket for both Briton Ferry Town and Swansea. Some good scores in League matches led to his call-up for the match with Surrey when Glamorgan found themselves short of a batsman on the eve of the game.

As a contemporary recalled, "he was tall, fair, slim and graceful with his methods smacking of the perfect wickets he had been accustomed to at Trent Bridge. His cover and off-driving were models of perfection." In June 1931 when Nottinghamshire were playing at St Helens, he invited his former team-mates on the Sunday to afternoon tea at his home in Briton Ferry and to meet his fiancée. The arrival of the famous cricketers caused something of a stir amongst the neighbours and it was not long before some were playing cricket with the professionals on the lawn of George's home.

He remained in South Wales for the rest of his life and, after retiring from professional sport, George joined the South Wales Constabulary. He also played for Glamorgan in their fund-raising friendly in 1945 against the Swansea Central League. In later life, he was also a noted breeder of bantam chicks.

George Harris takes guard at St Helen's in Swansea.

307
TAYLOR, Henry Thomas ('Tom')

Born – Cardiff, 7 July 1911
Died – Narberth, Pembrokeshire, 20 July 1970
Amateur
RHB
Ed – Cantonian High School, Cardiff
1st XI: 1932-1934
2nd XI: 1935-1950
Club: St Fagans, Glamorgan Nomads, Welsh Cygnets

Batting and Fielding Record:

	M	I	NO	RUNS	AV	100	50	CT	ST
F-c	3	4	1	17	5.67	-	-	1	-

Bowling Record:

	Balls	M	R	W	AV	5wI	10wM
F-c	12	0	11	0	-	-	-

Career-best:
First-class – 16* v Worcestershire at Cardiff Arms Park, 1934

Tom Taylor was one of the great characters of club cricket in the years either side of the Second World War. He had a fine record as a top-order batsman with St Fagans and on three occasions during the early 1930s he turned out for Glamorgan. He later served on the county committee and acted as a wise counsel to Wilf Wooller.

With Glamorgan looking to blood new talent, and Tom's good form as an opening batsman in club cricket, he was called up in June 1932 to make his Championship debut against Kent at Swansea. Batting at number five, he made 1 and 0 and was not chosen again for almost two years, playing against Worcestershire at the Arms Park when Maurice Turnbull was indisposed and Norman Riches was called up to lead the county at the ripe old age of 51!

Tom fared better against Worcestershire, making an unbeaten 16 in his only innings and was called up a fortnight later when Cambridge University visited the Arms Park. The county selectors hoped that the game would give Tom a further chance to convert his good form for St Fagans into runs at first-class level, but he was dismissed for a duck.

The insurance broker joined the Glamorgan committee during the late 1930s, and duly became a great friend of Wilf Wooller, when the Welsh rugby international joined the St Fagans club after moving to Cardiff during 1937. The pair enjoyed their time both on and off the field, with Tom one day after a game at Usk, betting Wilf that he couldn't remove all of the decorations around the walls of a pub by only using his fishing rod. Never one to spurn a challenge, Wilf used his rod, to the horror of the landlord and great applause from the St Fagans contingent, and successfully fished all of the ornaments off the walls and ceiling! The owner of a swish two-seater sports car, Tom frequently won the post-match race by St

Tom Taylor.

Fagans players back to the Plymouth Arms where the club's players would congregate after their sporting exertions.

Despite becoming the Manager of the Phoenix Insurance Company after the Second World War, Tom still devoted much of his spare time to cricket. He played for Glamorgan 2nd XI during 1949 and 1950, and used his vast knowledge of club cricket to advise Wilf and others in the Club's hierarchy about emerging players. He also helped his pal with various administrative tasks and remained on the committee until the early 1960s, besides acting as chairman of the cricket committee.

308
DAVIES, William David Edward

Born – Briton Ferry, 26 August, 1906
Died – Briton Ferry, 1 October, 1971
Professional
RHB, LBG
1st XI: 1932-1935
2nd XI: 1935-1937
Colts: 1923
Cap: 1935
Clubs: Briton Ferry Town, Neath

Batting and Fielding Record:

	M	I	NO	RUNS	AV	100	50	CT	ST
F-c	7	12	1	122	11.09	-	-	2	-

Bowling Record:

	Balls	M	R	W	AV	5wI	10wM
F-c	78	1	60	0	-	-	-

Career-best:
First-class – 32 v Gloucestershire at St Helen's, Swansea, 1932

Billy Davies had a fine record as a batsman in club cricket for Britton Ferry Town with his reputation for playing explosive innings with a flashing blade (*a la* Zorro) earning him the nickname 'Darro'.

Billy secured a place in the Briton Ferry side shortly soon after leaving school and joining his father (also Billy) in the local steelworks. His promise as a hard-hitting batsman also attracted the Glamorgan selectors who selected him for their Colts side in 1923. It was though to be nine years before the professional had his first taste of county cricket and came at a time when, under Maurice Turnbull's captaincy, the club were giving opportunities to homegrown talent rather than hired hands from England.

His big-hitting feats in the South Wales and Monmouthshire League led to his selection in 1932 for the match with Leicestershire at Cowbridge. He marked his debut with 8 in his only innings as Glamorgan won by an innings before, at number eight, making a lusty 32 against Gloucestershire at Swansea. He followed this up with a quick-fire innings of 21 against Hampshire at the Arms Park, but in his other two appearances, against both Northants and Sussex at Swansea, Billy showed the more reckless side of his character and was stumped in each match attempting rather ambitious blows.

He re-appeared in county cricket twice in 1935, firstly against Yorkshire at Bradford and secondly against Essex at Neath. The latter was only the second Championship match at The Gnoll and many of his friends turned up eager to see Billy unleash some off his ferocious cuts or massive straight drives. Overambition got the better of him in the first innings as he was bowled for a duck attempting to drive the leg-spin of Laurie

Eastman, but second time around he found the boundary ropes on several occasions and was unbeaten on 27 when Glamorgan, who were following-on, were all out.

In 1935 Billy also posted an assertive 31 for the Second Eleven in their match against their counterparts from Middlesex at Pontypridd. However, he only played once more for Glamorgan, in their Second Eleven fixture with Cheshire at Briton Ferry in 1937, with contemporaries suggesting that with greater patience and self-discipline at the crease, Billy could have featured far more often at first-class level.

309
WHITMAN, Eric Ioan Emlyn
Born – Barry, 31 July 1909
Died – West Norwich Hospital, 5 December 1990
Amateur
RHB, RM.
Ed – Barry Boys Comprehensive School; University College, Cardiff
and Bristol University
1st XI: 1932
Cambridgeshire 1937
Clubs: Barry, Bournemouth Sports
Hockey for Wales

Batting and Fielding Record:

	M	I	NO	RUNS	AV	100	50	CT	ST
F-c	2	3	0	27	9.00	-	-	-	-

Bowling Record:

	Balls	M	R	W	AV	5wI	10wM
F-c	318	8	172	3	57.33	-	-

Career-bests:
First-class –   16 v Leicestershire at Aylestone Road, Leicester, 1932
         2/113 v Warwickshire at Edgbaston, 1932

Eric Whitman.

Eric Whitman had a brief career with Glamorgan, with the young seamer opening the bowling with Jack Mercer against Leicestershire and Warwickshire during Glamorgan's 'tour' to the Midlands during 1932.

The son of John Emlyn Whitman, a schoolmaster from Aberdare, Eric showed great promise as a bowler in university sport when a science undergraduate in Cardiff, besides impressing in club cricket for Barry. He was also a talented hockey player and represented Wales.

Despite his brief foray into county cricket, and the offer of professional terms with Glamorgan, Eric opted to follow his father into the world of education and after training as a science teacher at Bristol University, he taught at schools in the Home Counties as well as in Cambridge where he also had the opportunity during 1937 of playing Minor County cricket for Cambridgeshire against both Norfolk and Lincolnshire.

During the Second World War, he was a pilot officer with the Royal Air Force, and after hostilities were over, he taught in Dorset, besides playing cricket for Bournemouth Sports. He then became Headmaster of Sutton Coldfield Grammar School and later Aldridge School in Walsall. In later years, he acted as Vice-Principal of Bourneville College. He had married Madge Trowell in 1936 and, after retiring from playing cricket, Eric became a useful golfer.

310
THOMAS, David John
Born – Swansea, 25 November 1911
Died – Swansea, 1 September 2001
Amateur
RHB, LM / SLA
Ed – Swansea University
1st XI: 1932
Colts: 1930-1931
Club and Ground: 1933
Clubs: Pontarddulais, Briton Ferry Town, Briton Ferry Steel

Batting and Fielding Record:

	M	I	NO	RUNS	AV	100	50	CT	ST
F-c	1	1	1	10	-	-	-	-	-

Bowling Record:

	Balls	M	R	W	AV	5wI	10wM
F-c	102	1	63	0	-	-	-

Career-best:
First-class –   10* v Northamptonshire at St Helen's, Swansea, 1932

David Thomas had a fine record bowling left-arm cutters, as well as orthodox left-arm spin, in the South Wales Cricket Association either side of the Second World War. His success for Pontarddulais, and subsequently for Swansea University, attracted the attention of Glamorgan's talent scouts who were keen to give a chance to promising young Welsh cricketers. David duly played for Glamorgan Colts during 1930 and 1931.

The release of Frank Ryan in 1931 had given further opportunities to Wilf Jones, but when he lost form and confidence during 1932, David was given his chance in Glamorgan's match against Northamptonshire at Swansea. However, he failed to take a wicket in either innings. The subsequent success of Emrys Davies, and latterly Willie Jones, meant that David was not called up again for a County Championship match, despite an outstanding record in club cricket.

311
LINTON, James Edward Fryer, DSO ('Jef')

Born – Llandaff, 7 May 1909
Died – Roo, Cozumel Island, Mexico, 27 December 1989
Amateur
RHB, RM
Ed – Charterhouse School and RMA Woolwich
1st XI: 1932
Europeans 1931/32; All Egypt 1938
Club: Cardiff, South Wales Hunts, Gezira Sports Club

Batting and Fielding Record:

	M	I	NO	RUNS	AV	100	50	CT	ST
F-c	2	4	0	3	0.75	-	-	-	-

Bowling Record:

	Overs	M	R	W	AV	5wI	10wM
F-c	150	4	82	1	82.00	-	-

Career-bests:
First-class –   2 v Hampshire at Dean Park, Bournemouth, 1932
                1/34 v Middlesex at Cardiff Arms Park, 1932

Glamorgan's search for homegrown talent during 1932 saw them select for a couple of matches 'Jef' Linton, a young officer in the Royal Artillery and a member of a well-known family of solicitors from Cardiff. He did little of note but subsequently went on to enjoy a glittering military career, winning the DSO, besides escaping from a POW camp in Italy during 1943 and taking part in the Battle of Arnheim in 1944.

'Jef' Linton (reproduced courtesy of Charterhouse School Archives).

The son of James Mitchelson Linton, a Cambridge-educated solicitor who practiced in Cardiff and Newport, 'Jef' attended Charterhouse where he led the school's XI during 1927. On leaving school he went to Woolwich and continued his cricketing education by playing in various military teams. In 1929 he gained a commission in the Royal Artillery and was posted to India where he also played in domestic cricket, appearing for the Europeans in the Sind Trophy during 1931/32.

The following summer, 'Jef' spent time in Cardiff with friends and family and, after impressing whilst playing in some games for the South Wales Hunts, the all-rounder was drafted into the Glamorgan side for their games with Middlesex at the Arms Park and Hampshire at Bournemouth. He duly bagged a pair on his debut, before making 2 and 1 in his second, and what proved to be final appearance.

His cosmopolitan cricketing career continued when he was serving in the Middle East with the Royal Artillery from 1936. Whilst stationed in Egypt, he played twice against HM Martineau's XI in 1938, besides appearing for the Gezira Sports Club and the All Egypt side against the team of English amateurs. In 1939 his battalion returned to the United Kingdom, allowing 'Jef' to represent the Royal Artillery against the Royal Engineers at Lord's – a match during which he showed his full batting credentials with a fluent 41 as well as claiming a couple of wickets.

In 1941 'Jef' went with the 11th Royal Horse Artillery to North Africa and participated in a series of battles with German forces before taken prisoner in February 1942 at Antelat. Together with colleagues, he was transferred to an Italian POW camp, but he effected an escape during November 1943 and safely returned to the UK but only after climbing across a series of hills wearing thin civilian clothes and having two umbrellas to use as walking-sticks, before swimming across the River Sangro to reach Allied territory.

In 1944 'Jef' was posted as a Major to 1st Air Landing Light Regiment and commanded Number 2 Light Battery. He and his colleagues were dropped on the first evening of the Battle of Arnheim, with his unit being involved in nine days of fighting. He and fellow officers remained on the beaches to the very last, overseeing the loading of all the boats at the end of the skirmishes only to find that the last ferry had gone. They duly stripped off their uniforms and swam naked across the river, before safely landing on the other bank and acquiring what clothes they could muster from a group of locals.

His bravery and courage saw 'Jef' earn the DSO with his citation reading: "On 24th September, 1944 his gun position west of Arnhem was attacked by infantry and tanks. He showed the highest degree of initiative and determination in stemming the attack and organizing the defense of the sector, thereby preventing further enemy penetration. He set an excellent example under heavy fire and was to a great extent responsible for restoring confidence among the troops by his visits to all forward posts and by his own personal courage."

He was subsequently appointed Commander of the 1st Air Landing Light Regiment and travelled to Norway with the S.A.S. to accept the surrender of 350,000 German troops. With only 6000 troops at his disposal, the operation drew on all of his confidence and temperament. During 1947 and 1948 he served as Senior Instructor in anti-tank warfare at the School of Artillery before acting as Commander at the RMA Centre from 1949 until 1952. This was followed by time as Commander of the Royal Artillery (Home Counties) until retiring with the rank of Brigadier in 1957. He then became a farmer in Wiltshire where he enjoyed a more peaceful retirement.

In 1939 he married Pamela Kyrle Chatfield in Westminster with the couple having two sons. His younger brother Marcus also played for Glamorgan Colts, plus the county's Club and Ground side during 1935 before also serving with the Royal Engineers.

1933

By 1932/33 Glamorgan's debt stood at £4000. The Club were in dire straits and Ernest Tyler, the Treasurer, wrote an open letter to the Press in which he outlined how £1,500 was required to enable Glamorgan to play Championship fixtures in 1933. However, he added "if this is not forthcoming, the committee will have no option but to declare that it is impossible to maintain first-class cricket in Wales."

The "Save Glamorgan Cricket Campaign" duly began with a round of fund-raising events, dinners, whist evenings and all sorts of functions, all with the sole purpose of securing enough cash. Members and other benefactors were listed in the Club's inaugural Yearbook with the cost of producing the attractive annual being underwritten jointly by Brain's Brewery and the *Western Mail* in the first form of sponsorship in the club's history.

Thankfully sufficient funds were raised for the Club to continue but there was no upswing in playing fortunes. Maurice Turnbull's team ended the summer in 16th place with the sole victory in the Championship season coming as Stradey Park took first-class cricket into Carmarthenshire. The visitors to Llanelli were Worcestershire and it proved to be a lucrative experiment as around 4000 paying spectators attended and reveled in the way local men Emrys Davies and Trevor Every put the visitors bowling to the sword.

Despite these decent gate receipts, there was still much to be done off the field to seal Glamorgan's future with Maurice putting Club before Country by turning down an offer to join the MCC on their winter tour and to undertake instead another winter of junketing and fund-raising across South Wales.

An advert in the Western Mail *from 2 May 1933 promoting Glamorgan membership.*

HAINES, Claude Vincent Godby ('Bob')

Born – Bristol, 17 January 1906
Died – Lower Cwmtwrch, 28 January 1965
Amateur
RHB, SLA
Ed – King's School, Canterbury
1st XI:1933-1934
2nd XI:1935
Club and Ground: 1933-1935
Cap: 1933
Kent 2nd XI 1924; Sir Julian Cahn's XI 1936; British Empire XI 1941-44; Gentlemen
of Essex 1943; Home Guard (London District) 1942-1944; Devon 1946
Clubs: Barry, Ealing, Southgate, Frinton-on-Sea, Epsom, XL Club, Cross Arrows,
Swansea

Batting and Fielding Record:

	M	I	NO	RUNS	AV	100	50	CT	ST
F-c	12	20	2	350	19.44	-	2	3	-
Wartime	3	3	0	35	11.67	-	-	1	-

Bowling Record:

	Balls	M	R	W	AV	5wI	10wM
F-c	60	2	33	1	33.00	-	-

Career-bests:
First-class –   59 v Sussex at Cardiff Arms Park, 1933
                  1/15 v Leicestershire at Cardiff Arms Park, 1933

Bob Haines was another well-travelled amateur who played for Glamorgan during the early 1930s whilst working as a land agent in South Wales and playing club cricket for Barry. He subsequently moved to the Home Counties and acted as match secretary of the British Empire XI which raised money for a number of charities and good causes during the Second World War.

Born in Bristol and educated in Kent, Bob was the son of Alfred Haines who had played for Gloucestershire between 1901 and 1910 before becoming the professional and groundsman at Wye College shortly before the Great War. Bob inherited his father's love of cricket and shone as a schoolboy batsman, winning a place in the Public Schools team against The Rest at Lord's in 1924. Also that summer he played twice for Kent 2nd XI, making an assured 47 on debut against Norfolk, followed by innings of 46 and 47 against Wiltshire.

Bob then trained to be a land agent and surveyor, and whilst based in the Vale of Glamorgan played for Barry. His decent form led to his selection for Glamorgan's match against Nottinghamshire at Trent Bridge in May 1933 and, batting at number four in the order he made 12 and 20 in the drawn match. He also cut a favourable impression in his second appearance, against Sussex at the Arms Park, as he made a cultured 59 and shared a decent stand with Maurice Turnbull which helped Glamorgan secure a draw against a decent Sussex attack.

Bob Haines.

During June, he also made 52 against the 1933 West Indians at the Arms Park, and appeared regularly for the next month. Bob also made five appearances the following summer, but with less success, making 89 runs in eight innings, the last of which came batting at number seven in Glamorgan's away match with Somerset, staged at Downside School as Maurice used his growing influence within MCC circles to celebrate the retirement of his former Headmaster by staging a Championship match between the two counties at the famous public school to the south of Bath.

Bob also played for the county's 2nd XI against Berkshire at the Arms Park in 1935 before moving to work in the Home Counties. This saw him play for a number of leading clubs in the London area, including Ealing and Southgate, besides appearing for Sir Julian Cahn's XI during 1936. When the War broke out, Bob joined the Home Guard before using his wealth of contacts within club and county cricket to organize fund-raising matches for the War Effort involving a British Empire side.

As Edgar Hoskin wrote in *Shadows Over the Wicket*, the purpose of the Empire team, known initially as the Touring Club, was "to raise much-needed funds for the British Red Cross and St John Fund War Organization. The second consideration was to keep the noble game alive and as an added attraction, to enlist the help of as many Dominion and Colonial players as possible. And lastly, but by no means less important, a great endeavor was made to provide relaxation from the exigencies of War for the game's staunch followers."

They initially played against a number of clubs in the south-east of England and service teams, before diversifying their activities to include matches against scratch county teams including Nottinghamshire and Northamptonshire. Quoting Hoskin again "the match secretaryship was entrusted to the well-known Glamorgan amateur, CVG Haines. Most probably his reign [in 1943 and 1944] was the most difficult of all, as all-round conditions were truly uneviable by this time."

Bob also appeared in many of the matches with Hoskin also commenting how "his batting was a sheer delight. Deserved far more good fortune than he received.....His off-drives and cover-drives were an object lesson.....His highest innings was 80 v Wembley in 1943 but the most valuable effort was his 72 versus the Buccaneers at Lord's in 1942." Indeed, in the latter year, Bob's aggregate of 532 runs was only surpassed by the Essex duo of Harry Crabtree and Sonny Avery.

He also travelled to Cardiff to take part in Glamorgan's wartime matches at the Arms Park during 1943 and 1944, besides arranging a game over the Whitsun Bank Holiday in the latter year against the British Empire XI. After the War, Bob moved to briefly work in the Torquay area and during 1946 he appeared in Minor County cricket for Devon against Dorset, Cornwall and Oxfordshire. He then returned to South Wales to work in the Ystradgynlais area. He joined Swansea and acted as their captain during 1950. Bob's last match of note was playing for the Swansea club against Glamorgan at St Helen's in 1949. The same year, he also married Rachel Iris Impanni.

313
THOMAS, Hugh Wyndham Vaughan (also known as VAUGHAN-THOMAS), OBE
Born – Swansea, 13 May 1910
Died – Framfield, Sussex, 20 October 1986
Amateur
RHB
Ed – Bishop Gore Grammar School, Swansea and Exeter College, Oxford
1st XI: 1933
Club and Ground: 1933-1938
Club – Swansea

Batting and Fielding Record:

	M	I	NO	RUNS	AV	100	50	CT	ST
F-c	1	1	0	3	3.00	-	-	1	-

Career-best:
First-class – 3 v Gloucestershire at Gloucester, 1933

Vaughan Thomas, who played one game for Glamorgan during 1933, was the younger brother of the famous BBC radio and TV broadcaster Wynford Vaughan-Thomas. Born Hugh Wyndham Vaughan Thomas, within a year of his birth, his father David had taken the surname Vaughan-Thomas following his induction into the Gorsedd at the 1911 Eisteddfod in Carmarthen. It appears from family and college records that Vaughan later opted against taking the hyphen.

His father had been educated at Llandovery College and Exeter College, Oxford where he completed a degree in mathematics before becoming a teacher of music at Harrow and later a composer and professor of music at Swansea University. Indeed, music historians regard him as "one of the most important composers in Wales from the Victorian era to modern times."

Like his illustrious elder brother, Vaughan attended Bishop Gore Grammar School and was taught English by the father of Welsh poet Dylan Thomas, who was a contemporary of Vaughan's at Swansea Grammar School. He subsequently went up to Oxford to read

Modern History at Exeter College where he continued to show good promise as a cricketer, as well as a hockey player, appearing for the College for all four years when he was in residence, besides leading them in 1930 and 1931. Vaughan was also captain of the college's tennis team in 1932.

With the Glamorgan selectors blooding local talent, Vaughan was included in the team which travelled to the Wagon Works ground in Gloucester for the Championship match in 1933. Vaughan made 3 in what proved to be his only innings at first-class level, but he did feature that summer, and again until 1938 in Glamorgan's Club and Ground side.

Vaughan Thomas.

Vaughan subsequently went into teaching in Scotland and during 1941 he played for the British Army in their match against the Scottish Counties at Alloa. He also played hockey for Scotland, and served with distinction for the Royal Corps of Signals during the Second World War, acting as a member of Mountbatten's staff at Combined Operations and rising to the rank of Brigadier.

In particular, Vaughan became an expert on the landing of armoured assault craft, known as Buffalo's, and besides being involved in the Normandy Landings, he also helped oversee the crossing of the Rhine by these assault vessels. His expertise subsequently led to the award of a military OBE in 1946, as well as advisory work with the 1st Belgian Army Corps as they oversaw crossings in many parts of Germany and Eastern Europe.

In December 1948 in Westminster, he married Betty Margaret Pedrick. She was the daughter of a Devon-born Royal Naval engineer – it was her third marriage having previously married Charles Lankester in 1929 and Robert Brown in 1936. Vaughan subsequently became a successful businessman in Sussex and lived at Arches Manor in Framfield, besides having property in Egerton Terrace in Chelsea. He maintained his interest in cricket and became a Vice-President of the Blackboys club near Uckfield, besides serving on the committee of Sussex CCC from 1970 until 1983.

314
JONES, William Maxwell

Born – Alltwen, 11 February 1911
Died – Denbigh, 1 December 1941
RHB, RM
Professional 1933-1934
Amateur 1938
1st XI: 1933-1938
2nd XI: 1936-1937
Colts: 1929
Club and Ground: 1930-1933
Cap: 1934
Clubs: Pontardawe, Pontarddulais

Batting and Fielding Record:

	M	I	NO	RUNS	AV	100	50	CT	ST
F-c	11	15	3	116	9.67	-	-	1	-

Bowling Record:

	Balls	M	R	W	AV	5wI	10wM
F-c	353	9	214	6	35.67	-	-

Career-bests:

First-class – 51* v Worcestershire at Stradey Park, Llanelli, 1933
          3/11 v Sir Julian Cahn's XI at Rodney Parade, Newport, 1933

Bill Jones was an all-rounder who played in eight matches for Glamorgan during 1933 and 1934 whilst on the professional staff, before re-appearing as an amateur in three matches during 1938.

Bill Jones.

The son of a coal miner in the Clydach area, he had impressed as a young cricketer for Pontardawe in the South Wales and Monmouthshire League and appeared for the Colts, as well as the Club and Ground side from 1929 before joining the professional staff in 1933 as the Club made attempts to promote their homegrown talent.

Bill enjoyed a handsome first-class debut in late June 1933, against Worcestershire at Llanelli, where batting at number seven he made an unbeaten 51 besides claiming a couple of wickets as Glamorgan marked their first appearance at Stradey Park with a thumping win by an innings over their English opponents. However, he did not bat or bowl in the game against Middlesex in mid-July at Swansea, before appearing during the last week of August in the return fixture with Worcestershire. The game at New Road duly saw the home side gain revenge for their mauling in Llanelli by turning the tables on the Welsh county, winning by an innings with Bill making 13 and 0.

He played in five further Championship matches during 1934 but did little of note and was released from the professional staff at the end of the season. Bill continued to perform well in the Leagues, and on the back of some decent innings and bowling spells, he played for the Glamorgan 2nd XI against Middlesex at Briton Ferry in 1936, as well as featuring in the visit to Wimborne for the away match with Dorset.

Tom was chosen again for the 2nd XI in 1937 against Kent at Maesteg, before some further good performances in the League saw him being chosen for the three-day friendly with Sir Julian Cahn's XI in July 1938. The game at Rodney Parade saw Tom claim 3/11 with his lively medium-pace bowling and, with doubts over the long-term fitness and future of Jack Mercer, Tom was called up again twice during August for the visits to Bristol and Eastbourne.

He duly opened the bowling with Jack against Gloucestershire and claimed the wicket of Wally Hammond, but only after the great England batsman had made 140 with his side declaring on 503-9 before bowling Glamorgan out twice to win by an innings. Three weeks later at Eastbourne, he operated as first change but was put to the sword by John Langridge, who posted a fine double-hundred. He did claim the wicket of Jim Parks (senior) but the match proved to be Tom's final first-class appearance.

He was listed in the 1939 National Survey as an accounts clerk working in a tinplate factory at Pontardawe.

An advert for one of the fund-raising rugby matches organized by Maurice Turnbull on behalf of Glamorgan CCC.

1934

The upshot of the merger with Monmouthshire, as well as the flimsy finances, meant that Glamorgan further trimmed the wages of the professionals, besides choosing more local and young amateurs during 1934. Over a dozen new faces duly appeared in 1934 compared with just three the year before, with Glamorgan suffering a series of injuries during the summer.

Dai Davies was missing for much of the season after being rushed to hospital on the second day of the match against Kent at Gravesend having suffered a haemorrhage from a stomach ulcer. Johnnie Clay also suffered a leg strain and missed several games whilst Dick Duckfield and Maurice Turnbull were injured during the contest at Lord's. Indeed, the injury list was so long that 51 year-old Norman Riches was recalled for the match against Gloucestershire at the Arms Park.

GLAMORGAN
COUNTY CRICKET
CLUB

1934
OFFICIAL
YEAR BOOK
AND RECORDS
1921—1933

PRICE
6 D.

OFFICES:
9, HIGH STREET, CARDIFF

The cover of the Glamorgan *Yearbook for 1934.*

Given all of these distractions, it was a feather in Maurice's cap that Glamorgan rose up to 13th place in the Championship table, after recording three victories including an innings victory over Surrey at The Oval. Northamptonshire were also defeated at Pontypridd and Somerset at Swansea, where over £1000 was also taken in a lucrative match against the Australians. Further funds were raised through adverts in the Club's Yearbook which also boosted the membership drive by listing the names of the gentlemen and lady subscribers.

315
EVANS, Talfryn

Born – Sandy, Carmarthenshire, 10 June 1914
Died – Llanelli, 31 March 1944
Professional
LHB, SLA
1st XI: 1934
2nd XI: 1936-1937
Colts: 1933
Club and Ground: 1933-1936
Clubs: Elba, Llanelli

Batting and Fielding Record:

	M	I	NO	RUNS	AV	100	50	CT	ST
F-c	1	2	1	0	-	-	-	-	-

Bowling Record:

	Balls	M	R	W	AV	5wI	10wM
F-c	32	0	25	0	-	-	-

Career-best:
First-class –   0* v Kent at Gravesend, 1934

Tal Evans was an enthusiastic young cricketer who played alongside his uncles, Harry and Sid Harries, in the Llanelli team of the 1930s. He also had a brief spell as a professional on Glamorgan's staff, and made one Championship appearance during 1934.

As a child, Tal had suffered from rheumatic fever which left him unable to fully use his right arm. Consequently, he concentrated on bowling with his unaffected left-arm and, after practicing with an orange in the back garden of his home in Llanelli, he developed prodigious powers of left-arm spin. His success with bowling chinamen and googlies for Llanelli in the early 1930's led to his selection for the Glamorgan Colts team, plus the Club and Ground side.

A few concerns were raised about his abilities in the field and holding a bat, but these did not stop Gloucestershire also giving him a short trial. The thought of the teenager joining the West Country side concerned Maurice Turnbull and Johnnie Clay, especially as they were doing their utmost to promote native talent so Tal was offered a professional contract with Glamorgan for 1934.

He subsequently joined the staff and also underwent an intensive programme of batting practice with Arthur Webb, the former Glamorgan and Briton Ferry cricketer who was the professional at Christ College, Brecon. Tal duly made his Championship debut against Kent at the Bat and Ball Ground in Gravesend, but he made little impact. Batting at number ten, Tal was unbeaten on 0 in the first innings and run out without scoring in the second. Tal also didn't bowl in Kent's first innings before bowling 5.2 overs in their second, conceded 25 runs but did not take a wicket. His limitations in the field were also exposed at Gravesend but Glamorgan hoped that with further experience and confidence, the youngster could develop into a useful bowler. Having a 2nd XI competing in the Minor County Championship was a massive bonus and during 1936 Tal played against Berkshire, both at Reading and Barry Island, as well as against Cheshire at Ebbw Vale. The following year he played for the 2nd XI against Cheshire at Boughton Hall, as well as against Middlesex at Ebbw Vale.

He also appeared for the Colts against the Welsh Schools during 1937, but at the end of the summer, the Club had to make a difficult decision. The emergence of batsman Willie Jones as a left-arm spinner had reduced Tal's opportunities and, with doubts still remaining about his fielding and his inability to fully use his right arm, the Club regrettably had to release him.

In 1939 he was also passed as unfit for National Service in the Army. Sadly, Tal collapsed and died at his aunt's house in Sandy Road, Llanelli at the end of March 1944 at the age of 29.

316
DICKINSON, Harold John ('Harry')

Born – Barry, 26 November 1911
Died – Hammersmith, London, 2 June 1997
Professional
RHB, RM
Ed – Barry Boys School
1st XI: 1934-1935
2nd XI: 1935
Club and Ground: 1934-1935
Cap: 1935
Clubs: Barry, Maesteg Town

Batting and Fielding Record:

	M	I	NO	RUNS	AV	100	50	CT	ST
F-c	7	13	6	37	5.28	-	-	3	-

Bowling Record:

	Balls	M	R	W	AV	5wI	10wM
F-c	612	16	335	6	55.83	-	-

Career-bests:
First-class –   14* v Lancashire at St Helen's, Swansea, 1935
                3/91 v Cambridge University at Fenner's, Cambridge, 1934

Harry Dickinson was a promising young fast bowler who made seven appearances for Glamorgan during the mid-1930's as the Club looked to augment its resources from the pool of promising homegrown talent.

He had first shown promise as a talented young sportsman whilst at Barry Boys School, and then, whilst playing for the town's cricket club, his fiery performances drew the attention of Glamorgan's talent scouts. He duly joined the Glamorgan staff in 1934

Harry Dickinson standing third from the left in a photograph taken of the Glamorgan team at Worcester during 1934.

and made his debut for the Club and Ground XI as well as the first-class friendly with Cambridge University at Fenner's. Harry ended up with three wickets but each of his scalps had reached a hundred by the time he dismissed them, with the Light Blues beating the Welsh side by ten wickets.

During May 1934 Harry made his Championship debut at New Road and, as first change, claimed one wicket in what proved to be a watery draw. The following month he played against Lancashire at Liverpool, where he added another scalp in an innings defeat for the Welsh county, before re-appearing during July against Essex at Clacton-on-Sea where he went wicketless during a two-wicket defeat.

Despite these reversals during 1934, Harry had shown enough sparkle with the new ball to be offered terms for 1935, but the club's offer was a modest one and, with his parents hoping he would secure a decent wage, and job security, Harry opted to join the Great Western Railway as a draughtsman.

He left South Wales to begin his apprenticeship but nevertheless agreed to help out whenever needed during 1935. However, all three of his appearances that summer ended in Glamorgan defeats, firstly at Tunbridge Wells where opening the bowling with Jack Mercer he claimed one victim in the four-wicket defeat against Kent. His dismissal though of Frank Woolley for 53 proved to be his last scalp in county cricket as the games against Lancashire at Swansea and Warwickshire at Edgbaston saw the youngster from Barry go wicketless in seven-wicket and 123-run defeats respectively.

Whilst at school, he had played rugby alongside Ronnie Boon, before playing for Barry Romilly RFC. After opting to join the Great Western Railway, he lived at Northolt, Middlesex for 52 years with his wife Joan and raised three daughters and nine grand-children.

LING, Anthony John Patrick ('Pat')

Born – Skewen, 10 August 1910
Died – Eastbourne, 12 January 1987
Amateur
LHB
Ed – Stowe School
1st XI: 1934-1936
2nd XI: 1936-1937
Club and Ground: 1933
Cap: 1934
Wiltshire 1928-1932; Cumberland 1930; Somerset 1939
Clubs: Trowbridge, Carlisle, Stoke Limpley, Somerset Stragglers

Batting and Fielding Record:

	M	I	NO	RUNS	AV	100	50	CT	ST
F-c	9	13	3	192	19.20	-	-	1	-

Bowling Record:

	Balls	M	R	W	AV	5wI	10wM
F-c	12	0	12	0	-	-	-

Career-best:
First-class – 41* v Leicestershire at St Helen's, Swansea, 1934

Pat Ling was a forceful left-handed batsman who played nine matches for Glamorgan during the mid-1930s, as well as in five matches for Somerset in 1939.

Pat Ling.

He was the son of John Richardson Ling, a civil engineer living in Skewen, whose family hailed from North-west England. Pat captained the Stowe XI in 1928, before winning a place in Wiltshire's side where he impressed many with his attractive strokeplay and played in Minor County cricket until 1932. He subsequently moved back to North-west England and whilst playing club cricket for Carlisle, Pat also played for Cumberland as well as for the Border League in 1933 for their annual match against Scotland.

He returned to South Wales during 1934 and with the Glamorgan's selectors keen to give chances to young Welsh amateurs, the Skewen-born batsman made his Glamorgan debut in May 1934 against Cambridge University. In thirteen subsequent innings for the Welsh county Pat failed to register a half-century with contemporaries believing that his main downfall was going for an over-ambitious shot too early in his innings. Pat also played for Glamorgan's 2nd XI in their Minor County matches during 1936 and 1937, before his family's farming activities saw him return to Somerset where he became a pig and poultry farmer based at Limpley Stoke. He duly played in five matches for the county, but again did little of note. Pat remained in the West Country after the War with his final match of note being Somerset Stragglers against the Old Cliftonians at Clifton College during August 1947.

318
REED, George Henry

Born – St Fagans, 8 August 1906
Died – Whitchurch, Cardiff, 11 December 1988
Professional
RHB, LFM
Ed – Cantonian High School, Cardiff
1st XI: 1934-1938
Club and Ground: 1935
Cap: 1934
Clubs: St Fagans, Cardiff, JHP Brain's XI, Welsh Cygnets

Batting and Fielding Record:

	M	I	NO	RUNS	AV	100	50	CT	ST
F-c	25	25	12	65	5.00	-	-	6	-

Bowling Record:

	Balls	M	R	W	AV	5wI	10wM
F-c	4234	143	1941	62	31.30	1	-

Career-bests:
First-class –   11 v Sussex at The Saffrons, Eastbourne 1938
              5/30 v Sussex at St Helen's, Swansea, 1936

George Reed was a brisk left-arm seamer and lower order right-handed batsman who played as a professional with both St Fagans and Cardiff, before joining the Glamorgan staff and appearing in 24 matches for Glamorgan between 1934 and 1936 before an injury curtailed his county career, and resulted in just one more appearance in August 1938.

George grew up on the western outskirts of Cardiff and during the mid-1920s joined the St Fagans club where he played in their 1st XI as a hard-hitting left-arm bowler. He was subsequently made a decent offer to join Cardiff as their professional and assistant groundsman, and duly became their regular opening bowler. He took 7/45 against Neath in his first season

George Reed.

with the club, followed by 8/18 against Gloucester in 1931 and 9/37 against Newport in 1933. However, his finest summer for the city club was 1934 when he established a new record with 74 wickets.

From 1929 he also featured in Pat Brain's team which annually met the Glamorgan side for a pre-season practice match at the Arms Park. These matches gave him a chance to impress the watching Glamorgan hierarchy and together with his success with the Cardiff club, he was selected for the Welsh county's match against Lancashire at the Arms Park at the end of May 1934. It was something of an inauspicious debut as the Red Rose county rattled up 514-7, but George claimed his maiden wicket as he clean bowled Frank Booth.

George kept his place in the Glamorgan line-up for the visit to Hull to play Yorkshire where he took 3/39, followed by a return of 4/81 against Worcestershire at the Arms Park. The latter game saw hm bowl a feisty post-lunch spell in the visitors first innings, claiming the wickets of Bernard Quaife and Cyril Harrison from successive balls before seeing Dick Howorth dropped off the next, depriving the bowler of a hat-trick in his first summer of county cricket

These performances saw the 28 year-old join the county's full-time staff for 1935, with many believing that George might be a long-term replacement for Jack Mercer. He promised much during his first year on the staff, taking 4/42 against Sussex at the Arms Park and 4/83 against Worcestershire at Swansea, before taking his maiden 'five-for' against Sussex at Swansea, claiming 5/30 in the visitors second innings. In fact, it proved to be his only five-wicket haul at first-class level as he ended the season with 28 wickets at 25 runs apiece.

Over the winter of 1936/37 George sustained an injury to his left shoulder and he missed the following season. He never fully recovered and subsequently bowled at a less lively pace in club cricket for Cardiff. During his association with Glamorgan, George had also been less than impressed by the modest terms of his employment. In 1934 his modest match fee had been part of a row between Cardiff and Glamorgan which culminated with the club refusing to release the fast bowler to play against Leicestershire at Hinckley. Relations between the two parties had become strained following another rise in the amount Glamorgan paid for the use of the Arms Park for county games. Their decision to play instead at Pontypridd and subsequently at Cowbridge had fueled the debate, and with George unhappy at the amount he was getting, the Cardiff officials told Glamorgan that they wanted him as fresh as a daisy for their club matches.

It was perhaps no surprise that at the end of the 1937 summer George left the Glamorgan playing staff. He did re-appear in one match during August 1938 against Sussex at Eastbourne, by which time he had become a policeman with the South Wales Constabulary. In his youth, George had also been a talented footballer and had trials with Cardiff City, with some confusing him with the Irishman George Reid who played as a centre-forward for the Bluebirds. Sadly, in later life, George suffered from dementia and died during December 1988 whilst a patient at Whitchurch Hospital in Cardiff.

319
DAVIES, David <u>Aubrey</u>

Born – Swansea, 11 July 1915
Died – Exeter, 25 July 1994
Professional
RHB, LBG
1st XI: 1934-1938
2nd XI: 1935-1937
Club and Ground: 1933-1938
Cap: 1935
Devon 1946-1950
Clubs: Swansea, Exeter, Torquay

Batting and Fielding Record:

	M	I	NO	RUNS	AV	100	50	CT	ST
F-c	46	64	16	600	12.50	-	1	28	-

Bowling Record:

	Balls	M	R	W	AV	5wI	10wM
F-c	1115	15	760	14	54.28	-	-

Career-bests:
First-class –   55 v Surrey at The Oval, 1937
                3/63 v Warwickshire at Edgbaston, 1938

Aubrey Davies was a talented all-rounder with Swansea during the 1930s with the right-handed batsman and leg-spinner also playing for Glamorgan between 1934 and 1938, before moving to Devon for whom he played in Minor County cricket after the Second World War.

After some fine performances in club cricket, Aubrey made his debut for Glamorgan's Club and Ground side during 1933 before joining the county's professional staff and making his first-class debut against Leicestershire at Hinckley in 1934.

Over the course of the next few seasons, Aubrey played some promising innings in their middle-order, although he only scored one half-century, against Surrey at The Oval in 1937. His leg-spin, whilst being effective at club level, saw him take only 14 wickets at county level.

Aubrey appeared regularly for the 2nd XI in the Second Eleven Championship during the mid-1930s with the Club's selectors hoping that greater experience would improve his game, but it did not do the trick and he left the Glamorgan staff at the end of 1938.

Aubrey Davies, seen during 1936.

Aubrey subsequently moved to Devon having secured professional appointments with Exeter and subsequently Torquay. He also got married in Exeter during 1945 before playing Minor County cricket for Devon from 1946. His last game of note came during 1950 when he played against Surrey 2nd XI at The Oval.

His father George had been a weighing machine fitter who hailed from Tredegar.

320

ROBERTS, John Frederick ('Fred') CBE, OBE

Born – Pontardawe, 24 February, 1913
Died – Uplands, Swansea, 20 April 1996
Amateur
LHB
Ed – Pontardawe Grammar School
1st XI: 1934-1936
2nd XI: 1935-1937
Club and Ground: 1933-1934
Combined Services 1946-1949, RAF
Clubs: Pontardawe, Watford, Cheltenham, MCC

Batting and Fielding Record:

	M	I	NO	RUNS	AV	100	50	CT	ST
F-c	5	6	1	86	17.20	-	-	3	-

Career-best:
First-class – 47* v Warwickshire at St Helen's, Swansea, 1934

'Fred' Roberts had an illustrious career with the Royal Air Force and, if the left-handed batsman had not opted for a military life, he could have had an equally successful career with Glamorgan. The youngster had a decent record as a schoolboy with Pontardawe and played for Glamorgan's Club and Ground side during 1933. The following year he made his first-class debut against Warwickshire at Swansea and, with Maurice Turnbull absent on England duty, Fred batted at number six and impressed with an unbeaten 47. He kept his place for the next match, against Somerset at Downside School but, as his military training began, he only played once in 1935, and twice during 1936.

During this period he also played for the County's 2nd XI in their Minor County Championship fixtures, besides making his debut for the RAF during 1939 in their annual contests against the Royal Navy and The Army. He duly

Fred Roberts.

rose to the rank of Air-Vice Marshall, besides acting as the Director of Personnel Services for the Ministry of Defence (Air). Between 1966 and 1968 Fred also acted as Director General of RAF Ground Training, and was awarded both the CBE and OBE for his efforts

After the Second World War, Fred also played for the Combined Services between 1946 and 1949, and showed what Glamorgan had missed by scoring 52 against the 1947 South Africans at Portsmouth. His last major game was during August 1950 when he played for the RAF against The Army at Lord's.

321
CARR, Harry Lascelles

Born – Lambeth, 8 October 1907
Died – Marylebone, 18 August 1943
Amateur
RHB, WK
Ed – Clifton College and Trinity Hall, Cambridge
1st XI: 1934
HDG Leveson Gowers XI 1931
Clubs: Cardiff, Richmond, MCC

Batting and Fielding Record:

	M	I	NO	RUNS	AV	100	50	CT	ST
F-c	1	1	0	6	6.00	-	-	-	-

Career-best:
First-class –   6 v Cambridge University at Cardiff Arms Park, 1934

Harry Carr, the son of a newspaper magnate, played once for Glamorgan during 1934 in their friendly against Cambridge University at Cardiff. At the time, the Club were seeking a replacement after Trevor Every's unfortunate affliction, but Harry was not called upon again.

The son of Sir Emsley Carr, the owner of the *News of the World* newspaper, Harry had attended Clifton College where he represented the school at cricket and rugby, before going up to Trinity Hall where he gained Blues in billiards and golf. Harry also represented his College at cricket, where he proved, as at Clifton, to be an able wicket-keeper and batsman,

Harry Carr, seen on his wedding day.

but did not win any cricket Blues whilst in residence between 1924 and 1926.

After graduating, Harry remained in the Home Counties as he began his training as a journalist besides keeping wicket for Richmond and the MCC. During this time he also appeared in two first-class games for HDG Leveson Gower's XI, against Oxford University in June 1931 and the following month against Cambridge University at Fenner's.

Harry married Eileen Mary Bracewell Smith during April 1933 and, soon afterwards, moved to South Wales. This resulted in his appearance during the final week of June 1934 in the Welsh county's side which met Cambridge University at the Arms Park. Some felt that he could be in the running to be a long-term replacement for Trevor Every, but he was never called up again by the Glamorgan selectors.

During the Second World War, Harry was commissioned into the RAF Volunteers Regiment where he rose to the rank of Flight Lieutenant, He duly worked with the intelligence branch for two and a half years before being taken seriously ill. Flying Officer Harry Carr died in August 1943 in a nursing home in Marylebone following an operation.

322
DUNCAN, Anthony Arthur ('Tony').
Born – Cardiff, 10 December 1914
Died – West Surrey, 3 January 1998
Amateur
RHB
Ed – Rugby School and Balliol College, Oxford
1st XI: 1934
Club: Cardiff

Batting and Fielding Record:

	M	I	NO	RUNS	AV	100	50	CT	ST
F-c	2	3	1	16	8.00	-	-	-	-

Career-best:
First-class –   15* v Somerset at St Helen's, Swansea, 1934

Tony Duncan was one of Wales' leading amateur golfers after the Second World War. He also enjoyed a distinguished military career and, besides being the first Welshman to captain the Great Britain and Ireland team in the Walker Cup during 1953, he also played cricket twice for Glamorgan during 1934.

He was the second son of John Duncan, the Managing Editor of the company which published the *South Wales Daily News* (which Tony's grandfather had founded in 1871) as well as the *South Wales Echo*. In his youth, John had played rugby for Cardiff but golf became his passion, with the journalist winning the Welsh Amateur Championships in 1905 and 1909, and becoming regarded as one of the founding fathers of golf in Wales, serving as Chairman of the Welsh Golf Union for over twenty years, besides being a founding member of Southerndown Golf Club.

Tony's brief flirtation with county cricket stemmed from a successful time as a schoolboy in the Rugby XI in 1933. He duly played that year for the Lord's Schools against The Rest, and followed it up with a century in the Oxford Freshman's Match. He failed to make the Dark Blues side in 1934, but some useful innings for the Authentics, as well as for Cardiff, saw his inclusion in the Glamorgan side which met Gloucestershire at Llanelli in early July. Batting at number seven, Tony made 1 and 0, and a fortnight later at Swansea re-appeared in the match with Somerset at St Helen's. He duly made an unbeaten 15 as Glamorgan won by nine wickets.

Tony made one appearance for Oxford University during 1935, scoring 1 in both innings of the game against Leicestershire. A hand injury whilst playing for the Authentics in 1935 meant that the Oxford selectors did not call on him again, nor the Glamorgan selectors as, encouraged by his father, golf became Tony's leading recreation. He was in the Oxford side in 1934, 1935 and 1936, whilst between 1933 and 1959 Tony represented Wales on 51 occasions in home internationals. He also won the Welsh Amateur Championships in 1938, 1948, 1952 and 1954, before becoming a Walker Cup selector and Chairman of the Welsh selectors.

Tony Duncan.

During 1953 he became the first Welshman to captain a Walker Cup team, losing 9-3 to the United States, though Tony was so busy with administration that he declined to play himself in the Anglo-American tournament. Indeed, in one of the foursomes, James Jackson, who was pairing Gene Littler in the US team against James Wilson and Robbie MacGregor, was discovered to have sixteen clubs in his bag, two too many.

Tony, as a Corinthian sportsman, decided against pressing for the player to be disqualified saying, "this is ridiculous. We have not come 3000 miles to win a 36-hole match by default on the second hole!" Together with other officials they thumbed through the rulebook and found one which said that in exceptional circumstances, the penalty may be ignored. The following morning, with a clever pun on a line from *Rule Britannia*, a local newspaper headline proclaimed "Great Britain waives the rules!"

Tony had gone up to Oxford in the autumn of 1933 to read Mathematics, but after a year he switched to History and, on coming down from Oxford, he joined the Welsh Guards and commenced a distinguished military career. Had his father not sold his publishing empire, Tony may well have become a journalist instead. Joining the Welsh Guards also meant that in 1941 he also played cricket at Lord's, alongside Maurice Turnbull and the famous racehorse trainer Peter Cazalet, in a one-day match against the Grenadier Guards.

Between 1945 and 1959 Tony acted as Assistant Quartermaster General of London District before acting until 1962 as the non-NATO officer to the British Defense staff in Washington. He then returned in 1963 to serve as the Army representative at RAF Staff College in Bracknell before being appointed in 1968 to the position of Commandant of the Nuclear, Biological and Chemical Warfare School. Between 1970 and 1979 Lieutenant-Colonel Duncan acted as the Retired Officer at Staff College, Camberley.

He married Ann Patricia Krabbe who, as an above average golfer herself, enjoyed and shared his passion for the sport. In October 1966 Tony was referee in the Piccadilly World Matchplay Championships at Wentworth, with the final seeing Jack Nicklaus from the USA meeting the South African Gary Player. On the ninth, Nicklaus hit an enormous drive which would have been out of bounds had there not been a ditch along the out of bounds boundary. Nicklaus' stroke ended up in the ditch, so Tony allowed him to drop two club lengths inside the out of bounds line under penalty of one stroke. He duly did this but then saw, some 50 yards ahead, an advertising sign and asked for relief under line of sight rule. Tony stood behind Nicklaus' ball and decided that the sign was not in line between the ball and the pin and refused to allow a drop.

As they walked to the next tee, Nicklaus told Tony that his decision had been wrong, but Tony stuck to his guns, believing that his request was nothing more than an excuse to re-drop the ball. There were acrimonious letters between the two men for a few months after the Championships, but for many others in the golfing world, Tony's decision had been spot on, with Henry Cotton saying "I wish there were more referees like Tony Duncan. He is fair, knowledgeable and experienced." Tony Duncan and Jack Nicklaus, who lost to Gary Player in the final, never met or spoke after 1967.

323
WENT, Gwilym John Hubert

Born – Barry, 25 March 1914
Died – Braintree, 1 June 2005
Amateur
RHB, LBG
Ed – Barry Boys School
1st XI: 1934
2nd XI: 1935-1938
Club and Ground: 1934
Club: Barry

Batting and Fielding Record:

	M	I	NO	RUNS	AV	100	50	CT	ST
F-c	1	2	1	14	14.00	-	-	1	-

Bowling Record:

	Balls	M	R	W	AV	5wI	10wM
F-c	30	1	14	0	-	-	-

Career-best:
First-class – 14* v Gloucestershire at Stradey Park, Llanelli, 1934

Gwilym Went played once for Glamorgan during 1934 as the Welsh county promoted their homegrown talent. He had a decent record for Barry and this led to his selection during 1931 for the county's colts side. Some further impressive innings for

Gwilym Went.

the colts as well as the Club and Ground side led to his selection in 1934 for the match against Gloucestershire at Stradey Park. He made an unbeaten 14 in the first innings, but was dismissed for a duck second time around as Gloucestershire won by seven wickets.

Despite the reverse, Gwilym remained in the selectors thoughts and played in a couple of 2nd XI matches during 1937, including the matches with Berkshire at Barry Island as well as Cheshire at Boughton Hall. He never though played again for the 1st XI.

324
MORGAN, *Edward Noel*

Born – Garnant, 22 December 1905
Died – Cardiff, 27 August 1975
Amateur
RHB
Ed – Christ College, Brecon
1st XI: 1934
Club: Cardiff

Batting and Fielding Record:

	M	I	NO	RUNS	AV	100	50	CT	ST
F-c	1	1	0	1	1.00	-	-	-	-

Career-best:
First-class –   1 v Essex at The Gnoll, Neath, 1934

Noel Morgan was the elder brother of Guy Morgan and played once for Glamorgan during 1934. Educated at Christ College, Brecon, Noel played in the school's XI during 1923 – a season which also saw him make a century insides seventy minutes against Hereford Cathedral School – before going into the world of banking. He duly secured a position in Cardiff and became a leading figure in the financial world of the dockland community.

A series of useful innings for the town club led to his county call-up for the match against Essex at Neath during 1934 but Noel only made a single during the first innings and was dismissed for a duck in the second.

His subsequent career in banking took him to Exeter and Hereford, but he was not called up again by the Glamorgan selectors. He was also a useful rugby playerand represented Cardiff RFC.

Noel Morgan, as seen in 1920, as a fifteen-year-old in the Christ College, Brecon 1st XI.

226

BLACKMORE, David

Born – Swansea, 19 December 1909
Died – Swansea, 15 June 1988
Amateur
RHB
1st XI: 1934
Club and Ground: 1935
West of England 1944
Clubs: Swansea, Elba Works

Batting and Fielding Record:

	M	I	NO	RUNS	AV	100	50	CT	ST
F-c	1	1	0	34	34.00	-	-	1	-

Career-best:
First-class –   34 v Somerset at St Helen's, Swansea, 1934

David Blackmore, seen in his Swansea football jersey.

David Blackmore was a talented footballer and cricketer in the Swansea area during the 1930s, who made a single Championship appearance against Somerset at St Helen's in 1934. He was a prolific run-scorer in the South Wales and Monmouthshire League with Swansea and Elba Works, but declined approaches to turn professional with Glamorgan and play county cricket on a regular basis, largely because the cash-strapped club could only offer modest terms, compared with his far more lucrative employment at the Elba tinplate works.

The youngest son of Thomas Blackmore, a blacksmith's labourer, David duly agreed to appear on a match-by-match basis for the Welsh county, and made his debut against Somerset at Swansea during 1934. David showed his talents with a well-composed innings on what proved to be his sole appearance in a Championship match, leaving the Glamorgan officials ruing the fact that they could not make a more lucrative offer to secure David's services on a more regular basis.

In 1935 he played in the Club and Ground match which the Glamorgan organized between the East and the West of the county, whilst in 1944 he appeared for the West of England in their fund-raising matches. He also played football for the St David's club in Swansea and had trials for Swansea Town FC.

326
CARLESS, Ernest Francis ('Ernie')

Born – Barry, 9 September 1912
Died – Barry, 26 September 1987
Professional
RHB, occ WK
Ed – Cadoxton School, Barry
1st XI: 1934-1946
2nd XI: 1935-1936
Colts: 1930
Club and Ground: 1933-1934
Devon 1947-1949
Clubs: Barry, Cardiff, Briton Ferry Town
Football for Cardiff City and Plymouth Argyle

Batting and Fielding Record:

	M	I	NO	RUNS	AV	100	50	CT	ST
F-c	3	3	0	35	11.67	-	-	1	-
Wartime	17	17	0	225	13.24	-	-	7	7

Career-best:
First-class –   25 v Surrey at Cardiff Arms Park, 1934

Ernie Carless.

Ernie Carless was a talented all-round sportsman either side of the Second World War, playing football for Cardiff City and Plymouth Argyle FC., besides playing county cricket for both Glamorgan and Devon.

He had shown rich promise as a batsman wicket-keeper in club cricket for Barry and Cardiff during the early 1930s. With Trevor Every having been forced into premature retirement, Ernie was called up twice for Glamorgan during 1934, against Middlesex and Surrey, each time at the Arms Park. He made an assured 25 in the latter contest and with the emergence of Tom Brierley behind the stumps, it wasn't until June 1936 that Ernie got another opportunity at first-class level, this time against Essex at Chelmsford.

The son of Charles Carless, a mineral agent at Barry Docks, he played for the Glamorgan Club and Ground side between 1933 and 1935, besides working as the Head Groundsman at Jenner Park. He married Lillian May Thomas in 1935 and continued to work additionally at Ninian Park during the wartime years.

After the War he looked after Home Park for Plymouth Argyle FC besides playing Minor County cricket for Devon from 1947 until 1951, He then returned to South Wales during the mid-1950s and helped coach Barry Town FC, besides acting as the groundsman at Jenner Park.

JONES, Emrys *Closs*

Born – Briton Ferry, 14 December 1911
Died – Briton Ferry, 14 April 1989
Amateur 1934-1936
Professional from 1937
RHB, OB
Ed – Cwrt Sart School, Neath
1st XI: 1934-1946
2nd XI: 1936
Club and Ground: 1934-1945
Cap: 1935
The Rest 1937; Western Command 1942; West of England 1944
Clubs: Briton Ferry Town, Briton Ferry Steel, Neath, Swansea, Maesteg Celtic, Elba

Batting and Fielding Record:

	M	I	NO	RUNS	AV	100	50	CT	ST
F-c	100	142	30	2016	18.00	2	7	42	-
Wartime	7	7	2	126	25.20	-	-	1	-

Bowling Record:

	Balls	M	R	W	AV	5wI	10wM
F-c	6443	165	3299	102	32.14	6	1
Wartime	?	?	?	4	-	-	-

Career-bests:
First-class –   132 v Cambridge University at Swansea, 1938
                7/79 v Sussex at Cardiff Arms Park, 1937

Had his career not been interrupted twice, off-spinner Closs Jones would surely have won Test honours with England. The off-spinner from Briton Ferry played initially as an amateur during 1934, claiming a couple of wickets in his eight appearances before agreeing to turn professional for 1937.

His move to the paid ranks produced immediate dividends as he took 62 first-class wickets during his maiden season as a professional. Closs began with five-wicket hauls against Kent and Lancashire, followed by 7/79 against Sussex, and a hugely impressive haul of 10/94 against the 1937 New Zealanders at Cardiff as Glamorgan defeated the tourists by six wickets.

As wicket-keeper Haydn Davies later recalled "Closs was a superb foil to Johnnie Clay. Johnnie had a high, classical action and loop, whereas Closs was slightly flatter and quicker through the air. They both spun the ball appreciably with Closs' top-spinner surprising many good batsmen."

His fine form resulted in selection for The Rest side which played the MCC in their 150th Anniversary match at Lord's as the England selectors took the chance to assess the credentials of the 25 year-old Welshman. But during the game, he jarred his shoulder and after claiming the wicket of Hedley Verity, was unable to take any further part in the game. He returned to county cricket and continued to play for Glamorgan, but without being able to give the ball a proper rip, he only took 14 wickets during the last two months of the season.

After plenty of rest over the winter months, Closs attempted to regained his bowling form in the Glamorgan side. But he ended up taking just 18 wickets during 1938 and 17 in 1939 as he was unable to recapture the zip and dip he had before the injury in May 1937. Some contemporaries felt he pushed himself too hard to rediscover these skills, but there is no doubt that his work over the winter months, saw his batting improve in leaps and bounds. Closs reaped the rewards in 1938 as he struck a forthright 132 against Cambridge University at Swansea, before making an unbeaten 105 the following year against Kent at Tonbridge.

Closs Jones.

But just when he seemed poised to forge a new career for himself in Glamorgan's middle-order, his career as a professional cricketer was halted again by the outbreak of the Second World War. Closs appeared in several of the county's fundraising friendlies, playing for the Western Command in 1942 and the West of England during 1944, before playing for Glamorgan teams in 1945.

By the time the County Championship re-started in 1946, Closs realised that his future lay away from professional cricket but, as a loyal Welshman, he agreed to help the county out during 1946. His last appearance for Glamorgan came at Rushden in July 1946 as he featured in the match against Northamptonshire. Closs duly retired from professional cricket at the end of the summer. His knowledge and skills were not lost to the game as he continued to mentor the rising talent in the Neath and Briton Ferry area for many years.

1935

A year to remember both collectively and individually as the Club's indebtness started to drop, whilst on the field Maurice Turnbull's team won six of their 26 Championship games. In all, it was Glamorgan's best summer since 1926 and their second best overall, with the inaugural visit to Newport producing one of the six wins. The game against Leicestershire at Rodney Parade saw the Welsh county win by 153 runs having earlier in the week demolished Hampshire by ten wickets at the Arms Park with Cyril Smart feasting on the visiting bowlers.

Haydn Davies, who made his Glamorgan debut during 1935 to begin what proved to be an illustrious career with the Welsh county.

At an individual level, Maurice typically led the way with 1642 first-class runs, whilst Johnnie Clay was deservedly – or belatedly in some people's eyes – called up by the England selectors to play against South Africa. It proved to be his sole Test but it was a mark of the coming of age of Glamorgan Cricket that one of their stalwart bowlers was considered to play at representative level.

The name of Emrys Davies had also entered the notebooks of the Test selectors as the all-rounder enjoyed a vintage summer with both bat and ball, and during the closing match of the summer against Worcestershire at New Road became the first Welshman to complete the coveted Double of 1000 first-class runs plus 100 first-class wickets.

1935 also saw Glamorgan continue to consolidate their Welsh identity by blooding more young talent from Carmarthenshire and Monmouthshire. Haydn Davies, a graduate from Aberystwyth University and Llanelli successfully made the transition from club and Minor County cricket into the Championship side, whilst Len Pitchford, Jack Cope and Wilf Hughes all progressed from appearing for Monmouthshire into the Glamorgan line-up. In the case of the latter two, each had a never-to-be-forgotten debut in first-class cricket, but for very different reasons!

328
PITCHFORD, Len

Born – Leighton Buzzard, 4 December 1900
Died – Clydach, 10 May 1992
Professional
RHB, RM / OB
1st XI: 1935
2nd XI: 1935
Monmouthshire 1933-1934
Clubs: Todmorden, Clitheroe, Church, Barrow, Rishton, Ebbw Vale, Elba

Batting and Fielding Record:

	M	I	NO	RUNS	AV	100	50	CT	ST
F-c	2	3	1	24	12.00	-	-	-	-

Bowling Record:

	Balls	M	R	W	AV	5wI	10wM
F-c	18	1	4	0	-	-	-

Career-best:
First-class – 14* v Warwickshire at St Helen's, Swansea, 1935

Len Pitchford was the professional at Ebbw Vale during the 1930s, and in 1935 the right-handed batsman made two first-class appearances for Glamorgan. His selection followed an innings of 226 for Glamorgan's 2nd XI against Berkshire in a Minor County match at Cardiff Arms Park.

Born in Buckinghamshire, Len had trials with Bedfordshire after the Great War before joining Lancashire, on the recommendation of George Baker, the former professional with the Red Rose county who was coaching at Harrow and had seen Len bat and bowl in club cricket in Bedfordshire. After being released from the Old Trafford groundstaff the right-handed batsman played League cricket for Church, Clitheroe, Barrow and Rishton before moving to South Wales and joining Ebbw Vale in 1931

Over the course of the next couple of seasons Len played Minor County cricket for Monmouthshire and in 1933 he made an unbeaten 247 during their match against Dorset at Abercarn, besides taking nine wickets in the match with his seam bowling.

Following Monmouthshire's merger with Glamorgan, he was called up for Glamorgan's Championship match against Yorkshire at The Gnoll in May 1935. Batting at

Len Pitchford.

number six in the order, he made 9 in his sole innings in the drawn game. He was recalled during July to play against Warwickshire at Swansea – a match which saw Len, batting at number seven, make an unbeaten 14 and 1. A couple of weeks later, he also represented the Welsh county's 2nd XI and made another double-hundred against Berkshire at the Arms Park in 1935.

Len then spent a season in the West Midlands before returning to South Wales as player-coach with Elba. After the Second World War, Len acted initially as the assistant groundsman at the St Helen's ground in Swansea, before moving to BP Llandarcy where he lovingly tended the square for over twenty years.

His brother Harry played for Buckinghamshire and the MCC, besides acting as groundsman at the Ascott Park ground owned by the Rothschild Family. Len married Amy Frodsom in Blackburn during June 1924. He also served with the auxillary fire service in the Neath area during the Second World War.

329
HUGHES, David _Wilfred_

Born – Ebbw Vale, 12 July 1910
Died – Southampton, 21 April 1984
Amateur
RHB, RFM
Ed – Ebbw Vale Secondary School and University College of North Wales, Bangor
1st XI: 1935-1938
2nd XI: 1935-1937
Club and Ground: 1934-1936
Cap: 1935
Monmouthshire 1929-1934; Dorset 1946-1949
Clubs: Ebbw Vale, Kettering, Poole

Batting and Fielding Record:

	M	I	NO	RUNS	AV	100	50	CT	ST
F-c	22	33	8	274	10.96	-	1	6	-

Bowling Record:

	Balls	M	R	W	AV	5wI	10wM
F-c	2873	68	1692	52	32.33	2	-

Career-bests:
First-class –   70* v South Africans at Cardiff Arms Park, 1935
                5/70 v Leicestershire at Aylestone Road, Leicester, 1936

Wilf Hughes was another cricketer from Monmouthshire to have a taste of first-class cricket during 1935, although in the case of the young seam bowler from Ebbw Vale, it came rather belatedly with the 25 year-old having opted to go into teaching after some promising appearances in Minor County cricket for his native county. His debut has subsequently gone down into cricketing folklore as the schoolmaster together with big-hitting Cyril Smart, turned the tables on the touring South Africans with a record-breaking stand for the last-wicket.

He had left South Wales believing that his prospects of playing county cricket were over, and secured a post as a science teacher in Northamptonshire besides playing in club cricket for Kettering. When Glamorgan duly visited the town in late May 1935 to play a Championship match, Ben Bellamy, the long-serving wicket-keeper with the East Midlands side, spoke to captain Maurice Turnbull "Have you heard about the young Welsh lad whose playing here in Kettering? I think you ought to have a look at him as he's getting a big bag of wickets every week and scoring runs as well!"

GLAMORGAN COUNTY CRICKET CLUB.

6, HIGH STREET,

CARDIFF.

DEAR SIR,

You have been selected to play for Glamorgan .... versus *South Africa and Leicester* at *Cardiff and Leicester (resp)* on *June 8ᵗʰ & 14ᵗʰ*

Play commences *11.30* { Beat ———————— at ———

{ Find your own way ~~there~~ *Cardiff*

Yours faithfully,

M. J. TURNBULL,

Secretary.

Please fill in and return the attached card by return or as soon as possible.

The invitation from Glamorgan's selectors to Wilf Hughes to play for Glamorgan during 1935.

Maurice duly made contact with him as well as speaking with Tom Williams, a leading figure in Monmouthshire cricket and the county's representative on the Glamorgan committee. Tom confirmed that Wilf had shown great promise before seeking the security of a teaching post, so Maurice wrote to Wilf inviting him to a trial at the Arms Park. For his part, Wilf did not want to give up his teaching job, but he had always wanted to see whether or not he was good enough to play at county level, so thinking that the trial might result in him playing for the 2nd XI during the school holidays, he travelled to Cardiff for a trial at the Arms Park over the Whitsun Bank Holidays in front of Bill Hitch, the Club's coach, Johnnie Clay and Maurice himself.

All went well and the schoolmaster was given a further chance to display his talents in the county's next game against the touring Springboks at Cardiff, as well as the Championship match against Leicestershire. After a lively new ball spell against the Springboks, Wilf had done little of note, but when Glamorgan were forced to follow-on, he hit the headlines on the final morning. When play began, just six Glamorgan wickets were remaining, and things swiftly got worse as Maurice was dismissed inside the first hour, and despite some stubborn resistance from Cyril Smart, Glamorgan had slipped to 114–9 when the virtual unknown player arrived in the middle with the South Africans poised to celebrate an innings victory.

The clatter of wickets prompted some spectators to leave – how they must have wished they had stayed as the all-rounder launched a blazing counter-attack and added what at the time was a record 131 runs during a dramatic ninety-minute passage of play. Realising that he had nothing to lose, Hughes unleashed a salvo of blows and belied his inexperience by thrashing the bowling to all parts of the Cardiff ground. His rousing and uninhibited blows saw him race to fifty in just 45 minutes and as the fourth of his mighty sixes sailed out of the ground, Nomad of the *Western Mail* wrote Hughes dominated the game to such a degree that even the eager and enterprising [Cyril] Smart was overshadowed as the South African attack was cut to ribbons."

Cyril then joined in with the fun by lofting a delivery into Westgate Street for six. Shortly afterwards, he completed his own century, greeted with huge applause and a hearty slap on his back from his partner. By lunch Cyril had reached 114, with Wilf on 70, and the pair were given a standing ovation as they left the ground, with many of the crowd hoping that Hughes might emulate his partner and completed a century on his first-class debut. But they never got back onto the field, as rain started to fall during the

Wilf Hughes.

interval, before intensifying in the early afternoon. By the tea interval, a number of pools of standing water had formed and the umpires had the formality of calling play off.

With Harold Dickenson opting against a career with Glamorgan, Wilf got further opportunities in the Welsh county's line-up. Whilst he never repeated his feats of big-hitting, Wilf developed into a useful partner for Jack Mercer and, although he continued to only to play in the school holidays, he proved a steady foil to his more experienced new-ball partner, besides claiming a couple of five-wicket hauls.

COPE, John James ('Jack')

Born – Ellesmere Port, 1 August 1908
Died – Brynmawr, Ebbw Vale, 28 January 1995
Professional
RHB
Ed – Ty Llwyn School, Newport
1st XI: 1935
2nd XI: 1936-1950
Club and Ground: 1935
Monmouthshiren 1931-1933
Clubs: Ebbw Vale, Radcliffe
Football for Bury, Ipswich, Cardiff City, Ebbw Vale and Llanelli

Batting and Fielding Record:

	M	I	NO	RUNS	AV	100	50	CT	ST
F-c	3	5	1	27	6.75	-	-	1	-

Career-best:
First-class – 14* v Hampshire at Cardiff Arms Park, 1935

Born in Cheshire and raised in Newport, Jack Cope played as a professional in both League football as well as first-class cricket, making three appearances for Glamorgan during 1935.

Jack's family had moved to South Wales when he was four years old, living initially in Newport before moving to Ebbw Vale when his father was promoted to a new position in the steel industry. He soon showed rich promise as a schoolboy footballer and cricketer, and initially joined Ebbw Vale FC where he played for the princely sum of £1 a week. His success however saw him subsequently move west to play for Llanelli AFC where he earnt £4 a week.

For the next few years he mixed playing as a left-half with Llanelli during the winter months and playing as a professional with Ebbw Vale in the South Wales and Monmouthshire Leagues. In July 1931 he was called up by the Monmouthshire selectors for their Minor County Championship match against Dorset at Abercarn. He subsequently became a regular in their line-up, batting at number three, and making 98 against Warwickshire 2nd XI at Edgbaston in 1933, in addition to 56 against Oxfordshire at Merton College.

Jack Cope.

Whilst playing Llanelli in 1933, Jack was spotted by a talent scout from Bury FC and he duly signed professional terms with the Lancashire club and moved to north-west

England. He also got an opportunity to play cricket – as an amateur – at weekends for Radcliffe in the Bolton League, in addition to playing during the week – as a professional – for Monmouthshire in their Minor County games.

In July 1934 he also made a favourable impression on the Glamorgan selectors when he top-scored with 42 in the Welsh county's friendly with Monmouthshire at Pontypool. Later in the year, the two county's affiliated and when, in the last week of June, Maurice Turnbull found himself a batsman short for the away match with Kent, he contacted Tom Williams, the former Monmouthshire captain and Glamorgan committee member, regarding giving an opportunity to a player from Monmouthshire in the match at Tunbridge Wells. Maurice suggested to Tom that he might like to play, but he declined and suggested Jack instead, knowing that a few weeks before the right-hander had shared an opening stand of 230 with Len Pitchford in a club match for Ebbw Vale. He also reminded Maurice about his decent innings against Glamorgan the previous year, so the net result was that Jack travelled overnight by train to the south-east and made his Glamorgan debut the following morning.

Given his weariness, it was not surprising that he only made 2 and 8, but with other batsmen still unfit, he kept his place for the next match against Hampshire at the Arms

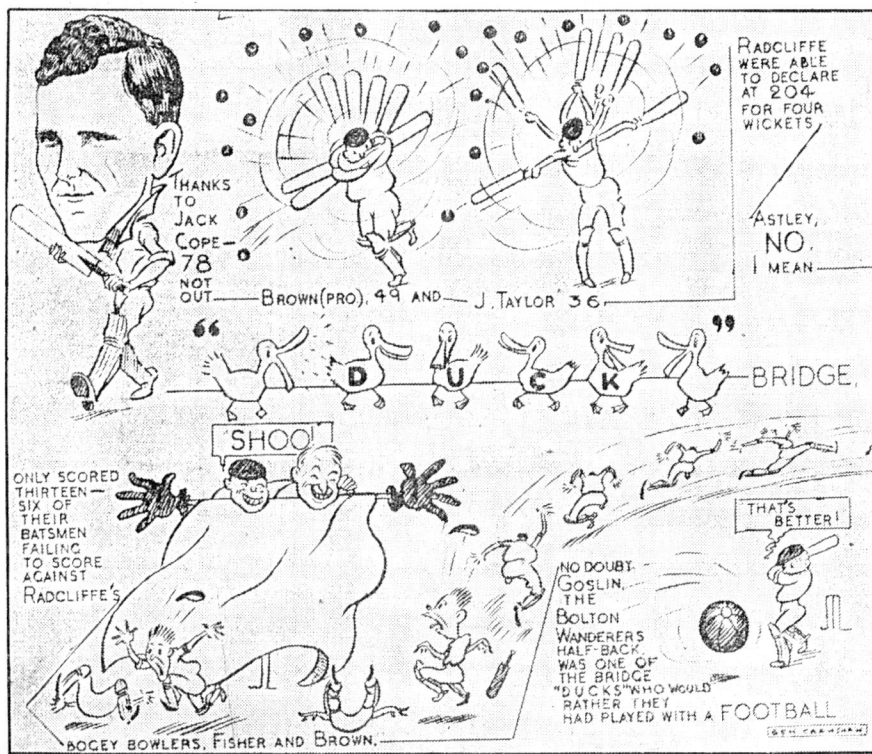

A cartoon celebrating the batting exploits of Jack Cope in the Lancashire League.

Park. He made an unbeaten 14 in his only innings in a match which Glamorgan won by ten wickets. Jack also played for the county's Club and Ground side against the Cardiff and District League at the Melingriffith Sports Ground, before three weeks later playing against Lancashire at Swansea but made just 2 and 1 as Lancashire eased to a seven wicket victory.

During 1936 he played for the Glamorgan 2nd XI against Cheshire at Neston with his selection stemming from the fact that he was now based in Lancashire. He remained with Bury until the end of the 1937/38 season during which time he had made 67 appearances in their Second Division matches besides scoring two goals. Whilst with Bury, he also came close to winning a Welsh cap. He was chosen to play in an international against Ireland, but only hours before kick-off, the selectors realized that he had been born in England and, being ineligible to play, was removed from the intended starting line-up.

During June 1938 Jack agreed terms with Ipswich Town who, at the time, were in the Third Division (South) and he duly made six appearances for them during the 1938/39 season before joining Cardiff City for the start of 1939/40. He remained in Cardiff during the wartime years and in 1945 secured a coaching post with their nursery team, based at Aberdare. He continued to play cricket for Ebbw Vale, and in 1950 appeared again for the county's 2nd XI against their counterparts from Gloucestershire at Bristol.

After retiring from cricket, Jack worked as a clerk at the British Steel plant in Ebbw Vale. In 1932 he had married Elizabeth Pudner, the daughter of the manager of the Ebbw Vale sheet mills. They had three daughters and a son, Michael, who was also a talented cricketer and footballer and coached the Ebbw Vale FC team.

331
DAVIES, Haydn George

Born – Llanelli, 23 April 1912
Died – Haverfordwest, 4 September 1993
Professional
RHB, WK
Ed – Llanelli County Grammar School and Aberystwyth University
1st XI: 1935-1958
2nd XI: 1935-1937
Colts: 1932-1937
Club and Ground: 1934-1958
Cap: 1936
West of England 1941; Army 1941-1943; Western Command v RAAF 1944;
The Rest 1946; MCC 1947-1948
Clubs: Llanelli, Morewoods

Batting and Fielding Record:

	M	I	NO	RUNS	AV	100	50	CT	ST
F-c	423	596	95	6515	13.00	-	11	581	203
Wartime	7	9	1	148	18.50	-	1	6	3

Bowling Record:

	Balls	M	R	W	AV	5wI	10wM
F-c	18	0	20	1	20.00	-	-

Career-bests:

First-class –   80 v South Africans at Cardiff Arms Park, 1951
                 1/20 v Nottinghamshire at Trent Bridge, 1951

Haydn Davies is regarded by many players and long-time supporters of Glamorgan CCC, to have been the finest wicket-keeper to represent the Welsh county, and when in the twilight of his career in 1955 he took a record eight dismissals in the match against the South Africans at Swansea.

He was also one of the best keepers never to have won Test honours, with the nearest he got to higher recognition was selection in the 1946 Test Trial at Lord's. Haydn kept for The Rest whilst Billy Griffith was behind the stumps for England, but it was Godfrey Evans who proved to be Haydn's nemesis. The Glamorgan gloveman was at the peak of his career at the same time as Godfrey with the England selectors preferring the more flamboyant Kent wicket-keeper whose batting talents were superior. A few commented though that Haydn's unconventional catching technique of lining up the ball with his right hand and dropping his left over it like a rat-trap when completing the catch had raised a few eyebrows amongst the purists at Lord's.

Haydn might also have played for Gloucestershire had Maurice Turnbull not intervened at the end of the 1935 season when the young keeper received an approach from Gloucestershire. At the time, he was a junior professional on Glamorgan's staff and had kept wicket for the 2nd XI in their Minor County Championship games, in addition to having made his first-class debut as a specialist batsman against Sussex at Hastings in early August. The previous month Haydn had displayed his abilities with the bat and behind the stumps by playing for the South Wales and Monmouthshire League against Glamorgan in a pair of one-day games at Maesteg, but Haydn batted at number nine in the match at Hastings with Tom Brierley remaining in possession of the gloves.

Others had noted his abilities behind the stumps, and in early September the young Welshman was chosen to keep wicket in a

Haydn Davies, as seen at a function in Ebbw Vale during 1956.

239

friendly for William Wickford's XI against Wiltshire at Swindon. Also in the scratch team were Gloucestershire's Tom Goddard and Wally Hammond, as well as Bev Lyon, the captain of the West Country side. All were impressed by Haydn's neat glovework and after the game, Bev spoke to the Welshman about joining Gloucestershire and playing regular 1st XI cricket as their wicket-keeper.

Believing that nothing more than a junior contract was on offer with Glamorgan, Haydn answered in the affirmative but thought nothing further about the conversation until late September when a national newspaper carried a story that Gloucestershire had secured the services of the highly promising Welsh wicket-keeper. With Swansea playing the All Blacks at St Helen's the following day, Maurice sent Haydn a telegram asking him to join him for lunch in a Swansea restaurant ahead of the match.

Worried by what Maurice would say, Haydn stressed that Bev had only asked him if he would like to play 1st XI cricket and that he had not signed any paperwork or spoken further to any Gloucestershire officials. "That's good to hear" replied the Glamorgan captain who subsequently agreed enhanced terms with Haydn for 1936 and said that he would select him behind the stumps for the Welsh county after he had served his apprenticeship

Haydn – the young rugby player.

in the 2nd XI. True to his word, Maurice gave Haydn an opportunity to keep wicket against Leicestershire at Swansea in 1936 as well as in the match against the 1937 New Zealanders at Arms Park. He became the regular behind the stumps from the middle of 1938, starting with the match against Lancashire at Old Trafford on 11 June.

This was not the only time that Haydn had considered changing clubs in order to keep wicket on a more regular basis. Whilst a youngster with Llanelli he had played plenty of 2nd XI cricket for the town club but had found his way blocked into the 1st XI by the more experienced Sid Phillips. Over the winter of 1933/34 he received an approach from the town's other major cricket club – Morewood's, who were based at the tin plate works on the Machynys Peninsula – about keeping wicket for them the following summer, so Haydn switched from playing at Stradey Park to turning out at Beach Road.

From an early age, Haydn had shown himself to be a talented and technically correct batsman and whilst a pupil at Llanelli County Grammar School, he had received several awards for his batting. The first came when he was presented with a bat having scored 75 against a team from Pontyberem, but when handing over the prize, Haydn's Headmaster also chided him for not going on to make a century. Suitably chastened by this admonishment, Haydn made 118 in his next school match, against Carmarthen Grammar School and was duly presented with a voucher for £2.

During his first year as a Chemistry undergraduate at Aberystwyth University, Haydn had kept wicket for the Glamorgan Colts against the Welsh Secondary Schools at Barry

Island, whilst he was also chosen for the county's Club and Ground side during the next couple of seasons. Having impressed for Morewood's, Haydn joined Glamorgan's junior staff in 1935, and over the next couple of seasons, continued to develop his glovework until the tutelage of 2nd XI captain Trevil Morgan and Club coach Bill Hitch before taking over from Tom Brierley during 1938

Haydn had been a multi-talented sportsman in his youth and during the winter months had played rugby as a hooker for Llanelli, besides winning Welsh schoolboy honours. He also kept goal for Llanelli AFC, whilst in the summer, in addition to his cricketing exploits, Haydn had shone at tennis, and in 1932 was Junior Lawn Tennis champion of Carmarthenshire besides appearing at Junior Wimbledon.

Haydn's abilities on the tennis and racquets court had not gone unnoticed by Maurice, and when meeting with the ambitious wicket-keeper in the Swansea restaurant in September another enticing offer came his way besides playing 1st XI cricket for Glamorgan. At the time, Maurice was contemplating how he was going to maintain his own fitness over the winter months having been forced into premature retirement from rugby with a wrist injury. Specialists in Cardiff had told him that he was risking his future as a batsman if he sustained another fracture so having enjoyed playing squash when an undergraduate at Cambridge, he had formed a limited company to create a squash club in Cardiff.

Haydn – the adroit wicket-keeper.

He duly told Haydn that the company had bought land and an old farmhouse in Ryder Street, just a short walk from the Arms Park in the inner suburb of Canton. With building work due to start over the winter months and the creation of two courts, Maurice told Haydn that a professional would be required and invited him to augment his cricket earnings by acting as the new club's professional. Whether or not, this was the incentive to remain with Glamorgan as their reserve wicket-keeper rather than throwing his lot in with Gloucestershire is not known, but the opportunities presented by being a squash professional helped to boost Haydn's reflexes and overall dexterity behind the stumps. It also helped to forge an all-to-brief friendship with Maurice – the pair enjoyed many games of squash between them, with contemporaries believing that Haydn was one of a small handful of people who could give the great and multi-talented Glamorgan captain a good game.

During the years leading up to the Second World War, many of the visiting cricketers took the opportunity to play at the Ryder Street club. On one occasion when Yorkshire played at Cardiff, Norman Yardley challenged Haydn to a game after play. The challenge attracted many wagers, with the Glamorgan camp being convinced that Haydn would

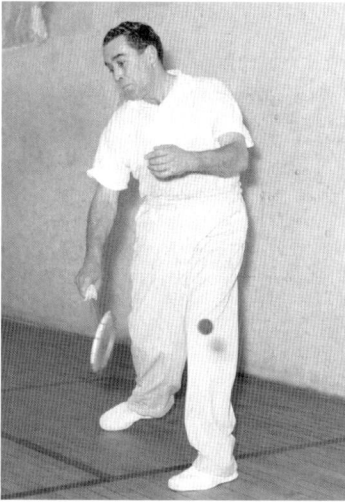

Haydn – the squash professional.

defeat the Englishman. It proved to be a very evenly matched contest, and all after a hectic day for both of the players. Watched from the gallery by many of their colleagues, Haydn and Norman matched each other stroke for stroke. Neither gained the upper hand, and with the score one-all, the two exhausted players shook hands and, after a shower, joined their friends in the Squash Club bar.

Another very popular feature of the Ryder Street club was its friendly bar and it was here that Haydn, together with Maurice and Wilf Wooller mixed and socialized with their many sporting friends – of both sexes – as well as giving Haydn a base, as their model professional, where he could pass on tips to the Club's members and his tutees, helping them to improve their game. Haydn proved to be a perceptive and jovial coach, always ready to provide helpful words of advice and a measure of the quality of his guidance can be gauged from the fact that Wilf and other members of the Ryder Street club, like Haydn and Maurice, represented Wales at squash.

Haydn's powers of analysis were also razor-sharp in cricket and he proved to be a wise lieutenant to Wilf, especially during his formative years as the Welsh county's captain. Indeed, it was Haydn who helped to keep up Wilf's morale midway through 1948 following a crushing 301-run defeat on a green wicket against Derbyshire had ended their good early season form and dented their title aspirations. The team were staying in Derby with Wilf and Haydn chatting late into the night about the teams prospects and forthcoming opponents. As Wilf recalled, "Haydn kept telling me it can be done. It's going to be our year. Further victories are going to come if we stay positive and if so, the title is there for the taking. Haydn's words were vindicated as we won five of our six games during June and it was from this time that we began our Championship campaign."

It was Haydn who also helped Jim McConnon when the footballer turned off-spinner went through several dips in his confidence. Haydn, from his position behind the stumps could pass on praise and encouragement, besides reminding the spinner to stick to the basics and not become too impatient if wickets were not looking like coming his way. A classic example came at Swansea in the match with the 1951 South Africans – a game which Haydn regarded as the highlight of his career. At tea, Jim was fretting with the tourists on 54-0 chasing 148 to win, but walking back out to the middle, Wilf and Haydn went up to Jim and said "just drop the ball on that rough spot outside off stump and we will win." Haydn duly applauded every ball that the spinner landed in the right place, and boosted by this vocal support, Jim settled into what proved to be match-winning line and length, claiming 6/27 including a hat-trick as ten wickets swiftly tumbled to give the Welsh county a remarkable victory.

Haydn Davies completes a catch in somewhat unorthodox fashion behind the stumps, much to the delight of Allan Watkins at slip.

It was Haydn who also helped Don Shepherd change styles having noticed during 1955 how the fast-medium bowler was not hitting the seam with as much regularity as in previous years because of a floppy wrist. "Did you ever see Johnnie Clay?" Haydn asked Don as he drove the bowler and Bernard Hedges to an away game. "Johnnie had a loose-wristed bowling action, just like you and switched to spin because he could not hit the seam all the time." A short conversation took place but Wilf was rather sceptical about the idea and felt that Don needed to continue learning his trade as a fast bowler and adapt his grip. But Haydn, as senior professional, duly won him around and after getting the Skipper's approval, Haydn gave up his spare time to work in the nets with Don as he experimented with off-cutters. His reward was seeing at close range Don's almost magical blossoming into the Welsh county's greatest ever wicket-taker.

The wicket-keeper and apprentice spinner shared many car journeys during which the question of whether Haydn should stand up to the off-cutter or stand back. As Don explained in later years, "because I was so quick through the air and got a lot of thick edges that no keeper would ever catch standing up, Haydn, by design not lack of ability, opted to stand back. He was able to make more ground and easily take catches in a normal first slip position. It also meant Gilbert Parkhouse, at first slip, could also go a bit wider and with Allan Watkins at leg-slip also going a bit squarer, we covered a lot more ground."

Haydn also gave plenty of advice to young Peter Walker when the man, regarded by many as the Club's finest-ever close to the wicket fielder, took his first steps in county cricket. As Peter recalled in his autobiography "one day when we were discussing fielding skills, Haydn asked me 'What do you catch with Peter?' My reply was 'obvious isn't it, my hands!' He smiled condescendingly and said 'No, you pillock, it's your eyes. They tell you where your hands should go. That's why I keep telling you to stand still at short square-leg to give your eyes a chance.' "

Haydn played in every County Championship match between 1947 and 1957, often playing with broken fingers strapped and bandaged. Despite having spent many hours behind the stumps, Haydn was always prepared to act in emergency as an opening batsman or fulfil the role of night-watchman if wickets fell shortly before the close of play. On his day, Haydn could be an explosive hitter and he struck a career-best 80 in his Benefit Match against the 1951 South Africans at the Arms Park.

1951 was also the summer when Haydn claimed his sole first-class wicket. It came during the away match with Nottinghamshire where, not for the first time, Wilf and Reg Simpson locked horns. Wilf had been irritated by Reg's vociferous boasts, and other barbed comments about the enhanced facilities at Trent Bridge, especially a swish new scoreboard. As the final day unfolded, the home side – who were following-on – were guided to safety by a century by Cyril Poole. With the contest moving towards a draw,

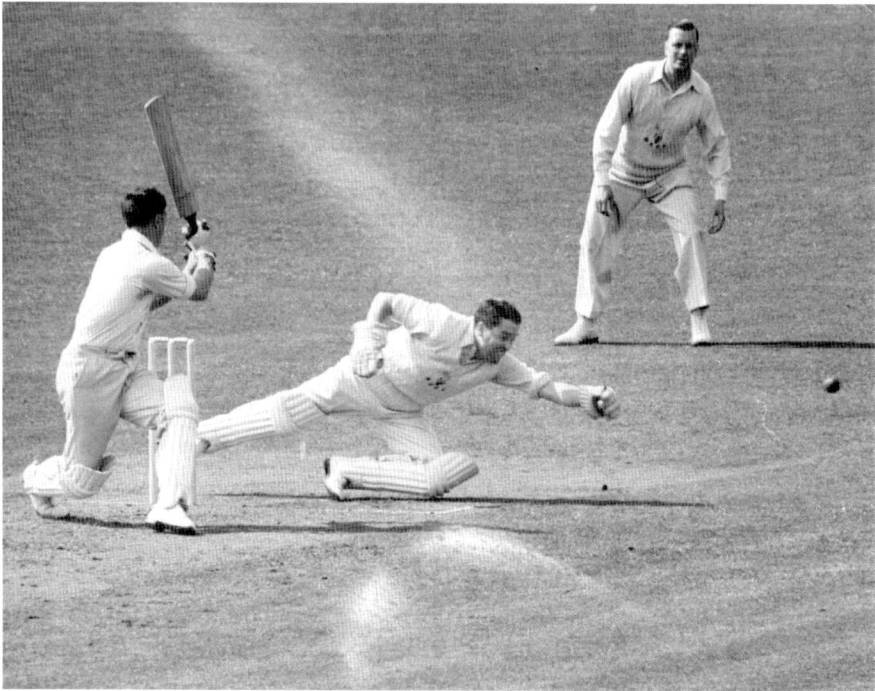

Haydn Davies deftly saves runs aplenty as he dives down the leg-side.

and a Notts declaration unlikely, Wilf brought on his occasional bowlers. Their names filled up the new slots on the scoreboard but, as Haydn whimsically told Wilf in between overs, "Hey Skipper, there's only room for ten names!"

As the game moved towards its conclusion and all ten slots filled up, Wilf – with a beaming smile – threw the ball to his wicket-keeper and said, "Now it's your turn Haydn". There was much mirth, as the scoreboard operators desperately tried to accommodate the eleventh bowler and in the hilarity, his opposite number Eric Meads obligingly hit his own wicket. Soon afterwards, the players walked off and shared handshakes, with Wilf going up to Reg and saying "Don't think much of your new scoreboard. It can't accommodate all of the wicket-takers!"

Haydn – the batsman!

Known to one and all as 'The Panda' because of his squat physique, and shuffling gait, Haydn's high quality wicket-keeping and penchant for hitting sixes made him a very popular figure with Glamorgan's supporters. Indeed, amongst the highlights of Glamorgan's performance in the field would be Haydn's vociferous appealing, or his joyful and deft stumpings as opponents completely misread the spin of the likes of Johnnie Clay, Len Muncer, Jim McConnon or, in later years, Don Shepherd.

A far more gregarious character than his namesake Emrys, Haydn was also something of a night-owl with many close friends and casual acquaintances across the country. On one occasion, the Glamorgan team were staying in the Midlands at a small hotel with no night porter and when Haydn returned in the wee small hours, he couldn't get back in. Having gently tapped the front door without a response, he started whistling hoping that one of his colleagues might hear. To his delight he got a return whistle so he responded with another one of his own. Again there was a reply but there were still no footsteps to be heard coming down the stairs or in the lobby.

Haydn whistled for a third time and got another reply. The same happened to his fourth and fifth which now were more like loud raspberries than melodic shrills. After a response to the sixth whistle, Phil Clift pushed up a window, looked down and came downstairs to help his team-mate. Haydn was delighted to see Phil but just as he was thanking him, Haydn looked across the lobby and saw the source of the replies to his whistles – a large parrot in a cage next to the receptionists desk!"

1958 proved, for several reasons, to be Haydn's final season of county cricket. It certainly was not because of his fitness as, aged 46, that summer had also seen him challenge three of the New Zealand tourists to games of squash at the Ryder Street Club. Each were provincial standard players but 'The Panda', in his trademark maroon tracksuit, defeated each without breaking into a sweat. The real reasons for his departure from county cricket lay in the murky doings associated with the cloak-and-dagger campaign, led by Norman Riches and a faction of committee members to replace Wilf as the Club's captain.

Haydn had always held ambitions to succeed Wilf as captain and, when told of the plan to oust Wilf, Haydn indicated that he would be keen to take over and during the closing years of his career, help to mentor the new captain, very much in the way that Johnnie Clay had helped to groom Wilf after the Second World War. As the summer unfolded, tensions developed between the pro-Wilf and anti-Wooller parties, culminating in the appointment on a trial basis during August of Tolly Burnett, an Old Etonian who had won a Cambridge Blue in 1949

The experiment was an abject failure and, as Wilf remembered in his memoirs, "Even Haydn Davies, who fancied the chance of leading the club and one of my oldest colleagues, seemed to be turning against me and siding with the opposition." Matters were not helped when it was revealed that Tolly was also sending secret reports on the Glamorgan squad to senior Club officials and, with newspapers carrying full accounts of the affair, a special general meeting was held in October at Bridgend Town Hall at which it was decided to hold a referendum to settle the issue of whether Wilf remained.

When the ballot papers were counted, Wilf had a clear majority of 1098 votes to 795. With Wilf having successfully rebuffed the coup, there was plenty of acrimony in the air during the subsequent months with Haydn deciding to retire from professional cricket and take up a post at the Edinburgh Squash Rackets Club. His last match had been in mid-August at Loughborough – a match which Leicestershire won by an innings off the penultimate ball. Having been told during the visit to Leicestershire that David Evans would be playing in the final three games of the summer, Haydn had tried his damnedest to prevent the Welsh county from losing. Batting at number nine he had restrained his attacking instincts in a bid to save the game.

When the final over began, he was defiantly unbeaten on ten with Peter Gatehouse set the face the last six balls with last man Don Shepherd hoping he would not be called upon to bat. But Gatehouse swished at the first ball of the over and spooned a catch to Terry Spencer. Don then saw out the next four balls, before hoisting the fifth ball of the over high in the air to long-on where Jack van Gelovan ran some fifteen yards to complete the catch. A crestfallen Don trudged off with the veteran wicket-keeper who turned to the master bowler and said, "You know what, Shep. The buggers have dropped the wrong man!"

It was not the way Haydn's glorious county career should have ended, and his legion of supporters at Swansea and Ebbw Vale duly watched his understudy as the selectors gave David Evans a chance to impress. The internal politics of the Welsh county were left behind as Haydn moved to Edinburgh and put his heart and soul into his new role. An indication of his success can be gauged from the fact that during Haydn's time in Scotland, the Club's membership rose from 250 to around 1400.

Haydn returned to Wales during 1974 and took over the Alma public house in Pembroke Dock. After retiring as mine host, Haydn moved to the Pembrokeshire village of Cosheston and restored his links with Glamorgan which he had severed in the aftermath of the disappointing events of 1958. In particular, he attended the regular gatherings of the Glamorgan Former Players Association and reveled in the opportunity to mingle again with Wilf and many of his former colleagues from the Championship-winning summer.

During the Second World War, Haydn served with the Army and was based with their Transport Corps at Llandrindod Wells where his chief role was training dispatch riders and others in the correct use of motorbikes. Haydn also played cricket for the Army between 1941 and 1943, besides playing for West of England and Western Command. His brother Roy, who he had legally adopted during the Second World War, played once for Glamorgan in 1950. His nephew Andrew Davies won a Blue at Cambridge in 1984 besides playing for the Welsh county's 2nd XI, whilst his great-nephew Jack has played for England Under 19 and is currently on the staff of Middlesex.

Haydn Davies, as seen during his final summer of county cricket in 1958.

1936

The euphoria of 1935 had evaporated into disappointment long before the end of the 1936 season as Glamorgan slid back down the Championship table. Their sole victory in the Championship did not come until early July at Swansea with Leicestershire being defeated by ten wickets at a ground where the following month the Welsh county inflicted an innings defeat on the Indians. Johnnie Clay had spun Glamorgan to victory over the tourists at St Helen's as on the final day he claimed 8/43 after Maurice Turnbull and Cyril Smart had each made half-centuries in what proved to be Glamorgan's only innings of the game. In the tourist's first innings Jack Mercer had been a thorn in the Indian's side having taking 7/48 to continue a purple patch of form which in the previous game, away to Worcestershire, had seen the lion-hearted seamer become the first – and still – only bowler in Glamorgan's history to claim all ten wickets in an innings.

Jack ended the summer with a deserved 127 wickets in first-class matches for the Welsh county, whilst on the run-scoring front it was Emrys Davies who led the way with a tally of 1479 runs and saw the all-rounder further consolidate on his achievements the previous year.

The visits to Neath, Newport and Pontypridd saw decent crowds but these matches at the outgrounds were not as lucrative as in previous years. But it wasn't all doom and gloom as further young players were bloodied in the 1st XI having impressed in the county's 2nd XI who continued to play with credit and enthusiasm in the Minor County Championship.

The Glamorgan team which played Breconshire in a one-day friendly during June 1936. Batting first, the image shows that only five of the Glamorgan have got changed – Emrys Davies (seated front left), Maurice Turnbull (seated third right), Johnnie Clay (seated second right) and Dai Davies (on the far right of the first row). Still in their civvies are Tom Brierly (standing second left), Dai Davies (standing second on the balcony), Dick Duckfield (third on the balcony), Haydn Davies (fourth on the balcony), George Lavis (fifth on the balcony), Jack Mercer (sixth on the balcony) plus Aubrey Davies (standing far right in the doorway).

HODGES, Albert Edward ('Bert')

Born – Newport, 29 January 1905
Died – Newport, 23 September 1986
Amateur
RHB
1st XI: 1936
2nd XI: 1935
Club and Ground: 1936
Wales 1930
Club: Newport

Batting and Fielding Record:

	M	I	NO	RUNS	AV	100	50	CT	ST
F-c	1	2	0	3	1.50	-	-	-	-

Career-best:

First-class –   3 v Gloucestershire at Rodney Parade, Newport, 1936

Bert Hodges, a leading batsman with Newport from the mid-1920s until the immediate post-war years, made one appearance for Glamorgan during 1936, appropriately enough on his home turf at Rodney Parade as the Welsh county met Gloucestershire.

The son of a Carmarthenshire-born ironworker, Bert followed his father into the heavy industry, working on the heavy rollers in the hot strip mill at the Orb Works. His cricketing prowess saw him play for the Monmouthshire Colts against their counterparts from Glamorgan during 1925 before Bert made his Minor County debut the following year in the away match with Cornwall at Penzance.

Bert continued to play for Monmouthshire until 1935, with his career highlights including 100 against Oxfordshire at Ebbw Vale in 1926, plus innings of 66 and 65 against Surrey 2nd XI at The Oval in 1929 and 1930. In the latter summer, he also made his first-class debut as he played for Wales against the MCC at Lord's. Batting at number seven, Bert scored 8 and 3 as the Welsh side lost by an innings. The following year, he met with more success with the bat as he opened the batting for the South Wales Cricket Association in their two-day contest against the Birmingham League at the Mitchell and Butler's ground.

His continued success for Newport saw Bert play for Glamorgan 2nd XI during 1935 against Middlesex 2nd XI at Osterley. With Maurice Turnbull playing for the South against the North at Lord's in mid-June 1936, Bert was drafted into the Glamorgan side, led by Johnnie Clay, for the match with Gloucestershire at Newport. Batting at number four, he made 3 and 0 in a match which, besides seeing the visitors win by 97 runs, was his sole appearance for the Welsh county in Championship cricket.

Bert married Sophia Fletcher in 1927 – they had four children.

333
PORTER, Arthur

Born – Clayton-le-Moors, 25 March 1914
Died – Newport, 20 February 1994
Amateur
RHB, RM/OB
Ed – Mount Pleasant School, Accrington
1st XI: 1935-1949
2nd XI: 1936-1950
Club and Ground: 1947
Cap: 1946
Clubs: Enfield, Newport

Batting and Fielding Record:

	M	I	NO	RUNS	AV	100	50	CT	ST
F-c	38	64	7	1292	22.67	2	5	16	-

Bowling Record:

	Balls	M	R	W	AV	5wI	10wM
F-c	966	24	480	16	30.00	-	-

Career-bests:

First-class – 105 v Surrey at The Oval, 1946
4/25 v Gloucestershire at Cardiff Arms Park, 1946

Arthur Porter played regularly for Enfield in the Lancashire Leagues from 1928 until 1934 before joining the police force and moving to Newport. He duly joined the town's club besides making his debut for Monmouthshire in 1935 in their match against Glamorgan during which he top-scored with an unbeaten 47.

With his name having gone into the notebooks of the Glamorgan selectors, Arthur made 45 and 47 in mid-May for the county's 2nd XI in their match against Middlesex 2nd XI at Finchley. With Maurice Turnbull absent for the match at Neath against Worcestershire at the end of June, Arthur was called up for his first-class debut. However, he made only a modest impact scoring 0 and 4, but a fortnight later Arthur was chosen in the party for the visit to Hove. Once again, he played a bit part, scoring 5 and 4 as Sussex recorded a five-wicket victory.

In both of the games for Glamorgan, Arthur had been fortunate enough to secure time-off from his

Arthur Porter.

police duties, but as the international situation deteriorated he had less and less time for cricket, and following the outbreak of War in 1939 he became a military policeman, overseeing operations at Newport Docks.

After being demobilized in the spring of 1946, he agreed to help Johnnie Clay and play on a regular basis for Glamorgan as they resumed their activities. In all, he played in eighteen matches and appeared regularly at number four in the order. Despite his modest previous record in county cricket, Arthur showed that, like a fine wine, his cricket had matured and in mid-July he scored his maiden century with an unbeaten 100 against Lancashire at the Arms Park. Just for good measure, he also claimed 4/25 with his off-cutters, whilst in the following match against Surrey at The Oval, Arthur reached three figures again as he posted 105 against an attack which included Alec Bedser and Alf Gover.

Boosted by his success with the bat, Arthur made a further sixteen appearances during 1947 – a summer which saw him fail to add to his tally of centuries, but nevertheless saw him play some useful innings, headlined by a fine 89 against Essex at Westcliff-on-Sea. His sojourn as a county cricketer came to an end in September 1947 as he secured a post as a Welfare Officer with the recently-formed British Steel Corporation in Newport.

However, Arthur was able to secure enough leave to play in one match during the Championship-winning summer of 1948, as well as the game in 1949 at Stradey Park, Llanelli, fittingly enough against Lancashire. Arthur also played regularly for the county's 2nd XI during his summer holidays with his final county appearances taking place in the early 1950s. After retiring from playing, Arthur acted as Newport's scorer for many years, whilst his son Brian followed in his father's footsteps by also appearing for the town club and Glamorgan 2nd XI.

334
SAMUEL, Glyndwr Ninian Thomas Watkin ('Glyn')

Born – Swansea, 26 October 1917
Died – Hastings, 14 April 1985
Amateur
RHB
Ed – St Helen's Primary School, Swansea and Uppingham School
1st XI: 1936
2nd XI: 1936-1937
Colts: 1934
Club and Ground: 1938
Club: Swansea
Rugby for Swansea

Batting and Fielding Record:

	M	I	NO	RUNS	AV	100	50	CT	ST
F-c	3	4	0	41	10.25	-	-	-	-

First-class –   22 v Leicestershire at St Helen's Swansea, 1936

Glyn Samuel was a promising schoolboy sportsman who had been in both the Uppingham cricket XI and rugby XV during 1934 and 1935, before playing at the age of eighteen on three occasions for Glamorgan in 1936.

Given the fact that his father ran The Cricketers Arms, overlooking the St Helen's ground, it is not surprising that young Glyn soon developed a love of ball games. His sporting talents were later honed at Uppingham School, with the youngster making his debut for Glamorgan Colts during 1934, besides playing at the Arms Park in a scratch Public Schools XI against the Welsh Secondary Schools. In 1935 he scored an impressive century for Uppingham against a touring Canadian schools side, and together with some decent innings for the Swansea club, he played regularly for the county's 2nd XI in their Minor County Championship matches during 1936 and 1937.

In mid-July 1936 the teenager played in three matches for Glamorgan, starting with the game at Swansea against Leicestershire. Batting at number nine, he made a composed 22 in his only innings as the Welsh county won by ten wickets. He retained his place for the away games with Sussex at Hove, and Nottinghamshire at Trent Bridge, but made 7, 2 and 10 in three nondescript innings and was never called up again.

During the late 1930s Glyn continued to play both cricket and rugby for Swansea, but like many of his generation he lost his best years to the Second World War. He was a talented fly-half for the All Whites, with the Uppingham School magazine recounting in 1935 how Glyn was "an excellent stand-off with a natural ability for the game. Did much towards the success of the side by his unselfish play."

Glyn Samuel.

Glyn initially worked as a turf accountant, before moving to East Sussex where he worked as a clerk in the Environment Department of Hastings Borough Council.

1937

The doom-mongers who had been in abundance around the grounds during 1936 were silenced as Glamorgan bounced back in 1937 from a moderate summer the year before to enjoy, by far, their best summer to date. 11 of the 28 Championship matches ended in victory as the Club yo-yoed back up to 7th place in the table. In addition, they twice defeated the New Zealanders with the game at Swansea helping to catapult Austin Matthews, their acquisition from Northamptonshire into the Test side.

Maurice Turnbull also struck a career-best 233* during a batting masterclass against Worcestershire at Swansea, whilst Arnold Dyson and Emrys Davies shared a record opening stand of 274 against Leicestershire where the latter also achieved the rare feat of a century and a hat-trick in the same game.

But, as commendable as these efforts were, the standout performance of the summer came from Johnnie Clay who recorded the record-breaking analysis of 17/212 against Worcestershire at Swansea, and all on a shirt-front wicket at St Helen's in a summer when he set a new Club record of 176 first-class wickets.

Willie Jones and Phil Clift also joined the conveyor belt of talent to emerge from the 2nd XI – from Carmarthenshire and Monmouthshire respectively – onto places in Glamorgan's 1st XI but despite these healthy moves forward and the plethora of individual records, 1937 also saw the Club sustain a loss of £1779 largely through a fall in membership and rise in the cost of staging 2nd XI games.

A signed scorecard of the match at Leicester during 1937 when Emrys Davies achieved the rare feat of a century and a hat-trick in the same match. As far as the latter was concerned, he dismissed George Geary, Fred Bowley and Haydon Smith in the home team's second innings.

335
JONES, William Edward ('Willie')

Born – Carmarthen, 31 October 1916
Died – Gloucester, 25 July 1996
Amateur 1937-1938
Professional 1946-1958
LHB, SLA
1st XI: 1937-1958
2nd XI: 1936-1957
Club and Ground: 1938-1957
Cap: 1937
West of England 1944; United Services 1944; South of England 1949-1956
Rugby for Llanelli, Neath, Penarth and Gloucester. Wartime international
cap for Wales
Clubs: Carmarthen, Morpeth

Batting and Fielding Record:

	M	I	NO	RUNS	AV	100	50	CT	ST
F-c	340	555	63	13270	27.00	11	76	117	-
Wartime	12	12	1	312	28.36	-	2	1	-

Bowling Record:

	Balls	M	R	W	AV	5wI	10wM
F-c	11558	438	5620	189	29.73	3	-

Career-bests:
First-class   212* v Essex at Brentwood, 1948
5/50 v Kent at Gravesend, 1949

The shy and mild-mannered Willie Jones was the first batsman in Glamorgan's history to hit a pair of double hundreds within the space of a fortnight. His achievement, which has only been equaled once (by Mike Powell) came in 1948 with 207 against Kent at Gravesend, followed by an unbeaten 212 against Essex at Brentwood, during a record breaking partnership of 313 for the third wicket with Emrys Davies.

Born and raised in Carmarthen, the diminutive left-handed batsman and spin bowler had a decent record for the Welsh schoolboys team and played as an amateur in the Glamorgan 2nd XI in the Minor County Championship between 1935 and 1937 as the Welsh county carefully groomed their next generation of players. His first chance at 1st XI level came in June 1937 when he played, batting at number 8, in Glamorgan's victory over Hampshire at Swansea. His elevation followed a series of attractive half-

Willie Jones.

centuries in the game with Cheshire, and he subsequently appeared in a further seven Championship matches in 1937 and eight during 1938.

He confirmed his rich promise with 74 against Essex in 1937, besides impressing with his swift fielding and safe catching in the outfield. As John Arlott wrote, "Quick and eager to start, he picks up at full speed and is always on balance for a fierce low throw before, under the applause, he toddles rather self-consciously back to his place."

His admirable athleticism came as no surprise because Willie was also an outstanding rugby player, and prior to the Second World War, it looked as if Willie might win international honours with the oval ball. Having played junior rugby for Llanelli, he became Neath's first choice fly-half from 1937/38 and the following season won a place in the first Welsh trial in 1938/39. He was promoted to the senior side for the second match in which *The Times* newspaper named him "outstanding player of the match." However, the Possibles turned the table on the Probables in the final trial, winning 21-6 and Willie missed out on selection for the Welsh XV. His dream of winning a Welsh cap had also seen him turn down an offer to turn professional and play rugby league for Salford.

After the outbreak of War, Willie played regularly for Neath during the fragmented 1939/40 season and on 9 March, 1940 Willie appeared in the first wartime International against England at Cardiff Arms Park. After joining the RAF, Willie spent time in Northumberland during which time he played cricket for Morpeth during 1942 and 1943 before being transferred to RAF Innsworth, near Gloucester. In November 1944 Corporal WE Jones was also one of three travelling reserves chosen by Wales for the match against England at Swansea, but this was the closest Willie got to international honours and, by the time the Five Nations Championship resumed after the War, his chance of a full International cap had gone.

Missing out on a full Welsh cap only added to Willie's anxious manner He never quite believed in his own ability, and Willie was so lacking in confidence that he would ask his wife to ring up the Glamorgan office to find out whether or not he had been selected to play. He was also a great worrier and when asleep in bed, Willie would often nudge his wife whilst deep in dreams saying "Run up, there's three there!"

An offer to join Gloucestershire also weighed heavily on his mind following his move during 1946 to play rugby for Gloucester. The Gloucestershire secretary had contacted Willie with a quite decent offer, especially relating to payments if he

Willie Jones demonstrates his batting abilities at the Arms Park.

was injured and unable to play cricket. His contract with Glamorgan was not so generous and led to Willie being as thrifty as possible on away trips and saving every penny in case of a rainy day. The more comprehensive and lucrative terms of the Gloucestershire offer led Willie to start thinking about switching to the West Country side. But this only set Willie off worrying about Wilf Wooller's reaction, as well as what his friends in the Glamorgan side would say. He decided to continue playing cricket with the Welsh county but ended up also appearing in county rugby for Gloucestershire.

Willie had played again for Neath against the touring New Zealand Army team on 3 November at The Gnoll, but when club rugby resumed in 1946/47 season he joined Gloucester, largely as a result of his time at RAF Innsworth. His fine form led to his selection for Gloucestershire and in the semi-final of the County Championship at the Kingsholm ground in Gloucester, he celebrated St David's Day by kicking 18 points in a 24-17 victory.

Two weeks later In the final against Lancashire at Blundellsands Willie dropped kicked two goals in the 8-8 draw. He also played well in the replay at Kingsholm which Gloucestershire narrowly lost, before the following season again kicking Gloucestershire to the semi-final of the County Championship where they lost to Eastern Counties at Bristol. In all games that season, Willie kicked a total of 214 points, earning him the epithet of "a kicking genius" by one journalist. His preference to kick rather than pass did however lead to some criticism, with one writer also commenting that Willie had "scant sense of an opening or constructive play."

Alongside his prowess with the oval ball, Willie became the mainstay of Glamorgan's middle order against the smaller, red leather ball. "Willie Bach", as he was known to one and all, was a gifted and wristy strokemaker, always ready to punish any wayward deliveries and possessing a rasping square-cut to anything short outside off stump. Having played in some of Glamorgan's wartime friendlies, courtesy of being a short car ride away at RAF Innsworth, he turned professional at the end of hostilities and joined Glamorgan's full-time staff for 1946. His maiden first-class hundred came in 1947 with 132 against Essex at the Arms Park, and the following year he went from strength to strength as during the Championship-winning summer he topped the batting averages and amassed 1655 runs.

Despite having a solitary hundred to his name, 1948 saw Willie record his maiden double-hundred against Kent at Gravesend. After returning to the pavilion with 207 runs to his name, he acknowledged the back-slapping and praise of his colleagues by saying "I'll never do that again!"

Yet a fortnight later at Brentwood, he and Emrys Davies shared a record stand of 313 for the third wicket with the pair confusing the hapless Essex fielders by calling to each other in Welsh. Both scored double hundreds, with Willie's contribution being an unbeaten 212. Again there was plenty of hand-shaking when Willie wearily returned to the Glamorgan changing room, with the modest batsman turning to Wilf and saying "Dieu, everybody's going to expect me to score 200 every time I bat!"

The following day there was a veritable avalanche of telegrams and letters of congratulations awaiting Willie in the Glamorgan changing room. He began to open some of the envelopes, but then stopped. "Why don't you carry on opening them?" enquired a curious colleague to which Willie replied "I'm going to keep them for when I have a bad day."

Like several others in the Glamorgan team, Willie was in awe of Wilf and his prowess on the rugby field. This led to a lot of friendly banter and leg-pulling in the dressing room, with others teasing Willie that, given his outstanding record at drop-kicking goals for Gloucester, he was actually a better kicker of a rugby ball than Wilf. Indeed, rugby historians believe that Willie's record was one of the reasons why the dropped goal was reduced in value from 4 to 3 points from the winter of 1948/49.

On occasions after play, and with several drinks inside him, Willie would throw down a wager with Wilf over who could kick the furthest, and there are tales of the players gathering in the evening gloom at the Arms Park or St Helen's, as Willie and Wilf held a kicking contest on the rugby field. Their colleagues would ensure fair play by measuring each kick and if Willie was still behind, he would tenaciously continue until the ground was bathed in moonlight.

Willie Jones – the left-arm spinner.

But his winter recreation impacted on his cricket, just when he seemed poised to press for a place in the England side as during November 1948 he damaged his knee whilst playing rugby for Gloucester. After treatment, he returned to club and county rugby but after enduring further pain, the medics advised him that he would be jeopardizing playing for Glamorgan during 1949 if he continued. In February 1949 Willie duly told Gloucester RFC that his season was over and he put all of his efforts into preparing help Glamorgan defend the county title.

Willie's success with the bat in 1948 and his decent early season form in 1949 led to his selection in the South XI which met the North XI in the Test Trial at Edgbaston. The three-day encounter saw Willie bat at number four with his county colleague Allan Watkins at number five. Willie did not disgrace himself with innings of 2 and 24 in the drawn game, but he missed out on selection in the first two Tests of the summer against the New Zealanders before his season came to a juddering halt as he aggravated his knee injury again whilst fielding in Glamorgan's match during the first week of July against Lancashire at Old Trafford.

A broken patella was diagnosed, forcing him onto the sidelines for the rest of the summer, besides ending his rugby-playing career. His knee injury also restricted his bowling opportunities, with his haul of 47 invaluable wickets during 1948 remaining his best, and most important contribution with the ball. Despite having an operation to fuse his broken kneecap, the injury also ended any aspirations he held about playing Test cricket as, after regaining fitness in 1950, no further opportunities came his way to impress at the highest level.

He continued though to be a consistent run-scorer, passing the thousand mark on five occasions during the 1950s, whilst in 1953 – Willie's Benefit Year – he etched his name once again into the county record books with a sixth-wicket stand of 230 with Len Muncer at New Road. Both batsmen scored hundreds and, with the Welsh county benefitting from their efforts to the tune of a first innings lead of 148, Worcestershire were left fighting to save the match on the final day.

Despite having so many years of experience behind him, plus several batting records to his name, Willie still remained a bag of nerves, sat whilst waiting his turn to bat, chain smoking with trembling fingers, and almost unable to speak. On occasions, his fragile temperament saw him back away from fast bowling. But if he got hit on the shoulder or backside, Willie responded by unfurling some classical and perfectly-timed strokes.

His great pal during the 1950s was Jim McConnon, another player who at times lacked confidence and self-belief. Indeed, Phil Clift recalled how the pair would support each other when the players gathered

Willie Jones plays forcibly through the covers.

after play, either in the changing rooms, or a hostelry, to discuss the days events. "Willie was never too timid after a couple of drinks to voice an opinion", the former batsman and Club Secretary recalled, "But it was Jim McConnon who made the bullets and it was Willie who fired them!"

Willie's nervousness and shaking hands prevented him from being a catcher close to the wicket, but his running skills which had allowed him to play rugby at almost the highest level meant he was a good fielder at cover, mid-wicket or in the deep. But there were days when he erred and Peter Walker recalled one during the mid-1950s when Willie, at deep square-leg dropped a catch off Wilf's bowling. "Willie was inconsolable but a couple of overs later another catch came to him off Wilf's bowling, and down went that chance too. Now he could barely stop shaking: what would Wilf be thinking and surely it couldn't happen again? But it did. This time the batsman middled a powerful sweep, and like a bullet, the ball flew at head high straight at Willie. Seeing another probably dropped catch, Willie stood stock still, opened his arms wide and shouted "Hit me!" Luckily the ball brushed the top of his cap en route to the boundary and even Wilf joined in the general roar of laughter!"

Willie retired at the end of the 1958 season. He might have carried on for at least another year but as the summer progressed, he became more and more concerned by the off-field politics and bickering about the future of Wilf. Matters were not helped by the arrival of the rather haughty Tolly Burnett and with the latter sending reports on each player to the committee, the offer of a coaching position at Dean Close School in Cheltenham, led to Willie announcing his retirement.

To many, Willie Jones will be remembered as the nearly man, and the person who came so very close to being a double international. His dreams of a Welsh rugby cap thwarted by the outbreak of the Second World War, and his quest of a England cricket cap ended by a fractured patella. Others, especially those weaned on cricket in the immediate post-war era will remember the way, at 5 foot 5 inches, he epitomized the way Glamorgan, as the Championship minnow's, lowered the honours of the so-called county giants. Those closer to him will also remember his warm heart and compassion, as well as his puckish sense of humour which in one game at the Arms Park saw him overtake his lumbering partner Haydn Davies, as the pair ran three – much to the confusion and, if truth were known, the mirth of the umpires!

A photograph from the mid 1950s showing Willie Jones (right) plus Norman Riches and Western Mail journalist Bryn Thomas on the rugby field at the Arms Park.

336
CLIFT, Phil Brittain

Born – Usk, 3 September 1918
Died – Cardiff, 22 May 2005
Professional
RHB, OB
1st XI: 1937-1955
2nd XI: 1936-1970
Colts: 1936-1958
Club and Ground: 1936-1955
Cap: 1938, (1947)
Coach 1955-1977, Secretary 1978-1982
Clubs: Usk, Abertillery, Maesteg Celtic, Neath

Batting and Fielding Record:

	M	I	NO	RUNS	AV	100	50	CT	ST
F-c	183	306	21	6055	21.24	7	28	169	-
Wartime	2	2	0	83	41.50	-	1	-	-

Bowling Record:

	Balls	M	R	W	AV	5wI	10wM
F-c	1325	37	675	11	61.36	-	-

Career-bests:
First-class – 125* v Derbyshire at Cardiff Arms Park, 1949
3/6 v Sussex at Llanelli, 1951

1948 was a momentous year for both Glamorgan CCC and Usk as the small Monmouthshire town which – with a population of 1500 – supplied two members of the Welsh's county's Championship winning squad in Phil Clift and his great pal Allan Watkins.

Their emergence, as county cricketers of note, more than justified Glamorgan's decision back in 1934, to merge with Monmouthshire with the entry of a 2nd XI in their name into the Minor County Championship the following summer allowing the likes of Phil and Allan to make the transition from club cricket to county level. In the case of Allan, he went on to win honours in international cricket, but for Phil, it was also the start of a lifetime of service to Glamorgan Cricket as he acted as a player, coach, scorer and secretary for the Welsh county.

Phil Clift.

News about Phil's prolific form as a sixteen-year-old batsman had reached the ears of Glamorgan officials via rather unorthodox means, as it originated not from officials of the Usk club but from Father Hodges, the local Catholic priest, who was only too delighted to pass on details to Maurice Turnbull, the Glamorgan captain and an influential figure in the religious community of South Wales. After extolling the virtues of the youngster, who had struck 120 against Ross-on-Wye, Father Hodges said he would be only too happy to bring Phil for a trial in nets at the Arms Park. This duly took place and did not need divine assistance as Phil suitably impressed both Bill Hitch, the Club's coach, as well as Maurice himself who was only too glad to thank Father Hodges for his recommendation. Shortly afterwards, Phil was chosen in the Glamorgan Colts side to play their counterparts from Somerset. He confirmed his rich potential by scoring 137, besides taking eight wickets, and the following week he received a congratulatory letter from Maurice inviting him to an interview in the Club's office to discuss terms as a junior professional.

It was quite awe-inspiring experience for the schoolboy and, as he remembered, "I nervously sat outside until Miss Poole, Maurice's secretary, told me to go in. She also said, just stand in front of the desk and let Mr Turnbull speak to you. I duly did what I was told and stood in front of Maurice's huge writing desk – 'Well, Clift, why do you want to be a cricketer?' he said, to which I replied 'I love the game of cricket, sir, and want to play it every day.' There was a pause and then Maurice said 'We will find out about that' and then scribbled down a few details about me. The following week, a letter arrived at my home, offering me a contract with the terms of £2 10 shillings a week in the summer, and £1 a week in the winter. I was delighted to accept."

The following summer Phil made his Championship debut against Kent and besides playing some free-scoring innings, he impressed with his swift fielding and smart catching close to the wicket. By the time, the Second World War broke out in 1939, Phil seemed destined to post a maiden first-class century but he had to wait another eight years before reaching this personal milestone. He joined the Royal Air Force and his rich promise as a cricketer was recognized by his selection for an Anti-Aircraft side against the RAF at Blackpool in 1943 as well as for a Services XI against the Eastern Counties at Edgbaston the following summer.

His cricketing progress was also interrupted by a bout of TB but he recovered and after rejoining the Glamorgan staff in 1947, he registered his maiden hundred against Nottinghamshire at Trent Bridge. The following summer, the 29 year-old batsman so impressed the touring Australians with a composed innings for Glamorgan at Swansea against the fiery pace of Ray Lindwall and Keith Miller, that when asked by the English Press to name some of the uncapped batsmen who had impressed them most during Australia's tour to England in 1948, one of the names given by no less a judge than Don Bradman was Phil Clift.

He confirmed the opinion of the legendary batsman by enjoying a fabulous summer in 1949 – a year which saw him pass a thousand runs for the first time in his career, with his tally including 104 against Kent at Swansea, followed the next match by an unbeaten 101 against Essex at Ebbw Vale, and then later in the season Phil registered a career-best

125* in the six-wicket victory over Derbyshire at Cardiff.

However, by his own admission, his finest innings that summer was the hundred at Ebbw Vale after Essex's captain Tom Pearce had set Glamorgan a stiff target of 177 in just 105 minutes. As Tom headed back to the pavilion, the visiting leader said to Wilf Wooller "Now let's see what your fast scoring batsmen can do!" Phil responded by swatting Trevor Bailey, the England all-rounder for a massive six in the opening over, before striking a further 14 boundaries with a sparkling innings of 101 as Glamorgan galloped to their target for the loss of one wicket, and all in the space of just 79 minutes.

With the ball having been dispatched by Phil to all parts of the Welfare Ground, the Essex team were rather shell-shocked as they trooped up the steps to the small pavilion and shook hands with the

Phil Clift in a specially posed photograph batting at the Arms Park.

delighted Glamorgan side. As Tom shook hands with a jubilant Wilf, the home captain loudly said "Well Tom, my batsmen are pretty bloody quick when they try, aren't they!"

By this time, Phil had become an important member of the Glamorgan leg-trap, with the Usk-born professional standing fearlessly at backward short-leg, whilst Wilf stood alongside at forward short-leg, and his friend Allan Watkins at leg-slip. This trio of alert fielders rarely let anything miss their grasp, and the excellence of the close catching was one of the most important factors in Glamorgan's emergence in the County Championship after the Second World War, as well as a stunning victory over the 1951 Springboks at Swansea where Phil held some vital catches in the South African's fateful second innings.

1951 also saw Phil reach three figures again as he made 109 against Middlesex at Swansea, followed in 1952 by 100 at

Phil Clift seen batting against Gloucestershire during 1950.

262

Northampton and then the following year by an unbeaten 111 in the away match with Nottinghamshire. But by the time of this century at Trent Bridge, Phil had been affected by further bouts of illness which coupled with his diabetes left him feeling quite drained after long days in the field. With a decent crop of young batsmen emerging, he opted to retire from playing in 1955 and become the captain of Glamorgan 2nd XI and the Club's Assistant Coach.

The sudden death the following July of George Lavis saw Phil elevated to Head Coach and for the next two decades, in his caring and sharing way, he helped to groom and inspire the next generation of county cricketers. His reward for the long hours in the Indoor Schools in Neath, Ebbw Vale and Cardiff Arms Park was Glamorgan's success during the 1960s, culminating with the Championship title again in 1969, in addition to back-to-back victories over Australia in 1964 and 1968, with all of the home-grown players in the Championship-winning team having come through Phil's hands and being taught, in his own words, the correct way to play the game – "Hard, but fair".

In 1959 Phil also combined his coaching duties with work as the county's Assistant Secretary. It followed a summer of upheaval within the Club and his close friendship with Wilf meant that he became his trusted right-hand man in the office. In 1977 Phil duly stepped into Wilf's shoes as Glamorgan Secretary after his friend retired. Phil himself retired in 1982 after a lifetime's service to the Club. But this did not end his association with Glamorgan Cricket as over the course of the next dozen years, he acted as a talent scout, as well as scoring for the youth teams, besides on occasions, acting in this important capacity for the senior side.

Phil died in Cardiff after a short illness during May 2005 and it

Phil Clift catches Bert Wolton as Glamorgan's leg-trap claims another victim.

was a measure of his immense popularity that so many of the players whose career he had helped to guide were present at the Memorial Service held near his home in Whitchurch. As Mike Fatkin said in his capacity as Glamorgan's Chief Executive "Phil was a legendary figure within the Club and a very nice man to boot, who always had the best interests of the club at heart."

337
MATTHEWS, Austin David George

Born – Penarth, 3 May 1904
Died – Penrhyn Bay, Llandudno, 29 July 1977
Professional
RHB, RFM
Ed – St David's College, Lampeter
1st XI: 1937-1947
Club and Ground: 1923, 1938
Cap: 1937
Northamptonshire 1927-1936; England 1937 (1 Test);
Clubs: Cardiff, Penarth, Undercliffe, The Pterodactyls
Rugby for Penarth and Northampton; Table Tennis for Wales

Batting and Fielding Record:

	M	I	NO	RUNS	AV	100	50	CT	ST
F-c	51	71	24	691	14.70	-	-	12	-
Wartime	2	1	0	1	1.00	-	-	1	-

Bowling Record:

	Balls	M	R	W	AV	5wI	10wM
F-c	9380	355	3607	277	15.88	16	4
Wartime	?	?	?	4	-	-	-

Career-bests:
First-class –   37 v Essex at Chelmsford, 1946
             7/12 v Somerset at Ynysangharad Park, Pontypridd, 1946

Austin Matthews was playing Test cricket barely three weeks after making his Glamorgan debut in 1937. His remarkable elevation followed a most impressive spell of fast swing bowling against the New Zealanders, and a return of 14-132 against Sussex on a plumb wicket at Hastings. As a result, he was drafted into the England side for the Third Test at The Oval, where he dismissed Walter Hadlee in both innings.

Austin had initially emerged as a talented young sportsman during the early 1920s playing cricket for Cardiff and rugby for Penarth, besides representing Wales at table tennis. In 1923 he appeared alongside his lifelong friend Maurice Turnbull in the Glamorgan Club and Ground teams, as well as for The Pterodactyls – a team of promising schoolboys and young students – as the county's selectors ran their eye over the emerging talent. Austin also declined a fairly modest offer to join

Austin Matthews, as seen on a cigarette card.

Glamorgan's junior staff in preference to completing his college studies and pursuing his rugby career playing as a forward with Penarth RFC.

But after graduating from Lampeter, he joined Northampton RFC where his success with the oval ball also saw Austin win a place in a final Welsh Trial in 1929, thereby emulating the feats of his father Frederick who had also played rugby for Penarth and had appeared in a final trial in 1896. By this time, and with the possibility of winning a Welsh cap, Austin opted to stay fit over the summer months by playing club cricket. His success as a seam bowler in the local leagues came to the attention of the Northamptonshire selectors and in 1927 he made his first-class debut against the 1927 New Zealanders at Kettering.

He became a regular in the East Midlands side in 1928, but despite his appearance in the Welsh trial, nothing came of a place in the Welsh rugby team. As one door closed, another opened as Austin became the spearhead of Northamptonshire's new ball attack, claiming 76 first-class wickets in 1931, 70 in 1932 and 93 in 1933 during a summer which saw him claim 7 five-wicket hauls. His partnership with Nobby Clark, the left-arm quickie, added spice to what hitherto had been an attack dominated by medium-pace.

Austin Matthews –
Northamptonshire,
Glamorgan and England!

Austin enjoyed another good summer in 1936, claiming 84 first-class scalps, but a difference of opinion over the financial terms of a new contract led him to sever his links with Northamptonshire. It appeared that his career in county cricket had come to an abrupt end as he secured a coaching appointment at Stowe School. At the end of the Summer Term in 1937, he returned to his family's home in Penarth believing that his days of professional cricket were behind him. But once again, he met with good fortune having after making contact with Maurice, the highly influential Glamorgan captain.

News of Austin's return to South Wales came as manna from heaven for Maurice as Glamorgan were facing something of an injury crisis. Jack Mercer, their long-serving opening bowler was carrying a leg injury, whilst other seamers were out of form or injured as well. Maurice was eager to find a replacement and with nothing else planned for the rest of the summer, Austin agreed to help out.

After the MCC had swiftly ratified his signing, Austin made his Glamorgan debut on 28 July, against Gloucestershire at Newport and he soon made an impact, taking two wickets for just ten runs in a fiery opening burst. His pace and movement also caused problems for the New Zealanders when they made another fruitless journey to South Wales, going down to a massive 332-run defeat as the Glamorgan bowlers scythed through their batting once again with Austin taking four wickets in their first innings, before Johnnie Clay and Emrys Davies claimed five apiece in their second innings.

Austin continued his purple patch during the next Championship match against Sussex at Hastings, as he took seven wickets in each innings. His career-best return of 14/132 on a perfect batting strip sent many tongues wagging, and not just in the Glamorgan camp as England selector Percy Perrin had travelled to the South Coast, ostensibly to watch Emrys who was enjoying a fine summer with both bat and ball. Although Emrys struck a sound hundred, it was Austin's bowling that caught Percy's eye. He duly followed this up with a further six wickets against Somerset at Weston-super-Mare, and on 9 August – just thirteen days after his Glamorgan debut – the England selectors drafted him into their squad for the Third Test match.

With the selectors looking ahead to the visit of the Australians in 1938 and with Bill Bowes and Ken Farnes both injured, and Freddie Brown out of favour, Austin got his chance at The Oval. He opened the bowling with Alf Gover and bowled Walter Hadlee, besides later in the Kiwi's innings catching Lindsay Weir. When England replied, he batted at number 9 and was unbeaten on 2 when England went past the New Zealand total of 249. He again dismissed Hadlee, courtesy of a catch by Denis Compton, and returned figures of 8-2-13-1 as the game ended in a draw.

A. MATTHEWS Glam.

With England not touring in 1937/38 he did not get a chance to add further to his Test caps and instead returned to Stowe to continue his coaching duties, besides agreeing to help out Glamorgan during the second part of the summer. He duly claimed 30 wickets in seven appearances including a ten-wicket match haul against Kent at Maidstone as he returned figures of 10/128.

Austin then had a spell coaching at Cambridge University in 1939 prior to claiming 50 wickets in eleven matches for the Welsh county, with the highlight of his summer coming at Swansea where he had a match return of 10/76, including figures of 7/21 in the first innings, but his efforts were not quite enough to see Glamorgan to victory as the tourists won a low-scoring encounter by two wickets.

A cartoon caricature of Austin Matthews.

Following the outbreak of the Second World War Austin joined the Royal Air Force and rose to the rank of pilot officer. Based in the south-east of England, he was able to appear for the RAF in various fund-raising matches besides playing for an England XI in a special contest against The Dominions in 1944 as well as travelling back to South Wales to take part in several of the special games which Glamorgan had organized.

After being demobbed, he made himself available to Glamorgan as county cricket resumed in 1946. He duly enjoyed another purple patch of form, with some dubbing him the renaissance man as he ended the summer with 93 wickets at just 14.29 as Glamorgan ended the summer in the top half of the table. He also helped with the coaching duties and the young bowlers could have had no finer tutor as he claimed half a dozen five-wicket hauls including career-best figures of 7/12 against Somerset on a rain-sodden wicket at Ynysangharad Park. In addition he completed a match return of 11/77, with figures of 6/67 and 5/10 against Lancashire at Old Trafford.

Glamorgan's officials had hoped he would agree to play again in 1947, but with another coaching offer from Cambridge University, plus work on various training manuals, he was only able to turn out in five games in 1947 before calling time on his varied and successful career as a professional cricketer, with his final appearance coming for Glamorgan against Nottinghamshire at Trent Bridge.

Maurice Turnbull and Don Bradman head out to the middle at St Helen's for the toss ahead of Glamorgan's game against the 1938 Australians at Swansea.

1938

Hopes were high of another productive summer but the Club only won 5 of their 24 Championship fixtures and slipped back to 16th place in the table. Whilst the Glamorgan captain of the 1920s would have been very satisfied with five victories, it was now very different, especially as Maurice Turnbull and others had talked up the emergence of promising young talent and had sweet-talked the Club's bankers about the overall improvement.

There were however mitigating circumstances, much to Maurice's relief as Johnnie Clay, Wilf Hughes, Cyril Smart, Jack Mercer and the Glamorgan captain himself were all struck down by various ailments, with the Club's leader ironically injuring his left leg whilst turning sharply in a game of squash on the courts at Cardiff Squash Club which he himself had helped to create in Ryder Street in a bid to boost the city's sporting facilities and where the players, could stay fit as well as enjoying the racquet sport!

After an operation on his damaged cartilage, Maurice was back in the Glamorgan side for the match against Yorkshire at the Arms Park – a game which in the wider history of the Club and sport in Wales as a whole proved to be a totemic one as Wilf Wooller, the Denbighshire and Cambridge University all-rounder made his debut in Glamorgan's colours. The man who was the star in Welsh rugby, and who subsequently led the county to higher honours after the Second World War enjoyed a productive time and was amongst a batch of other amateurs who had their first taste of county cricket during 1938.

But 1938 did not see the Glamorgan 2nd XI play in the Minor County competition as the costs became too prohibitive. In fact, the rising debts over 1937/38 led to a deputation from the club, including Sir William Reardon-Smith, an influential shipowner in Cardiff and Vice-President of Glamorgan CCC, meeting with the Manager of the Midland Bank to discuss the situation. To ease the situation the Manager gave Glamorgan an unsecured overdraft for nine months, allowing some 2nd XI friendlies to be staged in 1938.

338
WOOLLER, Wilfred

Born – Rhos-on-Sea, 20 November, 1912
Died – Cardiff, 10 March, 1997
Amateur
RHB, RM
Ed – Llandudno County Grammar School; Rydal School and Christ's College,
Cambridge
1st XI: 1938-1962
2nd XI: 1961-1965
Captain: 1947-1960; Secretary 1961-1977
Denbighshire 1930-1934; Lancashire 2nd XI 1932; Cambridge University 1935-1936
(Blue both years); MCC 1947-1948; South 1947; Gentlemen 1947-1953; HDG Leveson
Gower's XI 1947; England XI 1955
Clubs: Colwyn Bay, St Fagans, JHP Brain's XI, MCC, XL Club
Rugby for Cambridge University, Sale, Cardiff and Wales 1932/33-1938/39 (18 caps)
Football for Cardiff City and squash for Wales

Batting and Fielding Record:

	M	I	NO	RUNS	AV	100	50	CT	ST
F-c	400	630	72	12692	21.60	5	61	392	-

Bowling Record:

	Balls	M	R	W	AV	5wI	10wM
F-c	54472	2330	23511	887	26.50	40	5

Career-bests:
First-class – 128 v Warwickshire at The Gnoll, Neath, 1955
            8/45 v Warwickshire at Ebbw Vale, 1953

Wilf Wooller was a bit like Marmite – you either loved or loathed him! To the latter camp, he was an outspoken and trouble-making autocrat, a combative and argumentative bully, prone to explosions of outrageous political incorrectness whilst to the former he was an inspirational and supreme captain, tough as titanium and a man who always lead from the front and stood up, like a crusader in the Middle Ages, for what he perceived to be right.

Whichever camp you are in, you cannot decry Wilf's achievements for Glamorgan, or Welsh sport in general. If Maurice Turnbull was the architect of Glamorgan during the 1930s, Wilf was the man who laid the post-war foundations and watched the Club flourish from 1948 when, under his astute leadership, the Welsh county won the Championship. Over the

Wilf Wooller.

269

next 50 years, Wilf lived and breathed Glamorgan cricket, fulfilling every role within the Club, from player to secretary and latterly as President. As one sage of the Pressbox wrote "If he strolled through the corridors of cricket power with an almost arrogant air, few would question his well-informed background of the game he loved and the rich knowledge he contributed to its well-being."

What would have been his maturest years as an all-round sportsman were lost to the Second World War, much of which he spent in Japanese-run Prisoner of War camps. His grim time in captivity, where life and death were seamlessly intertwined, had a transformational change on his character. He had gone to War as a carefree and happy-go-lucky sportsman, but returned as a tough and uncompromising personality who viewed cricket as a battle of wills and mental ruthlessness, often standing fearlessly at short-leg or silly mid-on and snarling words of advice inter-mixed with contempt to opposing batsmen.

Peter Cranmer, his colleague as an undergraduate for Cambridge, and later an opponent with Warwickshire, also observed how the post-War Wooller was very different to the pre-War one. "If Wilf now felt strongly about something and considered it would be beneficial to Glamorgan, he did it, regardless of whether it heaped criticism on himself – and God knows, there were plenty of occasions when it did. But no amount of criticism shook him. He believed in himself and Glamorgan, though not necessarily in that order."

When Wilf led Glamorgan to the Championship in 1948, it was said that whilst his players idolized him; those in other teams loathed him. Even some of the London press could barely believe that the Welsh county had won a competition dominated by the big English counties. Everyone based west of Offa's Dyke had a broad smile on their face as under the 'Wooller way', success finally came to a county for too long considered to be the Cinderella of the cricket world. Under Wilf that summer, they certainly went to the ball!

Born in Rhos-on-Sea during the year the *Titanic* sank and Captain Scott came second in the race to the South Pole, he was the second of five boys born to Wilfred and Ethel Wooller. Wilf's father had run a successful building enterprise in Eccles, near Lancashire before moving to Rhos-on-Sea to, quite literally cash in on the building boom in the resort town. Besides erecting some substantial properties, Wilfred senior also helped to create the ground used by Colwyn Bay CC (and latterly Glamorgan) off Penrhyn Avenue.

The Woollers. Back row – Roy, Pop, Jack and Wilf. In front – Gordon.

His father was also a keen cricketer, renowned as a fast, but erratic new ball bowler and tail-end hitter. 'Little Wilfred' and his brothers Jack, Roy, Gordon and Peter dutifully went along to watch their father play and play cricket with a tennis ball, but football was his favourite sport as a young schoolboy in Llandudno and he shone as a centre-forward in the school team. Some fifteen years later, Wilf also played in the same position for Cardiff City in their fund-raising matches. Having the football club's Chairman Sir Herbert Merritt as his employer no doubt helped Wilf's selection for the Bluebirds, together with his standing as the pin-up boy of Welsh rugby.

Wilf and his brothers had received a tragic jolt during 1924 when their mother died of septicemia a few days after giving birth to Peter. His father subsequently married Clara Brooks, the daughter of a well-to-do solicitor, who ran an infant school in Rhos-on-sea. It was Clara who helped to pave the way for Wilf to enter Rydal School, but at first, Wilf did not like his stepmother's idea as Rydal was a rugby, rather than a football school. However, he was won over as a boarder in Glanabber House by Donald Boumphrey who, besides being Housemaster, was also master-in-charge of rugby and cricket. He had played rugby to a high level, besides representing Cheshire and Denbighshire at cricket, and winning the Military Cross for bravery whilst fighting for King and Country in the bloody battles on the Somme and Passchendaele. As Wilf later recalled, "Through his influence I soon

Wilf, seen on the right during the Wales-England rugby international in 1933 at Twickenham.

forgot about football with Donald often wandering into our dormitory before lights out and talking at length to us about sport."

Given his sturdy physique, Wilf initially played as a prop forward for Rydal, whilst his tall frame allowed him to develop a high windmill-like bowling action and win a place in the 1st XI as a fast bowler. With the legendary SF Barnes living locally and spending time in the nets at Colwyn Bay, Wilf was able to pick up further advice, besides broadening his cricketing education with visits to watch Lancashire and England play at Old Trafford.

His good form for Rydal and Colwyn Bay led to his selection during 1930 for Denbighshire, whilst the following year he struck his maiden hundred for Rydal. However, it was his bowling that was his stronger suit. With Lord Colwyn also acting as President of Lancashire CCC, Wilf's name reached the ears of the Red Rose county and during August 1932 he played for the county's 2nd XI against Durham at Old Trafford. It was his sole appearance for them, although in 1949 they made an unofficial approach to Wilf to join Lancashire and take over the captaincy. By then, his heart was well and truly in South Wales so he declined the offer.

The 1930s also saw Wilf's rugby career take off with the strong-running inside-centre leading the Rydal XV in 1932/33 during his third-year in the Sixth Form as he completed his preparations to read geography and anthropology at Christ's College, Cambridge. He also played for Sale, alongside Claud Davey, the Welsh international, with the two forming a formidable pairing which earned them a place in the Possibles team for the final Welsh Trial at St Helen's. It was Wilf's first-ever visit to South Wales, and, as he travelled with his father by train to Swansea, the schoolboy had his first taste of the fervour surrounding Welsh rugby as two others in their compartment began discussing the players chosen, with the man sat next to Wilf saying to his companion "Who's this Wooller from up north?"

Nobody watching the game was left in doubt about the abilities of the youngster as he scored a fine solo try as the Probables were beaten 15-6. Both he and Claud were duly included in the team to

Wilf – the undergraduate at Cambridge on the right with a friend.

play England, alongside Glamorgan cricketers Maurice Turnbull, Viv Jenkins and Ronnie Boon, and a fortnight after the game at Swansea, Wilf celebrated the first of his eighteen caps by being a member of the first-ever Welsh side to win at Twickenham.

For the first of so many times during his epic sporting career, the Sixth Former proved that he was not a man for walk-on roles. Besides being part of a quick move which saw Wilf burst through and feed Ronnie on the wing to score the match-winning try, he also made some crunching tackles – one of which led a journalist to write "with long, raking strides Wooller went after Elliot and before the Englishman had covered half of the necessary distance, he crashed him to the earth with a tackle which neither England nor Elliot will soon forget."

Blessed with the physical attributes of wide shoulders, powerful hips and long, muscular legs, the fourteen-stone youngster was a formidable sight in full flow with ball in hand. As JBG Thomas, the doyen of rugby writers (and later a close friend of Wilf's) once wrote, "in full flight he scattered opponents to left and right, leaving them well behind as would a Derby winner to a selling plater. His tremendous pace and stride carried him past, around and through opponents, who scarcely believed such a powerfully built man could move so quickly."

Whilst up at Cambridge, Wilf formed an outstanding partnership with Cliff Jones, with the pair also enjoying life to the full. Their adventures included an action-packed three-week rugby tour of the United States besides many parties with the other young and virile undergraduates from Wales, one of which during Wilf's final year in residence landed him in hot water with the College's Senior Registrar, into whose flat below a number of partygoers tumbled as its ceiling collapsed under the weight of so many people who wanted to mingle with Wilf and his famous pal!

In November 1935 Wilf also earned the epithet 'The Dragon of Wales' as he played a key role in the totemic and nail-biting victory over the All Blacks at the Arms Park. It

Wilf Wooller walks out to bat.

came during the closing minutes as Wales were trailing 12-10. As Wilf later recalled, "we had already lost Don Tarr, our hooker, who was stretchered off with a broken neck, but in the final phase of the game, we gained a scrum in the middle of the park. Our seven forwards heeled the ball, and fly-half Cliff Jones, running flat out passed the ball on to me at inside-centre. I looked to pass the ball to Claud Davey outside me but noticed that his opposite number was running straight towards him. I held onto the ball and burst into the open towards the full-back before punting the ball over his head." Wilf sprinted past the Kiwi but could not gather the ball as it bounced back over his head from the semi-frozen turf in the in-goal area. Wilf tumbled helplessly into the straw, used the previous night to protect the pitch, which was piled up beyond the dead-ball line. "But as I fell, I heard a tremendous roar. Geoffrey Rees-Jones, the Oxford winger following up, had caught the ball as it was coming down and dived over in the corner. We had won on the stroke of time 13-12."

During the summer months, Wilf also won a place in the Cambridge XI, with his contemporaries including future England cricketers Norman Yardley, Billy Griffith and Paul Gibb, as well as West Indian 'Monkey' Cameron and Indian fast bowler Jahangir Khan. Wilf was also a member of the Light Blues side which defeated Oxford by 195 runs in the 1935 Varsity Match, and in true Wooller style, he celebrated becoming a Double Blue by heading with friends after the game in a journey across the English Channel to sample the nocturnal delights of Paris.

But Wilf's exploits on another occasion got him into trouble again. After a night of heavy drinking with his chums, they had celebrated the end of their final examinations by collecting a series of souvenirs to take back to their rooms, including the receiver from a telephone box outside the main college gates. But local police saw their antics, which resulted in Wilf and others being sent down from Cambridge after pleading guilty in the Magistrates Courts to acts of gross public disorder.

Wilf duly secured a job in Cardiff, after advice from Cliff Jones, with the graduate working for the coal exporting firm of Gueret, Llewellyn and Morgan. The company's managing director was Herbert Merrett, an avid supporter of rugby and football, besides owning many fine greyhounds who raced at the Arms Park. Under Herbert's guidance Wilf spent the next couple of years, playing rugby for Cardiff, and Wales, besides learning the coal trade in further detail by working in North Africa. At first, Wilf had little time for cricket, but when back in the UK, he joined St Fagans for 1938, finding, in his own words "the club, its ground and its members the ideal summer break for me." His fiery swing bowling, as well as his lusty hitting, soon attracted the Glamorgan selectors, with Jack Mercer, the veteran seamer, watching Wilf on several occasions in the belief that the Cambridge Blue could augment the county's injury-struck attack.

A photograph of Wilf in bowling action.

Maurice Turnbull, the Glamorgan captain was fully aware of Wilf's sporting credentials and supported Jack's view, so an invitation was sent to Wilf to play against Yorkshire at Cardiff in mid-June, After Herbert Merritt agreed to release him from his duties at the Docks, Wilf pulled on a Glamorgan sweater for the first time on 15 June, 1938. Once again, he had an immediate impact, taking 3/22 during a hostile opening spell before adding two later wickets to record a maiden county 'five-for'. His commitments with GLM meant he did not play again until July, but he impressed again, this time with the bat, striking a half-century in even time against Kent.

The following year at the Cardiff ground, Wilf hit 111 in a shade over two hours against the 1939 West Indians, besides claiming 5/69 to set up a 73-run victory. His all-round contribution led to joyous celebrations at the Cardiff ground, and later in the bar at the Cardiff Squash Club where Wilf had developed his racquet-playing skills, besides mixing with many of his sporting friends. But as war clouds gathered and Germany invaded Poland, it was time for the fun and frolics to end, as Wilf, and several of his sporting pals, joined the Territorial Army section of the Heavy Anti-Aircraft Regiment. As members of 242 Battery, they were based initially at Lavernock Point, guarding the ports of Barry and Cardiff, with training being mixed with some sport. The latter included a rugby match at the Arms Park during March 1940 between England and Wales, with Wilf leading the team in red shirts, followed a few weeks later by a game in Paris between the British Army and their French counterparts, with Wilf again in charge of the visitors.

But the realities of War were soon brought home to Wilf as he received the tragic news that his brother Gordon, a pilot in the RAF, was missing, presumed dead. Gordon had been a decent cricketer, playing for Denbighshire and Sir Julian Cahn's XI, for whom he worked in one of his furniture stores in Cardiff. Gordon's death hit Wilf hard, as his unit undertook further training in Swansea and Scotland, before hearing that they would be deployed to North Africa as part of 'K Force' to support the Desert Rats.

However, the night before they sailed from the Gourock Ferry Terminal, the Japanese attacked Pearl Harbour, and, by the time their liner had entered the Bay of Biscay, their destination had changed to Batavia in Indonesia. The plan had been to set up gun batteries in Java, but within a few weeks, the Japanese had overrun the island with Wilf and his colleagues being taken prisoner of war. After being held at various internment camps from

May 1942, Wilf and his unit were transferred to Changi in Singapore, and as they neared the notorious camp and saw the severed heads of Chinese and Malay civilians on street-corner gallows, all knew that their nightmare had only just begun.

The next three years saw horrendous spells of hard labour in searing temperatures on the notorious Burma-Siam Railway for Wilf and his colleagues. Deprived of food, many staved off death by foraging for food. Anything which crawled, wriggled or flew was caught and eaten. Lieutenant Wooller was quite enterprising, growing bananas on a strip of land by his hut, besides tending a pair of ducklings. Their eggs were a vital source of nourishment in the putrid conditions, where cholera and dysentery were rife, where lice feasted in the hair of the prisoners, where cuts swiftly developed into weeping ulcers, and where so many of Wilf's comrades met a slow and painful death.

Wilf Wooller welcomes Jimmy Eaglestone and Pete Hever to Glamorgan during the Spring of 1948.

Observing at first-hand the limits to which the human body could be pushed, and surrounded by emaciated bodies and appalling conditions, was a life-changing experience for Wilf. Through strong will and sheer fortitude, he survived with his nightmare in Changi ending in mid- September 1945. After being liberated, Wilf and his fellow survivors all received treatment in Singapore and Ceylon, before heading back to Southampton. Like everyone else on-board the makeshift hospital ships, their thoughts on the homeward journey were focused on rejoining their families and getting back to normal life.

For Wilf, he was hoping to resume his sporting career and rejoin Gillian Windsor-Clive, the daughter of the Earl of Plymouth, who he had married on 24 September 1941 after a whirlwind romance. But their marriage had proved ill-fated, with Gillian, after reading that Wilf was missing presumed dead in Java, having begun a new relationship with another man. As Wilf recalled in his memoirs, "my life was in ruins and I felt I couldn't carry on. Marital separations were very rare in those days, and even though I was the innocent party, I felt like a failure and full of shame. I was full of dark, gloomy thoughts." Fortunately, two of his old pals from Rydal, Edgar Bibby and Jack Townley, looked after Wilf for a while as he came to terms with what had happened, both in south-east Asia and back home.

Wilf duly returned to Cardiff hoping to resume his job with GLM, but with the coal industry about to be nationalised, Herbert Merrett suggested that looked elsewhere for employment. Seeking some ideas, Wilf spoke to GV Wynne-Jones, another old friend from the world of Welsh sport, who had been appointed Glamorgan's Treasurer as, under Johnnie Clay's guidance, the Club resumed their activities. "Why don't you play for Glamorgan this summer," said Geevers. "The county are starting up again soon and we could do with you off-field as well. Why don't you help Johnnie and me as our Assistant Secretary?"

Wilf duly accepted the offer and, with his loss of weight preventing a return to rugby, cricket became his principle sport for the next half-century. 1946 saw Wilf deputise for Johnnie Clay as the Club's captain against Essex at Chelmsford and Surrey at The Oval. After a winter of administrative duties and overseeing a fund-raising campaign, Wilf became the Club's captain in 1947, moulding a successful squad with a mix of local talent and astute signings from other countries. Officially an amateur, Wilf had the cricket brain of the wisest professional. He proved to be a ruthless and, at times, very outspoken captain, leading from the front and never afraid to ask anyone to do anything that he himself would not think twice about doing himself. Indeed, Wilf was ready to anything in the side's best interest, whether it was opening the batting, bowling for hour after hour as a stock bowler, or fearlessly standing at short-leg, letting the opposition batsmen know what he thought of them!

As John Arlott wrote "memory will always recall him, his wide, heavy shoulders, slightly stooped, shambling down the pitch to his place, little more than a stride from the batsman, at forward short-leg. There, eyes intent under a high forehead, jaw jutting, fists jammed truculently down on hips between deliveries, he dominated the outcricket." Contemporaries regarded him as one of the bravest short-legs in the immediate post-war years, and many opposing batsmen cowered and mentally disintegrated beneath his immense physical and loud verbal presence.

Indeed, it was Wilf who devised the pioneering leg-side attack, plus its ring of close catchers, as the Welsh county's bowlers became the first in the county game to exploit an in-slant attack. Norman Hever bowled in-swing with the new ball, whilst Wilf moved the ball both ways. Allan Watkins could bend the ball back in to the pads from left-arm over, whilst the off-spinners Len Muncer and Johnnie Clay feasted on the inside-edge, whilst left-arm spinner Stan Trick found the outside edge. In wicket-keeper Haydn Davies, Watkins at backward short-leg, Phil Clift or Jim Pleass at short

Wilf Wooller, seen at Scarborough during 1949.

square-leg, Wilf himself at silly mid-on, plus Arnold Dyson and Gilbert Parkhouse in the slips, Glamorgan had a ring of top-class catchers. As Wilf gleefully recalled "It won us the Championship. We weren't the best bowling or batting side, but by God, we caught flies."

Wilf loved the mental battle which ensued and there are many stories about the way he would curse and swear at opponents whilst fielding at silly mid-on or when bowling. Indeed, in one game against Sussex, Wilf had directed a volley of comments against the

Rev. David Sheppard (who later became the Bishop of Liverpool), after beating the outside edge of his bat on several occasions, an appeal for caught behind was turned down by umpire Alec Skelding. Although Sheppard later admitted, that he had indeed edged the ball, Skelding gave him the benefit of the doubt, much to Wilf's anger. It prompted another outburst from Wilf, with Skelding turning at the end of the over to Sheppard and saying "Excuse me, sir, you are a man more qualified to judge on these matters than myself, and you will presumably recognize him if you saw him, but is this the very Devil behind us?"

Wilf may have played hard on the field, terrorizing young and inexperienced captains, as well as opposing batsmen but he was always the first to buy them a drink and socialize after play. As Colin McCool of Somerset and Australia wrote, "Wilf Wooller must be the most shambling, contrary hunk of cussedness ever to step out of Wales. For five years we bristled like fighting cocks every time we stepped on to the same cricket field. We goaded and taunted each other ceaselessly, waiting to see who would break first. For five years we mumbled and muttered and cursed…. And then we'd laugh and call a truce until the next time we met. He would have trampled roughshod over a baby for the good of Glamorgan cricket, but it was all forgotten once he had climbed out of his flannels."

His colleagues also came in for a few choice words if they got things wrong, as in 1955 in the case of Tony Lewis, then a schoolboy just a month on from his seventeenth birthday who joined Wilf as he was approaching a deserved century against Warwickshire at Neath. On 99 Wilf glanced a ball backward of square on the leg side, to which Tony shrilled 'yes'. But the youngster had never seen the speed over the ground of Norman Horner, who threw at Wilf's end. Wilf was well out of his ground as the ball bounced over the top of the unattended stumps. After regaining his breath, Wilf raised his bat, acknowledged the applause for his century and then walked down the pitch to Tony. As the schoolboy later recalled, "In the clubhouse afterwards my friends asked if Wilf had said to me you will do that one day. I told them what he actually said was 'you do that to me again and I'll have your cloth-eared head off!'"

Don Shepherd had also irked Wilf during a game at Lord's in the early 1950s when Middlesex's John Dewes was edging Don – then a fast-medium bowler – through and over the slip cordon. The frustrated Glamorgan captain duly positioned everyone bar himself into catching positions behind the wicket. "Don't pitch anything up," was Wilf's advice to his bowler before taking up his normal post at silly mid-on. But as Don remembered, "The inevitable happened as I bowled a half-volley which Dewes drove towards the long-on boundary. Wilf looked round, realizing he was the only one anywhere near it, and set off in pursuit with those famous knees going like pistons. As he passed me, he turned and said, "Shepherd, you must be the dullest bugger who ever played for Glamorgan."

Umpires also came in for an ear-bashing if they erred, as in the case of a game at the Arms Park where Harry Baldwin was called to account by Wilf for signaling a no-ball believing there to be too many fielders on the leg-side. This was an era of restrictions to the number of fielders on the leg-side. "What was that for, Harry?" asked Wilf, to which the umpire pointed to five on-side fielders, before saying "There you are and that

A photograph showing Wilf Wooller at a special function at Dowlais CC. Bryn Thomas of the Western Mail *is on the left.*

one makes six!" To which Wilf retorted "But that sixth one is a chap going around the boundary edge selling scorecards!"

Wilf may have won that particular verbal joust in Cardiff, but he lost the repartee in a match against Derbyshire at Chesterfield during 1951. Glamorgan amassed over 400 on the opening day but, to the delight of a large crowd at Queen's Park, he was dismissed for nought and was given plenty of verbal advice on his way back to the pavilion. The wags were back in position on the second day as Derbyshire launched their reply, and after a while they had plenty to amuse themselves as a duck waddled up from the lake beyond the boundary at the Town End and accompanied Willie Jones who was fielding at long-on.

Shortly afterwards, Willie moved across to long-off and was joined again by his feathered friend, much to the delight of the spectators and the Glamorgan team. Wilf then joined in the fun by moving Willie back to long-on, with the duck duly waddling after him. "Who's your new pal?" Wilf loudly shouted whereupon a loud voice boomed out in reply from the home crowd "That's not his. That's thine Wooller after your batting on Saturday!" For once Wilf was speechless as his players doubled-up in laughter. But he had the last laugh as Glamorgan won by an innings on the second day as Len Muncer followed up his century on the opening day by taking five wickets in each Derbyshire innings.

Wilf was also responsible, albeit in rather unusual fashion, for Peter Walker fielding at short-leg for the Welsh county from the late 1950s onwards. It came when Peter was a raw teenager in a game when Glamorgan were under the cosh with the opponents having passed 300 for the loss of just two wickets. As Peter recalled, "I was fielding at third man at each end which gave me a long run between overs. At the end of one over Wilf decided to make a bowling change and to bring on Jim McConnon, and I just about reached the strikers end when I noticed, so I asked him where I should go next. Given the scoreline Wilf was a bit exasperated. He gave me a look and said "Just spit in the air and go where it lands!" You did what Wilf said, so I spat up in the air and it landed at short-leg. To the second ball, the batsman gave me a catch and I fielded there for the next 25 years or so!"

To some, especially his fiercest critics, Wilf was a manufactured cricketer. He certainly worked hard at his cricketing skills and, by dint of sheer application and tenacity, Wilf made himself into an excellent all-rounder. A measure of both his ability and durability was that in 1954, as an amateur, he achieved the coveted Double at the age of 41! He thereby became one of only five men to achieve the feat solely for the Welsh county and reached the coveted landmark against Warwickshire at Edgbaston with host chairman Alec Hastilow walking out to the middle with a bottle of champagne and glasses on a tray.

1948 had been a very special year for Wilf, not least in leading Glamorgan to the county title, but also for the fact that he married Enid James, an optician in Cardiff on 29 September 1948. The pair had met the summer before, and after the deep personal sadness of his first tryst, his marriage to Enid was the polar opposite as she became his loyal and faithful companion, the mother of three boys and two girls, as well as the proud matriarch of a happy flock of grandchildren.

Wilf's family commitments, as well as his work with both Glamorgan and the insurance brokerage he had also set-up, meant that he had to decline an invitation to tour South Africa in 1948/49 but his consolation at missing out on playing for England was being appointed a Test selector, under the Chairmanship of Gubby Allen from 1955 until 1962, and choosing a series of highly successful England teams. The highlight was the 2-1 series victory over the 1956 Australians, with the fruitful recalls of David Sheppard and Denis Compton for the matches at Old Trafford and The Oval, plus the decision to let Jim Laker and Tony Lock loose on a spin-friendly surface at Manchester.

It was a tactic which also saw fruit at Swansea in 1964 and 1968, as Glamorgan famously became the first (and probably only ever) county to defeat the men in baggy green caps. By this time, Wilf had retired from first-class cricket, having hung up his boots at the end of the 1960 season but, as the Club's Secretary, he was still very much in charge and took great delight from these famous victories at Swansea.

Wilf Wooller, seen in Glamorgan's office at number 6 High Street in Cardiff.

The victory over the 1951 South Africans at St Helen's, in front of over 20,000 spectators, also meant much to Wilf. The two-day victory encapsulated his never-say-die attitude after both teams had been dismissed for 111 in their first innings. With the wicket starting to take spin, a positive approach was needed, although for his part, Wilf needed few invitations to attack the bowling and if there was anyone who was not going to go down without a fight, it was the Welsh county's leader. He hit a typically aggressive 46, and together with doughty support from Jim Pleass, Glamorgan were able to set the tourists a target of 147. By tea, the South Africans had reached 54 without loss and the game appeared to be heading away from Glamorgan, as neither of their spinners seemed able to pierce the defence of Springbok openers John Waite or Russell Endean.

During the interval, Wilf spoke to his team in the dressing room, cajoling them for one last effort, and telling them that all that was needed was one wicket, as others would quickly follow. His words proved prophetic as a quite remarkable passage of play then followed in front of an increasingly animated crowd, as all ten wickets fell within the space of three quarters of hour for just 29 runs. Len Muncer claimed 4/10, and Jim McConnon 6/10, with each aided by some breathtaking catches close to the wicket, including one by Wilf himself at silly mid-on, where, after deflecting a firm on-drive from Clive van Ryneveld, he clutched onto the rebound inches from the turf. The end came when Gilbert Parkhouse, fielding as substitute for Emrys Davies, caught Percy Mansell off a top edge, despite nursing a wrist injury before the jubilant Glamorgan team were mobbed by an equally joyous crowd with Wilf carried shoulder-high from the field with the Welsh National Anthem echoing out from the Pavilion.

It had been a repeat of the bowling and fielding skills which had secured Glamorgan's first title in 1948 as well as a masterclass in the leadership skills and nous of a man whose

Wilf (third left), the England selector at Lord's, with Jack Flavell, Doug Insole, Norman Gifford and Len Coldwell during the 1964 Ashes series.

pre-match preparations at Swansea also involved consulting groundsman (and long-term friend) George Clements about the tide-times, aware that changes in the tide could add a capricious element to the conditions and assist the swing bowlers. Indeed, Wilf (and George alike) were irked by the comments of a few misguided individuals when looking at the pitch at Swansea ahead of a game. "How much sand have you put on this?" was an oft-heard comment from visiting players, unaware of the grounds history and its reclamation from a sandbank. Wilf never wasted any opportunity, even when fielding at short-leg, to put them right!

Despite having hung up his boots two years before, Wilf came out of retirement in July 1962 for the match with Middlesex at Rodney Parade. He scored 2 and 5, besides claiming the wicket of Ted Clark in the drawn game, but his most memorable contribution came with the dismissal of Bob Gale for 200 at the end of the Middlesex innings. As the batsman headed off towards the Rodney Parade pavilion, Wilf marked his 400th and final appearance for the Welsh county by shouting out in a booming voice "That's the worst bloody two-hundred I have ever seen!"

The incorrigible Glamorgan captain had used the same line, and at the same ground in August 1956, when Gloucestershire's Tom Graveney made a double-century against the Welsh county. It had brought many smiles and a few laughs, especially between the pair when they shared a drink together after play in the Rodney Parade pavilion, but there had been few smiles earlier that summer when Wilf was involved in a couple of on-field incidents. The first saw him accused by the Press of unsporting behaviour during the match against Surrey at The Oval. It followed a passage of play when Peter May drove a ball to Bernard Hedges at mid-on. Bernard dived and appeared to catch the ball, whereupon May started to walk back to the pavilion, but Bernard then signalled that he had not held the ball. By now, Peter had walked past Ken Barrington at the non-striker's end, and seeing that Peter was well out of his ground, Wilf shouted to Bernard to throw the ball to Haydn Davies to effect a run out.

The Surrey man did not complain, instead wryly smiling to himself that Wilf had played hard but fair. Up in the Press Box however, a different story emerged with one of the London-based writers filing a story that Wilf – an England selector – had duped Peter, who at the time was the England captain. Soon the telephone wires buzzing with stories about a cheating Welshman, but not everyone in the Press Box agreed. Alf Gover, the former Surrey and England bowler popped down to the Glamorgan changing rooms at tea and told his good friend what was unfolding. Peter also approached Wilf and said "Don't worry Wilf. There was really a single there and Ken should have run. He was the one to blame and if he hadn't been watching the ball, we'd have all been OK!"

However, the editions of the national papers made unpleasant reading the following morning and the story dragged on for several days as Glamorgan visited Sussex where Wilf was involved in another spat . After the home side had made 379-9, Glamorgan were bundled out for 64 as a sea fret hung over the ground. It had cleared by the time they batted again, but Wilf's instructions were clear and precise – "We just defend and stay at the wicket". He set the tone himself, batting for seven hours in making an unbeaten

79 as Glamorgan amassed 200-1 in 138 overs to save the game. Robin Marlar, the Sussex captain, used all of his eleven as bowlers, and even bowled several overs of high lobs which Wilf and Bernard Hedges gently patted back.

From a Glamorgan perspective, the end justified the means but Wilf was castigated in the Press for a second time in the space of a week, whilst the Sussex Chairman sent a tersely worded letter of complaint to the Glamorgan committee about the fact that many people had left the ground, bored by the proceedings, whilst others had demanded a refund of their admission money. Matters were not helped by the correspondent of the *London Evening Standard* writing "Glamorgan are the most hated side on the county circuit."

Wilf – the Glamorgan Secretary.

These incidents started to fuel the fires of discontent during 1957, with Wilf also losing friends in the home camp as he led a campaign to take county cricket from the Arms Park to Sophia Gardens. An opportunity arose for the Welsh county to develop a headquarters of their own, with proper facilities in the parkland at Sophia Gardens, but the thought of Glamorgan moving away from the Arms Park appalled Norman Riches, the President of Cardiff Athletic Cub and a stalwart traditionalist (Vol.1. p183-188). He duly persuaded the City's Lord Mayor to use his casting vote at the Council's meeting to scupper the plans for Glamorgan's move away from the Arms Park.

During the autumn of 1957, Wilf – now aged 44 – began to consider his future with the Club and he informed the committee that he would be happy to stand down as captain if a suitable replacement could be found. The problem was that there were no obvious long-term successors in the amateur ranks, but undetered by this, Norman and a faction of committee members, began a covert plan to oust a man they regarded as a trouble-making tyrant. Approaches were made to players at Oxford and Cambridge University, as well as Billy Sutcliffe of Yorkshire, only for his father Herbert to talk him out of moving to South Wales. Johnnie Clay also entered the debate and, drawing on his own experience, suggested that Wilf should remain as team manager and help to groom a successor, in the same way he had operated back in 1946. But Johnnie's suggestion was misconstrued and the debate escalated when the committee agreed to offer Wilf a post as part-time consultant /advisor at a salary of £500. In essence, they wanted Wilf's advice but not his authority, and at half the salary. Realising that the knives were out for him, Wilf tendered his resignation as captain-secretary with effect from the end of 1958.

Norman Riches responded by persuading Tolly Burnett, a 33 year-old science master at Eton who had a won a Blue at Cambridge in 1949 to have an eight-match trial during August and early September as Glamorgan's prospective new captain for 1959. Tolly had never played in Championship cricket and, not surprisingly, the experiment proved to be an embarrassing failure. With more and more details about the internal wranglings reaching the newspapers, a special general meeting was held during October at Bridgend

Town Hall, at which it was agreed to hold a member's ballot to settle the issue of whether or not the Club should retain Wilf's services. It resulted in a majority in favour of retaining Wilf, who responded by withdrawing his resignation and agreeing to continue both playing for, and captaining, the Welsh county.

After retiring from playing on a regular basis at the end of the 1960 season, Wilf continue to mix his administrative duties with running an insurance brokerage as well as sports journalism. He had already become a respected writer on cricket and rugby initially for the *News Chronicle* and subsequently the *Sunday Telegraph*, besides broadcasting for BBC Wales. Indeed, it was Wilf who was commentating when Garry Sobers struck Malcolm Nash for six sixes at Swansea in August 1968 with his words "and it's gone all the way down to Swansea" accompanying footage of the sixth six and a place in broadcasting history.

Wilf also had the microphone in hand twelve months later when Glamorgan defeated Worcestershire at Sophia Gardens to clinch the 1969 Championship under Tony Lewis – the man who Wilf had identified back in the mid 1950s as the person to lead the Club to fresh honours. Once again, his description of Don Shepherd claiming the final wicket of a daffodil-golden summer and the post-match celebrations have been preserved for future generations into the BBC vaults, whilst those present in the ramshackle commentary box at Sophia Gardens were privileged to witnessed a more tender side of Wilf's character as he uttered these famous words with a veritable river of tears flowing down his cheeks.

His forthright views on air or in print ruffled a few feathers, but showed that Wilf still passionately wanted Glamorgan to taste success. He continued to be annoyed by what he perceived to be negative play, such as the time in the early 1970s when Somerset, under Brian Close, adopted a go-slow policy whilst batting at St Helen's. An irate Wilf eventually announced over the tannoy that any spectator wanting a refund of their entrance money should report to the club office adjacent to the Pavilion. Yet despite several whiffs of controversy, especially over the departure of Majid Khan as the Club's captain during 1976, Wilf's tenure as Glamorgan secretary saw the Club defeat Australia on consecutive tours, win the County Championship in 1969, besides reaching the final of the Gillette Cup in 1977 and bringing international cricket to Wales in 1973.

During these years, Wilf also roared to the defence of white South Africa in 1970 and retained a steadfast belief in the value of sporting links, whilst he also locked horns in print and on radio with Peter Hain who championed the anti-Apartheid campaign. Whilst Wilf took delight in getting his points across in public, his private life was very much that. Indeed, it is doubtful if Wilf's restoration to normal life after his wartime incarceration would

A jovial Wilf Wooller at a Glamorgan Former Players Re-union at Sophia Gardens during the late 1980s.

have been so successful had it not been for Enid and the oasis of calm she created in their family home in the Cardiff suburbs. At times of turmoil, when Wilf to the general public seemed to be floundering between a rock and a hard place, Mrs Wooller and their children provided a haven of tranquility.

In later life, Wilf played bowls besides mellowing (albeit very slightly!) into a benevolent patriarch of the Club, acting as a Trustee and later President from 1991 until his death, a month before the start of the 1997 season and the summer when Glamorgan lifted the Championship crown for the third time. As Tony Lewis commented in his obituary of the man who had been his guide and mentor, "Whatever his office, Wilf was always in attendance at home matches at Cardiff, sharing his firm opinions with both committee members and general public, latterly making Robert Croft his main target for extra tuition as the young off-spinner moved towards Test selection. In heart and mind, he never actually relinquished the captaincy of Glamorgan."

339
DALY, Guy Nolan (also known as O'DALY)

Born – Bramley, Hampshire, 4 September 1908
Died – Basingstoke, 29 September 1991
Amateur
RHB, RM
Ed – Imperial Service College, Windsor
1st XI: 1938
2nd XI: 1936
Club and Ground: 1935
Club: Abergavenny

Batting and Fielding Record:

	M	I	NO	RUNS	AV	100	50	CT	ST
F-c	1	1	0	9	9.00	-	-	-	-

Bowling Record:

	Balls	M	R	W	AV	5wI	10wM
F-c	42	1	17	0	-	-	-

Career-best:
First-class – 9 v Cambridge University at Swansea, 1938

Guy Daly, who played once for Glamorgan during 1938, had an outstanding record in club cricket with Abergavenny, and would have played more frequently for the Welsh county had he not sustained an injury whilst delivering his brisk away-swingers.

The son of an Irish doctor based in Hampshire, Guy and his cousins had attended Haileybury School (then known as Imperial Service College) where he played cricket with some success. He joined Abergavenny during 1935 after purchasing a poultry farm in the area. He soon had an impact as, in the final game of that season, he posted a hundred against Newport. His abilities as a hard-hitting all-rounder had already won him a place

Guy Daly.

in Glamorgan's Club and Ground side, whilst in 1936 he made his debut for their 2nd XI against their counterparts from Middlesex at Finchley, in addition to playing in the away match with Dorset at Wimborne.

In 1937 Daly scored 1171 runs and took 138 wickets for Abergavenny to eclipse all of the club's previous records. His feats once again did not go unnoticed by the Glamorgan selectors and when Cambridge University visited St Helen's in mid-June 1938, Daly was one of several promising talents who were given a chance to impress. However, he injured himself after bowling just seven overs and took no further part in the game.

Guy combined the role of coach-groundsman at Abergavenny for several years either side of the Great War.

340
SILKIN, Samuel Charles
Born – Neath, 6 March 1918
Died – Oxford, 17 August 1988
Amateur
RHB, LBG
Ed – Dulwich College and Trinity Hall, Cambridge
1st XI: 1938
Club and Ground: 1936-1937
Cambridge University 1938; Surrey Young Amateurs, Middlesex 2nd XI
Clubs: Southgate, Cambridge Crusaders

Batting and Fielding Record:

	M	I	NO	RUNS	AV	100	50	CT	ST
F-c	1	2	0	2	1.00	-	-	1	-

Bowling Record:

	Balls	M	R	W	AV	5wI	10wM
F-c	54	0	60	1	60.00	-	-

Career-bests:
First-class –   2   v Cambridge University at St Helen's, Swansea, 1938
             1/27 v Cambridge University at St Helen's, Swansea, 1938

Sam Silkin, who between 1979 and 1985 served as Attorney General, was good friends with the brother of Maurice Turnbull, and during 1938, the Glamorgan captain tried to help Sam win a place in the Cambridge University side for the Varsity Match by selecting the Neath-born spinner in the Welsh county's side for their friendly at Swansea with the Light Blues.

It proved to be Sam's only first-class appearance for Glamorgan, and followed his frustration at still being on the fringe of the Cambridge XI for the game against their counterparts at Oxford. He had been a talented leg-spinner for Dulwich College and in 1936 Sam was the captain of their 1st XI. His success with the ball saw him chosen for both the Young Amateurs of Surrey and Middlesex 2nd XI whilst, during both 1936 and 1937, when visiting family and friends in South Wales, he played for Glamorgan's Club and Ground side, chiefly through his friendship with the Turnbull family.

A photograph of Sam Silkin taken during 1937.

In May 1938 Sam made his first-class debut for Cambridge against The Army, but he only scored 2 and claimed a solitary wicket. He failed to keep his place in the Light Blues side, and during the lead-up to the Varsity match, he desperately wanted another chance to claim a place in the Cambridge XI. With Johnnie Clay injured for the friendly against the Light Blues at St Helen's, Glamorgan were looking to blood a young spinner so knowing about Sam's aspirations, Maurice chose his brother's close friend in the side to play in the match at Swansea. Once again, Sam took just one wicket from nine overs, besides making 0 and 2 and failed in his bid to play at Lord's in the Varsity Match.

Sam was the second son of Lewis Silkin, the first Baron Silkin who acted as Minister of Town and Country Planning in Clement Attlee's government from 1945 until 1950, before setting up Lewis Silkin and Partners, the London-based law firm. After completing his education at Trinity Hall, Cambridge, Sam followed his illustrious father into the world of law and politics and served as a barrister in London. In 1964 he was elected as Labour MP for Camberwell, and during the late 1960s he led the United Kingdom delegation to The Council of Europe. Between 1970 and 1974 he was the opposition front bench spokesman on law and from 1974 until 1979 served as Labour MP for Southwark.

He accepted a life peerage in 1985 and as Lord Silkin of Dulwich, he became the Opposition spokesman on legal matters in the House of Lords until his death in 1988. In 1941 he had married Elaine Stamp with whom he had two sons and two daughters. After her death in 1985, Sam married Sheila Swanston.

In his youth Sam had also been a decent fives player and during 1934 reached the finals of the Public Schools Doubles Tournament. Despite his great fame and success in the political world, Sam regarded one of his greatest achievements as dismissing Jack Hobbs whilst playing for the Young Amateurs of Surrey.

HARRIS, Wilfred Ernest ('Ernie')

Born – St Fagans, 24 April 1919
Died – Cardiff, 4 December 1996
Amateur
Ed – Canton High School, Cardiff
1st XI: 1938-1947
2nd XI: 1937-1939
Colts: 1936
Club and Ground: 1937
Clubs: St Fagans, XL Club, Cardiff University Staff

Batting and Fielding Record:

	M	I	NO	RUNS	AV	100	50	CT	ST
F-c	5	8	0	59	7.37	-	-	1	-

Bowling Record:

	Balls	M	R	W	AV	5wI	10wM
F-c	84	1	43	0	-	-	-

Career-best:
First-class –   25 v Kent at Tonbridge, 1939

Ernie Harris was a loyal stalwart of St Fagans, playing for the club from the mid 1930's until the 1980s. He had made his debut as a schoolboy batsman and medium-pace bowler, and played his final match over fifty years later having developed – but as he modestly admitted never quite mastered – the art of leg-spin.

Ernie was amongst the clutch of schoolboys to be identified by Bill Hitch and other coaches as having a possible future in the county game. Bowling accurately at a brisk pace, he formed a useful foil to Wilf Wooller who at the time also played club cricket for St Fagans. It also helped Ernie's cause that the Glamorgan talent scouts were keeping an eye on the Welsh rugby international who they hoped would agree to turn out for Glamorgan.

His athletic prowess in the field also caught the eye, and after some promising performances for Glamorgan Colts and their Club and Ground side during 1936, Ernie was selected for the county's 2nd XI in their Minor County Championship matches against their counterparts from Kent at Sittingbourne and in the return match at Maesteg.

A photograph of Ernie Harris taken at his retirement function at Cardiff University.

The following summer, Ernie was called up by the county's selectors to appear in the County Championship matches against Kent at Maidstone and Warwickshire at Rodney Parade in Newport. Ernie was overjoyed to appear in both games and he dutifully followed the instructions of Maurice Turnbull and the senior professionals – even to the extent when his turn came to bat at The Mote to persuade umpire Frank Chester that conditions were too gloomy. Dai Davies, his batting partner had already spoken to the Test umpire and after an unsuccessful attempt, Dai told his young colleague to have a word as well. Chester duly replied "Tell Dai that he doesn't have a chance and that the shop will stay open as usual until 6.30pm!"

Ernie made two further appearances during June 1939 but his best years were lost to the War and after service with the Army, Ernie secured a clerk's post at University College, Cardiff. How-

Ernie Harris, seen on his wedding day during 1943.

ever, he continued to play with great success at weekends for St Fagans and during May 1947 he gleefully answered an SOS to help out Wilf and the Glamorgan side at Bramall Lane, after a spate of injuries was set to ravage the Welsh county's line-up. It was an inauspicious return to county cricket as he made 0 and 2 in a game which the powerful Yorkshire side won by nine wickets.

He returned to his job at the university where he subsequently rose to the rank of Registrar, besides being the shining light behind the university's staff cricket team. Even when well into his sixties, Ernie still cut a dapper and athletic figure in the field, cheerfully bowling well-flighted leg-spin and, proudly wearing his Glamorgan sweater, besides batting in a spritely way with a flowing cover drive.

Ernie also served on the Welsh county's committee during the 1960s and 1970s. In 1973 he was the Club's Match Manager for the One-Day International between England and New Zealand at Swansea – the first international match ever staged in Wales.

342
JONES, David Alfred

Born – Aberkenfig, 9 March 1920
Died – Pen-y-fai, Bridgend, 18 April 1990
Amateur
RHB, RM
Ed – Ebbw Vale Secondary School and King's College, Taunton
1st XI: 1938
2nd XI: 1938
Club and Ground: 1937
Club: Ebbw Vale

Batting and Fielding Record:

	M	I	NO	RUNS	AV	100	50	CT	ST
F-c	1	1	0	6	6.00	-	-	-	-

Bowling Record:

	Balls	M	R	W	AV	5wI	10wM
F-c	84	3	43	2	21.50	-	-

Career-bests:

First-class –   6 v Sir Julian Cahn's XI at Rodney Parade, Newport, 1938
                2/22 v Sir Julian Cahn's XI at Rodney Parade, Newport, 1938

David Jones was a lively right-arm seam bowler who played in the first-class friendly against Sir Julian's Cahn's XI at Newport during July 1938. It came a few weeks after the youngster had left King's College, Taunton where he had showed great promise as an all-rounder and had won a place in both the Welsh Schools team as well as Glamorgan's Colts team.

Indeed, the school's magazine for 1937 commented how "David has served the side well as a change bowler. He is a forcing bat, but his defence needs tightening before he will make runs". With Glamorgan looking to blood young talent, the youngster was also given opportunities to play for the county's 2nd XI in 1938. However, he opted for a career away from cricket and the game against Sir Julian's team was his only first-class appearance.

David Jones, as seen during 1937.

343
JARRETT, Harold Harvey ('Hal')

Born – Johannesburg, 23 September 1907
Died – Pontypool, 17 March 1983
Professional
RHB, LBG
Ed – Highgate School
1st XI: 1938-1947
Warwickshire 1932-1933
Club: Newport

Batting and Fielding Record:

	M	I	NO	RUNS	AV	100	50	CT	ST
F-c	1	1	0	0	-	-	-	1	-
Wartime	2	1	0	0	-	-	-	1	-

Bowling Record:

	Balls	M	R	W	AV	5wI	10wM
F-c	54	1	45	4	11.25	-	-

Career-best:
First-class – 3/18 v Sir Julian Cahn's XI at Rodney Parade, Newport, 1938

Hal Jarrett claimed a wicket with his first ball for Glamorgan against Sir Julian Cahn's XI at Newport in 1938, catching Australian Harold Mudge of his own bowling at the Rodney Parade ground where he was employed as groundsman.

Born in South Africa and educated in London, Hal had initially played county cricket for Warwickshire during 1932 and 1933, with the all-rounder striking 45 on his first-class debut against the Indian tourists at Edgbaston. Having a longer run-up than a classical leg-spinner, Hal's best performance with the ball came later in 1932 against Leicestershire at Hinckley where he claimed 8/187 against Leicestershire. He re-appeared during 1933 but his subsequent appearances were restricted by the emergence of Eric Hollies.

After being released by Warwickshire, Hal mixed playing and coaching during the winters in Kenya, with a professional appointment in Scotland, before accepting a

Hal Jarrett.

similar position with Newport in 1937. He remained in South Wales for the rest of his life and re-appeared for the Welsh county during their wartime friendlies during 1944.

After the Second World War, he combined his duties as the groundsman at Rodney Parade with work for Henry Giles whose sports goods emporium was based in Skinner Street in Newport. Gilesports were the sole agents of Warsop-Hendren cricket bats and stockists for equipment from national suppliers such as Stuart Surridge, Gray Nicholls, Gradidge, Sykes and Sugg, and were looking for innovative means to promote and advertise playing kit and other equipment. Following a meeting with Wilf Wooller, an idea was developed for the creation of a magazine promoting cricket in the area.

As a result, the *South Wales Cricketers Magazine* came into being with Hal acting as one of the editors of a magazine which Gilesports helped to subsidise by paying for lavish adverts of their own, besides persuading others in the cricket industry to take out promotional space. Hal also collated plenty of news about the Welsh county, their 2nd XI, the coaching opportunities plus an extensive round-up from club cricket, with news from the South Wales and Monmouthshire Cricket Association, the Swansea Central League, the Newport and District Amateur League, as well as the leagues in the Aberdare and Rhymney Valley, plus updates on youth and schools cricket, including the Welsh Secondary Schools Association.

The magazine duly became a mouthpiece which united the efforts of Glamorgan officials and other key figures in recreational cricket, allowing Glamorgan to showcase how they were wisely spending the money from the Nursery and Development Fund which had been set-up to improve the facilities, especially at the Arms Park.

His son Keith also played twice for Glamorgan during 1967 and won fame as a rugby player for Wales and the British Lions.

344
DAVIS, Brian Henry Stevens

Born – Beaconsfield, 16 January 1909
Died – Docking, 2 February 1977
Ed – Lancing College
1st XI: 1938
Club and Ground: 1938-1939
Buckinghamshire 1928. Berkshire 1929-1937
Clubs: Cardiff, South Wales Hunts, St Fagans, Beaconsfield

Batting and Fielding Record:

	M	I	NO	RUNS	AV	100	50	CT	ST
Friendly	1	1	0	23	23.00	-	-	-	-

Bowling Record:

	Balls	M	R	W	AV	5wI	10wM
Friendly	24	0	23	0	-	-	-

Brian Davis, a petroleum technologist, played for Glamorgan during mid-July 1938 in their two-day friendly against Sir Julian Cahn's XI at his private ground in West Bridgford, Nottingham.

Born and raised in Sussex, Brian had been in the Lancing XI in 1926 before moving to the Home Counties and playing Minor County cricket for Buckinghamshire as well as Berkshire. He was subsequently promoted to a post in South Wales and after some decent performances in club cricket, Brian appeared for Glamorgan's Club and Ground side, as well as in their friendly against Cahn's XI.

In later life, he changed his surname to Stevens-Davis.

BHS Davis.

Brian Davis (third right in the middle row) together with other members of the Glamorgan squad and students at UCW Aberystwyth as the county cricketers prepare for the 1938 season by undertaking their pre-season training at the university town. Maurice Turnbull, in his suit, is sitting in the centre of the middle row.

1939

All looked rosy in the world of Glamorgan Cricket in May 1939 with victories by Maurice Turnbull's team over Essex at Ilford plus Northamptonshire at Kettering prior to a win by 73 runs over the touring West Indians at the Arms Park. It was a game that saw Wilf Wooller complete his maiden hundred for the county, before taking 5/69 to seal a famous victory and lead the team off the field to a tumultuous reception not far short to that which four years earlier he had experienced when the Welsh rugby team defeated the mighty All Blacks on the adjoining rugby ground.

1939 was also a memorable summer for Emrys Davies as during the game against Gloucestershire at the Rodney Parade ground in Newport, he scored an unbeaten 287 which was the Club's highest individual score, surpassing Dick Duckfield's efforts at The Oval a few years before. Earlier in the summer Emrys had been sounded out by the England selectors for the MCC tour to India and Ceylon. They had been closely monitoring his performances over several seasons and all concerned with Glamorgan Cricket were very proud when the yeoman all-rounder was announced in the party for the winter tour.

But soon afterwards, the international situation became worse and the winter tour was cancelled as the outbreak of the Second World War loomed. Unlike the Great War, the end of season matches were played out with Maurice scoring a century in the closing match, against Leicestershire at Aylestone Road. His team ended the summer with six victories and a place in 13th spot in the Championship table, but there were more important matters than the future prospects of Glamorgan at the forefront of everyone's minds as the Club's valiant players swapped their cricket whites for the khaki of military uniforms.

Most of the playing squad were to safely return to Welsh shores during the subsequent years, with Allan Watkins – one of the debutants during 1939 and another product of the Monmouthshire nursery – going on to win Test honours with England. But, as military training began during the autumn of 1939, none could have imagined that Maurice had played his final innings for the Welsh county.

345
WATKINS, Albert John ('Allan')

Born – Usk, 21 April 1922
Died – Kidderminster, 3 August 2011
Professional
LHB, LM
1st XI: 1939-1961
2nd XI: 1961
Colts: 1937-1939
Club and Ground: 1937-1961
Cap: 1947
England 1948-1952 (15 Tests); MCC; Players
Club: Usk
Football for Plymouth Argyle and Cardiff City; Rugby for Pontypool

Batting and Fielding Record:

	M	I	NO	RUNS	AV	100	50	CT	ST
F-c	407	649	76	17419	30.39	29	89	390	-

Bowling Record:

	Balls	M	R	W	AV	5wI	10wM
F-c	45005	2011	17684	774	22.84	24	-

Career-bests:
First-class – 170* v Leicestershire at St Helen's, Swansea, 1954
7/28 v Derbyshire at Chesterfield, 1954

Allan Watkins.

Allan Watkins was the first Glamorgan player to appear in an Ashes Test Match, with the jovial and energetic all-rounder appearing in the final Test of the 1948 Ashes series, with Allan – after a string of outstanding performances in Championship cricket – appearing in the final Test of the series at The Oval. Whilst the match was his debut for England, it was also Don Bradman's final Test appearance for Australia, needing just four runs in his final innings to complete a batting average of 100, and the Usk-born all-rounder duly entered the record books as the last person to field a ball from the player regarded as the world's finest-ever batsman.

Standing close to the wicket at silly mid-off, he was right in Don's eyeline, duly following the instructions from captain Norman Yardley to stand so close that he could see the whites of his eyes. Allan duly picked up the ball after the Australian had defended his first delivery – an orthodox leg-break – from spinner Eric Hollies, before returning it to the bowler. The next ball was a googly which, for once, the great man failed to read and was clean bowled. The maestro returned to the pavilion for a very rare duck, with Allan for the rest of his life, clearly remembering the minute details of his part in the legendary batsman's final innings in Test cricket after he had been applauded all the way to the wicket by the England fielders and the massive crowd "there were no tears in his eye" he would tell those asking him about the events at The Oval in 1948, thereby dispelling an urban myth associated with Bradman's final innings.

It proved though to be an unhappy Test for the Usk-born professional as he made a duck in England's first innings and was hit on the shoulder by a ball from Ray Lindwall which left him bruised and in pain, allowing him to bowl just four overs in Australia's second innings – a personal and collective blow as Allan was regarded as the all-rounder in the England line-up, batting in the middle-order and opening the bowling with Alec Bedser.

His selection for the game at The Oval, as well the injury, meant that Allan missed the last few county games of the 1948 season including the title decider at Bournemouth where Glamorgan won the Championship title, beating Hampshire by an innings. Allan had stayed in London to get further treatment on his injured shoulder and on the Tuesday afternoon when his county colleagues were quickly polishing off the Hampshire resistance, Allan nervously stood at Hither Green railway station in Lewisham, buying every edition of the evening newspaper to keep up to date with events at Dean Park, only leaving the station when, at long last, the cricket scores in

A photograph of Allan Watkins batting against Australia.

the Stop Press section had told him the good news that Hampshire had been dismissed and that Glamorgan were County Champions.

Despite his modest Test debut, Allan was chosen for the MCC winter tour to South Africa and in February 1949 Allan became Glamorgan's first-ever Centurion in Test cricket, scoring 111 in the Fourth Test of the series against South Africa at Johannesburg with the Usk-born batsman putting the Springbok bowlers to the sword as he hit fifteen fours in a three and quarter hour innings. It was a feat which gave Allan immense pleasure, and one which he subsequently marked by calling his home 'Ellis Park' in memory of his wonderful feat at the Johannesburg ground.

Allan enjoyed an outstanding tour to the Cape, as in the First Test at Durban he took as astounding catch at short-leg to dismiss Dudley Nourse – it was described by some as "the catch of the century." However, after playing just one Test against the 1949 New Zealanders he fell out of the selector's favour, until being appointed as senior professional on the MCC tour to India, Pakistan and Ceylon in 1951/52. It was an under-strength side which visited the sub-continent and saw the jovial all-rounder wholeheartedly undertake the role of stock bowler, delivering long spells in the searing heat and on unresponsive surfaces.

It was a measure of his fortitude that Allan also finished the tour as the leading run scorer in the Test series with India, whilst his determination and stamina were also to the fore during a nine-hour vigil in the 1st Test at Delhi with his 137* saving England from defeat – an innings in the dry heat which was even more impressive given that for most of his sporting career, Allan suffered from asthma. His efforts also saw him win the prized accolade of Indian Cricket's Cricketer of the Year for 1951/52.

Allan's jolly disposition and ready humour was a huge asset, especially on long and arduous overseas tours and, unlike the more straight-laced Gilbert Parkhouse, Allan fitted in well into the England set-up and there were few clashes of personality. Allan subsequently played in three home Tests against the 1952 Indians and was preferred to Essex's Trevor Bailey. However, he enjoyed little success in this series, with a mere 52 runs and 3 modest wickets. He was chosen for The Rest in the 1953 Test Trial at Edgbaston, but went wicketless and scored just 10 in the drawn game. No surprise that with others in the ascent, and Len Hutton, the England captain, showing less belief in Allan's abilities, he was not called up again by the England selectors, with the 15th and last of his appearances in Test cricket having come at Old Trafford during mid-July 1952 against India.

He had been born thirty years previously in the small town of Usk, and with the local cricket club just 40 yards from his family's home, it was no surprise that the labourer's son

Allan Watkins demonstrates his catching abilities in a specially-posed photograph taken at the Arms Park.

quickly took a keen interest in ball games and each day after school, and throughout the summer holidays, he took part in all sorts of activities on the outfield until dusk. During these formative years, he was known to one and all as Albert, but following his rise into professional cricket, he found his Christian name quite cumbersome when signing autographs. "Why don't you sign as Alan instead" was the advice on one occasion from Wilf Wooller, his future captain, with the all-rounder inadvertently spelling his adopted name with a double 'l'.

Despite gaining a place at Usk Grammar School, the world of academia held little interest for him. "Albert is not interested in his lessons" said one school report whilst on one occasion, he was sent home from school for having made a cricket bat during a wood-work lesson rather than following the instructions of his teacher to make another item!

Allan had made his debut for the Usk 1st XI aged twelve and over the course of the next couple of years, the schoolboy's success with bat and ball led to his selection for the Monmouthshire Colts, alongside Phil Clift, his lifetime pal and fellow player from Usk. Allan's success, plus a few kind works from George Lavis – who was helping to coach the Colts – led to Bill Hitch, Glamorgan's head coach, visiting Usk during 1937 and putting Allan through his paces. Hitch liked what he saw and later that summer the fifteen-year old made his debut for Glamorgan's Club and Ground side.

With the Glamorgan hierarchy eager to make the most of their affiliation with Monmouthshire, Allan was delighted at the end of the 1938 season, to receive an offer to become a junior professional with Glamorgan, at the modest sum of 30 shillings a week. Fortunately, Phil Clift's father, who ran a photographer's shop in Usk, owned a car and Allan was able to save money by travelling to Cardiff alongside Phil, who was four years older and already a first-class cricketer. But there were many occasions when playing for the 2nd XI or Colts team when Allan would have to catch the bus from Usk to Newport and then travel on another service to Cardiff.

In mid-May 1939, and just three weeks after his seventeenth birthday, Allan made his debut in Championship cricket for Glamorgan, against Nottinghamshire at Trent Bridge. His selection did not stem from some dramatic early season games for the 2nd XI or Colts, but more through the unavailability of others. There had been a delay in the registration of Peter Judge, the former Middlesex seamer, whilst both Wilf Wooller and Austin Matthews were unavailable for the away match in Nottingham. Having impressed in the nets with his accuracy, the teenager was duly chosen to open the bowling with Jack Mercer.

Young Allan Watkins, demonstrating his bowling action during 1937.

Allan went wicketless on his debut and batted at number ten, arriving in the middle with his side on 112-8. He remained unbeaten as Glamorgan were dismissed for 130 before following-on. He did not bat or bowl again as the contest ended in a draw, but in his brief innings, he had impressed the watching journalists with one writing how "he showed the right temperament and some of his shots were real gems."

Allan kept his place for the next two games away to Essex at Ilford and against Sussex at Hove, and was thrilled to play once again alongside his pal Phil Clift. The two youngsters from Usk were known as 'Laddie' and 'Nodder' to Glamorgan's senior professionals with Allan having the latter monicker because of the way when playing he would nod his head up and down to prevent his long blond hair from flopping across his face!

With the difficulties over Peter Judge's registration having been ironed out, plus Wilf and Austin being available, Allan had few opportunities for the rest of the summer in the 1st XI. His swift fielding though meant that the teenager acted as twelfth man at a number of home games, with Allan making the most of this chance to watch the visiting professionals, including Yorkshire's Maurice Leyland, who was also of stocky build and on whom Bill Hitch had advised him to model his game. Allan was thrilled in early August to catch a few minutes with the England batsman during the match at the Arms Park and, in particular, was grateful for the fellow left-hander's advice about slightly changing his grip and stance so that he could stretch forward a further foot and a half.

However, it was a few years before Allan could put into regular practice Maurice's wise advice as the outbreak of the Second World War brought an abrupt end to the Championship season. The autumn of 1939 saw Allan return to Usk where he worked in the local bakery, besides playing at scrum-half for the town's rugby club. His deft passing and grubber-kicking also led to occasional games for Pontypool RFC, but with the international situation deteriorating, he joined the Royal Navy in the summer of 1940. After initial training in Malvern he was posted to Granby Barracks at Devonport, where he remained for the rest of the War.

With plenty of time on his hands, Allan found plenty of opportunities to play various

Allan Watkins seen playing football for Plymouth Argyle during 1939.

sports and, at left-half, he was a member of the Barracks team which defeated Plymouth Argyle in the local cup competition. His ball-skills and passing in other matches impressed the Argyle scouts and as soon as he was demobilized in 1945, Allan signed professional terms with the Plymouth club, with the winter of 1945/46 seeing him mix his time between working in the bakery in Usk and playing football for the Pilgrims.

Everything changed however during the spring of 1946 as he received an offer from Johnnie Clay to play for Glamorgan once his footballing duties in Devon had ended. As Allan later recalled: "At the time I wasn't really sure that I was good enough. I'd enjoyed playing in 1939 but I never thought anything would come of it with Glamorgan. Molly [his wife] encouraged me to give it a go, as did some school friends and my old Headmaster, so I wrote to Johnnie and said that I was available from mid-June until mid-August. He duly replied that a short-term professional contract had been drawn up, besides telling me that I was included in the Glamorgan squad for the away match with Essex."

It proved to be an inauspicious return to county cricket as Glamorgan subsided to an innings defeat at Chelmsford, before losing three of their next four games. First, they lost to Middlesex at Swansea, before being beaten by Worcestershire at Ebbw Vale followed by a defeat to Yorkshire at Sheffield. During this time, Allan could easily have been forgiven for thinking that he would have been better off getting himself ready for the forthcoming football season making doughnuts and bread in the Usk bakery besides going for occasional runs along the country lanes and playing cricket for the local club.

Allan only made modest contributions with bat and ball during this period, but with few others available and nobody else pressing a claim for a place, he had retained his place in Glamorgan's line-up and by mid-August was scheduled to return to Plymouth for their pre-season training. Despite his lack of runs and wickets, Johnnie wanted Allan to stay with the Welsh cricketers, especially as several others were struggling with aches and pains after their first full summer of cricket for many years. "Do you think you could stay for one more match?" said Johnnie, shortly after Allan had ironically said farewell to his team-mates. A phone-call was duly made to the Plymouth manager who agreed to release Allan for a few days from the pre-season training.

The match in question was against Surrey at Cardiff Arms Park and, in front of a crowd not far short of 10,000, Allan struck his maiden Championship hundred in just under three hours at the crease. "An innings of great promise" was one of the comments in the local press, before the following morning, his bowling colleagues forced the visitors to follow-on. They fared little better second time around as Johnnie claimed 6/71, and on the final afternoon, Glamorgan only needed two runs to secure a famous victory over the brown hatters. Given the modest target, Haydn Davies and Peter Judge opened the innings before the former departed in the opening over, so it was Allan who duly came in and gleefully struck the winning runs.

After returning to the pavilion, Allan quietly looked through the telegrams and other letters of goodwill which had been sent following his maiden century. Amongst the pile of mail was a telegram from Bill Hitch which said "I always believed in you. Well done!"

Another came from Trevor Arnott and said "keep your chin up and take your success calmly and you should have a good future." There was also a pencil-written note from his former headmaster in Usk which had been handed in via a steward. It said "I am delighted to have seen your first century. May you build a mighty successful career on today's great innings."

If Allan still held any self-doubts about a career as a professional cricketer, these were blown away by this innings at the Arms Park and the heartfelt show of support from Allan's friends and former coaches. A few weeks later, he agreed professional terms with Glamorgan for 1947, even though he was technically still under contract with Plymouth Argyle. But Allan had made his mind up that cricket came before football and when, during the spring of 1947, the Chairman of the Plymouth club told him that the season had been extended and that he had to continue playing football, Allan replied "Not bloody likely. I'm going to Wales. I'm playing my cricket!"

Having walked away from a professional football career, the all-rounder went on to enjoy an outstanding first full summer with Glamorgan. Allan struck four further centuries with 146 against Northamptonshire at Kettering followed by 111 as Worcestershire visited Ebbw Vale – a performance which saw him win his county cap. Allan then made 105 against Somerset at Weston-super-Mare, before posting yet another century against Surrey when the South London club visited the Arms Park.

Besides excelling with the bat, and being a more than useful bowler, Allan also developed into a key member of the county's fielding unit, standing at leg-slip alongside his good friend Phil whilst Wilf stood at forward short-leg to complete a formidable gaggle of close catchers. Standing close to the wicket was a completely new experience for Allan who, given his athletic abilities, had previously been stationed in the outfield. But during one game on a rain-affected wicket, he was summoned into the leg-trap as Austin Matthews found great assistance bowling on the damp surface. After finding the inside-edge and seeing the ball lob up gently into the leg-side, the bowler turned to Wilf and said 'I'd like to have a fielder there.' The captain quickly looked around, caught Allan's eye and motioned to him to move into leg-slip. It was in this position that he remained for much of the next decade.

Later in his career, Allan had the good fortune to coach Peter Walker – the man who subsequently took over

Allan Watkins and Wilf Wooller walking out to bat at the Arms Park.

300

the mantle of Glamorgan's leading close-to-the-wicket fielder in his native South Africa – yet Allan himself had never received any tuition on close-catching, and at first largely relied on his instinct. This was not unusual with professionals at the time, and it was Arnold Dyson, the veteran slip fielder and forward short-leg, who had acted as something of a mentor for Allan during his formative years, mixing a few words of guidance with, as Allan later recalled, a few sharp retorts. "I remember taking a catch one day having gone a long way to my left. I was on the floor with the ball in my left hand and Arnold at forward short-leg said 'How many times have I got to tell thee? Don't anticipate!"

But sensing what a batsman might do saw Allan once fling himself an estimated eleven feet to catch in his out-stretched left hand an inside-edge which Don Shepherd – then a seam bowler – induced from the bat of Sussex's John Langridge. It was feats of dexterity such as this, plus a seasonal tally of catches for which a wicket-keeper would have been proud, which led John Arlott in 1948 to write, "Allan is the best close-to-the-wicket fielder in the world. He has caught the uncatchable so often as to have the impossible his normal standard."

One of Allan's favourite tricks when making a catch in the Glamorgan leg-trap was to immediately put the ball in his pocket and then to turn around and look to the boundary, as if the ball was making its way to the ropes before, to the surprise of the batsman who was wondering where he had hit the ball, pulling it out of his pocket to a huge smile and roars of laughter from his colleagues.

During 1946 and 1947, Allan also turned out occasionally for Cardiff City's reserve team besides making a few appearances for their 1st XI in friendly matches. However, he became increasingly troubled by cartilage problems in his right knee, and given the fact that the England scouts were sounding out his availability for winter tours, he opted to focus on cricket. Allan subsequently developed into a solid and enterprising all-rounder who was regarded as one of the best in the county game.

As a left-handed batsman, he was especially powerful off the back foot, with powerful cuts and pulls, whilst as a bowler he was dubbed by colleagues as "Wat-Tosh", delivering brisk left-arm seam or swing with new ball *a la* Ernie

Allan Watkins, plus the rest of the MCC squad seen at Heathrow Airport after returning from the 1955/56 tour to India.

Toshack of Australia, before bowling cutters at a slower pace. If conditions permitted, Allan also had spells of orthodox left-arm spin in tandem with Don Shepherd's off-cutters.

During the winter of 1953/54 Allan was a member of the Commonwealth XI which toured India, alongside fellow county stalwarts George Emmett, Raman Subba Row and Peter Loader. He then returned to the United Kingdom and during 1954 recorded his career-best performances with both bat and ball. Firstly, at Swansea in late May, he made 170* against Leicestershire – an innings described by *Wisden's* correspondent as containing "magnificent forcing strokes which brought him three 6's and twenty-seven 4's" as Glamorgan won by ten wickets. In the final match of the season in late August, against Derbyshire at Chesterfield, his lively left-arm seam and swing saw Allan complete figures of 7/28 including a remarkable spell of four wickets in five balls as the Welsh county recorded another ten-wicket victory inside two days play.

1954 was also the first of two consecutive summers when Allan performed the coveted Double of 1000 first-class runs and 100 wickets with 1955 also seeing Allan take a well-deserved Benefit with the £4,750 raised on his behalf being invested in a dairy he had purchased in Usk as well as in his children's education. 1955 also saw Allan complete his best-ever bowling tally of 114 wickets and during the summer he was delighted to accept an invitation from the MCC to go on their A team's tour to Pakistan over the following winter as a senior professional alongside a couple of fellow wise heads in Leicestershire's Maurice Tompkins and Somerset wicket-keeper Harold Stephenson.

It was a difficult tour as the party, led by Donald Carr, faced some questionable umpiring, although Allan's good humour and ready wit helped to defuse some testing situations. However, during the closing weeks of the tour he contracted malaria, with the effects of this illness only manifesting itself when he was back in the UK. Although he missed only a handful of games, Allan enjoyed a relatively modest amassing just 834 runs – the first time since 1946 that he had not made over 1000 first-class runs.

Fortunately, Allan returned to form in 1957 with 1199 first-class runs before topping the 1300-mark in both 1958 and 1959. By this time, though, Glamorgan were beset by debates over the future of Wilf. Allan had become the Welsh county's senior professional following the retirement of Haydn Davies and he led Glamorgan when Wilf was unavailable. Allan though did not like captaincy, despite having been earmarked by Wilf as his successor. "I was worried that it was me going to be skipper," Allan later said "but I didn't want it."

Despite these misgivings, he was still senior professional in 1960 and stepped in as captain when Wilf was unavailable. He still didn't enjoy it and continued to be a chain-smoker on match days, often pacing up and down in the changing room before going out to bat. It was no surprise that he let both Gilbert Parkhouse and Don Shepherd take over the captaincy baton later in the summer.

With Ossie Wheatley taking over the captaincy on a full-time basis for 1961, Allan agreed to continue as senior professional and step in as captain whenever needed, but he was still racked by self-doubt. With no improvement in his asthma, which was exacerbated by his heavy smoking, his well-being continued to be something of a concern and it may have been a blessing that a flare-up of his knee injury in the away match with Kent during the last week of May, meant that the contest at Gravesend was his final appearance for Glamorgan.

Ossie, and others, tried to cajole Allan back into action but still racked by nerves, he refuted these offers and announced his retirement at what at the time was a relatively early age of 39 with his tally of 29 first-class hundreds being the seventh highest in the Club's history. Allan did appear in mid-September 1963 for the MCC against Hampshire at Southampton, but by this time he was working as a warder at Usk Borstal with special responsibility for sport.

However, Allan didn't enjoy his work with the miscreants and, with his wife also finding quite taxing her role as overseeing the operation of the dairy business, Allan secured a coaching post at Framlingham College. He had previously coached on a part-time basis at Christ College, Brecon, but this was a full-time post and in Eastern England, Despite being faraway from his friends and family in South Wales, Allan relished his new role and agreed to play for Suffolk in 1965 and 1966 – his performances for the Minor County even led to an offer to return to South Wales and play in one-day cricket for Glamorgan. He subsequently moved to Oundle School in 1971, following the retirement of his lifetime friend Arnold Dyson and, at the Northamptonshire school he continued to pass on his love of the game, as well as many traditional values about playing sport, to the pupils at the school and remaining, even in semi-retirement, a well-liked and jolly figure in the school community.

Allan, Molly and their children seen as the all-rounder returns to his family in Usk after a winter tour.

As a former pupil at Oundle fondly remembered, "Allan's great strengths were his enthusiasm, which was infectious, and his deep knowledge of the game which he would pass on with great care and skill. He was never over technical and allowed each individual to develop themselves without ever inhibiting natural talent. He taught us how to play the game in the spirit and manner in which he had played. Hard and fair was fine – cheating, lack of respect and poor manners were not. Molly ran the sports shop – a little wooden hut next to the cricket nets which was a treasure trove of goodies. The walls were covered in pictures of Allan and England cricket teams and Molly was always there with a friendly, warm and welcoming smile. I think it was Molly who had the business acumen too and she often said that if she had ever left the shop with Allan in charge he would give everything away!

Whilst at Oundle in 1991, Allan was deservedly appointed a Life Member of the MCC – the highest of many honours which came his way – whilst in May 2005 he was inducted into the Welsh Sports Hall of Fame. He had married Molly, née Shankland, in 1942, who had been his childhood sweetheart and the sister of one of his cricket-playing friends at Usk. They had two sons and two daughters, with Molly tending the brood for much of the year whilst Allan was playing cricket, either at home for Glamorgan, on tour with the MCC or on coaching assignments in South Africa. She pre-deceased him in 2003 and as Allan readily admitted "she was the one with the brains. She looked after me and she did everything for me."

His death in August 2011 came the day before the Glamorgan Former Players Association annual meeting, during the County Championship match against Essex at Cardiff. At the start of the lunch break, the players from both sides, together with the umpires and over fifty of the Welsh county's former players stood in a minute's silence to mark the passing of a true Glamorgan legend.

346
THOMAS, Dillwyn

Born – Neath Abbey, 13 February 1905
Born – Neath, 29 August 1996
Amateur
LHB, RM
1st XI: 1939
Clubs: Neath, Elba

Batting and Fielding Record:

	M	I	NO	RUNS	AV	100	50	CT	ST
F-c	2	2	1	14	14.00	-	-	1	-

Bowling Record:

	Balls	M	R	W	AV	5wI	10wM
F-c	216	4	99	5	19.80	1	-

First-class – 14* v Yorkshire at Bradford Park Avenue, 1939
   5/64 v Essex at Ilford, 1939

Dillwyn Thomas emerged during the 1930s as one of the top young all-rounders in league cricket. However, he had a steady and relatively well-paid job as a timekeeper in the tinplate works at Skewen and turned down approaches to play professionally for Glamorgan.

He had a fine record with the ball for both Neath and Elba, and deservedly had a reputation for being able to deceptively swing and cut the ball. With injuries to other bowlers in mid-May 1939, Dillwyn agreed to take time off and play for Glamorgan against Essex at Ilford. Despite interruptions from the weather, Dillwyn enjoyed a decent debut at Ilford, opening the bowling with Jack Mercer and claiming 5/64 as Essex were dismissed for 109. He re-appeared in June 1939 when Johnnie Clay was unavailable for the visit to Yorkshire. This time, Dillwyn met with less success, going wicket-less as the Welsh county went down to a heavy defeat by an innings.

347
JUDGE, Peter Francis

Born – Cricklewood, 23 May 1916
Died – London, 4 March 1992
Professional
RHB, RFM
Ed – St Paul's School, London
1st XI: 1939-1947
Club and Ground: 1939-1947
Cap: 1934
Middlesex 1933-1934; Buckinghamshire 1935; RAF 1940-1944;
RAF (Southern Command) 1942;
British Empire XI 1940-1941; Bengal 1944/45-1945/46; Europeans 1944/45; DCS
Compton's XI 1943; Essex Services 1944; London Counties 1941-1944
Clubs: Burnley, Scarborough, Elland, Carlisle

Batting and Fielding Record:

	M	I	NO	RUNS	AV	100	50	CT	ST
F-c	54	67	24	332	7.12	-	-	29	-
Wartime	5	2	0	42	21.00	-	-	3	-

Bowling Record:

	Balls	M	R	W	AV	5wI	10wM
F-c	8001	221	3475	138	25.18	3	-
Wartime	?	?	?	7	-	-	-

Career-bests:
First-class –   40 v Worcestershire at Ebbw Vale, 1946
   8/75 v Yorkshire at Bradford, 1939

A photograph of Peter Judge during his days with Middlesex.

Peter Judge had a unique claim to fame – he was dismissed twice in the space of three balls during Glamorgan's match with the Indians in 1946, and having been dismissed twice in the space of a minute, he holds the rather unwanted record of the quickest pair in first-class cricket.

This unusual distinction took place at the Arms Park on the final day of the tourist match, and after Peter was bowled by the last ball of Glamorgan's first innings, captain Johnnie Clay decided to reverse the batting order in order to inject life into the fixture which was heading for a tame draw, and provide some entertainment for the sizeable crowd. With the umpire's having been informed, Peter and Johnnie stayed out in the middle as the Indian captain reset the field, but barely a minute after being bowled, Peter was on his way back to the Cardiff pavilion after being bowled again by the second ball of the second innings!

Peter had begun his cricket career with Middlesex in 1933 by enjoying an action-packed debut, just weeks after leaving St Paul's with the seventeen-year-old seam bowler returning figures of 5/77 and 4/62 against Surrey at The Oval. In all, Peter played eight times for Middlesex as an amateur between 1933 and 1934, before playing for Buckinghamshire for a couple of seasons, besides appearing in more informal types of cricket playing for teams such as The Jesters, the Buccaneers and the MCC.

He enjoyed these games and the socializing associated with them, but close friends urged him not to waste his talents as a bowler and, following their urgings, the tall and debonair gentleman turned professional. Peter duly appeared in League cricket in Yorkshire and Cumbria for a few years, before agreeing to join Glamorgan for 1939. His debut was delayed until the fourth week of the season – it was reported at the time that there were delays with the paperwork associated with his registration; others have suggested that it was due to Peter sorting out his rather complex marital status!

Whatever the reason, once everything had been finalized Peter enjoyed a decent first summer in the Welsh county's ranks, claiming 69 wickets, including career-best figures of 8/75 against eventual champions Yorkshire at Bradford Park Avenue.

During the Second World War, he served with the Royal Air Force, initially at airbases in the Home Counties and Gloucestershire, before being posted to India where he further added to his list of first-class teams by appearing for Bengal in the Ranji Trophy and the Europeans in the Bombay Communal Tournaments of 1944/45 and 1945/46.

He re-joined Glamorgan for 1946, and claimed 64 wickets in a further 27 matches, including 7/23 against Derbyshire at the Arms Park during 1946. The following summer he was hampered by an injury to his Achilles tendon in his left foot and appeared in just three games. It came as no surprise that he retired from county cricket at the end of the 1947 season and accepted professional terms for the following summer with Burnley in the Lancashire League.

Peter duly left Glamorgan with 138 wickets to his name – a tally which would have been much higher had the War not intervened. As a result, Peter will be most remembered for that rather unique distinction with the bat against the 1946 Indians. In later life, he lived near St John's Wood and was confined to a motorized wheelchair. Despite his limited mobility, he was a frequent visitor to Lord's and sat at the front of the Warner Stand, happily recalling his time in county cricket and, with a twinkle in his eye, sharing with passers-by his unusual claim to fame!

Peter Judge bowling in the nets at Cardiff.

348
PARKHOUSE, Richard John

Born – Pontardawe, 26 January 1907
Died – Hereford, 1 January 1984
Amateur
RHB
Ed – Ystalyfera School, Swansea Municipal School and Aberystwyth University
1st XI: 1939
2nd XI: 1933-1935
All Egypt 1938/39; Nigeria 1946/47-1949/50
Clubs: Clydach, Llanelli, Gezira Sporting Club, Madi Sports

Batting and Fielding Record:

	M	I	NO	RUNS	AV	100	50	CT	ST
F-c	2	1	0	0	-	-	-	-	-

Dick Parkhouse, a schoolmaster by profession, played twice for Glamorgan in 1939 but failed to score in his only Championship innings against Hampshire at Southampton. However, he did have the distinction that year of scoring a century in international cricket – albeit for All Egypt!

Born in the Swansea Valleys and educated at Aberystwyth University, the assertive top-order batsman had first come to the attention of the Glamorgan selectors when playing club cricket for Clydach.

He duly appeared for the county's 2nd XI in 1933 but, by this time, he was teaching in Egypt and playing regularly for the Gezira Sports Club. With his family having moved to Llanelli, Dick switched his playing allegiances to the Carmarthenshire club in 1934 when on his summer holidays and some decent scores for Llanelli saw him play again for Glamorgan 2nd XI.

Dick's success with the bat for both the Gezira and Madi Sports Clubs saw him win selection for the All Egypt side who met HM Martineau's XI in 1938/39. With the tourists having Bob Wyatt, Freddie Brown and Tom Pearce in their ranks, Dick made 110, and having impressed these fine judges, Dick accepted an offer to play for Glamorgan during July 1939 against Hampshire at Southampton and Surrey at The Oval.

The outbreak of War stifled his ambitions to play again for Glamorgan, and the following year Dick joined the Royal Air Force, for whom he was promoted to the rank of Flying Officer. After being demobilized, he opted to teach overseas once again, and secured a post in West Africa.

He subsequently played for Nigeria between 1947 and 1949, besides captaining them during the latter season. Dick subsequently returned to the UK during 1950 where he taught and coached in Scotland.

349
EVANS, Gwynn.

Born – Bala, 13 August 1915
Died – Leicester, 1 April 2002
Amateur
RHB, RM
Ed – St Asaph College and Brasenose College, Oxford
1st XI: 1939
Cap: 1939
Denbighshire 1933-1935; Oxford University 1938-1939 (Blue 1939); Leicestershire 1949; Oxford Past and Present 1942
Clubs: St Asaph; Leicester Ivanhoe

Batting and Fielding Record:

	M	I	NO	RUNS	AV	100	50	CT	ST
F-c	7	14	1	164	12.61	-	-	5	-

Bowling Record:

	Balls	M	R	W	AV	5wI	10wM
F-c	592	3	331	5	66.20	-	-

Career-bests:

First-class –   36 v Surrey at St Helen's, Swansea, 1939

1/27 v West Indians at St Helen's, Swansea, 1939

Gwynn Evans is amongst a small band of people to progress from club cricket in North Wales to a place in the Glamorgan side.

Born in Bala and brought up in St Asaph, he was the eldest son of the Rev. Thomas Evans and first appeared in county cricket for Denbighshire in 1933 as a steady right-arm seam bowler, making his debut against Lincolnshire in Scunthorpe. He appeared in a further nine Minor County matches, also appearing alongside Wilf Wooller and his brother Roy, before going up to Oxford to read Jurisprudence at Brasenose College.

He subsequently impressed in college cricket and won a place in the Oxford XI in 1938. He duly made

A photograph of Gwynn Evans taken around 1944 (reproduced with thanks to Brasenose College, Oxford).

his first-class debut against Gloucestershire before appearing as first change, against the touring Australians. To his delight, he claimed three wickets including that of Don Bradman who he trapped l.b.w. for 58. However, he failed to win a Blue, but this was rectified the following year as the North Walian took 6/80 against Leicestershire.

Stocky in build, he impressed once again with his skiddy pace and an ability to extract lift from the surface whilst his forthright use of the bat saw him post a trio of half-centuries. On the back of these performances with both ball and bat, plus a recommendation from Wilf, Gwynn accepted an offer to play for Glamorgan for the rest of the summer, with talk of the Oxford undergraduate becoming a long-term replacement for Jack Mercer. He duly made his debut in early August against the West Indians at Swansea, before appearing in the remaining Championship matches. However, he only claimed four wickets and failed to reach fifty.

His last appearance came during the away game with Leicestershire and as the final contest of the summer meandered towards a tame draw, Maurice Turnbull juggled the Glamorgan batting order, and it was Gwynn who was Maurice's partner at the crease when the match ended as a thunderstorm broke over the Aylestone Road ground. As events tragically turned out, it was the final innings for both men in Glamorgan's colours.

Gwynn subsequently completed his degree and undertook his National Service with the Royal Artillery, rising to the rank of Staff Captain, before focusing on his career as a teacher. After accepting a post in Leicester, he moved to the East Midlands and having impressed in club cricket, he appeared for the Leicestershire Club and Ground side during 1948, before agreeing to turn out the following summer for their 1st XI. His Leicestershire debut came against the 1949 New Zealanders at Grace Road, followed by an appearance at Lord's in the Championship match with Middlesex.

Once his teaching duties were over, Gwynn turned out regularly for the rest of the season for Leicestershire and, following the abrupt departure of club captain Stuart Symington after the match against Lancashire, Gwynn captained the county for the remaining six matches of the summer.

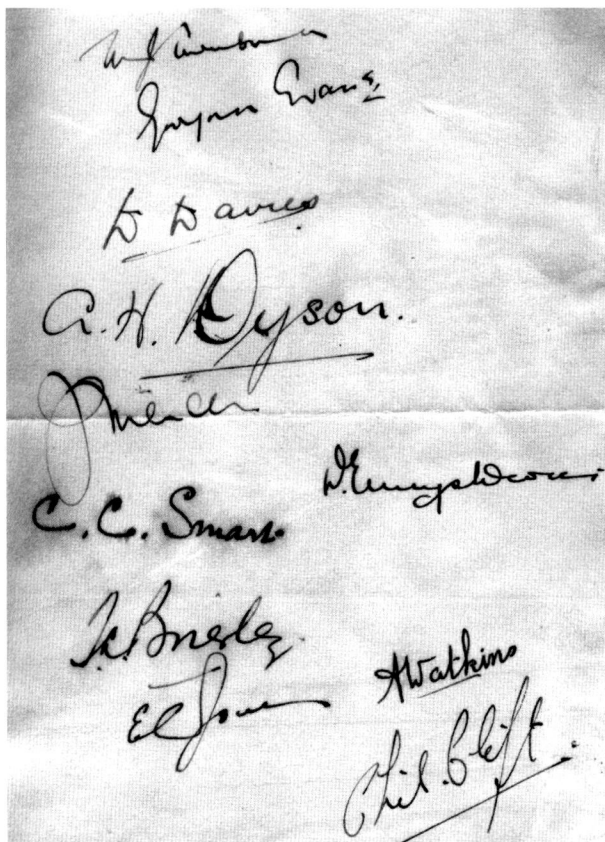

An autograph sheet from 1939 containing, second from the top, the signature of Gwynn Evans.

1940–1942

Almost as soon as War had been declared, the military authorities had moved into Cardiff Arms Park and St Helen's with plans being swiftly put in place for military training and other activities designed to prepare men for the War Effort. As neither cricket ground was the property of Glamorgan CCC, the Club's only concern during the winter of 1939/40 was the creation of an Emergency Committee to safeguard the practice equipment and financial assets.

With many believing that the War would soon be over, the Emergency Committee set in motion plans for a two-day fixture during the second week of August against a Somerset XI at Weston-super-Mare. As the dreadful events of the War unfolded, this was cancelled and it soon became clear that life would be disrupted for some time as the Government made impassioned pleas for factories to keep working and build up replacements for military equipment lost at Dunkirk and the hasty retreat from Northern France.

Maurice Turnbull with Bill Edrich seen at Lord's during 1942 in a fund-raising match organised by the Army.

During 1941 a pair of fixtures were agreed for early August against the London Counties team who had been staging exhibition matches to raise funds for the War Effort, but neither took place, despite the best intentions of the Glamorgan officials. Little changed during 1942 as the committee met again in the Club's offices at 6, High Street in the heart of Cardiff's central business district and talked once more about fund-raising fixtures.

With the constant threat of further attacks by Luftwaffe bombers on the nearby docks and the city itself, it was understandable that the minds of those present were distracted by events on the bigger stage as, once again, no matches were possible for the third successive summer.

1943

Conditions thankfully had eased by 1943 for a series of games to be staged both at the Arms Park as well as at Barry Island – the ground some 9 miles away adjacent to the popular promenade along Whitmore Bay and leased from the Earl of Plymouth at a peppercorn rent by Barry Athletic Club. Indeed, it was at Barry where on 12 June, and after several years of inactivity, Glamorgan staged a one-day friendly against the Anti-Aircraft Command which the Welsh county won by 21 runs.

Further games followed at the Arms Park although the contest on 10 July against the Western Command was washed out. The match though against The Army on 2 August went ahead in better weather in Cardiff and saw Glamorgan win by 129 runs, before a fortnight later also defeating the Royal Air Force at Barry Island at 26 runs in a match which saw the first appearance in Glamorgan colours of Gilbert Parkhouse, then a hugely gifted schoolboy batsman from Wycliffe College, who later became not only a regular in the Glamorgan side but a man who won Test Match honours with England during the 1950s.

These four friendlies, as well as the Present v Future match at the Arms Park during early August were small signs that life was gradually improving, but it would be three long and bloody summers before Championship cricket returned.

An image of the scorecard for the Glamorgan Present v Glamorgan Future game staged at the Arms Park in Cardiff during 1943.

350

CONTRACTOR, Dr Noshirwan Kaikhushro

Born – India, 5 June 1911
Died – Cardiff, 1 May 1987
Amateur
1st XI: 1943-1944
Club: Cardiff

Batting and Fielding Record:

	M	I	NO	RUNS	AV	100	50	CT	ST
Wartime	2	2	0	13	6.50	-	-	-	-

Bowling Record:

	Balls	M	R	W	AV	5wI	10wM
Wartime	?	?	?	1	-	-	-

Dr. Contractor.

351

WILLIAMS, Gwynfor Lloyd

Born – Kidwelly, 30 May 1925
Died – Talsarnau, Merioneth, 18 July 2007
Amateur
Ed – Christ College, Brecon and Brasenose College, Oxford
RHB
1st XI: 1943
2nd XI: 1949-1953
Somerset – 1955
Club: Llanelli, MCC, XL Club

Batting and Fielding Record:

	M	I	NO	RUNS	AV	100	50	CT	ST
Wartime	1	1	0	0	-	-	-	1	-

Lloyd Williams also played table tennis for Oxford University as well as squash for Somerset. He played frequently for Glamorgan's 2nd XI when based in Llanelli and after moving to the West Country he appeared for Somerset during their Festival week at Weston-super-Mare in 1955, playing against Surrey, Hampshire and Glamorgan.

Lloyd Williams.

352
PATTERSON, Arthur Sampson

Born – Cardiff, 8 August 1909
Died – Barry, 10 May 1975
Amateur
RHB, OB
1st XI: 1943
2nd XI: 1947-1948
Western Command 1942, London Counties 1944
Clubs: St Fagans, Barry, Glamorgan Nomads, MCC, XL Club

Batting and Fielding Record:

	M	I	NO	RUNS	AV	100	50	CT	ST
Wartime	2	2	0	19	9.50	-	-	-	-

Arthur Patterson was a stalwart figure in club cricket in South-East Wales with the inter-schools competition in the Cardiff area being named in his memory. In 1966 he was instrumental in creating the Welsh Club Conference. Sadly, he died in 1975 whilst playing in a cricket match at Barry.

Arthur Patterson.

353
JENNER, Lieutenant

1st XI: 1943

Batting and Fielding Record:

	M	I	NO	RUNS	AV	100	50	CT	ST
Wartime	1	1	0	0	-	-	-	-	-

354
SPURWAY, Robert John Vyvyan

Born – Woolwich, 21 July 1898
Died – Torbryan, Newton Abbot, 24 December 1951
Amateur
RHB
Ed – Forest School, Snaresbrook
1st XI: 1943
Clubs: Royal Navy, Free Foresters, Incogniti, MCC
Son of RP Spurway (Somerset and Natal)

Batting and Fielding Record:

	M	I	NO	RUNS	AV	100	50	CT	ST
Wartime	1	1	0	0	-	-	-	-	-

355
GREALY, John ('Jack')

Born – Kidderminster, 6 February 1915
Died – Worcester, 22 January 1982
Amateur
RHB, RFM
1st XI: 1943-1944
Clubs: Abergavenny, Abertillery, Ebbw Vale

Batting and Fielding Record:

	M	I	NO	RUNS	AV	100	50	CT	ST
Wartime	2	1	0	4	4.00	-	-	1	-

Bowling Record:

	Balls	M	R	W	AV	5wI	10wM
Wartime	?	?	?	4	-	-	-

Jack Grealy was a policeman who had a fine record as a fast bowler in club cricket in Monmouthshire.

SHEA, William _Dennis_

Born – Briton Ferry, 7 February 1924
Died – Ormskirk, 22 September 1982
Amateur
RHB, LBG
Ed – Neath Grammar School
1st XI: 1943-1948
2nd XI: 1939-1948
Colts: 1939
Club and Ground: 1948
Clubs: Briton Ferry Steel, Neath, Southport, Hightown

Batting and Fielding Record:

	M	I	NO	RUNS	AV	100	50	CT	ST
F-c	3	3	1	27	13.50	-	-	-	-
Wartime	6	4	0	37	9.25	-	-	-	-

Bowling Record:

	Balls	M	R	W	AV	5wI	10wM
F-c	306	5	180	5	36.00	-	-
Wartime	?	?	?	13	-	-	-

Career-bests:

First-class – 18* v Combined Services at Ynysangharad Park, Pontypridd, 1948
4/68 v Combined Services at Ynysangharad Park, Pontypridd, 1948

Dennis Shea was a batsman and leg-spinner who had a brief career with Glamorgan after the Second World War before moving to live and work in Lancashire where he enjoyed a successful career in the Liverpool Premier League.

Dennis was the son of William Henry Shea, a blast furnace worker at Briton Ferry Ironworks who lived in Ynysmaerdy, close to the home of Briton Ferry Steel. His father's sporting career had been affected by the Great War with William being wounded at Gallipoli whilst serving with the Royal Welsh Fusiliers.

Dennis Shea.

For Dennis, his National Service took him to north-west England where he met, and subsequently married Irene Cull in Southport during 1947. It was an eventful year for the former pupil of Neath Grammar School as Dennis also made his Glamorgan debut in the Championship match against Warwickshire at Swansea.

The leg-spinner had first played for the county's 2nd XI and Colts during 1939 having shown rich promise as a schoolboy cricketer in the South Wales and Monmouthshire League, playing for Briton Ferry Steel and Neath. He also appeared in some of Glamorgan's wartime matches in 1943 before undertaking his National Service in north-west England.

Dennis played for Glamorgan during 1948 against the Combined Services at Pontypridd, with the match at Ynysangharad Park seeing him record career-best performances with bat and ball. It proved to be his final appearance for the Club as the following year he moved to Lancashire and played with distinction for the next quarter of a century in league cricket, appearing for Hightown from 1950 until 1957, before joining Southport and Birkdale for whom he played between 1958 and 1974.

Dennis was the nephew of Alf Shea who played twice for Glamorgan during 1928 and was a stalwart of cricket in the Neath and Briton Ferry area

357
JENKINS, Arthur Ronald
Born – Pontypridd, 8 November 1921
Died – Bromley, 1 October 1999
Amateur
Ed – Pontypridd Grammar School and Jesus College, Oxford
1st XI: 1943-1945
Club: Pontypridd, Oxford University Authentics
Wiltshire 1946-1947

Batting and Fielding Record:

	M	I	NO	RUNS	AV	100	50	CT	ST
Wartime	8	8	0	77	9.63	-	1	2	-

Arthur Jenkins was a talented top-order batsman who, had it not been for the Second World War, would have probably played Championship cricket. He attended Oxford University and besides representing the university at football in 1942/43 (without winning a Blue), he played in the Varsity Match at Lord's during 1943 against Cambridge University. He played regularly in the wartime fixtures, including twice with his elder brother Tom, before moving to the Wiltshire area and subsequently playing for them in Minor County cricket.

Pontypridd Cricket Club in 1940. Arthur Jenkins is sitting front left and his brother Tom seated second right.

358
JENKINS, Tom Raymond

Born – Pontypridd, 8 August 1920
Died – Swansea, November 1995
Amateur
Ed – Pontypridd Grammar School
1st XI: 1943-1945
Colts: 1937-1945
Club: Pontypridd

Batting and Fielding Record:

	M	I	NO	RUNS	AV	100	50	CT	ST
Wartime	2	2	0	16	8.00	-	-	1	-

Besides playing in the wartime friendlies, Tom Jenkins also appeared for the county's Colts. His first game had been as a sixteen-year old: his last came in 1945 when he played against the Welsh Secondary Schools at the Arms Park.

359
NORTH, Alfred Stanley

Born – Newport, 5 May 1910
Died – Newport, 1 October 1992
Amateur
1st XI: 1943-1945
2nd XI: 1938-1948
Clubs: Newport, Whiteheads

AS North.

Batting and Fielding Record:

	M	I	NO	RUNS	AV	100	50	CT	ST
Wartime	10	11	1	210	21.00	-	2	6	-

Bowling Record:

	Balls	M	R	W	AV	5wI	10wM
Wartime	?	?	?	4	-	-	-

360
PARKHOUSE, William *Gilbert* Anthony

Born – Swansea, 12 October 1925
Died – Carmarthen, 10 August 2000
Amateur 1943-1945
Professional 1948-1964
RHB, RM
Ed – Brynmill School, Swansea; Ryeford Hall, Ross-on-Wye and Wycliffe College
1st XI: 1943-1964
2nd XI: 1962-1964
Club and Ground: 1948-1962
Cap: 1948
England 1950-1959 (7 Tests); Players 1950-1959; MCC
Club: Swansea, Saltburn

Batting and Fielding Record:

	M	I	NO	RUNS	AV	100	50	CT	ST
F-c	435	759	48	22619	31.81	32	123	312	-
List A	1	1	0	17	17.00	-	-	1	-

Bowling Record:

	Overs	M	R	W	AV	5wI	10wM
F-c	229	8	125	2	62.50	-	-

Career-bests:

First-class – 201 v Kent at St Helen's, Swansea, 1956
1/4 v Surrey at Stradey Park, Llanelli, 1952
List A – 17 v Essex at The Gnoll, Neath, 1964

Gilbert Parkhouse.

Gilbert Parkhouse was a graceful and gifted batsman who won seven Test caps for England, with his successful career as a professional cricketer with Glamorgan spanning the years from their first Championship title in 1948 to the introduction of limited-overs cricket in the early 1960s. During this time, he also became the first, and still only, batsman to score hundreds against every other Championship side, besides in 1961 scoring the fastest century on record for Glamorgan, racing to three figures in just 70 minutes at Northampton. No wonder that countless numbers of Welsh schoolboys called themselves Parkhouse when they played their own and more informal games of street cricket after the Second World War!

Gilbert was educated at Wycliffe College, near Stonehouse – a seat of learning in the shadow of the Cotswolds which was much in favour at the time for the sons of the well-to-do and *nouveaux riches* of South Wales. Gilbert shone as a young sportsman, with his prowess on the hockey pitch and rugby field winning him his school colours, as well a place in Swansea's junior rugby teams, as well as a Welsh hockey cap. His elegant and technically correct batting also led to offers of trials with Gloucestershire, but Gilbert's heart lay in South Wales and he remained loyal to Glamorgan

Sport was in his family's blood, with his uncles Jim and Jenkin Jones being leading members of Glais RFC, as well as decent club cricketers in their own right. Gilbert also spent his formative years at Brynmill School near the St Helen's ground, where from the age of seven he was coached in the skills of both rugby and cricket by Billy Bancroft, Glamorgan's first-ever home-grown professional back in their days as a Minor County and a man – quite curious in the hurly-burly of sporting life in South Wales – who was a professional cricketer during the summer yet an amateur in the winter when playing rugby for Swansea and Wales. (Vol.1, p17-20)

On many occasions during the 1930s, there had been a gleam in old Billy's eyes as he threw tennis balls to the young batsman in the cricket nets at St Helen's where Billy and his father had lived for so many years, besides tending the wicket at the ground overlooking Swansea Bay. He had coached many aspiring young cricketers but, as he told journalists during the late 1930s, he rated young Gilbert as the finest he had the privilege of coaching.

A young Gilbert Parkhouse being coached by Billy Bancroft on the rugby field at the St Helen's ground in Swansea.

After leaving Wycliffe, Gilbert joined the Army and, whilst undergoing his training as a Gunner, he played briefly for Saltburn in the North Yorkshire and South Durham League. During this time he also played rugby for the Army and Swansea, appearing at full-back for the All Whites in their matches during 1945 besides appearing in a number of Glamorgan Cricket's wartime friendlies,

On completing his National Service during the winter of 1947/48, Gilbert made his long awaited County Championship debut for the Welsh county the following summer. He soon showed class with the bat, amassing over 1200 runs in his debut season. Despite being slightly built, the youngster reeled off a wide range of high-class strokes, and swiftly became renowned as an immaculate timer of the ball. His craft and purity as a batsman was reflected in his refined strokeplay, crisply struck drives, powerful cuts and elegant deflections to fine-leg. All of this impressed the purists, whilst those who flocked to the Arms Park or St Helen's to watch him bat relished his appetite to take on opposing fast bowlers, leaning back with a visible relish to hook them to distant parts of the outfield, and enjoying any chance to make them look silly.

Gilbert Parkhouse and Phil Clift walk out to the middle to face the Somerset bowlers at Weston-super-Mare during 1948.

He was equally effective against pace or spin. Indeed, he was one of the first batsmen to regularly employ the sweep shot to balls of the right length outside off-stump – a stroke that exasperated many spinners, including Gloucestershire veteran Tom Goddard who christened him "a bloody Laplander!" As Tony Lewis later recalled, "Gilbert was a very special player. Like many class performers, he would take the ball late and run it off. The way he played [Frank] Tyson was beautiful because he could hook. Gilbert had amazing timing and footwork. He was one of those players who never slogged the ball – it just went, so gracefully!"

Despite not having previously played any Championship cricket, Gilbert's effortless batting was one of the factors behind the county's outstanding start to the season as Glamorgan won their first three games, against Somerset, Essex and Worcestershire. Given his many years of practice at Swansea, it was very fitting that his maiden Championship hundred should come at St Helen's as he posted 117 against Sussex, with his graceful efforts earning a few heartfelt words of praise from Billy Bancroft who was now sat as the steward on the player's gate to the steps leading up to the pavilion, with Gilbert's mentor giving his own personal vote of thanks before the enclosure rose as one to their new batting hero.

A second hundred followed later in the season as Gilbert made 103 against Yorkshire at Hull and featured in a team led by veteran spinner Johnnie Clay. A few weeks later, he was alongside Clay during the decisive games during August as Glamorgan defeated Surrey at the Arms Park before beating Hampshire at Bournemouth to lift the county title. However, Gilbert's contribution to these historic victories was modest as he was dismissed without scoring by Jim Laker in the game at Cardiff before making just 2 in his solitary innings at Dean Park. But by this time, he had already made a major contribution with runs in other games, besides showing that he had an exceptionally safe pair of hands in the slips. It came as no surprise that during the end-of-season celebrations Gilbert was awarded his county cap.

1949 saw Gilbert build on his success and exceed his tally from the year before. There were no second season blues as he twice improved his personal highest score with firstly 126 against Hampshire in the opening Championship game before in early July, making 145 on an easy-paced pitch against Nottinghamshire at Trent Bridge. At the end of the summer, Gilbert had 1491 runs to his name and it wasn't just events on the field which put a smile on his face, because in October 1949 he married Dorothy James in Swansea.

Gilbert had few pretentions as a bowler, in contrast to some of Glamorgan's other top-order batsmen including Emrys and Dai Davies, as well as Willie Jones or Wilf Wooller. Some colleagues privately wished that they could be like Gilbert,

Don Shepherd helps Gilbert Parkhouse change his bat at the Arms Park.

and stand at slip without having to think about bowling. "He could focus his thoughts on his batting," said one, "and at times during team meetings, he sometimes found it hard to appreciate that other batsmen also had a job to do as a bowler, and could be both mentally and physically tired as a result of their efforts with the ball."

He would sometimes let others chase balls which had flown past him in the slips rather than hurtling after them himself, but cricket needs individuals, and a streak of selfishness has been present in the DNA of many fine batsmen. For Gilbert, cricket was all about batting and, with Phil Clift unavailable through illness in 1950, Glamorgan shuffled their batting resources before, in June, moving Gilbert up from number three to open the batting with Emrys. The new pairing proved to be an instant success, with the two sharing a stand of 241 against Somerset at Swansea, as well as 233 against Surrey at Swansea. In his first match as an opening batsman, Gilbert scored 121 and 148 against Somerset, before making 127 in the next match against Combined Services. Just for good measure, he hit 161 against Surrey ten days later!

In all, Gilbert amassed 1742 runs that summer, including three consecutive hundreds, with his excellent run of form also leading to his selection for England against the 1950 West Indians. It was a disappointing summer for the national side with Gilbert's call-

up for the Second Test at Lord's arising from an injury to Denis Compton and further withdrawals by Reg Simpson and Trevor Bailey. Gilbert made his debut batting at number five, but after facing 30 balls without scoring he was bowled by Alf Valentine. Second time around, Gilbert featured in a rear guard action with Cyril Washbrook as England tried to save the game. Gilbert made 48 in the stand of 78 and was praised by *Wisden's* correspondent who wrote "Parkhouse showed encouraging confidence and a variety of strokes until he hit a full toss straight to silly mid-off in the last over of the fourth day."

His efforts though could not prevent defeat as the Caribbean cricketers won their first-ever Test on English soil, thanks to the spin of Valentine and Sonny Ramadhin. Gilbert was retained for the next Test and arrived at Trent Bridge on the back of making a typically handsome 162 for Glamorgan against Worcestershire at Kidderminster. The match at Nottingham saw him elevated to the number three berth, from which he made 13 in the first innings before an attractive 69 in the second, but again his efforts were in a losing cause as the Caribbean side won by ten wickets.

Gilbert Parkhouse is congratulated by Billy Bancroft and Emrys Davies after the Swansea-born batsman had been called up by the England selectors to make his Test Match debut.

With his star seemingly in the ascent, Gilbert then made 81 in the Gents-Players match at Lord's before being struck down with influenza. It saw him miss ten days of county cricket and he was one of an unprecedented eight changes to the England side for the next Test at The Oval. However, he remained in the selectors minds and, after his weight of runs in the Championship, he was named in the MCC party on the 1950/51 tour of Australia and New Zealand.

His selection for the winter tour Down Under, however, proved to be something of a poisoned chalice as the six-month long visit also revealed to a wider and far less tolerant audience, a few quirks in Gilbert's character. Described variously by county colleagues as "erudite", "quiet", and "self-contained", Gilbert was quite straight-laced and spoke with a refined English accent, often preferring to dine on his own after play, enjoying a good steak and a fine bottle of wine, rather than swilling beer, exchanging raunchy stories and chasing skirt. Jim Pleass, his room-mate for the first half of his county career neatly summed him up by saying " 'Parky' was a quietly spoken introvert who chose his friends and companions carefully, and did not suffer fools gladly. We had similar views on many things, so it seemed quite natural for us to room together on away matches."

These idiosyncrasies and a few alarms in playing the rising ball on fast, pacy pitches all contributed to an unhappy tour of Australia and New Zealand. There were rumours of clashes of personality with Cyril Washbrook and Len Hutton, as well as a possible altercation with Denis Compton over some apparently disparaging comments made about Emrys Davies, Gilbert's opening partner. Niggling injuries and illness also saw Gilbert miss out on selection for the First Test, but innings of 58 and 46* against an Australian XI helped secure a place in the Second Test at Melbourne.

Batting at number six, Gilbert scored 9 and 28, followed by an assertive 92 in the tour match against New South Wales. His services were retained for the Third Test at Sydney, but he made 25 and 15 and few eyebrows were raised when, with the series lost, the selectors chose David Sheppard instead of Gilbert for the remaining Tests against Australia. He did reclaim his place on the New Zealand leg of the tour, when injuries to others saw the Glamorgan batsman feature in the second of the two-match series, but in a low-scoring game, Gilbert made 2 and 20. It had hardly been a tour to look back on with relish and a very telling comment about Gilbert's winter in the Southern Hemisphere came from fellow batsman Phil Clift. "When he returned from the Australian tour, he barely mentioned it; others would have been full of their experiences."

We should not forget at the same time that Gilbert was neither boastful or a braggard, but he knew his worth, was proud to have played in Test cricket and, if need be, was not shy in reminding people of this fact. An example came after a heavy Championship defeat and a day when an irate Wilf was berating the team in the changing rooms. Injury had prevented Wilf from playing with Gilbert acting as his deputy. As the verbal tirade continued, a few asides were made about Gilbert's tactics. He could take it no longer and turned to Wilf saying " I'll have you know, Mr Wooller, that I have played for England."

It was over eight years before Gilbert played his next Test Match but England's loss during the 1950s was Glamorgan's gain. The gifted batsman passed the 1000 run mark every year during the decade besides posting a career-best 201 in the match against Kent at Swansea with his double-hundred typically featuring some flowing drives, assertive cuts and deftly-placed sweeps against the visiting spinners. Following Emrys' retirement in 1954 and experiments with others, the decade also saw Gilbert develop another fine opening partnership with Bernard Hedges. They had first opened together during July 1955 at St Helen's when Surrey visited Swansea with Jim Laker and the Bedser twins

Gilbert Parkhouse and Emrys Davies head out from the pavilion at the St Helen's ground during a County Championship match in 1952.

running amok through the home batting. It was not until 1957 that Gilbert and Bernard became the regular opening pair, with their partnership being sealed after handsome victories over Leicestershire at Coalville and Nottinghamshire at Stradey Park, as the duo mastered the wiles of Australian leg-spinner Bruce Dooland in the course of adding 156 in even time.

Their stirring efforts also laid the foundation for a victory by an innings and 120 runs, and one which put a huge smile on the face of Wilf, who on many occasions had clashed swords with visiting skipper Reg Simpson. Dooland had been the ace in the pack held by Simpson, with the Notts captain rating the Australian as the finest spinner in world cricket. But it was not his day at Llanelli as Gilbert and Bernard completely took him apart, with Wilf needing no invitation to scoff at Reg's assertions at the leg-spinner's standing in the world game.

There were several times though when Gilbert clashed with Wilf, although, as others in the team readily admitted, this was par for the course for Glamorgan cricket in these post-war years. Many of their exchanges came after the Welsh county ad been set a demanding target by the opposition on the last day, Wilf would sometimes say to Gilbert: "We're not going for them, so block it out." But Gilbert and the other top-order batsmen often found that they were in with a chance and with Gilbert's strokeplay to the fore, Glamorgan would go on to win. With more than a hint of resentment, Gilbert later reflected "Wilf would then take all the credit, despite his earlier instructions!"

A few clashes came during 1958 which was a difficult summer in many ways for the team, Gilbert and Wilf himself. With doubts over the future of Wilf as Glamorgan's captain, Gilbert was one of the names thrown into the ring when discussing who should take over. But 1958 was a relatively lean year with the bat for Gilbert, and despite passing the 1000 run mark, he failed to score a century in Championship cricket.

Fortunately, Gilbert was back to his very best during 1959 and topped the 2000 run mark in what was quite literally an Indian summer. In so doing, he broke his good friend Emrys' previous Club record of 1954 runs made in 1937, besides becoming the first Glamorgan player to reach this landmark.

It highlighted the rich vein of batting talent amongst the shires that the England selectors were able, season-after-season during the 1950s, to ignore the claims of the Glamorgan batsman. He had briefly re-appeared on the international stage in 1955 when acting as a substitute fielder in the Old Trafford Test against South Africa, and had run out Roy McLean to put England into a position from which they might have won the Test had other fielders not dropped catches. Any thoughts to the west of Offa's Dyke that this might prompt a recall for one of Swansea's favourite sporting sons proved far from the mark and it wasn't until his run-laden summer four years later that he donned an England sweater again.

1959 was different though and with doubts being raised over some of the England top order following a disastrous Ashes tour of Australia the previous winter, the selectors recalled Gilbert for the Third Test against the Indians at Headingley. By the time of his return to Test cricket, Gilbert had already four centuries to his name that summer for the Welsh county, and overall, with a young family to boot, was an older and wiser character. In keeping with the selectors policy of experimentation against a modest Indian side, Gilbert's opening partner was Geoff Pullar, the young left-hander from Lancashire. The game at Leeds was a success for the new pairing with *Wisden's* correspondent reporting how they "proved highly satisfactory" after the pair added 146 in the first innings – at the time a record for England against India and their best start in 26 Tests.

Gilbert Parkhouse seen batting against Nottinghamshire during 1958, with the East Midlands side employing a ring of leg-side catchers in the belief that the Welshman had a weakness against the short ball.

Gilbert's efforts delighted those who felt he had been unfairly ignored by the England selectors and with a chorus of "I told you so" emanating from west of Offa's Dyke, he retained his place with Geoff for the Fourth Test at Old Trafford. The match duly proved to be a personal triumph for Gilbert's partner who made 131 – the first century by a Lancastrian for England on his home ground. In contrast, Gilbert mistimed a hook and was dismissed for just 17 and, with the selector's minds turning to the winter tour to the West Indies, Gilbert's fallibility to the short rising ball was highlighted again.

Despite a score of 49 in the second innings against some less aggressive bowling by the Indians, Gilbert was replaced for the Fifth Test by Raman Subba Row, and was not chosen for the winter tour, with the game in Manchester proving to be Gilbert's last in England colours. The general consensus amongst his contemporaries on the county circuit was that if the England selectors had shown more faith in him, and fellow players accepting him for what he was, rather than what he wasn't, Gilbert could have made a huge impact at Test level.

The early 1960s saw Gilbert's consistency at county level being rewarded with special places in the Glamorgan record books. Firstly, in May 1960 he became the Club's first batsman to complete a full set of hundreds against each of the other first-class counties, reaching the milestone with 121 against Leicestershire, appropriately on his home turf at St Helen's. A few wags suggested another place in the annals later in the summer as he made 110 against Hampshire at Cowes – "it's our first hundred overseas", said one after the Glamorgan squad had travelled by ferry to the ground on the Isle of Wight!

Further centuries came in 1961 against Nottinghamshire and Northants before the following year 124 against Cambridge University with his 32nd century in Glamorgan colours beating what at the time was Emrys' Club record of 31. However, Gilbert's hundred at Fenner's also proved to be his last three-figure for the Welsh county, whilst 1962 also proved to be the final summer when he passed the 1000-run mark.

The following summer Gilbert was increasingly troubled by a back injury, as well as arthritis and made just 366 runs in 11 appearances. As Ossie Wheatley recalled, "he couldn't chase a ball or anything and, when you are playing six days a week that's pretty grim". Gilbert re-appeared in several of the early season games in 1964 but, after another flair-up of the ailments, he was on the sidelines for over two months, before making a farewell appearance on his home soil at Swansea against Nottinghamshire during mid-August.

In 1965 Gilbert accepted a position as coach of Worcestershire before moving the following year to Edinburgh where he coached at Stewarts-Melville College until 1987. However, in 1969 he came out of retirement to appear for Swansea in their one-day match against Barbados. Facing an attack which also included Wes Hall, the West Indian fast bowler, Gilbert made a cultured 57 and shared in a jaunty stand with Fred Trueman who was also guesting for the Swansea club. After retiring from county cricket, he proved to be a talented golfer, besides finding plenty of time to be with his wife Dorothy plus their son and daughter.

361
JONES, Harry Ogwyn

Born – Llangennech, 6 October 1922
Died – Llangennech, 20 March 1995
RHB, RM
Ed – Llangennech School
1st XI: 1943-1946
2nd XI: 1946
Club and Ground: 1945
West of England 1944
Clubs: Llangennech, Dafen, Llanelli, Pontarddulais

Batting and Fielding Record:

	M	I	NO	RUNS	AV	100	50	CT	ST
F-c	2	3	3	10	-	-	-	-	-

Bowling Record:

	Balls	M	R	W	AV	5wI	10wM
F-c	60	1	53	0	-	-	-

Career-best:
First-class –   7 v Worcestershire at Ebbw Vale, 1946

Harry Jones had a decent record as an opening bowler in the South Wales and Monmouthshire League. During his career, he appeared for his native Llangennech, as well as Dafen, Llanelli and Pontardulais, besides featuring in Glamorgan's wartime matches plus playing in two Championship games for the Welsh county.

Known to everyone as "H.O.", he first played in his early teens for Llangennech, before becoming a regular member of the club's 1st XI in 1938. After leaving the local school, Harry secured a clerk's post at the tinplate works in Llanelli. This

HO Jones.

328

reserved occupation meant that he was available for the series of fund-raising and morale-boosting contests which the Welsh county's emergency committee organized between 1942 and 1945. Harry featured in two games in 1943, before playing in nine games during 1944 plus a further eleven in 1945, including the Past v Future game at the Barracks Ground in Cardiff.

Bowling at a lively pace, he was Glamorgan's leading wicket-taker during these wartime games with his returns including 5/22 against the Royal Air Force at Barry Island in 1943, 4/34 against Sir Learie Constantine's XI at Barry Island, 4/32 in the match against the Royal Australian Air Force at Cardiff Arms Park in 1945, followed by 5/32 against Western Command at Briton Ferry, 4/31 against Constantine's XI again at Barry, plus 4/21 against the National Fire Service at Ynysangharad Park in Pontypridd.

These decent returns led to an offer from Glamorgan to join their full-time staff in 1946. His decent salary at the tinplate works, plus the fee for playing in the Leagues more than exceeded what the cash-strapped county could offer, but he told Johnnie Clay he was happy to lend a hand if they were short. This duly led to a couple of 1st XI appearances in June, against Essex at Chelmsford followed by the game with Worcestershire at Ebbw Vale, as well as the 2nd XI friendly with Gloucestershire at Barry Island during August.

Harry continued to play with great effect in the South Wales and Monmouthshire League and was a regular selection in their representative team. His final game for Llangennech came in 1965, and, like so many of his generation, his career at a higher level could have been very different had it not been for the Second World War.

362
JONES, Herbert Evan Lewis

Born – Pontypridd, 26 April 1916
Died – Brantford, Ontario, Canada, 29 January 1989
Amateur
All-rounder
Ed – Pontypridd Grammar School and the Welsh Medical School
1st XI: 1943-1945
Club: Pontypridd

Batting and Fielding Record:

	M	I	NO	RUNS	AV	100	50	CT	ST
Wartime	4	5	1	24	6.00	-	-	-	-

Bowling Record:

	Balls	M	R	W	AV	5wI	10wM
Wartime	?	?	?	1	-	-	-

Herbert Jones emigrated to Canada during June 1948 after completing his medical studies and remained in North America for the rest of his life.

363
VAUGHAN, Edgar Thomas
Born – Newport, 7 May 1920
Died – Clevedon, 11 September 2011
Amateur
1st XI: 1943
Colts: 1939
Clubs: Brecon, Llanelli

Batting and Fielding Record:

	M	I	NO	RUNS	AV	100	50	CT	ST
Wartime	1	1	1	3	-	-	-	-	-

Edgar Vaughan, a promising batsman from Llanelli, appeared in the friendly against the Royal Air Force at Barry Island in August on account of the youngster getting time off from his reserved occupation at Trostre Steelworks.

364
FOLLETT, G
Amateur
1st XI: 1943-1944

Batting and Fielding Record:

	M	I	NO	RUNS	AV	100	50	CT	ST
Wartime	1	1	0	1	1.00	-	-	-	-

1944

With matters slightly improving, Glamorgan's Emergency Committee were able to organize eleven fixtures between May and September 1944. All were one-day contests staged at Cardiff, Pontypridd, Barry Island, Swansea, Newport and Briton Ferry, together with an away game against the West of England at Gloucestershire's headquarters at Nevil Road in Bristol.

The West of England were one of three civilian teams which Glamorgan met, with the others being the British Empire XI, organized by Bob Haines, plus a side raised by Learie Constantine of the West Indies. Glamorgan also met five teams comprising servicemen – Western Command, The RAF, The Army, the National Fire Service and the Anti-Aircraft Command who were doing such a sterling job at the ports and other manufacturing establishments in South Wales.

All of the players in the teams, chosen by Glamorgan's Emergency Committee received a basic match fee and expenses, and included several from other counties, with the likes of Somerset's Bill Andrews, Gloucestershire's Bev Lyon and Kent's Ray Dovey all guesting for the Welsh county, because of their National Service commitments in the area, and being on hand to play in these fund-raising contests.

365
ANDREWS, William Harry Russell

Born – Swindon, 14 April, 1908
Died – Worlebury, Somerset 9 January, 1989
Professional
RHB, RFM
1st XI: 1944
Somerset 1930-1947; Forfarshire 1933; Devon 1950; England XI 1937; Under Thirty
1937; South of England 1946-1947; Rest of England 1947; 1950, Somerset 2nd XI 1957
Clubs: Stourbridge, Ebbw Vale, Keighley, Bingley

Batting and Fielding Record:

	M	I	NO	RUNS	AV	100	50	CT	ST
Wartime	6	6	2	52	13.00	-	-	3	-

Bowling Record:

	Balls	M	R	W	AV	5wI	10wM
Wartime	?	?	?	18	-	-	-

Bill Andrews, the well-known Somerset seam bowler, played for Glamorgan whilst stationed with the RAF at St Athan during 1944. He had a fine record with Somerset both before, and

then briefly after, the Second World War, during which the tall seamer, with a fine, high action claimed a total of 750 wickets at 23 apiece for the West Country side. He also had a brief spell with Forfarshire in Scottish county cricket in 1933 and 1934, before securing a new contract with Somerset.

Bill was a real character and well known for his greeting of "Shake the hand that bowled Bradman". He had indeed bowled the Australian maestro at Taunton in 1938 but it was, of course, a joke since Bradman had already scored 202.

During the War, he also played for a number of Services sides including the Royal Air Force and the United Services as well as for Blackpool Services in the Ribblesdale League, besides appearing for Keighley and Bingley in the Bradford League, plus

Bill Andrews.

various scratch elevens including an Empire XI, Tom Goddard's XI, George Duckworth's XI, a Combined Counties XI and the West of England.

Whilst stationed in Blackpool in 1943 he also appeared for a North Wales XI against an Empire XI at the Colwyn Bay Festival. After moving to South Wales in 1944 he played regularly for Glamorgan in their fund-raising games against the British Empire XI, Western Command, the RAF, Swansea Central League, The Army and the National Fire Service.

After retiring from county cricket, Andrews initially played for Stourbridge in the Birmingham League before appearing for Ebbw Vale in the South Wales and Monmouthshire Leagues in 1953 and 1954. He then returned to Somerset where he was 1st XI coach between 1955 and 1957, and latterly from 1964 until 1969, before coaching at Clifton College, Downside School and Millfield School.

Bill was also a good centre-half at football, playing for various teams including Glastonbury and Taunton Town, besides having a trial with Bristol City FC. He was also a keen golfer.

366
JAMES, Evan Llewellyn

Born – Barry, 10 May 1918
Died – Cardiff, January 1989
Amateur 1944-1945
Professional 1946-1947
RHB, RM
Ed – Gladstone Road School, Barry
1st XI: 1944-1947
2nd XI: 1948
Club and Ground: 1947
Clubs: Cardiff, Maesteg Town

Batting and Fielding Record:

	M	I	NO	RUNS	AV	100	50	CT	ST
F-c	9	12	4	232	29.00	-	2	10	-
Wartime	11	12	0	163	13.58	-	-	7	-

Bowling Record:

	Balls	M	R	W	AV	5wI	10wM
F-c	84	1	45	1	45.00	-	-

Career-bests:

First-class –   62* v Indians at St Helen's, Swansea, 1946
              1/8 v Essex at Cardiff Arms Park, 1947

Like many young cricketers during the late 1930s, Evan James lost his best years to the Second World War. The middle-order batsman and right-arm seamer had shown promise for the Welsh Schools team and also the Cardiff club during the 1930s. He was subsequently

Evan James, seen in a Glamorgan team group during 1946.

chosen to appear in the county's wartime fixtures in 1944 and 1945, and joined the county's junior staff for 1946 and 1947.

During this time, he appeared in nine first-class matches, with his finest moment in Glamorgan's colours coming in 1946 when he struck an unbeaten 62 against the Indian tourists at Swansea – a match watched by an estimated 50,000 people. However, Evan was dismissed in the second innings by CS Nayadu for a duck, before the tourists eased to a five-wicket victory.

Evan subsequently appeared in five further games for Glamorgan without making an impact with either bat or ball.

367
DOLMAN, Charles *Eric*

Born – Abertillery, 17 July 1903
Died – Bristol, 6 June 1969
Amateur
RHB, RM
Ed – Allhallows School
1st XI: 1944
2nd XI: 1936
Club and Ground: 1935
Monmouthshire 1922-1934, Wales 1926-1928
Club: Cardiff, Welsh Cygnets

Batting and Fielding Record:

	M	I	NO	RUNS	AV	100	50	CT	ST
Wartime	1	1	0	0	-	-	-	1	-

Eric Dolman, seen on the extreme right, with his mayor's chain, as Norman Riches formally opens the new pavilion at Sophia Gardens during 1967.

Eric Dolman was a prominent solicitor in Cardiff, besides being a Conservative City Councillor between 1949 and 1969. Eric also served as Lord Mayor of Cardiff during 1967 and was involved in various events as the cricket section of Cardiff Athletic Club, and Glamorgan CCC moved from the Arms Park to Sophia Gardens. In his youth he had also played rugby for Newport and Monmouthshire.

368
DOVEY, Raymond Russell
Born – Chislehurst, 18 July 1920
Died – Tunbridge Wells, 27 December 1974
Professional
LHB, OB
Ed – Eltham College
1st XI: 1944
Kent 1938-1954; Dorset 1955-1959; Commonwealth XI 1950/51
Club: Old Hill

Batting and Fielding Record:

	M	I	NO	RUNS	AV	100	50	CT	ST
Wartime	7	5	1	63	15.75	-	-	2	-

Bowling Record:

	Balls	M	R	W	AV	5wI	10wM
Wartime	?	?	?	9	-	-	-

Ray Dovey enjoyed a productive career for Kent with the bespectacled off-spinner taking 751 wickets in 249 first-class appearances for the English county. During the Second World War he initially served with the 30th Balloon Barrage in London before being stationed in South Wales. This move led to his seven appearances for Glamorgan during 1944. After the War, he toured India and Ceylon with the Commonwealth XI during 1950/51 and after retiring from county cricket with Kent, he appeared in the Minor County Championship for Dorset.

Ray Dovey.

369
PARRY, Raymond Howard

Born – Pontypridd, 13 June 1920
Died – Ascot, 1 October 2005
Amateur
RHB
Ed – Quakers Yard Grammar School and Jesus College, Oxford
1st XI: 1944
Oxford University Authentics 1944-1945; Devon 1950
Club: Pontypridd

Batting and Fielding Record:

	M	I	NO	RUNS	AV	100	50	CT	ST
Wartime	1	1	0	4	4.00	-	-	-	-

Raymond Parry read French and History at Oxford and, during his university vacation in June 1944, he played for Glamorgan against the Western Command at his home ground at Ynysangharad Park in Pontypridd.

370
VALENTINE, John James

Born – Chorlton, 24 May 1917
Died – Manchester, 1 September 1998
Amateur
LHB, SLA
1st XI: 1944
Anti-Aircraft Command 1944
Clubs: Cardiff, Newport

Batting and Fielding Record:

	M	I	NO	RUNS	AV	100	50	CT	ST
Wartime	1	1	1	14	-	-	-	-	-

A stalwart of club cricket in South Wales, the spinner was a late replacement in the Anti-Aircraft side which met Glamorgan at Rodney Parade, Newport for a one-day friendly during August 1944.

371
ORME, Samuel Edward ('Ted')
Born – Derby, 27 April 1917
Died – Derby, 9 November 1975
Amateur
RHB, LBG
1st XI: 1944
Derbyshire 2nd XI 1939; Derbyshire Club and Ground 1939
Clubs: Newport, Ebbw Vale, Derby LMS, Ilkeston, Duffield, Allestree

Batting and Fielding Record:

	M	I	NO	RUNS	AV	100	50	CT	ST
Wartime	1	1	1	59	-	-	1	-	-

Ted Orme was a talented young sportsman in Derbyshire during the late 1930s, playing 2nd XI cricket for his native county, besides being Derbyshire table tennis champion in both 1937 and 1938. Whilst on National Service in South Wales, Ted was chosen to play for Glamorgan against Sir Learie Constantine's XI at Barry Island during July 1944. He opened the batting with Willie Jones and carried his bat for an unbeaten 59 as his team beat the visitors from the Caribbean by five wickets.

372
THOMAS, D. Bryn
Amateur
1st XI: 1944
Club and Ground: 1949
Clubs: Llanelli, Grovesend Works, Neath
Hockey for Wales

Batting and Fielding Record:

	M	I	NO	RUNS	AV	100	50	CT	ST
Wartime	1	-	-	-	-	-	-	-	-

373
LYON, Beverley Hamilton
Born – Caterham 19 January 1902
Died – Balcombe, Sussex 22 June 1970
Amateur
RHB
Ed – Rugby School and Queen's College, Oxford
1st XI: 1944
Wiltshire 1920; Gloucestershire 1921-1947; Oxford University 1922-1923; Europeans 1924/25-1945/46; Sir Julian Cahn's XI 1936/37; West of England 1944-1945
Club: Pontypridd

	M	I	NO	RUNS	AV	100	50	CT	ST
Wartime	1	1	0	0	-	-	-	-	-

Bev Lyon had an outstanding career with Gloucestershire, leading the West Country side between 1929 and 1934, besides being one of *Wisden's* Cricketers of the Year in 1931. The Oxford graduate also toured Ceylon with Sir Julian Cahn's XI, in addition to playing in domestic cricket in India. Whilst on National Service in South Wales, Bev played club cricket for Pontypridd, where the town's Brown Lenox Steelworks was producing steel for the military, besides appearing for Glamorgan against The Army at Newport. He made a duck in his sole game for the Welsh county but, in all first-class cricket, Bev scored 10, 694 runs besides posting sixteen centuries.

Bev Lyon.

374
WILLIAMS, Dr Charles Derek
Born – Cardiff, 24 November 1924
Died – Cardiff, 19 September 2014
Amateur
RHB, RM
Ed – Canton High School, Cardiff; Cardiff Technical College and Merton College, Oxford
1st XI: 1944-1945
2nd XI: 1946-1953. Colts: 1945
Oxford University 1944-1946; Anti-Aircraft Command 1944, Berkshire 1949-1950
Clubs: St Fagans, Cardiff, Glamorgan Nomads
Rugby for Wales (2 caps), Oxford University, Penarth, Cardiff, Neath, London Welsh, Berkshire and The Barbarians

Batting and Fielding Record:

	M	I	NO	RUNS	AV	100	50	CT	ST
Wartime	6	7	1	74	12.33	-	-	-	-

'CD' Williams won two Welsh rugby caps, each against France during the 1950s. Having made his debut at Colombes in 1955, the back row forward played again on his home turf at the Arms Park in 1956 and late in the game scored the try which clinched the Five Nations title for Wales.

Whilst reading Chemistry at Oxford, Derek also won a boxing Blue and during 1948 he was one of the young athletes who ran into Wembley Stadium carrying the ceremonial torches for lighting the flames at the London Olympics.

Derek Williams.

The Glamorgan authorities had hoped that Derek would turn out for the county after graduating from Oxford, but he opted instead in taking a doctorate before pursuing a career as a chemical engineer. He continued to play rugby for Cardiff, whom he later captained and, later in life, was a member of Radyr Golf Club, besides serving as President of Cardiff Athletic Club.

375
PETERS, Harold George
Born – Swansea, 29th October 1918
Died – Swansea, 3rd March 1999
Amateur
RHB
1st XI: 1944-1945
Clubs: Swansea, Elba

Batting and Fielding Record:

	M	I	NO	RUNS	AV	100	50	CT	ST
Wartime	4	3	0	73	24.33	-	1	1	-

Harry Peters enjoyed a fine career as a batsman in club cricket in the Swansea area and was a member of the Swansea Central League team which defeated a Glamorgan Club and Ground side at St Helen's in July 1945. Opening the batting, he made 7 being dismissed for 7 by Closs Jones. His side ended up on 31 before dismissing the county's scratch side, led by Cyril Smart, for just 25 to win an extraordinary game by six runs.

He was a wagon repairer by trade and was employed at the Great Western Railway's depot at Landore to the east of his native town.

376
MORRIS, Robert John
Born – Penllergaer, 27 November 1926
Died – Harrow 29 December 2007
RHB, OB
Amateur
Ed – Blundell's School and St Catharine's, Cambridge.
1st XI: 1944
Cambridge University 1949-1951 (no Blue), Kent 1950
Clubs: Cambridge University Crusaders, Band of Brothers

Batting and Fielding Record:

	M	I	NO	RUNS	AV	100	50	CT	ST
Wartime	1	1	0	24	24.00	-	-	-	-

The son of Vernon Morris (Vol. 1, p.337-338), Robert was educated at Blundell's School and whilst at the famous public school in Tiverton, he won a place in the Public Schools XI which played at Lord's in August 1944. A few weeks later, the schoolboy made his Glamorgan debut against the Anti-Aircraft Command at Newport.

He enjoyed further success the following year for the Devon school, besides appearing again for the Public Schools at Lord's, before going up to Cambridge. His father had been a company director in Orpington since before the War so whilst an undergraduate, the talented batsman also played in second eleven cricket for Kent, before making two Championship appearances in August 1950. Both were against Derbyshire in consecutive games at Derby and Dover.

377
DAWES, James _Desmond_ Kneipp
Born – Ryton-on-Tyne, Durham, 28 December 1923
Died – Newcastle-on-Tyne, Northumberland, 13 October 1994
Amateur
Ed – St Cuthbert's Grammar School, Newcastle; King's College (Newcastle), Durham University
1st XI: 1944
Durham University 1943-1944

Batting and Fielding Record:

	M	I	NO	RUNS	AV	100	50	CT	ST
Wartime	1	-	-	-	-	-	-	-	-

Desmond Dawes was chosen in the Glamorgan side which played the Anti-Aircraft Command at Newport in 1944. At the time, he was starting his post-graduate medical studies whilst based briefly in South Wales but he did not bat or bowl in the game. Desmond subsequently became a doctor and a consultant ear, nose and throat specialist in the north-east of England.

378
YOUNG, John Albert
Born – Paddington, 14 October 1912
Died – St John's Wood, 5 February 1993
Professional
RHB, SLA
1st XI: 1944-1945
Middlesex 1933-1956; Leicestershire 2nd XI 1939; London Counties 1941-1945;
England 1947-1949 (8 Tests); MCC to South Africa 1948/49
Clubs: XL Club, Lord's Taverners

Batting and Fielding Record:

	M	I	NO	RUNS	AV	100	50	CT	ST
Wartime	4	3	0	25	8.33	-	-	-	-

	Balls	M	R	W	AV	5wI	10wM
Wartime	?	?	?	21	-	-	-

Jack Young.

Jack Young played for Glamorgan in four matches during 1944 and 1945 whilst on National Service in South Wales.

The spinner had first played for Middlesex in 1933, but had not secured a regular place in the team and had trialled with Leicestershire in 1939. When Glamorgan subsequently offered him terms on his demobilization in 1946, Jack accepted the offer, but the Middlesex hierarchy were unaware of his decision and did not like the loss of his services. They successfully managed Jack to change his mind, much to the angst of the Glamorgan officials, with the tensions between the North London side and the Welsh county being eased by the subsequent move to Glamorgan by Len Muncer, Pete Hever and Jimmy Eaglestone who were all colleagues of the spinner at Lord's.

Glamorgan's disappointment rose to the surface again when Jack duly won the first of eight Test caps as he made his England debut at Headingley against the 1947 Springboks. By the time Jack retired at the end of the 1956 season, he had taken 1361 first-class wickets at just 19 runs apiece.

379
LLEWELLYN, Ira William Thomas

Born – Briton Ferry, 19 November 1927
Died – Neath, 17 May 2019
Amateur
LHB, RM / OB
Ed- Cwrt Sart School, Neath
1st XI: 1944
2nd XI: 1948-1950
Southern Command 1946-1948
Clubs: Briton Ferry Town, Briton Ferry Steel, SCOW Margam, Thorneycroft's

Batting and Fielding Record:

	M	I	NO	RUNS	AV	100	50	CT	ST
Wartime	1	1	1	0	-	-	-	-	-

Bowling Record:

	Balls	M	R	W	AV	5wI	10wM
Wartime	?	?	?	1	-	-	-

A stalwart of the South Wales and Monmouthshire League, Ira Llewellyn had played for Glamorgan whilst still only sixteen against the West of England on his home ground at Ynysmaerdy in Briton Ferry. At the time, he was a seam bowler and claimed the wicket of Closs Jones. He later switched to off-spin and enjoyed a highly successful career in club cricket.

Ira Llewellyn.

380
BRADFORD, Colin H

Born – 1917
Amateur
Ed – Dover College
1st XI: 1944

Batting and Fielding Record:

	M	I	NO	RUNS	AV	100	50	CT	ST
Wartime	1	-	-	-	-	-	-	1	-

On completing his education, Colin Bradford worked for the Ministry of Agriculture and Fisheries in Battersea and spent time overseas visiting various farms and plantations. He spent part of his National Service in South Wales and was chosen to play for Glamorgan in their side against the West of England at Briton Ferry in 1944. He did not bat or bowl in the game but caught Bill Andrews off the bowling of Dennis Shea.

After the Second World War, he became a farmer in the East Midlands and appeared for Coalville and District in 1949 as well as the Derby and District Cricket Association in 1950.

381
DAVIES, Douglas

Amateur
RHB, WK
1st XI: 1944
Club: Dafen

Batting and Fielding Record:

	M	I	NO	RUNS	AV	100	50	CT	ST
Wartime	1	-	-	-	-	-	-	-	-

382

CROSSKEY, Thomas Roland ('Tom')

Born – Hastings, 4 July 1905
Died – Totnes, 25 March 1971
Professional
RHB, RFM
1st XI: 1944-1945
RAF 1943-1944; Scotland 1949-1950; Northumberland 1957
Football for Crystal Palace, Hearts, Albion Rovers, Cowdenbeath, Raith Rovers,
Morton and Montrose
Clubs: Carlton, Barry, Stirling, Edinburgh, Blyth, Ashington, Morpeth

Batting and Fielding Record:

	M	I	NO	RUNS	AV	100	50	CT	ST
Wartime	7	8	1	215	26.89	1	1	1	-

Bowling Record:

	Balls	M	R	W	AV	5wI	10wM
Wartime	?	?	?	5	-	-	-

Tom Crosskey was a fine all-round sportsman who mixed playing as a professional in both football and cricket. Besides playing for Glamorgan in their wartime friendlies, he also appeared in Don Bradman's final match on British soil as he represented Scotland against the 1948 Australians at Mannofield in Aberdeen.

Tom Crosskey, seen in his goalkeeper's jersey.

Born in Sussex, Tom's first professional appointment was as reserve goal-keeper at Crystal Palace FC, before moving to a similar position at Jack Harkness' understudy at Heart of Midlothian FC between 1928 and 1933. During this time, Tom also played cricket as a professional with Carlton in Edinburgh and met with success with both bat and ball.

During the Second World War, he served with the RAF and whilst based at the St Athan airbase he played seven times for Glamorgan during their wartime friendlies. Tom impressed with the bat and scored a fine 120 for Glamorgan against Western Command at Briton Ferry in 1945, besides playing some decent innings for Barry. Glamorgan sounded him out for a

A photograph of Tom Crosskey taken at Aberdeen in September 1948 when he played for Scotland against the Australians.

professional contract in 1946 but Tom had already secured a lucrative contract with a football club in the Scottish League and duly returned north of the border.

In 1948 Tom played for his adopted country in two one-day games against the Australians at the end of their tour. Tom scored 5 and 36 in the opening contest at Raeburn Place in Edinburgh before making 49 and 14 in the match at Aberdeen two days later. He subsequently appeared in four first-class matches for Scotland, against Yorkshire, Warwickshire, Sussex and the 1949 New Zealanders. He also played for clubs in the north-east of England, ending his career at Morpeth and representing Northumberland in 1957.

1945

With the war drawing to a close, the Emergency Committee of Glamorgan CCC were able to arrange a series of nine games during the summer months, including a couple of two-day encounters against the Royal Australian Air Force at the Arms Park as well as The Army at St Helen's.

All of these contests during 1945 took place on Welsh soil with matches also being staged at Newport, Briton Ferry, Barry and Pontypridd. The Glamorgan officials also arranged another Past v Present game, this time at the Barracks Ground in Maindy, Cardiff but hopes that the up-and-coming talent might prevail were dashed as the Past won a keenly contested game by seven runs.

The opponents during 1945 once again included the London Counties, the West of England and the West Indian eleven raised by Learie Constantine, as well as the various Service elevens which for 1945 included a game in late July at St Helen's against the New Zealand Services.

With matters still improving, it was pleasing for the long-standing supporters of Glamorgan Cricket to see Arnold Dyson and Emrys Davies turn out in some of these matches, but the match against the West of England at the Arms Park in mid-August in aid of the Maurice Turnbull Testimonial Fund reminded all concerned about the huge loss the Welsh county faced as they started to prepare for a return to normal during 1946.

WELSH
SPORTS LTD.

THE

SPORTS
AND ATHLETIC
OUTFITTERS

CASTLE ARCADE
CARDIFF

Telephone: Cardiff 1708

Score Card   Price 3d

In aid of
MAURICE TURNBULL MEMORIAL FUND

WEST OF ENGLAND XI
v.
GLAMORGAN

CARDIFF ARMS PARK

Saturday, 18th August, 1945
Commencing 11.30 a.m.

Western Mail & Echo Ltd., Cardiff.—6805N.

383
EVANS, William John ('Jack')
Born – Cardiff, 12 December 1907
Died – Rookwood Hospital, Cardiff, March 1982
Amateur
Ed – Cardiff High School
1st XI: 1945
2nd XI: 1935-1937
Club and Ground: 1924-1936
Colts: 1923-1926
Clubs: Cardiff, Briton Ferry, Welsh Cygnets

Batting and Fielding Record:

	M	I	NO	RUNS	AV	100	50	CT	ST
Wartime	1	2	0	15	7.50	-	-	-	-

A master builder by trade, Jack Evans appeared in the wartime friendly against the Royal Australian Airforce at the Arms Park in 1945, over twenty years after his first-ever appearance for the county's Colts team as well as their Club and Ground side. During the 1930s he had also appeared for Glamorgan 2nd XI in their Minor County Championship matches and was captain of Cardiff during 1938, 1940 and 1946.

Jack was also a noted rugby referee and during 1958 he officiated in two international games – Ireland v Australia and France v England.

Jack Evans.

384
ARCHER, Alfred Jacob ('Jake')
Born – Newport, 11 May 1912
Died – Caerleon, March 1972
Amateur
1st XI: 1944
2nd XI: 1935-1937
Monmouthshire 1931-1934; Anti-Aircraft Command 1944; West of England 1944
Clubs: Abercarn, Newport, Cardiff

Batting and Fielding Record:

	M	I	NO	RUNS	AV	100	50	CT	ST
Wartime	1	2	0	3	1.50	-	-	-	-

Jake Archer worked at Abercarn tinplate works and this reserved occupation allowed him to appear for the Welsh county against the Royal Australian Air Force during May 1945 at the Arms Park having the previous year played against Glamorgan for two other service teams.

During the 1930s Jake had played Minor County cricket for both Monmouthshire and Glamorgan but his well-paid job in the Abercarn works dissuaded him from becoming a professional with the Welsh county.

385
WILKINS, William Haydn

Born – Neath, 25 December 1916
Died – Cardiff, 17 May 2003
Ed – Gnoll Primary School; Neath Intermediate School
Amateur
RHB, RM
1st XI; 1944
2nd XI: 1938-1953
Colts: 1937-1939
Club: Cardiff, Glamorgan Nomads, MCC, XL Club, Welsh Cygnets

Batting and Fielding Record:

	M	I	NO	RUNS	AV	100	50	CT	ST
Wartime	1	1	0	7	7.00	-	-	-	-

Bowling Record:

	Balls	M	R	W	AV	5wI	10wM
Wartime	?	?	?	1	-	-	-

Born and raised in Neath, Haydn played for Glamorgan in their wartime friendly against London Counties at the Rodney Parade ground in Newport. Before the War, he had played for both the county's Colts team and their 2nd XI, and had it not been for the War, Haydn may well have won a place in the 1st XI. Although his prime years were lost to the War, he was still good enough to play in the county's 2nd XI until 1953.

He subsequently became a stalwart figure Cardiff Athletic Club. He also played rugby for Cardiff and was chairman of the city club during the 1960s. Haydn also served on the Glamorgan committee during the 1970s and 1980s at a time when his son Alan followed in his footsteps by playing county cricket for Glamorgan.

Haydn Wilkins, seated second left in a Glamorgan 2nd XI team photo from the early 1950s. John Riches is seated in the middle with Bernard Hedges seated second right.

386
MILDON, John Colin
Born – St Fagans, December 1921
Died – Redhill, Surrey 2010
Amateur
WK
1st XI:1945
2nd XI: 1946
Clubs: Cardiff, St Fagans

Batting and Fielding Record:

	M	I	NO	RUNS	AV	100	50	CT	ST
Wartime	1	1	1	6	-	-	-	-	-

387
THOMAS, Kenneth William
Born – Neath 1 July 1925
Ed – Cwrt Sart Secondary School, Neath and Swansea Technical College
Amateur
RHB, RM
1st XI: 1945
Clubs: Briton Ferry Town, Briton Ferry Steel

Batting and Fielding Record:

	M	I	NO	RUNS	AV	100	50	CT	ST
Wartime	1	1	0	2	2.00	-	-	-	-

388
MEREDITH, Glyn
Born – Newbridge, 6 August 1922
Died – Newport, 1 July 2006
Amateur
All-rounder
1st XI: 1945
Clubs: Newbridge, Wakefield, Pontllanfraith
Rugby Union for Newbridge RFC, Abertillery RFC; Rugby League
for Wakefield Trinity

Batting and Fielding Record:

	M	I	NO	RUNS	AV	100	50	CT	ST
Wartime	1	1	0	0	-	-	-	-	-

Glyn Meredith, who played for Glamorgan against the Royal Air Force at the Arms Park in June 1945, was a talented all-round sportsman who won fame as a fly-half for both Newbridge and Abertillery. His audacious play attracted the attention of scouts from rugby

Glyn Meredith.

league teams in Lancashire and Yorkshire, and in 1950 he was one of several Newbridge players to head north, leaving a position as a service worker in the local colliery to join Wakefield Trinity.

An ankle injury saw him retire three years later from rugby league and he returned to his native Newbridge. Despite the injury, he continued to play cricket for the town and the seam bowler claimed all ten wickets in an innings in a game during 1954.

389
FRY, Melvyn Hugh

Born – Newbridge, 22 August 1904
Died – Worthing, 1 May 1989
Amateur
WK
1st XI: 1945
Clubs: Newbridge, Elba

Batting and Fielding Record:

	M	I	NO	RUNS	AV	100	50	CT	ST
Wartime	1	1	0	11	11.00	-	-	-	-

390
ROBINS, Geoffrey George

Born – Pontarddulais, 26 November 1918
Died – Pontarddulais, 12 October 1987
Amateur
RHB, RM
1st XI: 1945
Clubs: Pontarddulais

Batting and Fielding Record:

	M	I	NO	RUNS	AV	100	50	CT	ST
Wartime	1	1	0	20	20.00	-	-	-	-

Geoff Robins had a fine career as an all-rounder in club cricket for his native Pontarddulais either side of the Great War. Remarkably, his one appearance for Glamorgan, against Sir Learie Constantine's XI at Barry Island during July 1945, came only a week after he had returned to British shores having been a Prisoner of War in Germany for the previous four years.

ROBINSON, Albert George ('Bert')

Born – Leicester, 22 March 1917
Died – Abingdon, 31 July 2009
Professional
RHB, RFM
Ed – Wyggeston Grammar School, Leicester
1st XI: 1945
Northamptonshire 1937-1946; Cambridgeshire 1948-1949; Berkshire 1951-1955
Clubs: Northampton, Wisbech Town

Batting and Fielding Record:

	M	I	NO	RUNS	AV	100	50	CT	ST
Wartime	1	1	0	0	-	-	-	-	-

Bowling Record:

	Balls	M	R	W	AV	5wI	10wM
Wartime	?	?	?	3	-	-	-

Bert Robinson is perhaps best known in the cricket world for having been cricket professional and coach at Radley College in Berkshire from 1949 until 2006. During his time at the famous Berkshire school he coached the likes of Ted Dexter, Andrew Strauss and Jamie Dalrymple during their formative years.

In 1945 he played for Glamorgan against Sir Learie Constantine's XI at Barry Island with his selection stemming from the fact that the brisk seamer who had played for Northamptonshire since 1937 was serving with the Royal Air France and stationed at the St Athan airbase. He made his 24th and final appearance in first-class cricket for the East Midlands county during 1946, before appearing in Minor County cricket for Cambridgeshire and Berkshire, as well as starting his lengthy career at Radley College.

RIPPON, Thomas John ('Jack')

Born – Swansea, 6 July 1918
Died – Sketty, Swansea, 29 December 1994
Ed – Brynmill School, Swansea
Amateur 1945
Professional 1946-1950
RHB, WK
1st XI: 1945-1948
2nd XI: 1947-1950
Colts: 1937
Club: Swansea

	M	I	NO	RUNS	AV	100	50	CT	ST
F-c	3	4	2	45	22.50	-	-	-	2
Wartime	1	1	0	4	4.00	-	-	-	-

Career-best:

First-class –   30 v Northamptonshire at Kettering, 1947

Jack Rippon was Haydn Davies' understudy as a wicket-keeper in the immediate post-war years and appeared twice in 1947 besides being behind the timbers in the friendly match against Somerset at the start of the Club's Championship-winning summer of 1948.

He was, quite literally a Swansea Jack, being the son of Thomas Rippon, a coal foreman at the town's docks, whilst he was educated at Brynmill School, close to the St Helen's ground where he played and kept score for over fifty years.

Jack shone as a young sportsman and aged fifteen he made his debut as wicket-keeper for Swansea's 1st XI during 1933. His prowess won him selection for the Glamorgan Colts during 1937, but like so many of his generation, his career was interrupted by the Second World War. For Jack, his war experiences were brief as the military fireman was taken prisoner in 1940 at Dunkirk and, for the rest of the War, he was in captivity in German Prisoner of War camps in France and Belgium.

After being released in the spring of 1945, Jack returned to South Wales and was fit enough to appear in July in Glamorgan's fund-raising match against the New Zealand Services at St Helen's, besides representing the Swansea Central League in their charity games. He joined the county's staff the following year as Haydn Davies' understudy, and during 1947 Jack, quite appropriately, made his first-class debut on his home turf at Swansea in the Welsh county's Championship match against Warwickshire. With Haydn on the sidelines, Jack appeared again in the away match with Northamptonshire at Kettering.

With Haydn returning to fitness and often playing through minor niggles, Jack's appearance against Somerset during May 1948 at Newport proved to be his last in the Welsh county's 1st XI, with Jack never claiming a catch, but completing a

Jack Rippon, seen in 1947 practising on the outfield at St Helen's ahead of Glamorgan's Championship match against Warwickshire.

trio of smart stumpings on his county appearances. The fireman continued to keep wicket for Glamorgan's 2nd XI until 1950, and was a regular in Swansea's side until 1958. He maintained his involvement with the club by acting as their scorer until the 1980s.

His loyalty to Swansea cricket is commemorated through the annual presentation of the Jack Rippon 1st XI Player of the Year Award. Through his mother Martha, Jack was also a cousin of Sir Harry Secombe who himself was a keen cricketer and a good friend of Don Shepherd, who chose Harry to play in his Glamorgan team in a Benefit Match during 1960 against a North Wales XI at Colwyn Bay.

ANDERSON, *Reginald Mervyn Bulford*

Born – Brynhyfryd, Swansea, 25 April, 1914
Died – Uplands, Swansea, 12 August, 1972
RHB, RFM
Amateur
Ed – Manselton Central School, Swansea
1st XI: 1945-1946
2nd XI: 1936
Clubs: Swansea, Llanelli, Morewoods

Batting and Fielding Record:

	M	I	NO	RUNS	AV	100	50	CT	ST
F-c	1	1	0	0	-	-	-	-	-
Wartime	4	3	1	1	0.33	-	-	-	-

Bowling Record:

	Balls	M	R	W	AV	5wI	10wM
F-c	108	4	60	0	-	-	-
Wartime	?	?	?	11	-	-	-

Reg Anderson was one of the fastest bowlers in the South Wales Leagues either side of the Second World War. He first played for Glamorgan 2nd XI in their Minor County matches in 1936, but his duties as a policeman in Swansea prevented him from appearing for the county on a regular basis. He did however play for Glamorgan in their wartime friendlies in 1945.

In 1945 he also showed his capabilities as a bowler by taking six wickets in the one-day friendly between the Swansea Central League and the Glamorgan Club and Ground side. His fine bowling dismissed the county side for just 25 as the League side recorded a famous victory. The following year, Anderson made his one and only first-class appearance, against Hampshire at Swansea. However, he failed to take a wicket or score a run in

Reg Anderson, as seen during 1937.

his only innings, and despite a good record in club cricket, besides appearing for the South Wales and Monmouthshire League, he was not called up again by Glamorgan.

394
BYFIELD, Clifford William
Born – Pontypridd, 24 January 1922
Died – Gravesend , 1 July 1984
Amateur
1st XI: 1945
Club – Pontypridd

Batting and Fielding Record:

	M	I	NO	RUNS	AV	100	50	CT	ST
Wartime	1	1	0	0	-	-	-	-	-

Cliff Byfield was a clerk at a colliery in Pontypridd and during July 1945 he played on his home turf at Ynysangharad Park for Glamorgan in their one-day friendly against the National Fire Service. He was dismissed without scoring in what proved to be his sole innings for the Welsh county.

395
HARRIS, Wilfred Edgar
Born – Swansea, 30 September 1913
Died – Swansea, October 1973
Amateur
1st XI: 1945
Club: Swansea
Rugby for Swansea

Batting and Fielding Record:

	M	I	NO	RUNS	AV	100	50	CT	ST
Wartime	1	1	0	8	8.00	-	-	-	-

Wilf Harris was a talented all-round sportsman playing rugby and cricket for Swansea either side of the Second World War, besides appearing for Glamorgan during August 1945 in their fund-raising friendly against the West of England at Cardiff Arms Park.

In September 1935 he had won fame in the rugby world by being a member of the All Whites team which defeated the All Blacks at St Helen's. Wilf converted a try in the famous victory by the Swansea rugby team. He was their captain in the 1938/39 season, and worked as a detective constable with Swansea Police.

Wilf Harris.

1946

As Glamorgan's players regrouped during the spring of 1946 it was re-assuring that Johnnie Clay should agree to oversee the arrangements for the first summer of county cricket for six long years. It was though a far from straight-forward task which faced the veteran from the Welsh county's inaugural summer of Championship action.

Bereft of Maurice Turnbull and his dynamic captaincy, Johnnie and his assistants spent plenty of time getting in touch with their professionals, some of whom were still abroad, to find out about their availability besides getting in touch with the amateurs whose National Service had ended or would soon be finishing uncertainty about the availability. There were also a few headaches about the venues which the Welsh county could use, to say nothing of bomb damage at the Arms Park and a small reserve of cash.

Given these handicaps and sundry distractions it was nothing short of a miracle that the Welsh county should enjoy one of their best-ever seasons in first-class cricket, rising up to 6th place in the Championship table, besides winning 10 of their 26 games. This included a previously unprecedented run of four consecutive Championship victories during July with the winning run starting away at Leicester before Worcestershire were defeated at Dudley prior to Gloucestershire being beaten at the Arms Park by eight wickets and then a seven-wicket win over Hampshire at Swansea.

Johnnie's shrewd captaincy was a vital element behind Glamorgan's success with the veteran cleverly handling his bowling resources and making subtle changes to the field. He was not afraid either to throw down some interesting challenges, as at Pontypridd during the rain-affected game against Somerset when, after agreeing to declare early, he saw Austin Matthews claim 7/12 as the visitors were dismissed for 53 before Glamorgan eased to an eight-wicket victory.

A scorecard from 1946 with the logo the Club used in the immediate post-war years.

GLAMORGAN COUNTY CRICKET CLUB
SCORE CARD

FIXTURES 1946
(Three Days Each)

Date		Opponents				Venue
Saturday,	May 11th	YORKSHIRE				Cardiff
Saturday,	May 18th	Lancashire				Manchester
Wednesday,	May 22nd	Gloucestershire				Bristol
Saturday,	May 25th	NORTHAMPTONSHIRE				Swansea
Wednesday,	May 29th	SUSSEX				Newport
Saturday,	June 1st	Sussex				Horsham
Saturday,	June 8th	INDIA				Cardiff
Wednesday,	June 12th	Essex				Chelmsford
Saturday,	June 15th	SOMERSETSHIRE				Pontypridd
Wednesday,	June 19th	MIDDLESEX				Swansea
Saturday,	June 22nd	WORCESTERSHIRE				Ebbw Vale
Wednesday,	June 26th					

396
ROBINSON, Maurice

Born – Lisburn, County Antrim, 16 July 1921
Died – Birmingham, 8 August, 1994
Professional,1946-1949
Amateur 1950
RHB, LM
1st XI: 1946-1950
Club and Ground: 1949-1950
Cap: 1946
Bombay Europeans 1943/1944; Hyderabad 1943/44; Europeans 1942/43 -1944/45;
Madras 1944/45; Combined Services 1946; Warwickshire 1951-52
Club: Moseley

Batting and Fielding Record:

	M	I	NO	RUNS	AV	100	50	CT	ST
F-c	66	106	7	2139	21.60	2	6	17	-

Bowling Record:

	Balls	M	R	W	AV	5wI	10wM
F-c	768	18	432	13	33.23	-	-

Career-bests:
First-class –   190 v Hampshire at Dean Park, Bournemouth, 1948
            3/17 v Sussex at The Saffrons, Eastbourne, 1949

Maurice Robinson played for Glamorgan for five seasons after the Second World War, during which he featured in a stand of 264 for the fifth wicket with Stan Montgomery against Hampshire at Bournemouth in 1949 – a partnership which still stands as a Club record – before playing briefly for Warwickshire, running a highly successful sports shop in King's Heath with his wife Cicely and becoming an international badminton coach with Germany and Holland.

A photograph of Maurice Robinson taken during 1946.

Born in County Antrim, the short and squat all-rounder showed sufficient promise to accept an offer in the late 1930s to join Warwickshire's junior groundstaff. This followed some promising performances in services cricket in the UK as well as in Egypt where he had served with the Army. Bowling at a steady medium-pace and with a sound batting technique, he showed promise as a top-order batsman for Warwickshire's 2nd XI during 1938 and 1939.

The outbreak of the Second World War saw Maurice join the RAF with Sergeant-Major Robinson initially training troops in Weston-super-Mare before in 1941 being posted to an airbase in Hyderabad in India. While stationed in Hyderabad, Maurice was summoned by the Nizam of Hyderabad to coach his daughters in badminton, besides making his first-class debut for the Europeans against the Indians at Madras in 1942/43. He played in a further seven first-class matches in India before being posted to RAF St Athan in South Wales.

The presence of the enthusiastic Irishman, with first-class experience, at the airbase in the Vale of Glamorgan soon came to the attention of the Welsh county's selectors and after an approach from them he duly agreed terms for 1946, making his first-class debut that summer against the touring Indians at the Arms Park. In all, Maurice appeared in fourteen matches for Glamorgan during 1946, plus a further eighteen in 1947, before being struck down with injury and missing all of 1948. He was restored to full fitness in 1949 and became a regular in the county's middle-order with the highlight of his efforts being a career-best 190 during a stand of 264 for the fifth wicket with Stan Montgomery with the Irishman watchfully batting for five and a quarter hours.

Maurice Robinson returns to the changing rooms after being dismissed during a match at the Arms Park during 1949.

The following summer, Maurice – playing now as an amateur – was affected by injury and only appeared in eight matches for Glamorgan before returning to the West Midlands where he and his wife had a sports shop. He had met Cicely before the Second World War whilst he was staying fit playing badminton at St Ambrose Church Hall. She was a very good badminton player, representing England in 1953 and, after getting married, the couple ran a successful sports shop in Kings Heath from November 1948.

After leaving Glamorgan at the end of the 1950 season, Maurice played in eight matches for Warwickshire during 1951 and 1952, but was past his best as a cricketer. He subsequently focused on badminton, travelling the world to train some of the games top players. Maurice also became the national coach for Holland with whom he went to the 1972 Munich Olympics and witnessed the horrors associated with the kidnapping by a Palestinian terrorist group of eleven members of the Israeli team, all of whom were eventually murdered along with a West German policeman. Maurice later coached badminton in Germany besides serving as President of the British Universities' Badminton Association, with his family's sports shop still surviving today and being run by his daughter.

397

JONES, Watkin Edward ('Wat')

Born – Gwauncaegurwen, 6 July 1917
Died – Morriston, Swansea, 23 August 1994
Amateur
RHB, RFM
Ed – Gwauncaegurwen School
1st XI: 1946-1947
2nd XI: 1949
Club and Ground: 1947
Clubs: Pontardawe, Pontarddulais, Clydach, British Police

Batting and Fielding Record:

	M	I	NO	RUNS	AV	100	50	CT	ST
F-c	5	1	0	0	-	-	-	1	-

Bowling Record:

	Balls	M	R	W	AV	5wI	10wM
F-c	564	9	342	13	26.30	1	-

Career-bests:
First-class – 7/92 v Kent at Rodney Parade, Newport, 1947

Wat Jones was a policeman in the Swansea Valleys, who had a fine reputation as a fast bowler in club cricket for Pontardawe, Pontarddulais and Clydach. He might have appeared for Glamorgan before the Second World War, but opted to pursue his training with the police rather than play for the Welsh county.

After the War, he got his opportunity to play for the Welsh county, making his first-class debut against Lancashire at the Arms Park in 1946. In all, he claimed six wickets in his debut season before taking 7/92 against Kent at Newport in 1947. However, his duties as a policeman prevented him from playing more often and his final games for Glamorgan were in their Minor County matches against Lancashire and Gloucestershire during 1949.

Wat Jones.

398
JOSEPH, Arthur Frederick

Born – Neath Abbey, 13 March 1919
Died – Briton Ferry, 2 January 2002
Amateur
RHB, LBG
1st XI: 1946
2nd XI: 1946-1951
Clubs: Briton Ferry Town, Briton Ferry Steel, Neath

Batting and Fielding Record:

	M	I	NO	RUNS	AV	100	50	CT	ST
F-c	1	2	0	8	4.00	-	-	1	-

Career-best:
First-class –   8 v Derbyshire at Queen's Park, Chesterfield, 1946

Arthur Joseph was a leading club cricketer in South Wales after the Second World War, who made one appearance for Glamorgan in 1946. Like many others of his generation, his playing career was interrupted by the War and, under different circumstance, the right-handed batsman and leg-spin bowler would certainly have made more than just one appearance for Glamorgan.

As a teenager, Arthur played many fine innings, for Briton Ferry Town and Briton Ferry Steel, but when he was twenty, War was declared, and for the next few years, Arthur saw active service with the Army in the Middle East. Whilst serving in Palestine, he played for the Army alongside Norman Yardley, the former England captain who was impressed by his spin bowling.

After the War, Arthur played several times for Glamorgan's 2nd XI in their Minor County fixtures, and in 1946 he was included in the county side for their Championship fixture against Derbyshire at Chesterfield. He made 8 and 0, did not take a wicket and was never called up again by the Glamorgan selectors.

Arthur Joseph.

He remained a leading figure in the South Wales Cricket Association, playing for Neath, and subsequently Briton Ferry Town whom he also captained for several summers. After retiring, from playing, Arthur remained in the game by umpiring in league cricket.

399
GRIFFITHS, William <u>Hugh</u>

Born – Marylebone, 26 September 1923
Died – Ockham, Surrey, 30 May 2015
Amateur
RHB, RFM
Ed – Charterhouse School and St John's College, Cambridge
1st XI: 1946-1948
Club and Ground: 1945-1947
Cambridge University 1946-1948 (Blue all three years); Free Foresters 1949.

Batting and Fielding Record:

	M	I	NO	RUNS	AV	100	50	CT	ST
F-c	8	11	2	34	3.77	-	-	-	-

Bowling Record:

	Balls	M	R	W	AV	5wI	10wM
F-c	1047	30	538	17	31.64	-	-

Career-bests:
First-class –   12 v Gloucestershire at Cheltenham, 1947
                  4/61 v Surrey at Cardiff Arms Park, 1947

The Right Honourable Lord Justice Griffiths had a brief career as a bowler of fast out-swingers with Glamorgan after the Second World War, including playing in their Championship-winning summer of 1948, before enjoying a most distinguished career in the judiciary, which saw him become a Life Peer and a Law Lord. Despite these duties, he retained his passion for cricket, and in 1991/92, he served as President of the MCC, thereby becoming the first Glamorgan player to achieve this honour with the most famous cricket club in the world.

Educated at Charterhouse, he was in the school's XI in 1940 and 1941, before joining the Welsh Guards as an eighteen year-old. In 1944, whilst serving as a Lieutenant in the 2nd Armoured Reconnaissance Battalion, he was awarded the Military Cross for bravery, having disabled a series of German tanks during the Guards advance from Brussels and their battle for the town of Hechtel. On the afternoon of September 8, a report was received that four Panzer tanks were approaching Allied positions – Hugh immediately volunteered to investigate and set off unaccompanied.

He soon came under fire, but made his way to a wood overlooking the road along which the tanks were advancing.

Hugh Griffiths, seen during his playing days with Glamorgan.

359

As the first tank approached he fired three shots and destroyed the lead vehicle. The other three retreated, and during his time in the wood, Hugh was also able to destroy two other enemy vehicles which preparing to mount a counter-attack on Allied positions

After the War ended, Hugh went up to St John's, Cambridge to commence his legal studies. Whilst at Cambridge, he was a Double Blue in cricket and golf. Between 1946 and 1948, he opened the bowling for Cambridge, recording career-best figures of 6/129 on his first-class debut against Lancashire at Fenner's in 1946. In his second game for the Light Blues he also clean bowled the Indian opening batsman Vijay Merchant, before later that summer making his County Championship debut against Kent at Dover, taking 4/61 in what proved to be his best performance for the Daffodil county.

His appearance against Kent – as the son of a Welsh surgeon from Monmouthshire – stemmed from his excellent performances for Cambridge University as well as the unavailability of Peter Judge for selection in the Glamorgan side. Years later Lord Griffiths quipped that his career with the Welsh county began because of a Judge, and ended a few years later when he started his career to become one!

With his on-going success with the new ball at Fenner's, he made further appearances for Glamorgan during his summer vacations in 1947, including the games against Surrey at the Arms Park, against Gloucestershire at Cheltenham and Nottinghamshire at Trent Bridge. The match at Cardiff duly proved to be his sole appearance at home for Glamorgan as, in 1948, he played in the matches at Northampton, Edgbaston, Grace Road and Hull – in the case of the latter, when Wilf Wooller was also unavailable.

Despite not seeing his performance against Yorkshire at Hull, the man who led Glamorgan to their first-ever Championship time later that summer held Hugh in high regard. "Hugh was a very talented fast bowler and someone who could deliver some very slippery spells of away swing," said Wilf. "He once struck Denis Compton in the face and with the new ball, his pace worried

Baron Griffiths of Govilon – the MCC's esteemed President.

some of the best batsmen in the land. He was, though, a very bright and talented fellow in areas away from cricket and, had he not opted for a legal career, I would have been delighted to have his services in our seam bowling line-up."

Indeed, later in 1948 when Allan Watkins was called up by the England selectors during August, Hugh once again came into the reckoning for a further county call-up as Glamorgan looked to consolidate their position towards the top of the Championship table. But Wilf and the Glamorgan selectors opted instead for the vast experience and nous of off-spinner Johnnie Clay for the match against Surrey at The Oval. It proved to

be a wise choice as the veteran almost single-handedly demolished the Surrey line-up at the Arms Park, before seeing Glamorgan to their famous Championship-winning victory against Hampshire at Bournemouth. Had Wilf and his fellow selectors opted to give youth its chance, history might have been very different.

After coming down, Hugh pursued a highly successful legal career, culminating in his elevation to a High Court Judge. After being called to The Inner Temple in 1949, Hugh cut his teeth on personal injury claims, before chairing the enquiry into the collapse of the Ronan Point tower block in Canning Town in 1968. As the recorder of Margate from 1962 to 1964, and of Cambridge from 1964 to 1970, he was also eager to give defendants another chance rather than send them to prison. His Liberal views were also apparent in 1971 when, after becoming a Judge of the High Court, he granted bail, pending appeal when overturning a previous decision under the Obscene Publications Act to jail the three editors of a magazine which had contained a lewd and salacious cartoon of Rupert the Bear.

In 1980 he refused to lift an injunction obtained by the Moors murderess Myra Hindley on the *Sun* newspaper from publishing extracts of her plea to the Parole Board, saying that he could think of nothing more damaging to the parole system than for prisoners to fear that their confidential submissions would be leaked to the Media. He also gave judgement in the famous 'Spycatcher' case during the 1980s about the memoirs of former MI5 officer Peter Wright. He came down in firm favour of the public interest for freedom of speech and a free press, adding with a certain amount of wit that it might be better to let the memoirs be published as it "was such a boring book!"

In May 1985 he became Baron Griffiths of Govilon – his family's home area – and a Law Lord. After retirement in 1993 he continued his work as an arbitrator, especially in cases of medical negligence, as well as working on international and commercial disputes. He was renowned as a good-natured and reforming arbiter, who often took a robust and independent line away from fellow judges. Experts in the judiciary were delighted when, in 1990, he was appointed to chair the Advisory Committee on Legal Education and Conduct.

During his time as President of the MCC, Lord Griffiths supported the introduction of women members, but the motion failed to gain the necessary two-thirds majority for a rule change. However, Hugh did not press the case further as he was comfortable that the members had democratically decided for themselves. In 1993 he was appointed captain of the Royal and Ancient Golf Club, and thereby became the first man to preside over both Lord's and St Andrews.

400
TRICK, William Mervyn Stanley ('Stan')

Born – Briton Ferry, 31 October 1916
Died – Morriston, Swansea, 27 October 1995
Amateur
RHB, LM / SLA
Ed – Cwrt Sart School, Neath
1st XI: 1946-1950
2nd XI: 1936-1964
Clubs: Neath, Briton Ferry Steel, MCC, XL Club

Batting and Fielding Record:

	M	I	NO	RUNS	AV	100	50	CT	ST
F-c	19	22	11	52	4.72	-	-	9	-

Bowling Record:

	Balls	M	R	W	AV	5wI	10wM
F-c	3094	186	1087	56	19.41	4	2

Career-bests:
First-class –   15 v Leicestershire at St Helen's, Swansea, 1949
6/29 v Somerset at St Helen's, Swansea, 1948

Stan Trick was a prolific wicket taker for Neath and Briton Ferry Steel in the South Wales Cricket Association either side of the Second World War, and on his few appearances at first-class level between 1946 and 1950, he proved to be a match-winning spin bowler.

As a schoolboy, Trick showed great prowess as a cricketer, bowling left-arm medium pace as well as spin, besides being a talented footballer, During the early 1930's, he won international football honours for Welsh Schoolboys and even agreed terms with Brentwood FC. However, he never turned professional and opted to stay in the Neath area, where he could work at his family's motor garage, and play cricket in the South Wales leagues.

His prodigious wicket-taking feats for Neath and Briton Ferry Steel brought him to the attention of the county selectors, and he made his debut in their 2nd XI in Minor County games in 1936. Despite some impressive performances, his work commitments prevented him from playing on a full-time basis and it wasn't until 1946, and after National Service in the Far East, that he made his first-class debut.

An image from 1931 of Stan Trick as a Welsh schoolboy football international.

Despite only appearing infrequently, Stan proved to be wily bowler in Championship ...owling on damper and greener surfaces, he would mix up his left-arm spin with little swingers – both in and out – often keeping the batsmen guessing as to what he was going to bowl next!

Stan was particularly useful on the dry, turning pitches at Swansea. Indeed, it was at the St Helen's ground in 1948 where he produced both a career-best and match-winning performance against Somerset and, in each innings, he claimed six wickets with his clever spin and subtle flight. The summer of 1948 also saw Stan record another ten-wicket haul at Swansea as he took 6/39 and 4/32 in the 278-run demolition of Kent. Two years later, he also claimed 5/18 against Derbyshire on his home ground at The Gnoll as the Peakites were beaten by 92 runs.

Stan Trick, as seen during 1948.

Although he made his fifteenth and final appearance in Championship cricket at St Helen's, against Lancashire at Old Trafford in May 1950 Stan continued to play with great success for many years for both Neath and Glamorgan 2nd XI. Indeed, his final game for Glamorgan's second string came in 1964, whilst he continued to appear well into his seventies for Neath, the MCC and the XL club.

One of the factors behind Stan's longevity was his smooth and sublime action. Indeed, Tony Lewis, who played many times during his formative years with Stan for the Neath club, once wrote "what a superb action Stan had! It was rhythmical, even elegant, but with bite in the delivery and tricky flight."

Stan was the cousin of Stanley Arthur Trick who played, chiefly as a batsman, for Essex between 1905 and 1919. Stan's father was Albert Thomas Trick who ran a chemist's business in Neath, whilst his grandfather was William Burrow Trick, an auctioneer and butcher, who was a leading figure with Neath, as well as its offshoot the Gnoll Park club, during the early 1900s.

1947

1947 was the start of the greatest era in the Club's history, as Wilf Wooller succeeded Johnnie Clay as Glamorgan captain. In reality however, it was business as usual given the fact that, whilst other English grounds had grandiose facilities and pristine outdoor nets, Glamorgan's cricketers were still the paupers of the county game using makeshift nets along the corridors of the North Stand, before venturing outside to use the grass nets at the Arms Park.

Nevertheless, their new leader guided Glamorgan to victory in eight of their 26 Championship matches, with their playing record including innings victories over Essex at the Arms Park, Kent at Newport and Northamptonshire at Swansea. Wooller's team also gave the South Africans a run for their money in the annual tourist match. It was a game which was watched by a crowd estimated at over 50,000 – much to the delight of the county's Treasurer and saw the Springboks leave Glamorgan a target of 252 on the final afternoon. At 39-6 another embarrassing defeat looked imminent, but 25-year old Allan Watkins led a counter-attack with a typically doughty 75. He received useful support from Maurice Robinson, the diminutive all-rounder, plus George Lavis and Haydn Davies, with the Celtic revival forcing the tourists captain to recall his frontline seamers to snuff out their resistance.

Len Muncer, Glamorgan's new signing from Middlesex, also enjoyed a stellar season and ended the year as the Club's leading wicket-taker with 107 wickets. The man, regarded as a long-term replacement for Johnnie Clay made some match-winning contributions, including 9/79 in Surrey's second innings as they subsided to a four-wicket defeat. Johnnie also enjoyed a fine summer in 1947, claiming 65 wickets at a cost of 16 runs apiece to finish the summer on top of the national bowling averages.

Johnnie's finest hour during 1947 came at the Arms Park as he took 6/5 during an eleven-over spell against a bemused and baffled Leicestershire line-up. During his spell, Glamorgan's close to the wicket fielders also took some smart catches as the foundations

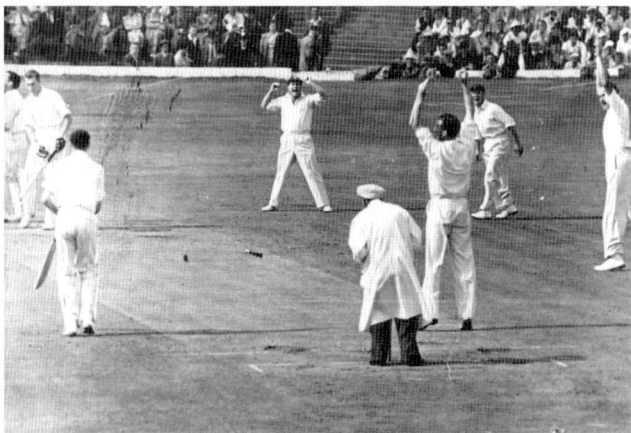

were laid for one of the vital ingredients in the Championship success the following summer.

The Glamorgan leg-trap in action at Swansea during 1951, with Messrs Watkins, Clift and Wooller all poised for action as Jim McConnon bowls to a South African batsman.

MUNCER, Bernard Leonard ('Len')

Born – Hampstead, 23 October 1913
Died – Camden, 18 January 1982
Professional
RHB, LBG / OB
Ed – Reading School
1st XI: 1947-1954
Cap: 1947
Middlesex 1933-1946; MCC 1935-1957; Players 1948
Clubs: Hampstead, Reading, Crewe, MCC

Batting and Fielding Record:

	M	I	NO	RUNS	AV	100	50	CT	ST
F-c	224	333	46	6460	22.50	4	21	111	-

Bowling Record:

	Balls	M	R	W	AV	5wI	10wM
F-c	38657	1919	14463	708	20.42	42	8

Career-bests:

First-class – 135 v Somerset at St Helen's, Swansea, 1952
9/62 v Essex at Brentwood, 1948

Len Muncer was a key member of Glamorgan's victorious team in the 1948 Championship. The off-spinner had made his debut for the Welsh county the previous summer, having moved to South Wales after a thirteen-year spell on the books of Middlesex. He had failed to command a regular place in the Middlesex XI and, with Johnnie Clay going into semi-retirement, the long-serving Glamorgan captain was able to secure Len's services courtesy of the MCC's Special Registration scheme.

It came at a time when Middlesex owed Glamorgan something of a favour as during 1946 they had agreed terms with Jack Young, a talented left-arm spinner who had played for Glamorgan during several of the wartime friendlies. He had been on Middlesex's books since 1933, and like Len, had never commanded a regular place in their line-up. In 1939 there had been talk of Jack joining Leicestershire and on hearing that the unsettled spinner was stationed in South Wales during the War, Johnnie met up with him and persuaded Jack to sign terms.

Len Muncer.

Everything changed however when Johnnie contacted Sir Pelham Warner with the news of Jack's signing and it was not long before the highly influential figure at Lord's persuaded the spin bowler to change his mind. In these modern days of litigation and lawsuits, Glamorgan would probably have had a good case for breach of contract, but it was a different era in the immediate post-War years and when Johnnie enquired about Len's availability, Middlesex did not stand in his way.

Len quickly impressed the Glamorgan hierarchy with his bowling repertoire, but during the pre-season matches in 1947, plus the early Championship encounters, there was much uncertainty about which was his most effective bowling style. For a while, he continued to mix his off-spin with leg-breaks but, after some sage advice from the gimlet-eyed Haydn Davies, it was agreed that Len should focus on off-spin.

He duly repaid Wilf and Haydn for their advice by topping the Club's wicket-taking list in 1947 with 107 wickets followed in 1948 by 139 wickets in the Championship, with the off-spinner being Glamorgan's leading wicket-taker with his tally being almost twice of that of Norman Hever who was second in the wicket-takers list.

He proved to be an indispensable weapon at Wilf Wooller's disposal, and a bowler who possessed the three virtues of length, flight and spin. At times during 1948, he was almost unplayable on the dry and spin-friendly pitches of South Wales, with a match haul of 15/201 in the game against Sussex at Swansea, and 11/82 against Nottinghamshire, also at St Helen's.

But Len was equally effective on turning pitches elsewhere and of his three ten-wicket hauls that daffodil-golden summer, his finest came at Brentwood where he completed his career-best return of 9/62 against Essex. He might even have emulated Jack Mercer by taking all ten, had he not caught Bill Morris, the ninth man to depart, off the bowling of Willie Jones.

As John Arlott wrote "on a turning wicket, he can make the spun ball cut back like a whip but, on a batsman's pitch, he has all the control and resource to keep down runs." In the mands of

A photograph from 1948 showing Len Muncer demonstrating his bowling action.

many, he was the most potent off-spinner in Championship cricket during 1948 and deservedly appeared in July at Lord's for the Players against the Gentlemen.

Higher honours never came his way, but Len showed that his success in 1948 was not a fluke by passing the hundred-mark once again in first-class cricket during 1949 with his impressive tally including returns of 12/94 against Somerset at The Gnoll in Neath, and 14/103 against Lancashire at Stradey Park in Llanelli. By this time, he had also developed his batting skills and, from a berth at number six in the order, he posted his maiden Championship hundred at Cardiff Arms Park in 1950, with 114 in three and a half hours, with 15 fours and a six.

He added three more in as many seasons, with an unbeaten 107 against Derbyshire at Chesterfield in 1951, 135 in the match with Somerset at Swansea in 1952, plus 128

against Worcestershire at New Road during 1953. A far cry from his early days in the lower echelons of the Middlesex line-up when in 127 innings he had struck just seven fifties, including 80, batting at number nine, against Kent at Folkestone in 1934 plus 85 from one place higher in the order against Northamptonshire at Kettering in 1937.

Given the fact that Len was also a capable slip fielder, he had become a genuine all-rounder by the early 1950s and in 1952 he became the second Glamorgan player to achieve the coveted Double of 100 wickets and 1076 runs in first-class cricket. The previous summer Len had also performed the match double by returning figures of 10/57 to go with his century in the away match with Derbyshire. A measure of his achievement at Chesterfield can be gauged from the fact that the only Glamorgan player to perform this feat in Championship cricket is Rodney Ontong, one of Len's proteges when coaching later at Lord's

Len's development into a decent all-rounder during the 1950s was quite heartening given that in August 1934 he had been knocked unconscious and forced to retire hurt on 45 after being struck on the head when batting against Nottinghamshire's Bill Voce who cocked a snook at the game's authority by bowling a spell of fast leg-theory during their Championship match at Lord's. As a traditionalist, Len had little time for Bodyline tactics but it was a measure of the man that he never held any grudges against the Northern paceman.

Len Muncer, seen bowling at Lord's during a match between Glamorgan and Middlesex.

Len was a model professional, described by John Arlott as having "a trim, almost military – air about his firm and rather burly figure with the precisely parted and smoothed hair, [plus] the neatly rolled sleeves." He was also a deep thinker on the game and fully earned the following tribute from Wilf – "There are many very fine cricketers who can bowl skillfully or bat brilliantly, or even do a little bit of both, but who cannot read a game intelligently. However, Len was not one of these and, like Haydn Davies, he could skillfully see how the game was going and work out tactics to help remove the better and more stubborn batsmen."

Kind words indeed, especially given the fact that Len had, on more than one occasion, stood up to Wilf and was not cowed by a tongue-lasing from 'The Skipper'. An example came during a match with Somerset when Wilf felt that Len was bowling a little too flat and should be giving the ball more air. After the occasional comment, Somerset's batsmen continue to prosper and after another boundary from Hughie Watts, Wilf's patience finally ran out and he snarled "For God's sake, Len, give them some bloody air!" But Len's reaction was to kick the ground and then bowl three slow full tosses in a row, helping Watts to reach his first, and what proved to be his only century.

This resilience no doubt stemmed from Len's experiences during the Second World War when he served as a sergeant in the Fifth Battalion of the Sherwood Foresters. After being posted with his battalion to South-east Asia, Len was taken prisoner in Singapore during mid-February 1942. He spent the rest of the War as a Prisoner of War and, from November that year, was forced to undertake laboring on the Burma-Siam Railway. His character and fortitude, as much as his stamina, helped him survive these difficult years, and despite losing many stone, he returned in a fit enough state to resume his career with Middlesex in 1946.

However, *anno domini* began to tell and Len missed six weeks of the 1953 season with a groin strain. With Jim McConnon emerging as a talented and younger off-spinner, Len realized that his career with Glamorgan was drawing to a close and, after taking a Benefit Year in 1954, which raised £3556, Len retired from the county game. To some, it was a premature end, with others also hinting that Len's decision was the result of being offered quite modest terms for the following season. "A strong character with strong opinions," was the verdict of one former colleague who, on more than one occasion, had heard Len speak his mind and, rightly or wrongly, believed he had a bit of a chip on his shoulder about the Club's committee.

After leaving the Welsh county, Len had a brief spell with Crewe in the Staffordshire League before securing a position as the MCC's Head Coach at Lord's. Len also combined his coaching duties, in these days before the Lord's Shop, by also overseeing the operations of Warsop's bat-making factory adjacent to the famous ground in a small property in Strathmore Court.

Len also stood as an umpire in 25 first-class matches, all at Lord's between 1957 and 1964, as well as a host of other one- and two-day games at the St John's Wood ground. In 1975 he also officiated in the World Cup warm-up game at Lord's between Middlesex and the Australians, whilst in June 1976, when Ray Julian was unable to officiate in the Sunday League match between Middlesex and Glamorgan, Len donned the white coat once again and stood with Alan Whitehead.

Len served as the MCC's Head Coach from 1955 until 1978, and during his tenure, he proved himself to be a popular figure. He was very much a traditionalist, insisting that the young cricketers in his charge always turned out for nets wearing the right clothing and practicing in the appropriate manner. He was slow to warm to the more unorthodox approach shown by some of the MCC groundstaff, including Ian Botham to whom he once famously said "you should have stuck to soccer, lad!" when assessing the prospects of the youngster who had been sent to Lord's by Somerset.

During his time at Lord's, Len recommended many young cricketers to Glamorgan including Rodney Ontong and Geoff Holmes, whilst he helped to improve the skills of several spinners including Barry Lloyd. Indeed, the off-break bowler from Neath was in the MCC Young Cricketers team which Len captained in 1971 against Scotland B at Perth. It was the last match of any note in which Len appeared, but he did not bat or bowl.

The same year he was awarded a Testimonial – which raised £2114 – in conjunction with Harry Sharp, his assistant in the Indoor School, and later the Middlesex scorer.

Like many professionals at the time, Len enjoyed playing cards and having a flutter. One of his most famous wagers came in 1950 when the West Indians visited Swansea to play the Welsh county in the sporting amphitheatre of St Helen's. Before the game started, Len had accepted a bet from Everton Weekes that the Caribbean batsman would score a hundred before lunch in the contest. Len therefore had a broad smile on his face when the gifted strokemaker was bowled by Allan Watkins for a single in the first innings. But Everton was unbeaten on 45 at the end of day two, and walking back to the Swansea pavilion, he gently reminded Len of the wager. With a series of flowing strokes and fierce pulls the next day, Everton duly reached 147 on the final morning and, as befitted a true gentleman, Len was pleased to honour the bet at lunchtime.

402
RICHES, John Dansey Hurry

Born – Cathays, Cardiff, 30 December 1920
Died – Cyncoed, Cardiff, 5 October 1999
Amateur
RHB, SLA
Ed – Repton School
1st XI: 1947
2nd XI: 1938-1957
Colts: 1935-1958
Clubs: Cardiff, MCC, Glamorgan Nomads, South Wales Hunts, XL Club,
Welsh Cygnets

Batting and Fielding Record:

	M	I	NO	RUNS	AV	100	50	CT	ST
F-c	1	2	0	5	2.50	-	-	-	-

Career-best:
First-class –   4 v Yorkshire at Bramall Lane, Sheffield, 1947

John Riches, who made one appearance for Glamorgan during 1947, was the son of Norman Riches, (Vol. 1, p.183-188) Glamorgan's first-ever captain in Championship cricket and he upheld the family's good name in club and representative cricket in South Wales, besides following in his father's footsteps by leading Glamorgan's 2nd XI between 1946 and 1954, as well as Cardiff in 1948.

Born the Christmas before Glamorgan's inaugural season as a first-class county, John attended Repton School in Derbyshire, and won a place in the school's XI during 1937 as a competent right-handed batsman and useful left-arm spinner, before the following summer winning a regular place in the Glamorgan Colts side.

After completing his National Service with the Army, John made his solitary first-class appearance for Glamorgan against Yorkshire at Sheffield during 1947, scoring 4 and 1.

John Riches, seen with John Davis and John Davies, at an event at Sophia Gardens during 2001.

He would probably have played on many more occasions for the county had it not been for the Second World War or the presence of legendary off-spinner Johnnie Clay and left-arm spinner Willie Jones.

Rather than following his father into the world of dentistry, John subsequently became a well-known solicitor in both Cardiff and Surrey. A quiet and genial man by nature, he was very proud of his father's achievements for the Welsh county. He would also smile when someone, albeit in jest, suggested that John's success as a spinner with Cardiff stemmed from the fact that Norman would often stand as the umpire in the Club's matches, with the whimsical suggestion that his illustrious father would answer John's appeals by raising his index finger and saying "That's out son!"

403
GOOD, Dennis Cunliffe
Born – Leeds, 29 August 1926
Amateur
RHB, RFM
Ed – Denstone School and Sheffield University
1st XI: 1947
Worcestershire 1946
Clubs: Rawdon, Windhill

Batting and Fielding Record:

	M	I	NO	RUNS	AV	100	50	CT	ST
F-c	3	5	2	47	15.67	-	-	1	-

Bowling Record:

	Balls	M	R	W	AV	5wI	10wM
F-c	360	11	225	7	32.14	-	-

Career-bests:
First-class –   21 v Derbyshire at Derby, 1947
                  2/34 v Derbyshire at Derby, 1947

Dennis Good, seen at the Arms Park, during 1947.

Dennis Good had a brief career with Glamorgan, playing in three matches during 1947 at a time when the Welsh county were rebuilding after the Second World War.

The Yorkshire-born pace bowler was educated at Denstone School, where he played in the XI between 1941 and 1943 before attending Sheffield University where he read textiles. Whilst at Sheffield, he also played for Windhill in the Bradford League and after impressing with his raw pace in club cricket he had a brief, but unsuccessful, trial with Yorkshire.

After graduating, Dennis undertook his National Service with the Royal Air Force and whilst based at RAF Hednesford in Staffordshire, he impressed some talent scouts from Worcestershire who were keeping an eye on the games. His lively performances with the new ball duly led to his selection for the West Midlands side against the Combined Services at New Road during July 1946.

The following summer, Dennis made the first of three appearances for Glamorgan, against the South Africans at the Arms Park. His selection resulted from injuries to Peter Judge and Austin Matthews, as well as recommendations from Worcestershire. 1947 also saw Dennis play against Surrey at The Oval and Derbyshire at Derby during which he claimed a further half a dozen wickets. Few doubted his pace or his eagerness to succeed but, with other and more accurate seam bowlers becoming available, the match in Derby proved to be his last first-class appearance.

Dennis subsequently returned to Yorkshire where he joined a Bradford-based textiles company before moving during January 1952 to Quebec in Canada where he subsequently set up his own textile import business.

An image taken in Canada during 1955 of Dennis Good.

404
TAMPLIN, Clifford

Born – Cardiff, 14 May 1920
Died – Leominster, 1 February 2006
Amateur
RHB, WK
1st XI: 1947
2nd XI: 1938-1949
Colts: 1936-1939
Club and Ground: 1947
Bengal 1942-1943
Clubs: Cardiff, Cardiff YMCA, Glamorgan Nomads

Batting and Fielding Record:

	M	I	NO	RUNS	AV	100	50	CT	ST
F-c	3	4	2	56	28.00	-	-	6	-

Career-best:
First-class – 40* v Kent at Rodney Parade, Newport, 1947

Cliff Tamplin was Glamorgan's reserve wicket-keeper during the years after the Second World War. Had it not been for Haydn Davies' outstanding and consistent efforts behind the stumps, and willingness to play even when suffering from bruised and cut fingers, Cliff would have enjoyed a successful county career himself.

Cliff had an excellent record playing for Cardiff before the War, besides playing for the Welsh Schools and Glamorgan Colts. During 1942/43 he made his first-class debut in Indian domestic cricket playing for Bengal in the Ranji Trophy at Calcutta whilst on National Service with the Army.

During 1947 he was called up by Glamorgan to play against the South Africans at the Arms Park, and he appeared in two other games in June 1947 when Haydn succumbed to injury, with Cliff playing against Kent at Rodney Parade in Newport and against Derbyshire at Derby.

After the War, Cliff regularly kept wicket for Cardiff as well as for Glamorgan in their Minor County matches during 1948 and 1949. He worked as a clerk in the Ministry of Labour and had married Thelma Eveleigh during 1942.

Cliff Tamplin, seen when playing for Glamorgan Colts during 1938.

MARSH, William Edward ('Bill')

Born – Newbridge, 10 September 1917
Died – Newbridge, 6 February 1978
Amateur
RHB, RFM
Ed – Monmouth School
1st XI: 1947
2nd XI: 1949
Colts: 1937-1938
Club: Newbridge
Rugby for Newbridge, Cross Keys and Monmouthshire

Batting and Fielding Record:

	M	I	NO	RUNS	AV	100	50	CT	ST
F-c	4	6	1	39	7.80	-	-	2	-

Bowling Record:

	Balls	M	R	W	AV	5wI	10wM
F-c	385	6	290	8	36.25	-	-

Career-bests:

First-class –   13 v Middlesex at Lord's, 1947
              3/70 v Worcestershire at Ebbw Vale, 1947

Bill Marsh was another promising sportsman from Monmouthshire who progressed from the county's colts to Glamorgan's junior teams prior to the Second World War before appearing for the Welsh county's 1st XI once hostilities were over. But whereas his contemporaries, Phil Clift and Allan Watkins, had long and fulfilling careers with the Welsh county, Bill only played in four matches.

The former pupil of Monmouth School was also a talented rugby player, and besides playing county rugby for Monmouthshire, Bill also appeared in a final Welsh trial. The schoolmaster was a brisk right arm bowler besides being a forceful batsman, who had played a series of hard-hitting innings for Usk for whom he played with great success after the Second World War.

With Peter Judge nursing an injury with his Achilles tendon and Hugh Griffiths still in residence at Cambridge University, Glamorgan turned to the whole-hearted Marsh for their visit to Lord's during June 1947. He duly opened the bowling with Wilf Wooller and claimed a couple of

Bill Marsh.

relatively expensive wickets as his new ball partner claimed 7/52 with Marsh also holding a couple of well-judged catches in the deep as Middlesex were dismissed for 102. It was not enough though to secure victory for the Welsh county as some lusty blows by Alex Thompson in the Middlesex second innings, saw the home side to a three-wicket victory.

Bill played again against Gloucestershire at Swansea and against Surrey at The Oval, before re-appearing a few weeks later in the contest against Worcestershire at Ebbw Vale. Despite returning his career-best figures he did not feature again in Glamorgan's Championship line-up.

406
PLEASS, James Edward

Born – Cardiff, 21 May 1923
Died – Cardiff, 16 February 2015
Amateur 1947
Professional 1948-1956
RHB, OB
Ed – St Fagans Primary School and Cantonian High School, Cardiff
1st XI: 1947-1956
2nd XI: 1948-1956
Club and Ground: 1947-1955
Cap: 1952
Clubs: Cardiff, Pontardawe, Hill's Plymouth, Briton Ferry Town

Batting and Fielding Record:

	M	I	NO	RUNS	AV	100	50	CT	ST
F-c	171	253	31	4293	19.30	1	11	77	-

Bowling Record:

	Balls	M	R	W	AV	5wI	10wM
F-c	24	0	15	0	-	-	-

Career-best:
First-class – 102* v Yorkshire at Harrogate, 1955

Jim Pleass was the longest-living member of Glamorgan's team which won the County Championship in 1948 by defeating Hampshire at Bournemouth.

Jim was the first son of Edward Pleass, an insurance salesman who became branch manager of the British General Insurance Company Limited. Edward, and his wife Eva lived initially in Splott, the bustling inner suburb adjacent to Cardiff Docks and it was here during May 1923 that Jim was born. Three years later, the Pleass family moved to the first of two homes in Fairwater, a more prosperous and leafy suburb to the west of the city, and locations from which Jim and his brothers were able to play all forms of ball games in the fields behind their home which ran down to the flood plain of the River Ely and the village of St Fagans.

It was whilst at the village's primary school that Jim further honed his ball-playing skills and, by the time he was a pupil at Cantonian High School, Jim showed great prowess as a schoolboy cricketer and footballer. His uncle Bill Pritchard had been a decent cricketer in his own right with the Cardiff club but his playing career had been interrupted by the War, and by the 1930s, he was a coach and umpire. Through his uncle's contacts, Jim played for the St Fagans Boys team, whilst some promising innings for the Cantonian school team saw Jim chosen for the Cardiff Schoolboys team.

A photograph of Jim Pleass taken during 1949.

His sporting education was further developed by trips with his uncle and other family members to watch Glamorgan play at the Arms Park in Cardiff, St Helen's in Swansea and at Ynysangharad Park in Pontypridd, whilst during the winter months, they also watched Cardiff City play at Ninian Park. Indeed, Jim's prowess with the round ball for his school side led to selection for Cardiff Corinthians FC, as well as trials with Cardiff City FC.

In 1939 Jim made his debut as a batsman and off-spin bowler for Cardiff and after attending nets at the Arms Park, he also received an invitation from Bill Hitch, the Glamorgan coach to attend some of the county's winter coaching sessions. The outbreak of War put a temporary halt to his county ambitions, and like thousands of other young boys, he initially joined the Home Guard before in 1941 joining the Royal Corps of Signals, largely because he had enjoyed Morse Code training with the Home Guard.

Jim duly undertook further training at Catterick Camp, besides representing the Army camp in their football matches, which included a game against Doncaster Rovers FC. He was subsequently promoted to a training camp in Huddersfield, followed by a posting to the West Coast of Scotland, where the newly-formed Combined Operations (Army, Navy and Air Force) were quartered near Ayr at HMS *Dundonald*. It was here that Jim and his colleagues practised amphibious landings before in the spring of 1944 heading south to Southampton.

On 6 June 1944 Jim duly took part in Operation Overlord, working as a wireless signaler in the invasion force and landing at Arromanches, or Gold Beach as it was designated for D-Day. Once the beachhead was established, Jim's job was to link the beach signallers with the heavily armed cruisers and helping to direct their fire at pin-pointed targets. Within forty eight hours, everything had been secured and, after a week working on patrol vessels, Jim and his colleagues returned to the UK and headed back to their Yorkshire base

It proved to only be a brief stay as Jim's unit were subsequently posted to Ceylon, Malaysia and Singapore before finally heading back home in January 1947 and resuming his work in the administration department of a tarmac-laying company. With his National Service completed, Jim also looked to resume his sporting career, and having kept in touch with Cardiff City's manager Cyril Spiers during the War, he headed to Ninian Park to see what the prospects were of securing terms with the football club. By now, a new manager was in post, and despite training with the team, no offers came Jim's way.

During the late spring of 1947, he also trained with the cricketers of Cardiff and acted as a net bowler at the Arms Park when Glamorgan were training. Jim's forte however lay in his batting and having scored four centuries for Cardiff, he was called up by the Welsh county for their away match against Derbyshire starting on the final Saturday of June. His steady batting against the lively Peakites attack led to a further four appearances, as an amateur, as well as a place on the end-of-season tour of Pembrokeshire, during which he posted a century against Pembroke County. His efforts had impressed Wilf Wooller and coach George Lavis and Jim was duly offered a contract for 1948 at a salary of £6 per week over the 22 weeks of the season.

Jim went on to write his name into the Club's annals by becoming a member of the first-ever Glamorgan side to lift the county title, defeating Hampshire at Dean Park in Bournemouth in late August 1948. For Jim, the delight in bringing the county crown to Wales was a worthy reward for the massive test of his own fortitude and strength of character he had shown four years earlier as a callow twenty-one year old youth during the Normandy Landings. Indeed, the names on the Glamorgan scorecard that day on the South Coast in 1948 might have been very different had lady luck not been on Jim's side, with the landing craft he was in

Jim Pleass demonstrates his forward defensive stroke at the Arms Park during 1947.

narrowly avoiding a German mine. An adjoining vessel in the flotilla was less fortunate, with Jim and his colleagues watching in horror as the other craft disintegrated before their very eyes, killing all of its unfortunate occupants.

After witnessing all of these events in Northern France, it was with sheer joy and pride that from April 1948 Jim, as a professional cricketer, went to battle on the cricket fields of England under the direction of the fearless Wilf Wooller, another man whose wartime experiences had transformed a happy-go-lucky amateur into a hard-nosed and tough cricketer. It was under this particular Field Marshal that Jim – by nature a quiet and self-effacing character – blossomed. His batting in the middle-order allied to his swift fielding won Jim a regular place in the line-up in 1948, and an indication of his value to the team duly came in June on his home patch at the Arms Park where his unbeaten 77 against Hampshire helped Glamorgan seal a 70-run victory.

Jim duly mixed football with Lovell's Athletic in the Southern League with professional cricket in the summer. He became an integral part of the Glamorgan side for the next few summers – a period which saw the Welsh county slide down to eighth in 1949, and then eleventh in 1950 before bouncing back up into fifth place in 1951. It was also a summer which saw Jim play a key role in one of the most remarkable victories in the Club's history as Glamorgan defeated the 1951 South Africans at Swansea. In fact, Wilf's team were the only county to defeat the Springboks on their tour, and even the most partisan of Welshmen would have been hard pressed to forecast a Glamorgan win when they were dismissed for 111.

With the St Helen's pitch assisting the slower bowlers, Len Muncer and Jim McConnon made early inroads before the tourists were also dismissed for 111. It was an eventful day as Glamorgan were batting for a second time shortly before the close and, after the loss of an early wicket, Jim was promoted up to number three and in a role of pseudo-nightwatchman he stoutly saw Glamorgan through to the close. On the second morning, Jim continued to defend watchfully and, at five foot eight proved to be a frustrating contrast for the tourists to Wilf who used his longer levers and taller frame to put bat to ball.

A deft cut by Jim Pleass against Percy Mansell's bowling during the famous contest between Glamorgan and the 1951 Springboks at Swansea.

This little and large combination shared what proved to be a match-winning partnership, besides show-casing Jim's outstanding abilities against spin bowling. Quick and nimble on his feet, Jim was able to defy the threats posed by the visiting spinners as Glamorgan left the tourists a target of 147. Second time around their top order batted with more assurance and confidence, guiding the tourists to 54-0 by the time tea was taken.

But a dramatic turnaround then followed after the interval. As Jim recalled in his memoirs, "within half an hour of the resumption after tea, South Africa were 54-1; 54-2; 61-3; 61-4; 68-5; 68-6 and 68-7 as Jim McConnon achieved a hat-trick. The bottom half of the South African batting order had change into "civvies", believing that they would not be needed, and, what with the mad scramble to change back into whites and don pads, their dressing room must have looked like the opening day of a quick-change artistes' convention!"

"But the wickets kept tumbling – 72-8 and 72-9 before Percy Mansell was caught off a top edge, and it was all over. We had won the greatest match ever by 64 runs. Then the euphoria; we were mobbed; the National Anthem was sung, and the champagne flowed!" It was undoubtedly the most thrilling game in which Jim had played with the celebrations matching those in Cardiff in August 1948 after the Glamorgan team had returned home from Bournemouth.

As far as Jim's fielding was concerned, his sharp and alert efforts at cover point when the quicker bowlers were operating also won rich praise. When the spinners came on, Jim would switch to a place in the leg-trap, carefully marshalled by Wilf with Jim and his colleagues snaffling many catches as the wily spinners found the edge of the bat.

Jim generally had a safe pair of hands, but there was one occasion, at Derby, which lived long in his memory when he spilled a catch and misfielded when at long-on in front of the Members enclosure as George Pope, the Derbyshire and England fast bowler, was batting. "Wilf decided to give him a few teasers to tempt him, and sure enough, George was tempted, I saw the ball climb steeply into the blue heavens and almost suspend itself for a moment, before dropping with ever increasing speed right into my hands – and straight out again! It hit the ground between my legs, and went for four. Raucous laughter from the Members; a broad grin from George Pope; a smirk or two from my team mates, but not from the bowler, and the game re-commenced."

"It surely couldn't happen again, but it did. This time I had to move about ten yards to my left, but the ball went up so high that there was ample time to get under it. I lined it up; waited patiently again for it; it dropped to earth, and I never even laid a hand on it as it evaded my desperate attempts and went for another four. The shame; the ignominy, the laughter (which was louder), the broad grins (which were now guffaws); the smirks (which were now grins), and the glowering malevolence (from the bowler). One well-meaning character in the Members' enclosure threw his hat towards me, and said; "why don't you use that next time." As if there would be a next time, but there was! Two overs later, up went the ball into the blue, and it was quite obvious to me where it was going to drop. This time, though, it was a happy ending. I clutched it to my chest, and redeemed myself!"

Jim won his Glamorgan cap in 1952, whilst in 1955 he scored his maiden first-class century at Harrogate as the Welsh county also secured their first-ever victory on Yorkshire soil. What made their win even more creditable was that Glamorgan were without Wilf, and had arrived in Yorkshire on the back of consecutive defeats to Hampshire and Leicestershire. They also had only just avoided the follow-on in their first innings and were indebted to a tenth wicket stand of 56 between Hugh Davies and Don Shepherd to avoid being asked to bat again.

Glamorgan were duly set a target of 334 on the final day, and with spinner Johnnie Wardle taking the first four wickets, a Yorkshire victory looked on the cards. But Jim's prowess against the slower bowlers was once again to the fore as he shared two productive stand with the other Jim's – Messrs. Pressdee and McConnon. Both seemed quite relaxed in the absence of Wilf, with whom they had clashed swords on more than one occasion, and they each helped Jim make serene progress as they chiseled away at the target.

Yorkshire's fielding also became rather complacent and some chances were spilled. As Jim later recalled, "To Yorkshire on that day, it all seemed a bit of a joke, but it was us who had the last laugh. All the wiles of Johnny Wardle, Brian Close and Ray Illingworth were of no avail, and when, late in the afternoon, I leg-glanced to the boundary to record my first "ton", my cup was full. Shortly afterwards it was over-flowing as the winning run was scored, still with twenty minutes remaining. We had beaten Yorkshire on their home ground for the very first time, and they did not like it. They quietly and quickly packed their bags and left the ground with not so much as a "well played" – with one exception – Norman Yardley, the Yorkshire captain and ever a gentleman."

Jim returned in an elated state back home with his wife Terry and young family, but he was brought back down to earth with a bump the following day in a friendly fixture at Merthyr Tydfil, against the Hoover Sports Club, who were celebrating the opening of their new ground at Pentrebach. But Jim had little to smile about as he was caught without scoring from the third ball of the match.

He retired from county cricket at the end of the following season having made 171 appearances in first-class cricket, scoring 4293 runs and taking 77 catches for the Welsh county. He continued playing for a while for Cardiff, often alongside his younger brother Allan, who also played for Glamorgan 2nd XI in 1952. For several years, he

An image of Jim Pleass taken during 2007.

had started developing a career as an insurance agent, initially working alongside Wilf – with whom he had played many games of chess on rainy days in cricket pavilions across the country – in the brokerage the Glamorgan captain had developed. Following his retirement from county cricket, Jim joined the Northern Assurance Company and worked for five years in London during the early 1960s, before returning to Cardiff and managing his own brokerage.

His return to South Wales also saw him take up golf, with Jim being a long-standing member of Llanishen Golf Club, besides rejoining Glamorgan CCC, and serving as a committee member. His duties included acting as match manager and announcer during one-day games at Sophia Gardens during the 1970s. The following decade he also played a key role in the creation of the Glamorgan Former Players Association, and until the year before his death, he was a regular and ever jovial face at the Association's annual gatherings.

407
HARRIS, Leslie John
Born – Cardiff, 20 July 1915
Died – Beckenham, 28 October 1985
Amateur
RHB, RM
Ed – Canton High School, Cardiff
1st XI: 1947
2nd XI: 1947-1948
Club and Ground: 1947
Clubs: St Fagans, Neath, Free Foresters, Buccaneers, Beckenham

Batting and Fielding Record:

	M	I	NO	RUNS	AV	100	50	CT	ST
F-c	3	4	2	7	3.50	-	-	1	-

Bowling Record:

	Balls	M	R	W	AV	5wI	10wM
F-c	51	7	183	5	36.60	-	-

Career-bests:
First-class –   5 v Derbyshire at Derby, 1947
          3/39 v Derbyshire at Derby, 1947

Leslie Harris was the elder brother of Ernie Harris, and during 1947 he emulated Ernie by playing in three matches for Glamorgan. The all-rounder however was perhaps better known as the founder father of the Primary Club and helped to raise millions of pounds for good causes including blind cricket.

He had first played in decent club cricket for St Fagans whilst at Canton High School, before switching his allegiance to Neath having secured a post with the Great Western Railway, no doubt through the influence of his father John who was an inspector with the company.

He later became a car salesman and, following the outbreak of War, he joined the Royal Engineers and served in Scotland. Whilst based in Edinburgh, he also found plenty of time to play cricket appearing for a Combined Services XI against a Scottish XI during 1944, besides appearing for the East of Scotland and an Anglo-Scottish XI in other wartime games.

After returning to South Wales and continuing his career with Neath, Leslie agreed to assist Glamorgan during 1947 following the retirement of Austin Matthews and Peter Judge. A decent seam bowler and a competent batsman, Leslie made his first-class debut during late June 1947 against Derbyshire at Derby – the first of three away games that summer in which the amateur played, followed in July by appearances against Northants at Kettering and Essex at Westcliff-on-Sea. He claimed three wickets on debut, but did little of note in his subsequent games. Nevertheless, Leslie agreed to help out Glamorgan again the following summer and regularly appeared for their 2nd XI during 1948, but with fewer injuries and a settled squad gelling under Wilf Wooller, Leslie was not called up again.

During the 1950s, Leslie moved to work in the transport trade in Kent, and joined Beckenham. So began a long and highly successful career in club cricket, with Leslie famed for his ability with in-swing. As one colleague recalled, "he was great to bowl with as he would rub a little of the Brilliantine he always wore on his hair onto the ball after which one side used to shine like a mirror! As a fellow swing bowler, it was wonderful to be handed a ball like that at the end of an over! Mind you, if you handed it back to Les in a worse condition, you didn't half get a bollocking!"

It was whilst associated with the Beckenham club that he helped to create the Primary Club during 1955. Set up by Leslie and a group of admittedly slightly inebriated members of the Beckenham club, who were frustrated by their ineptitude with the bat, it was agreed to invite those dismissed first ball in games involving the club to join The Primary Club and raise funds for Freddie Brown's recently established Fund for Blind Cricketers.

This most idosyncratic Club subsequently broadened its membership to those in any form of the game, and spawned a branch in Australia which Leslie and his wife Joan, thoroughly enjoyed

Leslie Harris (left) seen with his brother Ernie, each in their military uniform whilst on National Service.

linking up with for special matches. A measure of his success can be gauged by the fact that by the time of his death during 1985, the Primary Club had over 9000 members worldwide and annually raised over a million pounds for good causes.

Leslie also appeared for the Free Foresters and the Buccaneers and is reputed to have taken around 3500 wickets in club cricket. He frequently led touring teams from Beckenham and the other wandering clubs of which he was a member. In the words of a tribute in the Primary Club's newsletter shortly after his death "Leslie was a captain of authority, zest and plenty of humour."

408
EDWARDS, Aubrey Mansel

Born – Pen-y-Craig, Cowbridge, 4 July 1918
Died – Calgary, Alberta, 16 November 1997
Amateur
RHB, RM
1st XI: 1947
2nd XI: 1938-1947
Colts: 1937
Club and Ground: 1938
Alberta 1949-1952; Canada 1951
Clubs: Cowbridge, Swansea

Batting and Fielding Record:

	M	I	NO	RUNS	AV	100	50	CT	ST
F-c	1	1	0	0	-	-	-	-	-

Bowling Record:

	Overs	M	R	W	AV	5wI	10wM
F-c	126	4	74	3	23.67	-	-

Career-best:
First-class – 2/34 v Sussex at Hove, 1947

Aubrey Edwards, a member of a well-to-do family in the Vale of Glamorgan, played once for the Welsh county during 1947 before emigrating to Canada where he spent the rest of his life working in real estate.

Aubrey Edwards.

Born near Cowbridge, the young seam bowler had impressed in school and junior cricket and appeared for the county's Colts team during 1937. Further decent performances with the ball for Cowbridge also saw him play for Glamorgan's 2nd XI during 1938.

At the time, Aubrey had begun his training as a chartered auctioneer and estate agent in Cardiff, but this ended in 1939 as he joined the Welch Regiment. He subsequently rose to the rank of Major, serving in India and Burma, until being demobbed in the spring of 1947.

He duly returned to his family's home in Cowbridge and after good performances with the ball in club cricket, he won selection for Glamorgan 2nd XI against their counterparts from Worcestershire at the Arms Park. Returns of 4/18 and 3/22 saw Major Edwards swiftly being called up for Glamorgan's Championship match against Sussex at Hove in mid-July. With other seam bowlers injured, Aubrey bowled creditably with the new ball in tandem with Wilf Wooller.

It proved though to be his sole appearance as, after a couple of further appearances in 2nd XI games, he emigrated later in the year to the Alberta province in Canada. He duly joined the Calgary Real Estate Board and in 1955 formed with own real estate company called Aubrey M. Edwards Ltd., besides securing Canadian citizenship. He continued to play cricket and besides appearing for Alberta between 1949 and 1952, Aubrey also played twice for the Canadian national side against the MCC on their tour during August and September 1951.

Aubrey was also a decent golfer, besides playing hockey, rugby and football whilst living in Canada. He and his wife Margaret also had one son, David.

409
DAVIES, Gwynfor Llewelyn ('Gwyn')

Born – Cathays, Cardiff, 10 June 1919
Died – Cardiff, 1 April 1995
Amateur
RHB, RM
Ed – Cathays High School, Cardiff and University College, Cardiff
1st XI: 1947-1948
2nd XI: 1938-1950
Colts: 1937-1938
Club and Ground: 1952
Club: Cardiff
Rugby for Cardiff

Batting and Fielding Record:

	M	I	NO	RUNS	AV	100	50	CT	ST
F-c	2	2	0	9	4.50	-	-	1	-

Career-best:
First-class – 7 v Lancashire at Rodney Parade, Newport, 1948

Gwyn Davies, a schoolmaster in Cardiff, played twice for Glamorgan in Championship cricket, each time against Lancashire, in 1947 at the Arms Park and in 1948 at Rodney Parade in Newport.

Gwyn grew up in the Cathays suburb of Cardiff where his grandfather Daniel was a Methodist minister and his father Rhys was a local schoolmaster. Gwyn subsequently followed in his father's footsteps and taught Physical Education and Games for many years at Cathays High School.

He shone at an early age at both cricket and rugby, and made his debut for Cardiff as a sixteen year-old in 1935. After some decent performances as a right-arm seam bowler and orthodox right-handed batsman for Cardiff,

Gwyn Davies.

383

Gwyn made his debut for the Glamorgan Colts team during 1937 before progressing to the 2nd XI in the following summer. Like so many of his peers, his sporting career was halted by the Second World War, and after completing his training to be a teacher, Gwyn served with the Royal Engineers.

On returning home, Gwyn secured a teaching post and resumed playing rugby and cricket for Cardiff. His prowess with bat and ball saw him appear for Glamorgan 2nd XI until 1950, whilst during 1947, and again in Championship year of 1948, he helped out the Welsh county for the visit of Lancashire when others were injured or unavailable.

His sprightly fielding drew praise from the watching Press, but this was no surprise given the fact that he had been Cardiff RFC's full-back from 1946/47. Gwyn continued to represent the 1st XV until 1949/50 before joining the rugby club's committee, and together with his coaching duties at Cathays High School, he helped to groom a number of promising young players..

Gwyn continued to play cricket for Cardiff until 1967 – their first summer at Sophia Gardens after the move from the Arms Park the previous year. After retiring from teaching, Gwyn continued to be active with the Cardiff Schools cricket and rugby teams. His wife Agnes, nee Shepherd, predeceased him during September 1993 in Cardiff.

An advert, helping to raise funds for the Club from a scorecard in 1947 when Glamorgan played at Sussex.

1948

It was a seminal moment in Welsh sporting history as Wilf Wooller led Glamorgan to the 1948 Championship. His side won 13 of their 26 Championship games and, like a caterpillar emerging from of a cocoon, they shed their tag as the Cinderallas of the county game by clinching the title in late August at Bournemouth and all after the first day of the game against Hampshire had seen a handful of overs before rain descended on the resort town. After the rain clouds disappeared – moved as much by Welsh willpower and prayers as atmospheric processes – it was fitting that Johnnie Clay should take the final wicket at Dean Park, with the veteran coming out of semi-retirement to also played a key role in the innings victory over Surrey at the Arms Park which left Wilf and his team winning touching distance of the title.

It was a great summer for the small nucleus of players, augmented by just four new faces. Of these Gilbert Parkhouse made the greatest impact with the bat, with the Swansea youngster, having first appeared during the wartime games, playing some graceful innings as his team made a flying start to the season with victories during May over Somerset, Essex and Worcestershire.

June 1948 saw Willie Jones strike a pair of double-hundreds, besides sharing a record third wicket stand of 313 with Emrys Davies against a hapless Essex attack at Brentwood. These efforts all consolidated Glamorgan's position at the top of the Championship table with Wilf's team remaining in the title race during the course of July and August. Despite some unseasonal rain during the latter, and a series of draws, the back-to-back victories over Surrey and Hampshire saw the county title come to Wales.

With Wilf having been chosen to play for the Gentlemen of England against the Australians at Lord's, it was Johnnie who led the overjoyed Glamorgan squad as they headed home from Bournemouth by train to Cardiff. There was barely any space on Platform Three as their express arrived, with loud cheers greeting them as they alighted and joined the throng of delirious supporters. The happy party then walked to Cardiff Athletic Club for a celebratory party which, in the words of the famous Welsh melody "*Ar Hyd y Nos*" with their wives, girlfriends and other family members also in attendance. As Johnnie's wife later told a colleague, "he was quite beside himself with joy and really let himself go that night. I've never seen him in such a state. Thank goodness it's only once they've won the Championship!"

MATHEWS, Capt. Ian Guy

Born – Cologne, 19 March 1924
Died – Hereford, 1 May 2006
Amateur
RHB, RM
Ed – Abberley Hall; Wellington College; Staff College, Camberley
RHB, RM
1st XI: 1948
2nd XI: 1949
Club and Ground: 1948
Clubs: Barry, South Wales Hunts, The Army

Batting and Fielding Record:

	M	I	NO	RUNS	AV	100	50	CT	ST
Friendly	1	1	0	0	-	-	-	-	-

Bowling Record:

Balls	M	R	W	AV	5wI	10wM	
Friendly	48	1	29	0	-	-	-

Guy Mathews, a young Army officer, appeared for Glamorgan in their two-day friendly against Thomas Owen's XI at Cardiff Arms Park during April 1948.

The game, arranged by a local businessman saw a number of England Test cricketers play against the Welsh county, with the invitation side led by Norman Yardley, and the match umpired by Norman Riches and Douglas Jardine – the former England captain who had been involved in the Bodyline series in Australia during 1932/33.

Guy was therefore surrounded by a host of well-known players, with his selection stemming from his father's friendship with Charles Clay – the father of Johnnie – and through this link, Guy was given a trial by the Welsh

Guy Mathews.

county as they prepared for the forthcoming season. He failed to take a wicket during his eight overs and was dismissed without scoring by Eric Bedser.

He had been in the 1st XI at Wellington College, besides appearing in Services cricket for the Army as well as in club cricket for Barry. This followed his wartime exploits serving with the Ninth Gurka Rifles in India, Ceylon and Malaya, having parachuted into the latter with Force 136 during the country's occupation by Japanese forces.

Guy subsequently pursued a military career serving as a Captain with the Duke of Cornwall's Light Infantry in Germany, Ceylon, Cyprus, the USA, Aden, Canada and Norway. He subsequently worked at the US Command and Staff College at Fort Leavenworth in Kansas before returning to the UK and acting as a Lieutenant-Colonel in the First Battalion of the Somerset and Cornwall Light Infantry. After retiring from his military duties, Guy and his wife ran an antiques shop in Ross-in-Wye which specialized in Arms, Armour and Militaria.

411
EAGLESTONE, James Thomas

Born – Paddington, 24 July 1923
Died – Pinner, Middlesex, 14 October 2000
Professional
1st XI: 1948-1949
Club and Ground: 1948-1949
Cap: 1948
Middlesex 1947; MCC 1947
Club: MCC

Batting and Fielding Record:

	M	I	NO	RUNS	AV	100	50	CT	ST
F-c	50	78	7	1064	14.98	-	4	20	-

Career-best:
First-class –   72 v Sussex at St Helen's, Swansea, 1948

Jimmy Eaglestone had the distinction of being a member of consecutive Championship-winning teams, playing for Middlesex during 1947 and then Glamorgan the following year having joined the Welsh county for whom he also played in 1949.

His father William was a delivery driver for a Paddington-based drapers company and a cricketer with modest pretentions. Jimmy inherited his father's love of cricket and after impressing in schoolboy games, he made his debut for Middlesex 2nd XI in 1939. On leaving school, he immediately joined the MCC groundstaff with ambitions to become a professional cricketer.

Jimmy's first major match came during 1940 when he appeared in a Lord's XI against the XL Club. The following year he also featured in other games at Lord's including playing for The Rest against the RAF, and for Sir Pelham Warner's XI in their away matches against the Aldershot Barracks and Ealing. He retained his place on the groundstaff at Lord's and, like

Jimmy Eaglestone, seen in a specially posed photograph at the Arms Park.

other teenagers, joined the Home Guard with Jimmy involved in their work during air raids and manning the guns defending Central London. He also found time to assist in the warehouse of the company where his father worked who were now making and distributing military uniforms.

Once hostilities were over, Jimmy was able to focus on his activities at Lord's and accept an offer to join Middlesex's junior staff. In 1947 the left-hander was chosen in the MCC side with met Surrey at the St John's Wood ground. He marked his first-class debut with a sparkling 77 during a stand of 128 with Denis Compton and three days later, Jimmy won selection in the Middlesex side for the match against Somerset at Lord's.

He made a duck on his debut but in the next game against Warwickshire at Edgbaston he made 55, and shared a stand with Bill Edrich as the England batsman compiled an assertive double-hundred. Jimmy's half-century was the first of several cameos which Jimmy played during 1947, besides proving himself to be a livewire when fielding in the covers, However, Middlesex had a depth of batting talent at their disposal, and Jimmy was unable to secure a regular place in their line-up, often playing only when the stars were away on Test duty.

Leo Harrison, the Hampshire wicket-keeper, attempts to stump Jimmy Eaglestone during Glamorgan's historic Championship match at Bournemouth during August 1948.

Despite Middlesex being crowned county champions, Jimmy was frustrated by the lack of opportunities coming his way and accepted an offer to join Glamorgan on a two-year contract in 1948. The Welsh county's approach had followed discussions by Wilf Wooller and the Glamorgan hierarchy with Len Muncer, who had also been on Middlesex's books after the War. Aware of Wilf's desire to improve the county's fielding, Len readily put Jimmy's name forward, no doubt aware of his frustrations at only being a bit-part player in the set-up at Lord's as well as his alert and razor-sharp abilities in the field.

Norman Hever, another fringe member in the Middlesex squad was also approached and the spring of 1948 saw both men move to South Wales in search of furthering their careers. For Norman, it was an association which lasted for half a dozen years – for Jimmy it was a brief two year stay.

He quickly slotted into the job, making some outstanding contributions alongside Willie Jones in the covers or in the deep. With Haydn Davies on top form behind the stumps, Allan Watkins, Phil Clift and Gilbert Parkhouse all catching flies close to the wicket., plus Wilf's imposing presence at short-leg, Glamorgan had the finest all-round fielding unit in the country. These collective abilities in the field contributed greatly to Glamorgan's title-winning achievements. Jimmy's abilities in the field won him a regular place in the 1948 and 1949 side, during which time he played many attractive, but often short-lived innings, passing fifty on just four innings in 78 innings.

Having made 669 runs in the 1948 season, he made just 395 from 35 innings during 1949 with a solitary fifty. Although he took ten smart catches in both summers, Jimmy was not really enjoying his cricket. Some might point to the dominant (a few might say tyrannical) presence of Wilf, but there were other factors contributing to the way Jimmy's form tailed off during 1949.

With Stan Montgomery having joined the Club, and impressed with his forceful batting, there were hints from Wilf and the committee that, at best, Jimmy might only get a one-year contract for 1950. He was a Londoner at heart, whilst both he and his wife never really settled in the Welsh capital. When the offer duly came Jimmy's way of running a newsagents business near Paddington railway station, he decided to call time at the end of the 1949 season on his career as a professional cricketer.

412
HEVER, Norman George

Born – Marylebone, 17 December, 1924
Died – Oxford, 11 September, 1987
Professional
RHB, RFM
1st XI: 1948-1953
2nd XI: 1951-1954
Club and Ground: 1948-1953
Cap: 1948
Middlesex 1947; South, MCC
Clubs: Ferndale, Clydach, Maesteg Town, Cowbridge, Wallasey, MCC, XL Club

Batting and Fielding Record:

	M	I	NO	RUNS	AV	100	50	CT	ST
F-c	133	166	74	869	9.45	-	-	60	-

Bowling Record:

	Balls	M	R	W	AV	5wI	10wM
F-c	18829	629	7400	318	23.27	11	-

Career-bests:
First-class   40 v Leicestershire at Leicester, 1950
            7/55 v Hampshire at Swansea, 1952

A few critics at the start of 1948 had described Glamorgan as really being "Middlesex 2nd XI" following their acquisition of Norman Hever and Jimmy Eaglestone to join fellow ex-Middlesex player Len Muncer and the rest of Wilf Wooller's squad. However, the critics were forced to eat their own words as Norman became a highly potent strike bowler during their Championship winning season.

Norman Hever.

He proved to be a shrewd acquisition as the Welsh county carefully rebuilt their seam attack. With Peter Judge and Austin Matthews having retired, other bowlers had been tried during 1947. However, Hugh Griffiths was only available for part of the summer, whilst some of the homegrown seamers in the South Wales and Monmouthshire League were unwilling to agree professional terms with the Welsh county and forgive the security of their full-time jobs. Norman enjoyed an outstanding debut season in the daffodil sweater with lively fast-medium swing bowling claiming 84 wickets at just 17 apiece and deservedly brought him both his county cap, as well as selection in the 1949 Test Trial at Edgbaston.

Norman was the son of George and Elizabeth Hever, with his father working as a locomotive fireman for a local railway company. The family lived in Hampstead but hailed from Southborough in Kent, where Norman's uncle Harry had enjoyed a brief career during the 1920s as a left-arm spinner. On leaving school, Norman joined the Home Guard and served briefly in the London area before joining the MCC groundstaff.

In 1947 Norman secured a place on Middlesex's junior staff and in June 1947 he made his first-class debut against Hampshire at Lord's. It proved to be a successful first outing for the swing bowler as he claimed 5/26 in the visitors first innings with his efforts seeing Hampshire follow-on. He added three more wickets to his tally in their second innings as Middlesex eased to victory by an innings and 49 runs.

He played in a further eight matches for Middlesex that summer, but only added a further six wickets and lost his place in the Middlesex line-up in early August. With the prospect of another one-year contract with Middlesex for 1948, Norman was open to better offers from elsewhere and when Glamorgan offered terms for two years, he readily accepted. With his friend Jimmy Eaglestone also agreeing a two-year deal, Norman travelled to Cardiff during late March 1948 eager to secure a regular place in the Welsh county's line-up.

His in-swing added an extra dimension to the Glamorgan attack, with Norman offering something different to the brisk seam of Wilf, the nagging left-armers of Allan Watkins plus the raw pace of Hugh Griffiths. In the words of Don Shepherd, "he was a very big in-swinger of the ball. When he was bowling well, he was pretty lethal because he would have times when the ball would hit the seam and go away."

Norman duly became Wilf's new-ball partner, but given his assets, the Glamorgan captain was keen not to use the former Middlesex man as a stock bowler. Instead, Norman was used in short and what proved to be very effective bursts, and he failed to take a wicket in just one of the 25 matches in which he bowled. In all, he took 154 wickets during his first two seasons with the Welsh county and secured a contract extension into the 1950s.

Like other swing bowlers, he enjoyed bowling at Swansea and other coastal venues where the salty sea breezes appeared to assist him. Indeed, one of his best spells during 1948 came in August at Weston-super-Mare in the match with Somerset. The Clarence Park pitch traditionally assisted the spinners and, after the home spinners had twice dismissed Glamorgan, Somerset were left on with a target of 105 on the final day. Knowing that the spin of Len Muncer and Willie Jones would be a handful on the dry and sandy surface, Somerset's openers were looking to get early runs on the board against Wilf and Norman, but the latter singlehandedly reduced the home side to 15/3.

He began by dismissing both openers leg before with deliveries which jagged sharply back in, before bowling Bertie Buse with a ball that initially swung in, before hitting the seam and uprooting the batsman's off-stump. He added the scalp of Fred Castle during a second spell as the Somerset man sparred at a rising delivery and gloved the ball to a jubilant Wilf at forward short-leg. Despite some lusty blows from Maurice Tremlett, Len's off-spin filleted the lower order as Somerset slumped to 90-9. Wally Luckes and Horace Hazell then added a few singles as the tension mounted. One catch in the leg-trap was uncharacteristically spilled, but Len kept his nerve and found the inside-edge of Horace's bat with Allan, at leg-slip, diving to hold a catch which gave Glamorgan an eight-run victory and maintained their bid for the county title.

The two former Middlesex men duly led the Glamorgan side off the field to plenty of cheers from the multitude of Glamorgan supporters, many of whom had travelled over by Campbell's Steamer from Pier Head to cheer on Wilf and his men. For Glamorgan's players however, their mode of transport from the Somerset resort was a Great Western Railway service back to Bristol Temple Meads and then an express service to London Paddington for the match against Middlesex at Lord's the following morning.

Glamorgan's title ambitions were initially frustrated by rain, as the opening day of the contest at the St John's Wood ground was washed out by rain, before Jack Robertson and Bill Edrich posted hundreds to put Middlesex into the ascendancy. But after Wilf had taken the new ball, the home side dramatically collapsed from 260-2 to 306 all out as Norman claimed 5/34. He certainly enjoyed bowling against his former employers during 1948 as he had taken 5/39 against them earlier in the season when they met at the Arms Park.

With four matches remaining, Glamorgan were in pole position and large crowds turned up at the Arms Park for the next two contests against Northants and Surrey, eager to see further Welsh success. Norman briefly played a minor role in both games, each played on dry and cracked surfaces, with an indication that they would turn seeing Stan Trick, the talented left-arm spinner from Neath, being persuaded by Wilf to appear in the match with the East Midlands side, before Johnnie Clay came out of retirement for the visit of Surrey.

The Northants match was also blighted by the rain, but the game with Surrey ended in an innings victory for the Welsh county as Johnnie claimed a ten-wicket haul. Norman briefly played a hand with his in-swing clean bowling Laurie Fishlock and Stan Squires as the Londoners subsided to 47-9 by the close of a dramatic opening day before following-on the next morning and being dismissed for a second time by the Welsh spinners. It was then on to Bournemouth with Glamorgan needing one more victory to seal the title. Despite rain on the opening day, the fairytale came true, with Norman taking just one wicket in each innings as Len and Johnnie wove their magic again to seal an innings victory and clinch the title.

After his dramatic rise into county cricket, and his clever use in short bursts by Wilf, Norman appeared in the Test Trial at Edgbaston. He featured alongside Allan and Willie in the South side, but he only claimed one wicket and rather than his skillful bowling it was more down to the deft glovework of Kent's wicket-keeper Godfrey Evans who stumped Vince Broderick as the Northants batsman overbalanced to an in-swinger from Norman who, as with Haydn Davies, liked the keeper to stand up to the stumps when he returned for a second or third spell.

Although higher honours never came his way, Norman still claimed 70 wickets during 1949, followed by a further 57 in 1950 by which time others, such as Don Shepherd, were now opening the bowling. Norman had a brief renaissance in 1952 when he claimed 63 wickets, but he claimed only five in eight matches the following summer and appeared a spent force. In fact, he had only claimed one five-wicket haul in the previous two seasons, and spent 1954 playing just 2nd XI cricket and seeing out his contract.

Unlike the taller six-footers, Norman had a shorter and more squat frame. In modern parlance, his swing bowling would have described as "skiddy", but the efforts of previous summers had taken its toll. As Don recalled "Norman wasn't strong enough for the job,

An image from the mid 1990s of Norman Hever and other former Glamorgan players at the Club's Former Player's Association at Sophia Gardens. Norman (second left) is seen with Allan Watkins (first left), Jim Pleass and Wyn Walters.

day in, day out. There may have been other factors as well, as alluded to by Jim Pleass – "he loved life and he loved beer. He would drink beer, sometimes times till three or four in the morning and yet he would start bowling next day and pick up five wickets before lunch!"

During his final years with Glamorgan, Norman had dabbled in leg-spin and it was in this guise that he played as a professional for a number of Welsh clubs, before having a spell with Wallasey in the Liverpool Premier League in 1958 and 1959. He then trained as a groundsman and in 1962 secured a post at Wantage Road in Northampton. To his, and the club's delight, he won the Groundsman of the Year Award in 1964 and remained with the East Midlands county until 1973 when he took up a similar position at Wellingborough School.

Whilst in both posts, Norman had also acted as an umpire and stood in several of Northamptonshire's Second Eleven Championship matches. His name had been mentioned as going on the first-class list, but Norman opted to remain at Wellingborough School.

413
JAMES, David Harry

Born – Briton Ferry, 3 March 1921
Died – Margam, 22 February 2002
Amateur
RHB, RM
Ed – Cwrt Sart School, Neath
1st XI: 1948
2nd XI: 1947-1950
Club and Ground: 1948
Clubs: Briton Ferry Town, Briton Ferry Steel, XL Club

Batting and Fielding Record:

	M	I	NO	RUNS	AV	100	50	CT	ST
F-c	1	1	0	17	17.00	-	-	1	-

Bowling Record:

	Balls	M	R	W	AV	5wI	10wM
F-c	144	4	59	1	59.00	-	-

Career-bests:
First-class –   17 v Nottinghamshire at Trent Bridge, 1948
              1/59 v Nottinghamshire at Trent Bridge, 1948

David James, who played once for Glamorgan in 1948, was the son of Tuan James, one of finest left-arm spinners in League cricket in South Wales during the inter-war period and a man who briefly played for Glamorgan during their final year as a Minor County and later in first-class cricket (Volume 1 p.335). His uncle was off-spinner Harry Tomlinson who, like Tuan, also appeared for Glamorgan during the early 1920s

(Vol. 1 p.336-337).

Given this rich cricketing pedigree, it was only natural that David should play with success as an all-rounder for both Briton Ferry Steel and Briton Ferry Town in the immediate post-War years. Standing at just over six feet tall, he had been a capable batsman and bowler in schools cricket in the Neath area during the mid-1930s.

His father, an engineering patternmaker at Briton Ferry Tinplate works, would have dearly loved his son to secure a place on Glamorgan's staff, but with the financial uncertainties associated with the Welsh county at that time, it was not to be and after leaving school David sought monetary security by joining the Great Western Railway as a ticket office clerk.

Nevertheless, David still turned out regularly for Briton Ferry Steel but like so many of his generation, his playing career was blighted by the hostilities. Fortunately, his reserved occupation with the railway company meant that he did not have to fight on foreign fields and, when hostilities were over, he was able to secure sufficient leave to play for the county's 2nd XI as the Club regrouped after the War.

David James.

Between 1947 and 1950 David appeared in the county's 2nd XI in Minor County matches, as well as other friendlies whilst during 1948, he was drafted into the county's side for the Championship away match against Nottinghamshire. With Jim Pleass carrying an injury and the Trent Bridge pitch likely to assist the seam bowlers, the Briton Ferry bowler got the nod.

He didn't bowl in the Notts first innings but bowled 24 economical overs in their second innings as the game ended in a draw. He also caught and bowled Charlie Harris, whose century had helped the home side clear a deficit before rain brought a premature finish as a draw. Charlie was quite a fitting wicket, given the fact that David had played many times in closely fought games at St Helen's against his elder brother George who played for Swansea.

David continued to play cricket until into his sixties, appearing for the XL Club as an off-break bowler as well as for Briton Ferry Town. He had married Margaret Marshall during 1952, whilst in later life he became a noted and ever-genial local historian, writing the histories of both Briton Ferry clubs.

Index

ADDITIONS AND CORRECTIONS TO VOLUME ONE

p. 42 – **WH GWYNN:** b. 27 March 1856.

p. 46-47 – **CW DONNELLY:** b. Kimberley, 19 October 1865; d. Kimberley, 23 September, 1946.

p. 53-54 – **WM THOMAS:** d. Bridgend October 1931. Ed – Dean Close School, Cheltenham.

p. 79 – **RB SWEET-ESCOTT:** b. Essington, Staffordshire.

p. 81 – **SH BIGGS:** b. 2 April 1872.

p. 97 – **GA YOUNG:** b. 23 March 1886.

p. 121 – **TM BARLOW:** b. 3 November 1864.

p.126 – **D BINCH:** b. 12 October, Calverton, Notts; d. 12 December, Calverton, 1951.

p. 130-31 – **S LOWE:** d. Kirkby-in-Ashfield, 29 March 1947.

p. 138-39 – **RHT JOHNSON:** d. Cape Town 30 April, 1951.
He only played for Glamorgan during 1896, with RH Johnson (below) playing for the Welsh county between 1902 and 1908. RHT Johnson's amended career figures are as follows:

Batting and Fielding Record:

	M	I	NO	RUNS	AV	100	50	CT	ST
Minor	5	9	2	117	16.71	-	-	3	-

Bowling Record:

	Balls	M	R	W	AV	5wI	10wM
Minor	185	8	141	2	79.50	-	-

JOHNSON, Richard Hardwick. Born – Didsbury, Greater Manchester, 1 February, 1874. Died – Geelong, Australia, 27 October, 1924. Amateur. 1st XI: 1902-1908. Clubs: Penarth, Swansea, and Swansea Wednesdays.

Batting and Fielding Record:

	M	I	NO	RUNS	AV	100	50	CT	ST
Minor	5	8	1	53	7.57	-	-	1	-

Bowling Record:

	Balls	M	R	W	AV	5wI	10wM
Minor	18	0	18	0	-	-	-

Career-best: - 21* v Berkshire at Reading, 1905.

p.148-49: The 'B Lambert' who played for Glamorgan during 1897 and 1898 was not Bill Lambert, the former Middlesex, Hertfordshire and Northumberland but a young spinner called Bertie Lambert:

LAMBERT, Bernard Austin. Born – Bridgend, October 1876. Died – Johannesburg, South Africa, 15 March 1908. LHB, SLA. Professional. Clubs: Bridgend, Cardiff, Usk and Cowbridge.

p. 198 – TAL WHITTINGTON: d. 17 July 1944. He also served as the Honorary Secretary of the Welsh Cricket Union from 1927 until 1932.

p. 205 – RA GIBBS: b. 7 May 1882.

p. 210 – AE PEATFIELD: b. Retford, 13 April 1874.

p. 220 – A short note in the *Evening Express* newspaper for 30 July 1904 confirms that this player was WF Gibson of Cardiff Alpha and Cardiff, rather than WS Gibson of Swansea as previously thought. Whilst the statistics remain the same, the biographical details are as follows:

GIBSON, William Farquhar. Born – Cardiff, 1 April 1878. Died – Cardiff, 2 April 1971. Amateur.

Ed – Radnor Road Board School. 1st XI: 1904. Clubs: Cardiff Alpha, Cardiff. Brother of J Gibson.

p. 239 – J GIBSON: b. Cardiff, 10 July, 1879; d. Cardiff, 1951. Ed – Radnor Road Board School. Brother of WF Gibson.

p. 277 – J CHANDLESS: b. 23 August, 1884.

p. 299 – This was not KH Harris, as previously thought, but KF Harris. His playing statistics are the same, but his biographical details are as follows: **HARRIS, Kenneth Frank.** Born - Littleham, Exmouth, 7 October 1885. Died - Brynmill, Swansea, 29 October 1949. All-rounder. 1st XI: 1913. Devon 1903-1906; Perthshire 1907; Monmouthshire 1920-1931; Wales v MCC 1925. Clubs: Exmouth, Hill's Plymouth and Abercarn.

p. 328 – AE O'BREE: He died in the Maccauvlei Military Hospital in Vereeniging, South Africa on 27 December 1943.